SCARY MONSTERS
and
SUPER FREAKS

SCARY MONSTERS and SUPER FREAKS

Stories of Sex, Drugs, Rock 'n' Roll and Murder

MIKE SAGER

Thunder's Mouth Press

New York

For my parents,
Beverly and Marvin Sager,
and for my sister,
Wendy Sager

Introduction

I came to journalism for the stories.

I needed to write. I loved the words and the sentences; the rhythms and the sounds. I loved the typing–a desk, a good window, playing the keyboard, reading to myself in a low monotone that is not quite humming and not quite talking out loud. The keys go *clicka clack*. Twenty-six neutral symbols are willfully recombined. Text appears; something from nothing. It fills the page. And then the next . . .

But I was young. I needed something to write *about*.

With luck and perseverance—a great deal of perseverance—I was given my chance. I don't know how many stories I've published over the past two and a half decades. Thick files of them during six years at the *Washington Post*—back then, they kept the actual newsprint. They clipped each of your articles and taped it to a piece of yellow construction paper, one yellow paper per month. It was a way they had of monitoring your output. It was also thrilling evidence of your existence. You could pull your own clip file. You had proof: You were alive; you were creating; you were making progress. By the early eighties, I was writing upwards of twenty-five long magazine pieces a year. More recently, over the span of time represented in this collection—1988 through 2002—I have had the good fortune to be associated with the kinds of magazines and editors who have allowed me to take my time and to hone my craft—to tell a story, to get it right, to make it resonate.

Each of the pieces in this collection represents at least five months of reporting and writing. Each was a journey of discovery, of course—that is the nature of journalism: you start from zero. I remember as a fledgling reporter being assigned to write a story about mortgage interest rates. My first source had to explain to me the difference between interest and principal. The next morning, upwards of one million people were reading my account on the front page. Over time, I have learned many things, this among them: It is not shameful to be ignorant, only to remain so; truth is more important than pride.

Though I came to journalism for the stories, for something to write about, I have reaped much more. I am who I am today because of journalism—a man crafted by his craft, as it were: a found-art assemblage of disparate notions and sensibilities and odd, useless tidbits of information, all of it collected from the multitude of lives through which I have been allowed to pass, all of it welded helter-skelter onto the framework of the twenty-year-old kid who waded out into the real world 27 years ago with a Radio Shack micro-cassette recorder in hand to report his first piece as a pro: a story about a man who lived on a diet of wild plants. You have to start somewhere, no?

—Mike Sager

The Devil and John Holmes

John Holmes was a porn star. Eddie Nash was a drug lord. Their association ended in one of the most brutal mass murders in the history of Los Angeles.

Deep in Laurel Canyon, the Wonderland Gang was planning its last heist. It was Sunday evening and the drugs were gone, the money was gone, the situation was desperate. They'd sold a pound of baking soda for a quarter of a million dollars: There were contracts out on their lives. Now they had another idea. They sat around a glass table in the breakfast nook. Before them were two pairs of handcuffs, a stolen police badge, several automatic pistols and a dogeared sheet of paper, a floor plan. They needed a score. This was it.

There were seven of them meeting in the house on Wonderland Avenue, a jaundiced stucco box on a steep, winding road in the hills above Hollywood. Joy Audrey Miller, 46, held the lease. She was thin, blond, foulmouthed, a heroin addict with seven arrests. She had two daughters, had once been married to a Beverly Hills attorney. A year ago, she'd been busted for dealing drugs out of the Wonderland house. Six months ago she'd had a double mastectomy. Her lover was Billy DeVerell. DeVerell, 42, was also a heroin addict. He had a slight build, a pockmarked face, a record of thirteen arrests. "He looked like a guy in a dive bar in El Paso," according to a neighbor.

Sharing the house with Miller and DeVerell was Ronald Launius, 37. Blond and bearded, Launius had served federal time for drug smuggling. A California cop called him "one of the coldest people I ever met."

The house at 8763 Wonderland rented for $750 a month. There was a garage on the first floor; the second and third floors had balconies facing the street. A stairway, leading from the garage to the front door, was caged in iron. There was a telephone at the entrance, an electronic deadbolt on the gate, two pit bulls sleeping on the steps.

Though elaborately secure, the house was paint-cracked and rust-stained, an eyesore in a trendy neighborhood. Laurel Canyon had long been a prestige address, an earthy, woodsy setting just minutes from the glitter and rush of Tinseltown. Tom Mix and Harry Houdini once lived there among the quail and scrub pine and coyotes. Later, in the Sixties, the canyon attracted writers and artists, rock stars and gurus. Number 8763 Wonderland Avenue had some history of its own: Paul Revere and the Raiders once lived there.

By the Eighties, former California governor Jerry Brown was living on Wonderland Avenue, and Steven Spielberg was building on a lot not far away. The house at 8763 had passed from a raucous group of women—neighbors recall naked women being tossed from the first-floor balcony—to the members of the Wonderland Gang. Things at the house were always hopping, someone was always showing up with a scam. Miller, DeVerell and Launius needed drugs every day. They were always looking for an opportunity. Jewelry stores, convenience stores, private homes—they would try anything, as long as it meant money or drugs.

"There was a lot of traffic, all day, all night," says a neighbor. "Everything from Volkswagens to a Rolls-Royce Silver Shadow. They threw brown bags of dope off the balcony. There was shouting, laughing, rock & roll twenty-four hours a day."

At the moment, on this evening of June 28th, 1981, Wonderland Avenue was quiet. Five men and two women were meeting in the breakfast nook, sitting in swivel chairs, leaning against walls. The floor plan before them showed a three-bedroom, high-end tract house on a cul-de-sac in the San Fernando Valley. It had a pool and a sunken living room, a white stone façade. Inside was a painting by Rembrandt, a jade and ivory collection, sterling silver, jewelry and, most appealing of all, large quantities of money and drugs.

The man who owned the house was named Adel Nasrallah. He was known as Eddie Nash. A naturalized American, Nash came to California from Palestine in the early Fifties. In 1960 he opened a hot-dog stand on Hollywood Boulevard. By the mid-Seventies, Nash held thirty-six liquor licenses, owned real estate and other assets worth over $30 million.

Nash had clubs of all kinds; he catered to all predilections. The Kit Kat was a strip club. The Seven Seas was a bus-stop joint across Hollywood Boulevard from Mann's Chinese Theaters. It had a tropical motif, a menu of special drinks, a Polynesian revue, sometimes belly dancers. His gay clubs were the first in L.A. to allow same-sex dancing. His black club was like a Hollywood Harlem, jazz and pinkie rings and wide-brimmed straw hats.

The Starwood, on Santa Monica Boulevard, featured cutting-edge rock & roll. In the late Seventies, Los Angeles police averaged twenty-five drug busts a month at the Starwood. One search of the premises yielded a cardboard box containing 4000 counterfeit Quaaludes. A sign on the box, written in blue Magic Marker, said, FOR DISTRIBUTION AT BOX OFFICE.

Nash was a drug dealer and a heavy user. His drug of choice was freebase, home-cooked crack cocaine, and he was smoking it at the rate of two to three ounces a day. He always had large quantities of coke, heroin, Quaaludes and other drugs at the house. His bodyguard, Gregory DeWitt Diles, was a karate expert and convicted felon who weighed a blubbery 300 pounds. According to one eyewitness, Diles once chased a man out of the Kit Kat and emptied his .38 revolver into the man's car. The car was on the other side of Santa Monica Boulevard, across six lanes of traffic. The time was 2:30 in the afternoon. No one was injured.

Nash and Diles were well known on Sunset Strip. "Eddie Nash assumed he deserved a certain amount of respect," says one denizen. "If somebody fucked with him . . ."

Now, in the breakfast nook, a tall, gaunt man with curly hair and a sparse beard pointed to the floor plan he had sketched.

"Here, this back bedroom, that's Diles's room," he said. "He keeps a sawed-off shotgun under the blanket. . . . Here, this is Nash's room. There's a floor safe in the closet, right . . . over . . . here."

"You sure about this, donkey dick?" asked Tracy McCourt, the gang's wheelman.

"Hey, it's cool," said John Holmes, 36, the man with the plan. "I know Eddie. Nash loves me. He thinks I'm famous."

John Holmes was famous, at least in some circles. What he was famous for was his penis.

In a career that would span twenty years, Holmes made 2274 hard-core pornographic films, had sex with 14,000 women. At the height of his popularity, he earned $3000 a day on films and almost as much turning tricks, servicing wealthy men and women on both coasts and in Europe.

Since the late Sixties, Holmes had traded on his natural endowment. His penis, when erect, according to legend, measured between eleven and fifteen inches in length. Recently, however, Holmes's biggest commodity had been trouble. He was freebasing one hit of coke every ten or fifteen minutes, swallowing forty to fifty Valium a day to cut the edge. The drugs affected his penis; he couldn't get it up, he couldn't work in porn. Now he was a drug delivery boy for the Wonderland Gang. His mistress, Jeana, who'd been with him since she was fifteen, was turning tricks to support his habit. They were living out of the trunk of his estranged wife's Chevy Malibu. Holmes was stealing luggage off conveyers at L.A. International, buying appliances with his wife's credit cards, fencing them for cash.

Holmes was into Nash for a small fortune. Now Holmes owed the Wonderland Gang, too. He'd messed up a delivery, had a big argument with DeVerell and Launius. They took back his key to Wonderland, and Launius punched him out, then hit Holmes with his own blackthorn walking stick. They told him to make good. He tried to think. Addled synapses played him a picture: Eddie Nash.

"So you go in," Launius was saying to Holmes, reviewing the plan. "You talk to Nash, whatever, you tell him you got to take a piss. Then what?"

"I leave the sliding door unlocked—this one," said Holmes, pointing to the floor plan, "here, in the back. The guest bedroom. Then I leave. I come back to Wonderland. Tell you it's all clear. Then you guys take him down."

And so the plan was fixed. At midnight, the Wonderland people scraped together $400, and Holmes, whose pretense for entrance would be buying drugs, drove off to Nash's house.

It was 1.6 miles from Wonderland Avenue to Dona Lola Place, which was fortuitous, because the stolen Ford Granada driven by the Wonderland Gang was running on empty. In the car were DeVerell, Launius, McCourt and a man named David Lind, a friend of Launius's. Lind and his girlfriend had come down three weeks earlier from Sacramento to stay at Wonderland. An ex-convict who'd served time for burglary, forgery and assault to commit rape, Lind had been invited to town, he would later tell a court, to practice his "profession," committing crimes.

McCourt drove up the hill on Laurel Canyon Boulevard, across Mulholland Drive, over the crest of the Santa Monica Mountains, down into the Valley. The sun was warm and diffuse. Sprinklers were ticking water across lawns. Rush hour was on. It was 8:30 Monday morning.

Though Holmes had left Wonderland at midnight, he had stayed at Eddie Nash's for six hours, smoking up the $400 he'd taken to spend, helping himself to a little more of Nash's largess. Nash was extremely hospitable. He always called Holmes "my brother." They'd known each other for three years.

As night stretched into morning, Holmes had an attack of conscience, a glimmer of an understanding that knocking over Eddie Nash might lead to a lot of trouble. Nash knew the Wonderland people. He'd never met them, but he had, through Holmes, given them a $1000 loan. Holmes muttered something to Nash about the gang. He wasn't specific, but it really didn't matter anyway. Nash hadn't slept in ten days. He hardly knew what Holmes was saying. And, as Holmes's supply of coke dwindled, his conscience was overruled by his jones. He excused himself, left the room and unlocked the sliding door.

Arriving back at Wonderland just after dawn, Holmes announced the coast was clear. The time was right, he told Lind.

There was one hitch. DeVerell, Launius and McCourt, all heroin addicts, were out cold.

Three hours later, everyone was finally awake. Holmes drove to Nash's again to make sure the sliding door was still open. This time, the gang decided not to wait for his return.

Now, as McCourt turned right, off Laurel Canyon Boulevard onto Dona Pegita, he saw Holmes driving back toward them. Both cars slowed, pulled even in the middle of the street. Holmes rolled down his window, McCourt rolled down his.

"It's time," Holmes said, and then he smiled and raised his fist "Get 'em, boys!"

John Curtis Holmes had the longest, most prolific career in the history of pornography. He had sex onscreen with two generations of leading ladies, from Seka and Marilyn Chambers to Traci Lords, Ginger Lynn and Italian member of Parliament Ciccolina. The first man to win the X Rated Critics Organization Best Actor Award, Holmes was an idol and an icon, the most visible male porn star of his time.

Holmes started in the business around 1968, a time when porn was just beginning to surface from the underground of peep shows and frat houses into mainstream acceptance. The Sixties, the pill, "free love," communes, wife swapping, the perverse creativity of mixed-media artists who were pushing the limit, trying to shock—all of these things created an atmosphere in which porn could blossom. The pivotal event in porn history was the release of *Deep Throat*, starring Linda Lovelace and Harry Reems, in 1972. Though the movie, when it began to appear at theaters around the country, was branded as obscene and closed down almost everywhere it played, its producers contested the charges in the courts and eventually won. In the end, *Deep Throat* was massively consumed by an enthusiastic public. With the release the same year of *The Devil in Miss Jones* and *Behind the Green Door,* porn became part of popular culture. Suddenly, Johnny Carson was telling *Deep Throat* jokes on *The Tonight Show.*

One day in 1970, Holmes met Hawaiian producer Bob Chinn. Up to this time, Holmes had been doing mostly photo layouts, stag films and 8-mm bookstore loops. He showed Chinn his portfolio of stills, then stripped. That evening, Chinn wrote a three-page screenplay; a partnership was born. This would lead, in the mid-Seventies, to Holmes's most successful role, as Johnny Wadd, the hard-boiled detective, porn's parody of Sam Spade. Holmes's character, said Al Goldstein in *Screw* magazine, was "a thin, bony, trench-coated shamus, outrageously horny, bedding down with client and quarry alike." In Goldstein's opinion, "it was a goofy, crudely made series," but it was wildly successful. In a way, Holmes was everyman's gigolo, a polyester smoothy with a sparse mustache, a flying collar and lots of buttons undone. He wasn't threatening. He chewed gum and overacted. He took a lounge singer's approach to sex, deliberately gentle, ostentatiously artful, a homely guy with a pinkie ring and a big dick who was convinced he was every woman's dream.

Holmes went on to make more than 2000 movies. *Teenage Cowgirls, Liquid Lips, China Cat* and *Tapestry of Passion. Eruption,* a porn remake of *Double Indemnity. Dickman and Throbbin,* a lampoon of Batman and Robin. *Hard Candy,* a 3-D thriller. A porn "documentary" of his life, made in 1981, was called *Exhausted.*

In time, Holmes became known as the Errol Flynn of porn. And like the leading men of yesteryear, what was known of him was mostly myth.

According to legend—largely of his own making—Holmes was born in New York and lived with a rich aunt who'd been married fifteen times. The aunt sent him to fencing school, dancing school, a school of etiquette. They lived in London, Paris, Michigan, Florida. He lost his virginity at the Florida house, when he was six, to his Swiss nursemaid, Frieda.

In high school, Holmes said, he slept with all but three girls in his class. He graduated from UCLA with majors, variously, in physical therapy, pediatric physical therapy, medicine and political sciences. His first porn film was made while he was working his way through college. A girl from the dorm recommended him. Also while in college, he said, he danced "nude modern jazz ballet" and drove an ambulance.

When he became established as a porn star, Holmes said, he had a half dozen agents pulling in work for him. He made films nonstop, and he took eighty to ninety telephone calls a day. He had twenty-seven fan clubs; people wrote for locks of his pubic hair. Men asked him to autograph their wives' breasts. Women asked him to deflower their daughters. One regular trick had him barge into her bedroom while she was watching TV, then tie her up and rape her. Her husband watched from the closet. Holmes said he'd had sex in airplanes, helicopters, trains, elevators, kitchens, bathrooms, on rooftops, in caves, storm cellars, bomb shelters in Europe, under a table in a restaurant filled with people, fifty feet underwater while wearing scuba gear. He'd been with three governors, two of their wives and one senator, who was "really a freak."

Holmes said he owned ten different businesses, that he was a gourmet cook, that he had written twenty-nine books, including a how-to manual combining cooking and sex. His penis, he said, was "bigger than a pay phone, smaller than a Cadillac."

Holmes's voice was sly and ingratiating. He sounded a lot like Eddie Haskell on *Leave It to Beaver* and bore some resemblance to the actor who played him. Above all, he said, he loved his work: "A happy gardener is one with dirty fingernails, and a happy cook is a fat cook. I never get tired of what I do because I'm a sex fiend. I'm very lusty."

John Curtis Holmes was born to Mary and Edward Holmes on August 8th, 1944, in Pickaway County, Ohio, the youngest of three boys and a girl. Edward, a carpenter, was an alcoholic. Mary was a Bible-thumping Baptist. John remembered screaming, yelling, his father puking all over the kids.

Holmes's parents separated when he was three, and Mary moved the family into a housing project in Columbus. They shared an apartment with another divorced woman and her two children. When Holmes was eight, his mother married Harold, a manic-depressive who worked for the telephone company. They moved to a house on five acres in wooded, rural Pataskala, Ohio. Harold drank a lot. Once, he rammed his own hand into a harvesting machine. He lost his thumb and three fingers. At the hospital, as he came out of anesthesia, he said to Mary, "I'll never have to work again." He didn't. Mary went to work on an assembly line at a Western Electric plant.

John was a shy and lonely kid who kept to himself and had perfect attendance at Sunday school. He lost his virginity at age twelve to a thirty-six-year-old woman who was a friend of his mother's. At home, Harold picked on John. There were backhands, lectures, drunken rages. By the time John's half brother was born, John was spending most of his time in the woods, hunting, trapping, fishing, staying away from Harold. Then one day Harold threw John down the stairs and came after him. John swung and knocked his stepfather out. On his sixteenth birthday, Holmes joined the army. He served in the signal corps, spending three years in Nuremberg, Germany. He never went home again.

After mustering out of the army, at age nineteen, Holmes went to work as an ambulance driver, and soon thereafter he met Sharon Gebenini. Sharon was a nurse at USC County General, working on a team that was pioneering open-heart surgery. She was twenty, an army brat. They were married in August 1965 at Fort Ord, California.

One summer day in 1968, Sharon came home a little early from work. Her new boss, a pediatrician, had shut down the office for the afternoon, and she'd gone to the market, planned a special dinner for her husband.

Holmes, in those days, was a string bean, six feet tall, 150 pounds, hair still cut in a military buzz. When Sharon and John were first married, she says, he was very naive, looking for the perfect relationship. "He was very possessive. He wouldn't even let me meet the people he worked with."

Recently, Holmes had been drifting from job to job, trying to find a niche. He quit the ambulance service and got work stirring vats of chocolate at a Coffee Nips factory in Glendale. Then he sold shoes, furniture, Fuller brushes door-to-door. He drove a forklift at a meatpacking plant in Cudahy until his lung collapsed from working in the freezer. Just recently, he had begun training to be a uniformed security guard.

Unbeknownst to Sharon, Holmes had also recently started in porn, following an encounter with a professional photographer named Joel in the bathroom of the poker parlor in Gardina. Holmes was doing sex pictorials, dancing in clubs.

Now, home early from her office, Sharon left her purse in the foyer, squeaked down the hall on white rubber soles to the bathroom of their one-bedroom apartment in Glendale. The door was open. Inside was her husband, John. He had a tape measure in one hand, his penis in the other.

"What are you doing?" she asked.

"What does it look like I'm doing?"

"Is there something wrong? Are you afraid it's withering and dying?" she said, laughing.

"No, I'm just curious," said Holmes.

Sharon went to the bedroom, lay down, read a magazine. Twenty minutes later, Holmes walked into the room. He had a full erection.

"It's incredible," said John.

"What?"

"It goes from five inches all the way to ten. Ten inches long! Four inches around!"

"That's great," said Sharon, turning a page of her magazine. "You want me to call the press?"

Her husband fixed her with a long stare. Finally he said, "I've got to tell you I've been doing something else, and I think I want to make it my life's work."

Holmes went on to say that he wanted to be best in the world at something, and that he thought pornography was it. Sharon had been a virgin when they'd met. She wasn't happy.

"You can't be uptight about this," John said, a refrain she would hear for the next fifteen years. "This means absolutely nothing to me. It's like being a carpenter. These are my tools, I use them to make a living. When I come home at night, the tools stay on the job."

"You are having sex with other women," said Sharon. "It's like being married to a hooker."

Holmes said nothing.

And so began the loops and the stags, and then Johnny Wadd was born. Holmes let his hair grow, started wearing three-piece suits. He and Sharon settled into a strange hybrid of domesticity. She paid for food and household expenses, did his laundry, cooked for him when he was home. John kept his porn money and spent it on himself. By 1973, John and Sharon were sharing the same house, even the same bed, but they were no longer having sex. Sharon had gone so far as to stop physical relations, but she couldn't bring herself to kick him out. "Let's face it," she says. "I loved the schmuck. I just didn't like what he was doing."

John bought himself an El Camino pickup and a large diamond solitaire that became his trademark in films. Then he designed a massive gold and diamond ring in the shape of a dragonfly, and a gold belt buckle, measuring eight by five inches. The buckle depicted a mother whale swimming in the ocean, her baby nursing beneath. John was into Save the Whales. He wore the buckle when he and Sharon sold bumper stickers door-to-door.

In 1974, Sharon became the resident manager of a ten-unit apartment court in Glendale. It was owned by the pediatrician she worked for; she and Holmes lived rent-free in an adjacent house. Sometimes he worked around the apartments as the handyman and gardener. He also renovated the house, outdoing himself in the master bathroom, recreating a backwoods outhouse, complete with a quarter-moon cutout, a shingled roof over the bathtub and a rough-hewn box around the commode.

Holmes was an inveterate collector of junk. He picked wire out of dumpsters and sold the copper. He went to garage sales and bought old furniture. He could repair anything, liked sketching and working in clay. He also collected animal skulls. Once, Sharon says, he got a human head from UCLA. He boiled it clean in a pot on Sharon's stove. They called it Louise. At Christmas, they decorated it with colored lights.

About this time, Sharon says, Holmes began working as a courier for the Mob. "He'd come home from one of his movie premières, take off his boots, peel down his socks and take out a wad of large bills. He'd say, 'Count this.' We're talking $56,000 in two boots."

Jeana Sellers (not her real name) arrived in Holmes's life in 1976. She was a teenager, and her parents had just divorced. She'd driven out from Miami with her father and younger sister. Along the way, in Colorado, Mr. Sellers picked up a hitchhiker who was going to Glendale to see his girlfriend. Mr. Sellers had no particular plan; Glendale sounded just fine. By the time they pulled into the apartment complex managed by Sharon Holmes, it had been decided. The Sellers would stay there.

The complex had ten free-standing cabana apartments, built around a courtyard. Holmes's half brother and his wife lived there; this little community was the personal fiefdom of John Holmes. One day, Jeana was visiting a neighbor when Holmes came by to deliver a bag of pot. Holmes talked a while, looked Jeana up and down. "Too bad you're so young," he said finally, then left.

Soon after, the courtship of Jeana began. Whenever he returned from days or weeks away, Holmes would bring gifts: stuffed animals, roses, a ring. For her sister Terry, who was fourteen and overweight, he brought what he called "Terry food," pounds and pounds of candy. Holmes hired the sisters to do gardening around the complex. When they'd finish work, he'd make sandwiches. John had a van by then, and soon he began organizing camping trips with Jeana, Terry and Terry's boyfriend, Jose. "I was really charmed," says Jeana. "I was just taken off my feet. He treated me very special." John was thirty-one, she was fifteen.

One night Holmes told Jeana to meet him at the van. They went to the beach. "I didn't know what was going to happen, but I knew what might," she says. "We sat on the rocks, the moon was just right. We sat for a long time, and he was very, very quiet. He just stared. I played in the water. When I got out, he said, 'Let's go,' and we drove toward home. And then, just as we got to this intersection, he slammed on the brakes. It was dark, and there wasn't any traffic. He said, 'Would you make love to me?' I literally shook to death. I said yes. I loved him. We did it in the van. After that I was his."

In time, Jeana's father went back to Miami and took Terry with him, and Jeana moved in with John's half brother and his wife, David and Karen. Jeana dropped out of Glendale High School. During the day, she worked in a nursing home. At night, she baby-sat for David and Karen.

By 1978, Holmes was freebasing cocaine all the time. He'd been turned on to the drug on a movie set in Las Vegas and had been smoking ever since. Now he never went anywhere without his brown Samsonite briefcase. Inside were his drugs, his glass pipe, baking soda and a petri dish for cooking cocaine powder into rock base, a bottle of 151 rum and cotton swabs for lighting the pipe. Jeana was doing freebase too, almost every night.

"When he did coke," says Jeana, "he'd do it until it was all gone, and then he'd scrape the pipe and smoke all the resin he could find, and then he'd take a bunch of Valium. He'd have me make these peanut-butter chocolate-chip brown-sugar butter cookies. All the sugar helped him come down. He'd have a big glass of milk, and we'd turn on the cartoons, and then he'd go to bed in Sharon's room. I'd usually fall asleep on the couch."

By this time, Sharon had befriended Jeana. "The poor girl was emaciated," Sharon says. Sharon's first act was to move Jeana out of Karen and David's and into a garage apartment in the complex. A few months later, Jeana moved into the guest room of the house. "I knew the whole picture," says Sharon. "He was picking on a kid that didn't know any better. I had to let her know there was another world out there, that John was not God Almighty.

"John was terrified that I was going to confront her. But I had no reason to confront her. Why? Why would I confront her? He meant nothing to me in that way."

Holmes was gone now more and more, making films in Europe, San Francisco and Hawaii, doing private tricks, traveling to film openings across the country. At the same time, Holmes was acting as an informant on matters of porn and prostitution for Sergeant Tom Blake, an L.A. vice detective. He began spilling to Blake in 1973, after he was arrested on a movie set. It is debatable whether or not Holmes ever told Blake anything he could use.

Also during this period Holmes spent much of his time with his best and only friend, Bill Amerson, in Sherman Oaks. Amerson, a menacing six feet four, 250 pounds, tells tales of his own involvement in drug dealing and organized crime. He says he played pro football and worked as a stunt man, specializing in motorcycle crashes. He was now in porn—writing, directing, producing.

Amerson and Holmes had met on a shoot in San Francisco in 1970; they were kindred egos ever after. "John was like a little brother to me," says Amerson.

Amerson named John the godfather of his children and gave Holmes his own room at his house. Holmes and Amerson went hunting, deep-sea fishing, camping. Mostly, says Amerson, he and Holmes excluded women. "John didn't particularly care for women. At times, I think, he disliked women. He would rather be out in the woods. He was really a simple kid. He liked going to Disneyland, he liked all the rides. He was really sensitive, but he didn't want anyone to know. A puppy getting hit by a car, a dead bird, strange things made him cry. We spent hours talking about reincarnation, about life, about God, or the lack of."

Holmes started to become erratic around 1978. On sets, he was harder and harder to deal with. He'd lock himself in bathrooms, in closets. People who worked with him joked that you had to leave a trail of freebase from the bathroom to the bedroom to get Holmes to work. Amerson would get calls from directors. He'd go to the set, usually a rented house in the San Fernando Valley. He'd find Holmes "going through drawers, looking for something to steal. He'd turned into a fucking burglar.

"John got strange," says Amerson. "He got wild eyed. He didn't make a lot of sense when he talked."

Soon the man who once claimed to be making almost $500,000 a year selling his sexual charms was working as a drug delivery boy for the gang of outlaws and junkies who lived on Wonderland Avenue. He stole luggage, broke into cars, visited old girlfriends and tricks and ripped them off, charged $30,000 worth of appliances to Sharon's credit cards. For a while, he and his half brother David tried to make a go of a combination antique store and locksmith service. Jeana ran the store, the Just Looking Emporium. It didn't last long.

The night the store closed its doors for good, says Jeana, John was strung out and paranoid. "That was the first night he punched the shit out of me," she says, and thereafter, the beatings were regular. "One time he beat me so I'd sleep with these two black guys from his answering service. I think he couldn't pay the bill. Then he beat me 'cause I slept with them."

By early 1980, Holmes and Jeana had moved out of the complex for good. They stayed in motels sometimes, but mostly they lived in Sharon's Chevy Malibu. Or at least Jeana did. "I was famous for waiting in the car," she says. "We'd drive somewhere to do a drug deal. He'd get out. I'd wait. Sometimes it would be two days. I'd have a six-pack of Pepsi and a coffee can to pee in. And my dog, Thor. He was a little Chihuahua. John and Sharon gave him to me."

So it went, until they were busted in January of 1981. At that point, Holmes had Jeana, now twenty, turning tricks. She was living in an apartment in the Valley with a porn actress and high-priced hooker named Michelle. In the early hours of January 14th, Jeana and Michelle were visiting an apartment in Marina Del Ray. While John was waiting for them in the parking lot, he stole a computer out of a car. Thus far, Holmes had been pretty lucky. His connection as an informant for the L.A. police had kept him clear of being busted. But now Holmes was committing felonies almost every day. His luck had run out. The cops got them in the parking lot.

The next day, Eddie Nash bailed them out. Jeana didn't want to go back to Michelle's. John insisted. She refused. He punched her in the stomach, dragged her through the door. "Get some sleep," he told her. "You gotta work tonight."

John went to take a bath. Jeana heard the water shut off, heard John get into the tub. She wasn't going back to this. Enough was enough.

"Honey!" called John from the bathtub. "Get me a cup of coffee, will you?"

She was halfway out the door when she heard his voice. She froze for a moment, then took a step back inside. She took a deep breath. Then she was gone.

Jeana ran, with Thor in her arms, to a Denny's restaurant. A little old man lent her a quarter. She called her mother in Oregon, asked for a bus ticket. Mom said okay, but it couldn't happen until tomorrow. Jeana sat down and cried. The man bought her a bowl of chili, then sneaked her into his nursing home. Jeana slept the night on the floor by his bed. The other residents thought it was the scandal of the age. In the morning, many of them brought her toast from the cafeteria.

Jeana said goodbye, then called the Glendale bus station. She told the ticket agent that John Holmes, the porn star, was looking for her and wanted to kill her. Please, she said, don't tell him anything. The agent agreed to help. Then he asked how she was getting to the station. He and his son came and picked her up.

As Jeana expected, Holmes showed up at the bus station. The ticket agent played dumb. Holmes followed the wrong bus all the way to San Francisco.

Tracy McCourt turned right onto Dona Lola Place, drove 100 yards into the cul-de-sac, parked, cut the engine. DeVerell, Lind and Launius pushed aside the chain-link gate to Nash's driveway and filed around to the right, behind the house. The sliding glass door was still open, as Holmes had said.

They went inside, opened the door of the guest bedroom, peered out. Lind took the lead and charged down the hall, a short-barreled .357 Magnum in one hand, a stolen San Francisco police detective's badge in the other. Diles and Nash were in the living room. Diles was wearing sweat pants, carrying a breakfast tray. Nash was wearing blue bikini briefs.

"Freeze!" yelled Lind. "You're under arrest! Police officers!"

DeVerell and Launius covered Nash. Lind made his way behind the shirt-less, blubbery bodyguard. He shifted the badge to his gun hand, his left, then took out the handcuffs with his right. As he fumbled with his paraphernalia and Diles's thick wrists, Launius came over to help, tripped, bumped into Lind's arm. The gun discharged. Diles was burned with the muzzle flash. The right side of his back, over his kidney, began to bleed. Nash fell to his knees. He begged to say a prayer for his children.

"Fuck your children!" said Launius. "Take us to the drugs."

Lind rolled Diles onto his stomach, handcuffed him, threw a Persian rug over his head. Then he joined the others in Nash's bedroom. Every-thing was where Holmes had said. Lind put his .357 to Nash's head, asked for the combination to the floor safe. Nash refused. Then Launius forced the stainless-steel barrel of his gun into Nash's mouth.

In the floor safe were two large Zip-lock bags full of cocaine. In a gray attaché case were cash and jewelry. In a petty-cash box were several thousand Quaaludes and more cocaine. On the dresser was a laboratory vial about three-quarters full of heroin.

Lind taped Nash's hands behind his back, put a sheet over his head. He found a Browning 9-mm under Nash's bed, then went to Diles's room, where he found more weapons. Meanwhile, Launius asked Lind for his hunting knife. He went over to Diles, pulled the rug off his head, edged the knife against his neck.

"Where's the rest of the fucking heroin?" he demanded.

"I don't know," said Diles.

Launius pulled the knife slowly across Diles's neck. Blood flowed.

Suddenly, outside, Tracy McCourt began honking the horn of the getaway car.

"Forget it!" said Lind. "Let's get out of here."

At 10:00 a.m., Lind, McCourt, Launius and DeVerell walked through the door of the Wonderland house.

Holmes jumped up from the couch. "So what happened? How did it go down?"

"Don't tell him anything," snapped Lind.

Launius, DeVerell and Lind went into Launius's bedroom. They'd decided, before leaving Nash's, that they would short Holmes and McCourt in the division of the loot. Working quickly, Launius removed about $100,000 in cash from the briefcase and hid it in his room.

Meanwhile, Joy Miller and Barbara Richardson, Lind's girlfriend, left the house and drove down the hill to the Laurel Canyon Country Store for gas and cartons of cigarettes.

When they returned, the men were at the glass table in the breakfast nook. Everyone was busy. Holmes and Lind weighed the cocaine. Launius counted the Quaaludes. DeVerell counted the money. On the table were eight pounds of cocaine, 5000 Quaaludes, a kilo of high-quality China White heroin and $10,000 in cash. The jewelry would later be fenced for $150,000. Lind, Launius and DeVerell, the three who'd carried out the robbery, were to receive twenty-five percent each. Holmes and McCourt went halves on the last share.

As soon as the weighing was done, Holmes went to the kitchen to cook some cocaine powder into rock, then went into the bathroom to smoke. The rest of the Wonderland people took turns injecting heroin and cocaine. After a while, Holmes came back into the living room. He complained about his share of the money. It was only about $3000. He knew that Nash had a lot more than that lying around the house.

An argument ensued. Launius punched Holmes in the stomach. "Get the fuck out of here!" he screamed.

For the first few months, while she was in Oregon with her mother, Jeana had refused to take Holmes's calls. She'd gotten a job at a nursing home and was paying her mom rent, trying to rebuild her life. But Holmes kept calling. He sent flowers, presents, photos of them with the dog.

By May, Jeana began taking his calls. By June, she was thinking, "Well, I'm not doing anything here." On June 27th, two days before the robbery at Nash's, she flew to Los Angeles.

John was carrying two suitcases when he met her. "Oh, shit," she thought, but she didn't say anything.

"I didn't want to believe I'd fallen for a line again," Jeana says. "He was sweet. He was great. There wasn't any trouble. We went to a motel, had a nice reunion. No drugs. It was really nice. He was like the old John. Then he left."

On the day of the robbery Holmes still hadn't come back. Management asked Jeana to leave. Holmes hadn't paid for the room.

Jeana packed her suitcase, gathered up her Chihuahua. She didn't have any money. She didn't know what to do. She couldn't call Sharon. They hadn't spoken in two years. Jeana was somewhere downtown. She didn't know where. She walked the streets, tried to think. A pimp tried to pick her up. Then another. Then she ran into a woman preaching fire and brimstone on a corner. The woman took her to her house, put her to work painting a wall. Meanwhile, Jeana called Holmes's answering service and left the number. Holmes finally called on the afternoon of the 29th, after the Wonderland Gang kicked him out. He showed up at the house in the early evening. "He had the biggest pile of coke I'd ever seen in my entire life," says Jeana. "He took over the kitchen. He cooked coke all night long. He even had the Holy Roller's sister smoking."

In the morning, they went out to get food. "When we came back, the door was locked," says Jeana. "The Holy Roller was up in the balcony, waving a Christian flag, praying and hollering, singing 'We Shall Overcome.' She said John had cut some coke with an old tarot card and she believed it was a sign from the devil. I said, 'Please, just let me get my clothes and my dog and we'll leave.' "

Gregory DeWitt Diles, six feet four, 300 pounds, barged through the front door of the house on Dona Lola, dragging John Holmes by the scruff of his neck.

"In here," said Nash.

Diles shoved, Holmes skidded across the carpet. Nash shut the bedroom door.

Wednesday afternoon, July 1st, two days after the robbery. Jeana was tucked into another hotel in the Valley. An hour before, Holmes had run into Diles. Holmes was wearing a ring that had been stolen from the boss.

Eddie Nash was fifty-two years old, six feet tall, gray haired, strong and wiry. His family had owned several hotels before the creation of Israel in 1948. Nash told a friend that he missed the moonlight and the olive trees of his homeland, that he'd spent time in a refugee camp, that his brother-in-law was shot by Israeli soldiers.

The youngest son in the family, Nash arrived in America with seven dollars in his pocket. He worked for others for a time, then opened Beef's Chuck, a hotdog stand on Hollywood Boulevard. Nash was on the job day and night, wearing a tall white chef's hat, waiting tables himself.

June M. Schuyler, an elementary-school teacher from Santa Barbara, remembers meeting the "nice-looking, very-light-skinned foreign man" at Beef's Chuck. She was living in Hollywood while her autistic son attended the Belle Dubnoff School for Brain-Damaged Children. The school was a block away from Nash's place. She'd often take her son there for lunch.

From then, wrote Schuyler, in a letter to a judge many years later, "Ed Nasrallah began a courtship that was as old-fashioned as they come. For many months he took me out to dinner, introduced me to his mother and other relatives. There never was a sexual relationship between us. I said 'No' and I meant it."

Over the next year, Nasrallah brought her grape leaves, hummus, pots of Turkish coffee. Schuykir said that Ed loved her son exceedingly and that he offered to "fix it up for you to take him to a top brain surgeon. . . . No strings attached."

By the mid-Seventies, Ed Nasrallah had become Eddie Nash and had amassed a fortune. He was also a drug dealer and a heavy user. His drug of choice was freebase; sometimes he mixed the crack with heroin. Nash was missing part of his sinus cavity, one of his lungs had been removed, and he had a steel plate in his head.

For the last several years, Nash had rarely left his white-stone ranch house in Studio City. At home, Nash walked around in a maroon silk robe, or sometimes in bikini briefs, his body covered with a thin sheen of sweat. His voice had a smooth Arabic lilt. "You want to play baseball?" he'd ask his ever-present guests, lighting his butane torch, offering a hit off his pipe.

"The consumption of alcohol and drugs was an ongoing, everyday affair," says an attorney who is a longtime acquaintance of Nash's. "The cast of characters would go from two or three to ten or more. It was amazing, the haphazard way in which people would come and go. You'd walk into the house, there were various girls walking around in various states of undress. Some were quite attractive. Others looked like they'd been sucking on the pipe a little too long.

"When you met with Eddie, you met at his place, on his terms. I believe that cocaine paranoia created within him the desire to stay within that closed environment that he had control over. If anything, one of the themes in Eddie's life has always been control. He wanted to be in charge. He wanted to be the Arab man in his tent. The master, the giver of hospitality. All his lawyers—I think he had maybe six or seven working on different things— all his managers, employees, customers, everyone, would come to him. He'd have Jimmie, the cook, prepare these elaborate spreads. You could walk up, whisper something in his ear, and he'd make it available. Whatever. You just had to ask, and he'd give."

According to court testimony, Nash had a fancy for young girls, whips and a game with a revolver called Russian roulette. One woman who had sex with Nash remembers "a lot of temptation. There were piles of cocaine in front of you. Jewelry, wads of money. You'd be left in a room for hours, and then you'd be called in. There were two-way mirrors in the bedroom, anything you wanted would be made available. In a way Eddie would assess you on what you took or didn't take."

In early 1981, Nash's second wife—the mother of his two sons, aged eight and five—filed for a protection order against Nash. After she left him, according to a court affidavit, "I took the children to Oklahoma to my aunt and uncle's farm, together with my parents. My husband hired a girl to follow us. She came to the farm to find out if a certain man was with me. After she left, my husband called on the telephone at the farm and said to come home immediately. When I refused, he said, 'Don't come back to California or I will have two men waiting at the airport to kill you, and I will have your parents killed.' "

Nash is said to have had political, police and crime connections. According to one Los Angeles law-enforcement official, "Ed Nash was a very well-known figure in the Sixties around Hollywood with police, and it was never an antagonistic relationship."

One of Nash's friends and overnight guests was, according to a law-enforcement official, an Israeli with a military background, "the so-called reputed godfather of the Israeli Mafia." A report by the California State

Department of Justice revealed that the Israeli Mafia was active in California during the late Seventies and early Eighties and was involved in drugs, arson, extortion, gun-running and a number of murders, including the death and dismemberment of two Israeli nationals at the plush Bonaventure hotel in downtown L.A.

During his six or seven years of heavy drug use, said the attorney, "Nash lost over a million a year directly attributable to drugs. His business empire totally atrophied as a result of the coke. What really cracks me up is people believe he was a dope dealer. That's bullshit. He was consuming it. At an alarming rate."

On the afternoon of Wednesday, July 1st, 1981, Eddie Nash was again consuming drugs at an alarming rate. He'd been ripped off for eight pounds of cocaine, but the Wonderland Gang hadn't found his private stash, and now he was bubbling his glass pipe furiously. He'd sent two of his minions out to score more drugs, but they hadn't yet returned. Two customers waited. They did hits off Eddie's pipe, eyed the door.

One of the customers was Scott Thorson. Thorson had driven from Lake Tahoe to score from Nash. Or perhaps he had flown from Las Vegas. In court testimony years later, he would say, in answer to this and many other questions, "I don't recall. I really don't recall." Thorson was the live-in lover of the entertainer Liberace. He was also in Liberace's Las Vegas act. Wearing jewel-bedecked livery, he would chauffeur Liberace onto the stage in a glittering mini-Rolls-Royce, open the door, take his master's fur coat. Then Liberace would make a joke about having the only fur coat in the world that had its own limo. During one special engagement, Thorson danced with the Rockettes. Liberace called him Booper, treated him like a son, a lover, a pet.

Thorson had been addicted to cocaine for several years. It began, according to Thorson's book, *Behind the Candelabra*, when Liberace ordered him to have cosmetic surgery. First, however, Thorson had to lose thirty pounds. A doctor of dubious practice prescribed a salad of different drugs to aid the weight loss. Pharmaceutical cocaine was one of the ingredients.

In time, the surgery was completed, and Thorson was made into a young vision of Liberace. He remained addicted to coke. At the moment that Diles barged through the door with Holmes in tow, Thorson was with Eddie in his bedroom, doing hits. Nash was very upset.

"I'll have them on their knees!" Nash ranted to Thorson. "I'll teach them a lesson! They'll never steal from anyone again!"

Thorson was excused, and Nash closed the door. Diles smacked Holmes, threw him across the room, shoved him against a wall. "How could you do this thing!" Eddie Nash screamed. Diles hit him again. "I trusted you! I gave you everything!"

Nash and Holmes had met three years earlier at the Seven Seas. Nash was a big fan of porn. He invested in movies, leased office space to several porn-related operations. Holmes was one of the greats in the business. Nash liked having him around. He introduced him to all his guests. "I'd like you to meet Mr. John Holmes," he'd say.

For his part, Holmes did anything he could for Nash. Frequently he brought him girls. On Christmas Day 1980, he'd even presented Jeana. Nash reciprocated with a quarter ounce of coke. Holmes thought Nash was the most evil man he'd ever met, but he couldn't quite figure him out, so he respected him.

Now things were not so friendly. Holmes was crumpled on the floor. Diles leveled a gun at his head. Nash was leafing through a little black book that Diles had taken from Holmes's pocket.

"Who's this in Ohio?" Nash screamed. "Who's Mary? Your mother? Who's this in Montana? . . . Is this your brother? . . . I will kill your whole family! All of them! Go back to that house! Get my property! Bring me their eyeballs! Bring me their eyeballs in a bag, and I will forget what you have done to me! Go!"

Thursday, July 2nd, 3:30 a.m. Sharon Holmes switched on the porch light, spied through the peephole. Christ, she thought, John. She hadn't seen him in three months. His clothes were ripped, he was bloody from head to toe. He stared straight ahead, unblinking. She opened the door, folded her arms against her chest.

"Well?"

"Accident . . . car . . . um . . ." he stammered. "Can I . . . come in?"

They went to the bathroom. Sharon, a registered nurse, rummaged through a well-stocked medicine cabinet, brought out iodine and cotton swabs. She reached up and took John's chin in her hand, turned his head side to side. Funny, she thought, no cuts, no abrasions. Just blood. "You had an accident in the Malibu?"

John looked down at Sharon. His eyes blinked rapidly. They'd been married sixteen years. Sharon always knew when he was lying. That's probably why he always came back. "Run me a bath, will you?" he said.

John eased into the tub. Sharon sat on the wood-covered commode.

"What now?" she thought. He dunked his head, put a steaming washcloth over his face. Then he sat up. "The murders," he said. "I was there."

"What do you mean you were there?"

"It was my fault," John said, his eyes welling with tears. "I stood there and watched them kill those people."

"What are you talking about?"

"I was involved in a robbery," John began, and he told the story. The setup, the robbery, Nash's threat to kill his whole family, Sharon included. "So I told him everything," John said. "I told where the robbers lived and how to get there. I had to take them there."

"Who?"

"Three men and myself."

"Okay, you took them there."

"I took them there. There was a security system at the house. I called up and said I had some things for the people inside and to let me up. They opened the security gate, and the four of us went up the stairs, and when the door opened, they forced their way inside. Someone held a gun to my head. I stood there against the wall. I watched them beat them to death."

"You stood there?"

"There was nothing I could do."

"John, how could you?"

"It was them or me. They were stupid. They made him beg for his life. They deserved what they got."

"Blood! Blood! So much blood!" Holmes was having a nightmare. Tossing and moaning, punching and kicking. "So much blood!" he groaned over and over.

Jeana was scared to death. She didn't know what to do. Wake him? Let him scream? It was Thursday, July 2nd, 1981. After bathing at Sharon's, Holmes had come here, to this motel in the Valley. He walked through the door, flopped on the bed, passed out.

Jeana sat very still on the edge of the bed, watching a TV that was mounted on the wall. After a while, the news. The top story was something about a mass murder. Four bodies. A bloody mess. A house on Wonderland Avenue. Jeana stood up, moved closer to the tube. "That house," she thought. Things started to click. "I've waited outside that house. Isn't that where John gets his drugs?"

Hours passed, John woke. Jeana said nothing. They made a run to McDonald's for hamburgers. They watched some more TV. Then came the late-night news. The cops were calling it the Four on the Floor Murders. Dead were Joy Miller, Billy DeVerell, Ron Launius, Barbara Richardson. The Wonderland Gang. The murder weapon was a steel pipe with threading at the ends. Thread marks found on walls, skulls, skin. House tossed by assailants. Blood and brains splattered everywhere, even on the ceilings. The bodies were discovered by workmen next door; they'd heard faint cries from the back of the house: "Help me. Help me." A fifth victim was carried out alive. Susan Launius, 25, Ron Launius's wife. She was in intensive care with a severed finger and brain damage. The murders were so brutal that police were comparing the case to the Tate-LaBianca murders by the Manson Family.

Holmes and Jeana watched from the bed. Jeana was afraid to look at John. She cut her eyes slowly, caught his profile. He was frozen. The color drained from his face. She actually saw it. First his forehead, then his cheeks, then his neck. He went white.

Jeana said nothing. After a while, the weather report came on. She cleared her throat "John?"

"What?"

"You had this dream. You know, when you were sleeping? You said something about blood."

Holmes's eyes bulged. He looked very scared. She'd never seen him look scared before. "Yeah, well, uh," he said. "Um, I lifted the trunk of the car, and I gave myself a nosebleed yesterday. Don't worry."

On July 10th, police knocked down the door of their motel room and arrested Jeana and Holmes. For the next three days, Holmes, Jeana and Sharon were held in protective custody in a luxury hotel in downtown Los Angeles. Armed guards in the lobby, in the hallway. Room service. Holmes tried to make a deal with the cops. He wanted witness protection, a new name, money, a home. He wanted new names for Sharon and Jeana, too. He offered the police secrets. Names of mobsters, drug dealers, prostitutes, pimps. The police wanted to know who killed the Wonderland Gang. Holmes wouldn't tell.

"With Holmes, it was like he was center stage and the lights and the camera were on," says a detective who was present. "It was like he was doing a movie. Here he is, he has two women with him. All three of them are sleeping in the same bed. He stroked us, jacked us around. He told us certain things. That we were on the right track, that this is indeed what had happened, that this was the motivation, that this was how it came down. He played it for all it was worth, then he said he wouldn't testify. We cut him loose."

The three went back to Sharon's house. Sharon cooked dinner. Holmes picked up Sharon's two dogs and Thor from the kennel. Later, the women dyed Holmes's hair black. Holmes and Jeana painted the Malibu gray with a red top. They used cans of spray paint. The finish was drippy and streaked, but it didn't matter. They were going underground.

Now it was midnight in the parking lot at the Safeway in Glendale. The Malibu was idling. Jeana sat in the front seat, Thor in her arms. Holmes leaned up against the back bumper, smoking a cigarette. Sharon stood with arms crossed. "Change your mind. Come with us, Sharon."

"No way, John."

"It can be the three of us, Sharon, like old times."

"You've got to be joking."

"You can't do this to me," he said.

"Why? Why can't I?"

"Because I love you."

Sharon looked at him. On their first date, he'd brought a bottle of Mateus and a handful of flowers. Sharon had watched through the window as he picked them from the neighbor's front yard. Now she shook her head slowly, walked around the car to the passenger side. Jeana leaned out the window, and they hugged. Over the years, they'd become like mother and daughter. "Take care of him," Sharon said.

"Hello, Jeana."

"Chris? Is that you?"

"How are you, Sis?"

"Fine. Where are you calling from? You sound close."

"I'm here."

"In Miami?"

"Yeah."

"What are you doing here?"

"Well, I, I, ah, came . . . with a friend. Listen. Tell me where you are. I'll pick you up."

Jeana hung up the phone. Her brother Chris, 16, lived in Oregon. She hadn't heard from him in, what, six months? Not since she was home. Now it was December 4th, 1981. After leaving California, Jeana and Holmes had gone to Vegas, then Montana, then headed south, visiting the Grand Canyon, the Painted Desert. Holmes broke into cars along the way.

The couple ended up in Miami, at a small run-down hotel on Collins Avenue. Everyone there was on some kind of slide. Big Rosie, the manager, let Jeana work the switchboard and clean rooms in exchange for rent. Holmes went to work for a construction company, painting a hotel down the strip. For extra money, Jeana solicited tricks on the beach.

"Everybody at the hotel got to know us," Jeana says. "We were real friendly. John was doing a lot of drawing. Drawings of the dog, of me. We'd have dinner with other people at the hotel, go to movies. We were like a normal couple. After a while, I said I didn't want to go out on the beach anymore. We had a big fight. I ran out the door, down to the pool, and he ran after me, the fool. Everybody was down there. He beat the shit out of me, then walked back up to the room. Everybody was just shocked."

The next day, while Holmes was at work, a delegation of residents came to see Jeana. A mother and daughter offered to help. The daughter had a kid and a job. She was moving to a house. Would Jeana want to be the live-in baby sitter? Jeana packed her bag, gathered up Thor, put Holmes' gun in her pocketbook.

Now it was December 4th, and she hadn't seen Holmes in two weeks. Her brother was in town; something weird was going on. Chris didn't have a driver's license. How could he rent a car?

They picked up a six-pack, went to a park, sat by a pond.

"Jeana, I've got to tell you. See that car over there? It's the cops."

"You little . . ." Jeana stood, walked away. Chris caught up.

"Listen," he said, grabbing her elbow. "People are after John, and they think you're with him. You're going to get hurt. Tell the cops what they want to know, 'cause otherwise John's going to be dead in a few days. You're probably going to be saving him."

When the cops got to his hotel, Holmes was there. "I've been expecting you," he said. He invited them in for coffee.

"How you doing, John?" said the man in the gray suit, leaning over the safety rail of the bed. "John? Remember me?"

February 1988, seven years after the murders. A sunny room in the Veterans Administration Hospital in Sepulveda, California. The man in the suit was Los Angeles Police Department detective Tom Lange. Behind him was his partner, Mac McClain. The Wonderland case was still open. They had a few questions for John Holmes.

"We want to talk to you about Eddie Nash," said McClain. "John? . . . Remember Eddie? . . . John? Are you awake?" Holmes's eyelids fluttered. He weighed ninety pounds, his fingernails were two inches long. He was dying.

Following his arrest in Miami, Holmes was tried for the murder of the

Wonderland Gang. His defense was simple: John Holmes was the "sixth victim" of the Wonderland murders, and Eddie Nash was "evil incarnate." "Ladies and gentlemen," his lawyer told the jury at the outset, "unlike some mysteries, this is not going to be a question of 'Who done it?' This is going to be a question of 'Why aren't the perpetrators here?' "

In the end, the most damaging evidence the prosecution could produce was a palm print on a headboard above one of the victims. Holmes refused to testify. The jury found him innocent.

Holmes remained in jail, however, on his outstanding burglary case. While awaiting that trial, he was ordered by a judge to tell the grand jury what he knew about the Wonderland murders. Because he'd already been tried, Holmes would not be able to invoke the Fifth Amendment. According to the law, he had to talk. He refused anyway. He'd underestimated Nash once, but he'd never do it again. Nash would kill him and his family if he talked, he was certain of it. He was held in the county jail for contempt.

In jail, Holmes went on a hunger strike. Two weeks later, it was reported that he'd lost only seven pounds. Jailers said other inmates were giving him candy bars. Later it was reported that Holmes interrupted his fast, ate a meal, then continued his fast.

Finally, on the afternoon of November 22nd, 1982, Holmes relented and testified. He'd been in jail eleven months in all, 110 days on the contempt charge. His attorney told reporters that he'd changed his mind because of "certain arrangements" that had been made and "certain circumstances" that had arisen. What he may have been referring to was the imprisonment, that very same morning, of Eddie Nash, on charges of dealing drugs.

Just after the murders, Nash and Diles had found themselves in a world of shit. Nash's house was raided three times. Each time, drugs, money and weapons were seized. Each time, Nash made bail. Then Nash was arrested with three others on federal charges of racketeering, arson and mail fraud, an insurance scam. Nash's three coconspirators were found guilty. Nash was acquitted.

In the end, both Diles and Nash went to jail. Diles got seven years on charges stemming from the drug raids. Nash was found guilty of possessing two pounds of cocaine for sale. At trial, his lawyer argued that the $1 million worth of coke was not for dealing, that it was strictly for personal use. During recesses in the trial, Nash would go out to his car and smoke freebase. Then he'd swallow a few Quaaludes and return. His lawyer hired a young associate to stick Nash with a pin whenever he nodded off in court.

The judge in the case was Everett E. Ricks Jr. It was obvious from his comments that Ricks, a hard-liner, considered Eddie Nash a plague. Ricks even came in from his sickbed to sentence Nash. Coughing into the microphone, Ricks called Nash "a danger to the public" and maxed him out. Eight years in prison, a $120,350 fine.

Two years later, Ricks reduced Nash's sentence to time served, and Nash was released. Ricks cited Nash's need for delicate surgery to remove a sinus tumor. "I wouldn't want to be operated on in San Quentin Prison," Ricks said sympathetically.

Two years later, Ricks, himself, was ordered held against his will for psychiatric observation. The fifty-two-year-old former jurist had been arrested after he allegedly punched his eighty-two-year-old mother and threatened to kill someone if she didn't give him keys to a car.

After his release, Nash told a friend that jail had saved his life. He moved to a modest condo in Tarzana and set about rebuilding, taking college business courses at night. Drugs, inattention, back taxes and lawyers' fees had depleted his fortune.

Holmes, meanwhile, had gone back to making films.

When he got out of jail, Holmes was jubilant. He greeted reporters, had dinner with his lawyer, then called Sharon. She told him to "get the fuck out of my life." He couldn't call Jeana. She was nowhere to be found.

Holmes had nothing to do and nowhere to go. His lawyer lent him a Volkswagen Beetle and $100, and Holmes showed up at his friend Amerson's house. While Holmes was in jail, Amerson had started a company called John Holmes Productions. He was marketing Holmes's old films on video. Like all porn actors, John had been paid per day and had signed away the rights to his own films. His old friend was happy to pick them up. "Let's face it," Amerson says, "John was a product. I marketed him. That's what it's all about. It's business."

With all the publicity from the murders, John Holmes had achieved almost mainstream celebrity. The video boom was just beginning, and Holmes became a kind of Marlon Brando of porn. No longer the leading man, he was now the featured oddity. In *California Valley Girls*, for instance, he had one scene. He came in, sat on a couch. A girl entered stage right. Then another girl, another. At the end, there were six working at once on his penis.

Early in 1983, Holmes was shooting *Fleshpond* at a studio in San Francisco. One of the actresses in the cast was Laurie Rose. Laurie was nineteen; she came from a small town outside Vegas. In the business she was billed as Misty Dawn, the anal queen of porn.

"That first time, we didn't get to work together," says Laurie, "but we were attracted. It sounds silly, but you know how you can meet someone for the first time and it's like you know them already?"

After the film, John and Laurie, who looked like Jeana, began dating. Usually, they smoked freebase and had sex. Then, says Laurie, "the third time I went up there, he came up to me with the mirror and said, 'You want a hit?' and I turned to him and said no. He looked shocked. He said, 'Why not?' and I said, 'Because it makes me feel funny and I can't talk.' So he went in the bathroom, and he locked himself in. He stayed in there like three hours, and I'm just sitting there, you know, twiddling my thumbs. Finally he came out and said, 'You know what? This stuff makes me feel funny too. I'm going to quit.'"

In time, John and Laurie moved in together at Amerson's. When Amerson raised their rent to $400, they got their own place in Encino. John continued to make films, but he made Laurie stop. "He thought one porn person in the family was enough," she says. "And the AIDS thing was just starting to come out. Nobody had gotten it yet; but it was still in the back of our minds. He thought, 'Well, if I'm going to take a chance, that's enough.'"

Apparently, Holmes had made good his promise and stopped doing drugs. John and Laurie stayed home a lot and watched videos. On weekends they went to swap meets and yard sales.

"Nobody ever came over," says Laurie. "Nobody knew where we lived. His words to me were 'Friends can get you killed.' We were very careful. Then, when Eddie Nash got out of jail, John was very, very worried. We went on twenty-four-hour watch. For like three weeks, one of us had to be awake at all times. It was like being in a movie or something."

By late 1984, John was working as an executive at Amerson's VCX films. He was supposed to be doing sales and pre-production, writing and editing, in addition to acting. Amerson says Holmes spent most of his time playing cards and shooting darts. When VCX cut off Holmes's salary, Amerson put up money to start Penguin Productions. Holmes was to run it. Laurie worked as a secretary. "John was tired of the whole industry," she says. "He wanted to make a million dollars so we could just leave and be done with it."

Then, in the summer of 1985, John tested positive for AIDS.

"He went fucking crazy" says Amerson. "He panicked, walked in circles around the doctor's office, threw his briefcase down. He said, 'I'm gonna die!' and drove off."

"When he came back," says Laurie, "he was laughing about it. We closed up the office and went to the beach. We played our favorite songs, walked, talked. John said he felt like he was chosen to get AIDS because of who he was, how he lived. He felt like he was an example."

John continued making films for a while. His last film was *The Rise and Fall of the Roman Empress*, starring Ilona "Ciccolina" Staller, a member of the Italian Parliament. By the time it was released, in 1987, Holmes's health had already begun to slide. The word in the industry was that he had colon cancer. Holmes was telling people that doctors had removed sixteen feet of his large intestine. In truth, Holmes was operated on for hemorrhoids. Around that time, he also began developing complications related to AIDS. Amerson, meanwhile, accused his friend of embezzling $200,000 from the company. He cut Holmes off, canceled his insurance.

"John was really sick by this point," says Laurie. "We moved around a lot because the rent kept going up. I was working as a computer programmer. John would just stay home. He was in so much pain, you couldn't touch him. He couldn't walk. His legs and feet would swell up, his ears would bleed, he had infections in his lungs. His surgery wouldn't heal up, either. He was very upset about the business. He'd made all these people millions and millions of dollars. We were really broke. He called some people, and they said, 'We'll help you out.' But we'd never get the money they promised."

On January 24th, 1988, John and Laurie were married in the Little Chapel of the Flowers, in Las Vegas. It was a simple ceremony. The bride wore white. "It was a big ordeal for him," says Laurie. "He knew he was dying. He knew we wouldn't have a life together."

In February, Holmes was admitted to the VA hospital in Sepulveda. Soon after, Detectives Lange and McCain called the hospital. They wanted to see Holmes. After seven years, the district attorney was reopening the Wonderland case, based, in part, on testimony from Scott Thorson, Liberace's ex-lover. Thorson, who was waiting to be sentenced on a drug-related armed robbery, had sought a deal with police. He was prepared to testify that Eddie Nash had sent Holmes and Diles to Wonderland Avenue and that Nash felt responsible for the "bloody mess" that resulted. Now the police wanted Holmes's testimony.

Laurie was standing at the door when Lange and McClain appeared down the corridor.

"John, they're coming," Laurie said in a stage whisper.

Holmes nodded his head, put out his cigarette, closed his eyes.

"He was incoherent," says Lange.

John Holmes died on March 13th, 1988. "His eyes were open," says Laurie, "and it looked like he had looked up to Death and said, 'Here I am.' It was the most peaceful look I ever saw in my life. I tried to shut his eyes like in the movies, but they wouldn't stay shut."

Holmes didn't want a funeral, but he did have a last wish. "He wanted me to view his body and make sure that all the parts were there," says Laurie. "He didn't want part of him ending up in a jar somewhere. I viewed his body nekked, you know, and then I watched them put the lid on the box and put it in the oven. We scattered his ashes over the ocean."

Six months later, on September 8th, 1988, Diles and Nash were charged with the murders on Wonderland Avenue. After a preliminary hearing in January 1989, at which Thorson, among others, testified, Nash and Diles were bound over for trial this summer; they are currently being held without bail in the Los Angeles County Jail. Nash's and Diles's attorneys maintain their clients' innocence and question the credibility of witnesses for the prosecution.

"You know," says Detective Lange, "there's no mystery here. Every time you read something, they say it's a big mystery. Or the local TV says it's a big mystery. Or that show out of New York, you know, *A Current Affair*. Big mystery. Like aliens or something. There's no mystery. John Holmes didn't go to his grave with anything but a very bad case of AIDS. He told us everything initially, right after it happened.

"But it's one thing to tell someone something," says Lange. "It's another thing to testify to it in court."

(1989)

Little Girl Lost

Savannah was a gorgeous porn starlet with a taste for handsome rock stars and expensive Bob Mackie gowns. When things fell apart, she could only see one way out.

Jason slammed the door shut, slumped back against it. His soft brown eyes were saucered with panic; his lightly muscled chest was pumping air. "She did not just do that," he groaned.

He smoothed his fingers down one of his Luke Perry sideburns, absently measuring its length against the bottom of his earlobe, wondering what to do next. He glanced around her closet: Bob Mackie gowns, Anne Klein suits, Chanel shoes, ripped Levi's on individual hangers, hatboxes, dozens of them. "Dude, this isn't happening."

He pushed himself off the door, began pacing the long walk-through closet—five steps forward, turn, five steps back—rerunning the scene in his mind. His knee hurt. What was she thinking? Driving the Corvette like a maniac, squealing around curves, him screaming in the passenger seat—*Slow down! Slow down!*—and the next thing you know, around this one corner, it was so weird, kinda slow motion, he's seeing this fence two inches from his window, this whitewashed fence with big, heavy boards, and she's just plowing it down, splintering board after board after board, the white fiberglass nose of her car crumpling, the awful shattering noise, and then *boom!* she hits the tree.

It was now about 2:30 A.M., July 11, 1994, an hour or so after the accident. Jason Swing paced the closet, forward and back, and then on one trip he continued all the way to the opposite door, the master bathroom. He went in.

The Jacuzzi was swirling, and the candles were lit, dozens of candles, reflected in a three-way makeup mirror. He walked around idly, picking up a false eyelash, a ceramic cat, the bottle of white Zinfandel. He took a swig. Shit! he thought. He coulda been boning by now. His eyes fell upon the view from the sliding-glass doors that made up the north wall of the room, down the slope toward the river of lights on the Hollywood Freeway, and in the distance, up on the hill, the amber glow of Universal City.

Jason took a deep breath, walked back through the closet. He stopped at the door he'd slammed. On the other side was the garage. He called out in a tentative voice: "Shannon? Savannah? Can you hear me?"

He pressed his ear to the door, listened.

Breathing. It sounded like she had asthma or a bad cold.

He opened the door slowly.

Back in time, four years ago, Shannon sitting on a black leather sofa. She's a platinum-blonde, pale as porcelain, arms hugging her knees to her chest, two-inch lacquered nails, her big blue eyes bloodshot and glassy, tears running down her smooth chipmunk cheeks, past her overdrawn red lips . . . drip, drip, drip, into the deep V neck of her sweater, her new breasts, the work of a Beverly Hills plastic surgeon, 435 cc of saline solution in a silicone pouch on each side, catching and heaving in silent anguish.

She'd been found out, and she knew it, but she didn't know what to do next, so she was doing the usual: nothing. She was a young woman who lived in the moment; there was nowhere else for her to go. When things got bad, this was her reaction: curling into a ball, letting the events flood, waiting to see where she washed up.

Billy sat at her feet, yoga-style on the shag carpet, his palms pressed together as if in prayer: "Come on, Shannon, tell me, babe," he pleaded. "It's okay, sweetie. Let it out."

Silver bracelets clanked and chimed on Billy's forearm. His fingers were long and sinewy; he played bass in a band. "Please, babe, you can tell me," he beseeched. "Stop crying. It's okay."

Billy never knew what to expect. Or maybe he did. She could be so childish and endearing and happy one moment, squeaking and giggling with joy, tilting her head to one side and winking a Maybellined eye, playing with Willie, the kitten—their son, she joked—and then suddenly, the dark curtain would descend, the tears, the silence, the pain. Sometimes, making love, Billy would raise his head and look at her face, so pretty, except for her eyes, glazed and staring like a doll's. Where she had gone he could only imagine.

They had met at the Ventura Theatre eighteen months earlier, the night after Halloween, 1989. Shannon Wilsey was 19, lived with her dad in Ventura, an hour northwest of Hollywood. Shannon worked in a boutique on

Main Street, went to the beach every day, studied for her GED. She had posters of rock stars on her walls, a subscription to *Guitar Player*, liked to dress the family dog in party clothes with her 6-year-old half sister. Five-foot-four, 105 pounds, pert breasts, killer little ass, 34-24-34, Shannon was the kind of girl the Beach Boys had had in mind, the archetype of the California girl, updated with a tiny thong bikini. She had a dozen of them, all the same: the top, two little triangles, with strings around the neck and back; the bottom, a snake of spandex peeking out from the smooth crease of her butt, slithering high over her hips, diving small and tight in front. Just before she met Billy, she'd entered her first bikini contest at the local Holiday Inn. She took third. She blamed her breasts. Her Tater Tots, she called them, giggling, then growing teary. That was before the surgery. Sometimes you can fix what you think is wrong with you. Sometimes not.

Anyway, Billy Sheehan was onstage at the Ventura Theatre playing with his band, Mr. Big, when he spotted her. He was the leader, a garage-product from Buffalo who'd gotten his break playing bass in David Lee Roth's post-Van Halen group. Now Mr. Big was about to tour with Rush; a gold album and a hit video were in Billy's future. Shannon had come especially to see him. "My favorite thing in my little life is rock and roll," Shannon would say in her squeaky-cute, syrup-sweet voice, Marilyn Monroe meets Betty Boop. Her ambition, she told her dad, was to marry a rock star. The notion that someone loved by millions would love only her: Ultimate attention, that was her ideal.

She was in the front row when Billy spotted her, this real, live, perfect Varga doll, right down to the neatly trimmed bangs veiling her forehead. The spotlights sought her out in the shadows like rays from heaven, and she glimmered and shone, an angel dwelling on the outskirts of the mosh pit.

When he awoke the next morning, she was sleeping there beside him, so sweet and so beautiful—the skin, the ass, the tattoo on her ankle, "GREGG." Man, I could spend the rest of my life with this, he thought.

Two months later, at the end of his tour, he called. She sounded surprised.

They reunited at a Denny's on Sunset Boulevard, Shannon waiting at the counter with her bag. For the next few weeks, they played house at Billy's, just having the greatest time. Shannon never talked about her past, never talked about much of anything. What was on TV, who was in concert, what she was doing this moment—that was her world. She seemed simple; she wasn't really. She was just too closed off to let you in. You could tell she was hiding something. You didn't want to know.

In time, Shannon got a little apartment she called the Hellhole, with a roommate but no furniture. Shannon and Billy came and went, he for tours, she for, well, he wasn't quite sure what. She'd just disappear for a few days, a week, then show up again. Maybe if she hadn't been so beautiful, he would have asked. Beauty does that: shuts you up, makes you cling, blinds you to things.

Like countless pretty, young hopefuls before her, Shannon began her Hollywood sojourn with a B movie, *The Invisible Maniac*. She took Billy to the premiere at the Ritz Theater, in August 1990. Billy thought Shannon looked great twelve feet high on the screen. At one point, she had this really cute dumb line, and the whole place roared. Billy thought she was wonderful. "Babe, you are a fucking star," he said. Shannon said nothing. She thought they were laughing *at* her.

Said the *Los Angeles Times*: "The youthful actresses bare their bosoms about every five minutes. . . . The morbid, puritanical effect, axiomatic in schlock exploitation fare, is that sex, represented by all that bared flesh, just has to trigger a wretched excess of violence."

Shannon disappeared.

A month later, she showed up at Billy's in hysterics. She told him this story about how she'd once been involved with rocker Gregg Allman. He wanted her to make a movie. She had signed the contract and taken the money, but now she didn't want to do it.

Billy said he'd talk to his lawyers. Shannon grew frightened. "No, no, that's okay," she said. "I just wanted to see what you thought."

Then she had the breast surgery, and Billy wondered where the money had come from, but this was, after all, Hollywood. It wasn't until she pulled up in a brand-new Mustang convertible that he started asking questions.

"Did you get the money from Gregg Allman?"

"Yeah, and I have money left over." She giggled, so proud. "You should see my new apartment!"

Soon after, Billy was browsing a newsstand when something called *Squeeze* magazine caught his eye. It cost $16. There on the cover was Shannon, his baby, wearing the little black dress he'd bought her. She had a guy's prick in her mouth.

Billy called his partner at Metal Blade Records, who called his wife, who worked at Flynt Publishing, the home of *Hustler*. She asked around.

Shannon had signed a movie deal with Video Exclusives, a low-end, triple-X distributor. The deal specified twenty-five pictures, $250 per scene, plus an additional $250 each time she appeared on a box cover.

Billy called Shannon, sat her down on his leather sofa, took a place at her feet. "Babe," he said, "I know where you got that car, the apartment. I know the whole thing. . . ."

"What?" said Shannon.

"Babe," he said, "I know all about the contract."

Deny. Deny. Deny.

"What's going on with you?" he asked. "If you want to do a love scene and show your body, that's okay. But to do a porn movie, babe—this is gonna affect your whole life. Don't do it. Please!"

Shannon went silent, and then the tears began to flow. Billy pleaded with her to talk. "Please, babe. Tell me."

Finally, exasperated, Billy decided to try a little game. He'd been to shrinks. He knew when someone needed one.

"Shannon," he said. "I'm gonna say something, and I want you to answer with the first thing that comes to your mind."

She cut her eyes toward him.

"Why can't you talk, Shannon?" he asked, his voice soothing and professional. "Who's holding you down?"

Shannon's eyes went wide. She blinked. She seemed to go into a trance. It was as if something deep inside had suddenly been unveiled, a dark memory that had eluded her. It was an amazing, sudden transformation. Billy didn't know if she was acting or if it was real. It was like she'd been hypnotized.

"My mom," she said, a soft monotone.

"What's she doing?"

"She's holding me down on the front seat. She doesn't want me. She wishes I wasn't born."

"Where are you driving?"

"To the hospital."

"Why, Shannon? Please, tell me. . . ."

Shannon's mom and dad met in Mission Viejo, California, in the middle of June 1969. Mike Wilsey, 17, was the son of a mailman. He was cruising with a friend in his souped-up VW Bug. Pam Winnett, 16, was the daughter of a nurse and a hippie painter. She was living with her maternal grandparents, hanging out with some girlfriends.

In the late Sixties, Mission Viejo was the frontier of Orange County. The high school had no sports teams, there was no movie theater. It was safe and clean and boring. Shannon Michelle Wilsey was born on October 9, 1970.

Mike suspected that the baby was not his, but he and Pam got an apartment anyway, tried to make a go of it.

In Mike's version of the story, he came in time to love Pam, but she was very unstable, very unfaithful. Finally, he couldn't take it any longer. He dropped Pam and the baby at her father's house and said good-bye. Shannon was 3.

Shannon's early memories were disturbing. At the core was the story she told Billy, later others. She was sitting on a beanbag chair in an apartment, she recalled. There was a man dressed in women's clothes. What came next ended with her mom screaming, cursing Shannon's existence, holding her down on the front seat of the car, speeding to the hospital.

After a time, Pam married and moved to Texas. Mike was hurt and angry. "I had been with Shannon long enough to fall in love with her, no matter whose kid she was." But at the same time he was relieved. "I just thought, farewell and good riddance."

Mike's next contact with Shannon was ten years later, when she came to live with him and his wife. The couple were Christians. He worked as a Roto-Rooter man; they lived with their two kids in Oxnard, California. When Shannon showed up, Mike was transfixed. The resemblance was unmistakable. All these years he'd been so sure she wasn't his. His guilt was overwhelming. He prayed.

Shannon was well-behaved at first, but then she started breaking curfew. Mike warned her and warned her. Finally, he turned his 13-year-old daughter over his knee and spanked her.

Shannon went straight back to her mom in Texas. Then she was caught sitting on her stepfather's lap. She was shipped off to her great-grandparents, in Mission Viejo.

So it went, back and forth. One night, in a restaurant in Texas, her mom noticed Gregg Allman a few tables away. "He's staring at you, Shannon. Go talk to him."

Mike's next contact with his daughter was a phone call. "I'm on the road with Gregg Allman," she said. She was 17.

Attorneys for Allman have requested that *GQ* not use his name in connection with Shannon's, but Shannon mentioned it frequently, had it needled into her ankle in blue ink. The details she told of this period were sketchy. Partly because she never told anyone much of anything, partly because it was a haze. She had discovered heroin. She called its effect "the warm fuzzies." Heroin made her feel numb and dreamy, luxurious, safe, timeless. It made her troubles go away.

She traveled around the country when the band was on the road, stayed other times in a high-rise apartment with a private elevator. Gregg came and went. Then there was a big scene with his wife. Shannon called her dad. "I want to come live with you guys."

For the first three months, Shannon adjusted well to family life. She found the job at the boutique, went to night school, kicked back at home.

Soon she became restless. She began going to the Ventura Theatre, staying out to all hours. She entered her first bikini contest at the Ventura Holiday Inn.

She finished third that fall night in 1989, and the shoulder she cried on was that of another contestant, Racquel Darrian. Racquel was with her boyfriend and a young photographer named Micky Ray. All three had just started in porn. Micky told Shannon that she was beautiful and that she should be a model. He would do her portfolio, he said, get her a shot with a legitimate agent.

Mike Wilsey suspected the offer, told his daughter she didn't have the background to be an actress or a model. "There's no such thing as 'instant,'" he said. Shannon called Micky. Her dad carried her bags to the curb.

At Micky's, Shannon lay on the couch for days, watching TV, blissed out on some Percodan she'd found in the medicine chest. She kept Micky running out for food, bourbon and cigarettes. They had sex, but she wasn't into it.

Then her dad relayed a message. Billy Sheehan had called.

Shannon got off the couch, asked Micky to drive her to the Denny's on Sunset. She was going to become a star.

A black-tie banquet in a Las Vegas hotel, the 1992 *Adult Video News* Awards, the Oscars of porn. Light splinters off a mirrored globe on the ceiling, showers the throng below: stars, industry types, pop-eyed fans from across the country, seated at tables of ten, chicken or fish.

Halfway into the program, Chi Chi LaRue has just concluded the entertainment. The six-foot, 300-pound transvestite, real name Larry, is known as the Divine of the industry—a director, gossip columnist, gadfly and chanteuse. Tonight she chose an auburn wig and leather pants with the cheeks cut out. She sang "Spank Me," accompanied by a cavalcade of female stars, a fractured take on a production number: Miss America goes triple-X.

They danced out of the audience, up to the stage, a conga line of porno queens, each one larger than life: bustier, naughtier, with higher heels and deeper necklines, the filmic embodiment of male fantasy and lust. Robin Byrd and Amber Lynn, Christy Canyon, Racquel Darrian, Jeanna Fine, Tori

Welles—maybe thirty of them. They spanked Chi Chi's fat pink butt, then turned on one another, swatting and goosing, giggling and mugging and hugging.

And right there, center left, was Shannon Wilsey.

"Where's that bitch Savannah?" called Chi Chi. "She needs a spanking!"

The crowd roared and Savannah stepped forward in her $8,000 Bob Mackie creation, a skintight, low-backed, sequined halter unitard, in rainbow colors with accompanying aquamarine gloves. She could afford the outfit. Savannah was making close to $200,000 a year having sex on film. She side-stepped Chi Chi's swipe, swatted him one.

Now the girls were seated. It was time for more awards. The presenters were two veteran actresses, Shanna and Sharon. The category: best new starlet.

"And the winner is . . ." they said in festive tandem, opening the envelope. Their faces fell. They emitted a brief, spontaneous moan. "Savannah," they announced.

Accepting her winged golden trophy, Savannah stepped to the microphone and smiled—a huge, dazzling smile, framed by red lips. Her eyes were closed; her lids fluttered. Perhaps it was a shy reaction to all the acclaim or the weight of the two pairs of false lashes she always wore. Or perhaps it was the Jack Daniel's, heroin and coke she'd done, her usual cocktail.

"Heeeloo-ooo," she trilled to the crowd in her ditzy way, her eyelids working open. "Aren't you happy for me?"

She let out a little snort, and then a giggle, and then a long, whiny laugh, a kid thumbing her nose, *tee-hee-hee.*

The role for which she'd won was that of Scarlet in *On Trial,* a film inspired by obscenity prosecutions over the past few years in small municipalities across the nation. It had been nominated for eleven awards, including best girl-girl scene, by Savannah and Jeanna Fine. The film won seven, including best picture.

Up at the podium, Savannah basked in her moment. People often said she needed a roomful of adulation. Here it was at last. She lingered at the microphone. "Thank you again," she said finally. "I love you all."

She blew a kiss, took a step to leave. Then she stopped, returned to the microphone.

"And if *you* don't love *me,* I'm sorry. . . ."

After her first photo shoot with Micky, Shannon tried nudes. She liked posing, and she liked the money. Soon, she decided to try films. Her first scene was a girl-girl in *Racquel's Addiction,* with Racquel Darrian from the bikini contest. Shannon billed herself as Silver Kane, an allusion to a syringe.

Shannon was two hours late to the set, but when the footage came in, the director was ecstatic. Shannon was the real thing in a field crowded with almost, not-quite beauties. As to her performance, well, the camera loved her, and she loved the camera back, had the self-absorbed exhibitionism of a high-fashion model. Watching her was like seeing a girl in a jeans commercial take off her clothes and start having sex.

Only the sex with Shannon wasn't very exciting. Once that part started, she seemed to excuse herself from her body. If actors sometimes admit to "phoning in" a performance, it would have to be said that Shannon substituted a cardboard cutout of herself. Editors dubbed in the moans and groans.

No matter. They sell fantasy in porn, and Shannon was the ultimate sweet little girl in the parlor, the girl you were hopelessly infatuated with, the girl you could never get. That she didn't act like a whore in the bedroom seemed to fit. It was almost what men expected, a kind of living doll to which you did things.

After two films, Shannon landed the contract with Video Exclusives. The company gave her the new breasts, the apartment on Laurel Canyon and the Mustang. She took the name Savannah from her favorite movie, *Savannah Smiles,* a children's story about a rich little girl who runs away from home and reforms criminals.

The company shot twenty-five scenes but released only ten. Since the advent of the VCR, the porn industry had changed and boomed. No longer relegated to seedy theaters and peep shows, porn films could now be watched in the privacy of people's own homes. By 1993, sales and rentals were at $1.6 billion. At the low end of the market were companies such as Video Exclusives. They pumped out title after title, sex scenes with no plot, something for everyone: black men with white women, women who squirt when they come, shaved pussies, huge breasts, obese people, chicks with dicks.

When her one-year contract was completed, in the fall of 1991, Savannah was sent by Video Exclusives to Vivid Video. Vivid was decidedly upscale, a combination of a modern marketing agency and an old-time Hollywood studio. It signed six very pretty girls a year, made about eight movies with each one, advertised like crazy. Owner Steve Hirsch hired mainstream art directors and fashion photographers for the box covers, spent more than

$100,000 a film, allowed six days to shoot a script. Vivid didn't just sell movies. It created porno supermodels, the Cindys and Christys and Kates of triple-X.

Six months into her contract with Vivid, Savannah had done about five films, and Video Exclusives had capitalized, flooding the market with its back catalogue. Savannah was ubiquitous: best new starlet in the industry.

Unfortunately, everyone hated her. They called her "ice queen," "cold bitch," "evil cunt."

They had reasons.

Savannah was by now a $200-a-day junkie. She carried her works in a cloth makeup bag, inside her leather backpack: black-market ten-packs of B-D .29-gauge, ultrafine insulin syringes; the leg from a pair of white tights to tie off her arm; a lacquer-handled tablespoon from Pier 1, charred on the bottom from cooking her brown Mexican tar into a solution.

Savannah had trouble showing up for work. When she did, she was late. Depending on when she'd had her last fix, she was either very animated or very detached. When she began dancing in upscale strip joints across the country, a big moneymaker for porn stars, she never brought along enough drugs. Club owners would find her jonesing on the floor of her dressing room. They'd have to send out a lackey to score for her.

On the set, she was known to be "difficult": "If that goddamn P.A. doesn't get me my coffee in two minutes, I want him fired!"; "I don't want ugly bitches like this in a scene with me!" She demanded script approval, casting approval, her own makeup man. And where was the goddamn ashtray?

They ran and got her an ashtray. The fact was this: Savannah's films outsold all the others' five or six times over—up to 20,000 units each. Whatever Savannah asked for, she got. She responded by demanding more. They responded by hating her more. It was the circle that defined her life.

Savannah liked the acting. She learned her lines, even suggested nuances: "Do you think I should, like, make my voice catch right as I'm saying this?" Her favorite role was the lead in *Sinderella*. On the last day of shooting, the prince didn't show. "It figures," she told the director.

Her sexual performance continued to be mediocre. Most women in the industry say they enjoy the sex, some more so, some less. But they agree that you have to like it a little or you'll lose your mind. You show up for work, and you just let yourself get carried away; you fall in love with your scene partner for as long as it takes to get the film shot. Then you go back home. It's like getting paid for a one-day affair.

Savannah didn't even try to get into the sex. One story had her on all fours on a bed, taking it from behind. Out of the frame, she was absently fingering the leaves of a potted plant on the night table.

"Come on, Savannah," said the director, Paul Thomas. "Say 'Fuck me' or something."

Savannah looked over her shoulder at the actor inside her. "Fuck me or something," she said, then went back to playing with the plant.

Thomas is Vivid's chief director. He worked with Savannah as much as anybody in the industry did. He echoes the general sentiment: "She was a real bitch. A selfish, selfish bitch. She reveled in putting people down. She didn't like giving of herself in any way, shape or form. She was irresponsible and flaky and selfish and stupid."

In a world of fragile egos and damaged psyches, Savannah made little effort. She rarely socialized with anyone in the industry, though she did often fuck the boss. She was considered the classic ice queen—haughty, distant, unapproachable.

Probably the biggest slight to people in the industry was her mainstream status, the by-product of her penchant for rock stars. Over time, she would be linked with Billy Idol; Vince Neil of Mötley Crüe; David Lee Roth; Danny Boy, leader of the rap group House of Pain; and Axl Rose and Slash, both of Guns N' Roses.

The *Star* reported Savannah's engagement to Slash: ". . . and she's flashing a three-carat ring to prove it." *People* had Savannah and Slash "engaged in full hit whoopee" in a crowded New York club called the Scrap Bar. She was on national television with Marky Mark at the Grammys. And then there was her longest, most publicized affair, with Pauly Shore. He took her to the MTV Video Music Awards, to the opening of the movie *Point Break*, on vacations in Hawaii.

Savannah clipped and saved every article, blacking out any mention of her real name, Shannon Wilsey, with a thick Magic Marker.

Now, at the *Adult Video News* Awards, Savannah left the stage, made her way through the crowd. She was sitting tonight with her girlfriend Jeanna Fine. They were lovers, fellow junkies. Jeanna was a few years older, a sort of journey woman in the industry who'd worked herself up to become a feature performer.

Jeanna knew Savannah was demanding. Sometimes, when Savannah started her shit—"Hon-eyyy, I'm getting piss-yyy!"—Jeanna would look at her and laugh. " 'Feed me, do me, buy me,' " she'd chant, "the Savannah national anthem." Jeanna had dark hair and dark eyes. Her film persona tended toward dominatrix; at one time she'd done private outcall as such, commanding $1,000 an hour. She could handle Savannah's bullshit, did it well enough to inspire the kind of puppy-dog loyalty of which Savannah was capable when she could muster some trust.

Jeanna said she was "totally, completely, in love with her." She went slowly, got to know Savannah as few did. Jeanna knew how fragile Savannah was, that her bitch thing was really a protective force field, that she was so insecure and needy that her relations with the world were skewed. Jeanna knew about Savannah's passion for fuzzy slippers and macaroni and cheese, and for pink things and flowered sheets and lace. Jeanna knew the way Savannah rubbed her tits all over after she shot up; the way to touch her, to talk to her, to make her moan. Savannah needed constant care. She was dead inside, very lonely. Jeanna pampered her, sometimes ordered her around. Jeanna knew that a woman's clit was really between her eyes.

Now, her moment in the spotlight just passed, Savannah returned to her table to find Jeanna in animated conversation with Amber Lynn. Amber had done three very good years of films, then quit and got into dancing, 800 numbers and products. She was a big name in the business, very well respected among the girls.

Savannah broke into the conversation, turned her back on Amber. "I don't *want* to hang out with Amber," she whined. "This is *my* night."

Amber was nonplussed. So this is Savannah, she thought, this surly little kid wearing her mommy's false eyelashes. She's got a few things to learn.

"What's your name?" Amber interrupted. "Shannon? Savannah? Come over here, sit down. Let me talk to you a minute."

Savannah looked Amber up and down, turned on her heel. "Good *night,* Jeanna," she said.

Up in her room, Savannah sat on the king-size bed in her spangly outfit. She swigged a bottle of whiskey, snorted a couple lines, set about reading some fan mail.

It was routine stuff—requests for photos and dinner dates, words of longing, poems of lust and admiration, a big thank-you from a wife who said that Savannah's videos had rekindled her sex life. Another envelope:

"Savannah, your terrible. Please retire. Stix R."

She ripped out a sheet of paper, answered in her round, careful school-girl print:

Stix,

You don't know me and you never will, all you know is what you
see on my movies, which you have obviously taken the time to see
in your pathetic "terrible" life. You know you could never be with
someone like me. I am the BEST/CLASSIEST woman to ever be
in this business. You should feel lucky just to have seen me fuck on
film. Get a fucking life, asshole!!! Save your hand for jerking off—
not writing stupid letters, you worthless piece of shit.

Savannah

"Yo," said Jason Swing, answering the black cordless phone, plugging the
opposite ear with a finger. It was 10 P.M., July 9, 1994. Jason was the personal assistant of Danny Boy. He was house-sitting while the white rappers were on tour, livin' large at the star's crib with some buds on a
Saturday night.

"Heeeloo-ooo, it's mee-eee!" trilled the voice on the other end of the line.

Jason searched his memory bank. "Me who?"

"Savaaan-nah," she said, a bit irritated.

"Oh. Oh, yeah," said Jason. "Whazz-up?"

Danny Boy was Savannah's latest crush. She'd been in the "Jump
Around" video. She was pretty stuck on him. He was noncommittal. It
was the pattern.

Ever since Billy Sheehan, Savannah had had a hard time with relationships.
Not long after the scene in Billy's living room, Savannah had gone out and
fucked Billy Idol. She'd confessed; he'd forgiven. Then she'd started up with
a member of Ratt. She'd lied about going to a party Ratt was throwing, forgetting that Mr. Big was on the same label. Billy had stood five feet from
Savannah, drinking a beer. She'd pretended he wasn't there.

Savannah wouldn't give her father her phone number; he'd written long
letters, in printing similar to hers: "Please don't think I don't care. I do very
much. I hope you can talk to me more. I'd like to have your phone number.
. . ." Her dad prayed, thought about hiring a private detective. Her mom continued to be indifferent, though Savannah showered her with presents and
money. When Savannah had gone home to Justin, Texas, and confessed her
heroin addiction, her mom dismissed it as a phase.

Savannah and Jeanna had parted ways after a big scene in Palm Springs.
They'd gone there with a sugar daddy. Savannah had been holding the stash
of heroin, thirty bags. The girls had had a little spat. Savannah wouldn't give

Jeanna her fix; Jeanna refused to beg. While Jeanna was waiting in the hotel lobby for a car to the airport, dope-sick, wishing she were dead, Savannah strutted past in a thong bikini, another girl on her arm.

For a while, there had been Shawn. He was stolen by Savannah's best friend, Julie Smith. The couple had moved into a house that Julie had rented and furnished with a $2,000 loan from Savannah. Then there'd been the married strip-club owner. The last night of a weeklong stint at his club, the two had dinner. He complained about his wife the whole time. When Savannah asked why he'd married such a bitch, he stomped off. He left her with the check, and refused to pay for her week's dancing.

Slash had disavowed their relationship and the "engagement ring." The ring, platinum with three rows of diamond baguettes, was actually from a businessman, during the days when they used to shut his office door for meetings. When she asked that the door remain open, her relations with that company began to sour.

And Pauly Shore? They'd dated for exactly eleven months. Pauly talked about marrying her, the whole sweet nug-and-picket-fence giggage. He also made videos of them having sex. "It just gets to a point where they either move in or you break up," Pauly later said. "I didn't want to get deeper into quicksand."

Now there was Danny Boy, kind of. Jason was the guy who took his messages. Savannah had met Jason a couple of times at Hell's Gate, a club Danny Boy owned with Mickey Rourke and some others.

Jason didn't know Savannah was *someone.* To him, she was just another blonde party girl with a one-name name and fake tits. Vivid dismissed her in the fall of '92, eight months after she'd won best new starlet. She had her breasts done again, this time with 600 cc of saline in each side, 34DD. She wasn't happy with the work. They wrinkled funny at the cleavage when she leaned over, rippled when she would lie on her back. The scar tissue around the areolae, where the implants had been inserted, was pronounced.

"Is Danny there?" asked Savannah.

"He's on tour in Europe."

"He's gone already?"

"Yeah, he left, like, a week ago."

"Oh," said Savannah, totally deadpan. She was silent a few moments. Then: "What are *you* doing tonight?"

Jason's father was an interior decorator who'd done Spielberg's house, among others. His mother was an artists' agent. Jason had been a yell-leader in high school in Encino. More recently, he'd gone to cooking school, done club promotions.

Six feet tall, Jason was 22, had soft brown eyes, a matinee idol's dimpled chin, Luke Perry sideburns, a black Volkswagen Corrado. He had this clean-cut, Beverly Hills hip-hop white-boy thing going—big pants, sparse goatee, moussed hair with carefree strands, backward baseball cap.

Jason was what they call a Face Boy, a handsome man-child of few words, the male equivalent of the beautiful blonde. He went to all the clubs, knew lots of first names: Arnold, Michael, Mickey, Tori, Pauly and Juliette, on and on. Tonight he was going to a birthday party for—what was his name? One of the two fat guys in the movie *Amongst Friends*, you know, the sidekick guys? One of them.

"A parrr-tyyy?" trilled Savannah, brightening. Already tonight she'd called four people. All of them said they were busy. Last night she'd ended up mud-wrestling at the Tropicana for $900. "A party. Realllly?"

She arrived with her Rottweiler, Daisy Mae, in her white Corvette, which had replaced the Mustang. She'd gotten the dog because of a prowler. At first, she'd found flowers trampled around the windows and sliding-glass doors of her house. Then, little things—a watch, a hairbrush—began disappearing. Then she came home one night and all the lights were on and the stereo and TV were blaring: They'd been off when she left. The next day, she went out and bought Daisy. A friend gave her a blue steel .40-caliber semi-automatic Beretta. She kept it by her bed.

Savannah was wearing bib overalls and tennis shoes. She carried a package for Jason: four of her videos, several signed T-shirts, a calendar.

"What are these?" asked Jason.

"A little present," said Savannah. "It's me!"

Over the past few weeks, Savannah had been spending quite a lot of time on "me." She'd organized her scrapbook, watched and catalogued and shelved the seventy-four films she'd done, redoubled her efforts to read her fan mail. She set about framing every picture of herself she could find.

After parting with Vivid, Savannah had gone back to Video Exclusives, signed to do twenty-one sex scenes at $4,000 per. By now, the only person in the industry who would or could work with her was Nancy Pera, a.k.a. Nancy Nemo. The birdlike, talkative, fiftyish porn director was a nurturing sort, an old-school Italian mother who'd never had kids of her own.

Nancy called her Savvy—Slash's nickname for her. Whenever Savannah said she needed money, Nancy would organize the scenes, book the sets and choose one of the five men Savvy was willing to work with. Then she'd call Savannah, call her six more times, roust her up, direct and edit the film. Whatever Savannah wanted, Savannah got. Drugs, food, a place on Nancy's couch beneath the knitted comforter when she was too depressed to move. Though some might have seen Nancy as an enabler, she was really more of a hairpin; she held the troubled girl together.

In the summer of 1993, after a boyfriend told Savannah that the needle tracks on her hands and arms were ugly, she decided to kick. She called all over the Valley, collected downers from friends—Valium, Xanax, Seconal, Vicodin—anything to put her out, to wash down with whiskey. One night, she ate so many pills that she passed out on the living-room floor. There were a bunch of people over. They sat around her prostrate body, talking, having cocktails. Savannah would convulse periodically, and then every once in a while she'd sit up, start crying, curse at everybody. Then she'd pass out again.

On the morning of the eighth day, Savannah woke up, took a shower, put on makeup, even her eyelashes. When Nancy came over, Savannah was beaming. "I did it," she said, so proudly. "Did I really do it? I did, didn't I? I did!"

For the next sixty days, she didn't drink or do drugs. Then she went on the road, dancing. She had vowed to stay off H, but she was scared; she needed something. She told Nancy she had to be fucked up to be slutty, and slutty was her whole routine. Never much of a dancer, she strutted the stage to songs like "Big Balls" and "Bad to the Bone," did the requisite floor work. She drank heavily, took Valium, added a few lines of coke. "Dancing medicine," she called it.

By the late summer of 1993, Savannah had stopped doing movies, but then she got an offer she couldn't refuse. For $9,000, she agreed to appear in *Starbangers 1*, the first in a popular series.

For the first time in her career, Savannah was a consummate professional on the set. Everyone in the industry was talking: Savannah the ice queen in a marathon gang bang. *Adult Video News* gave her the most enthusiastic review of her career:

> She's an active slut hound in this tape, taking on eight guys at once, sucking dick as though there were a penis famine in the Ladies' House of Corrections, allowing her body to be doused

in champagne, then immolated with the searing heat of jizz. And you thought Savannah was a boring fuck.

Said Savannah: "I wanted to shock people, because I know people would never, ever, think that I would do anything like that. Next, I'm going to do my first anal."

In January 1994, Shannon made the cover of *Adult Video News*, and by spring, she was out of films, touring her strip act for $5,000 or more a week. Having kicked heroin, she'd managed to save $25,000 in cash. She started hanging out with Soleil Moon Frye, television's Punky Brewster. One day, Savannah led an expedition to a tattoo parlor. She had the "GREGG" on her right ankle changed into an angel.

At tax time, she had to pay $11,000 to the IRS. She bought a $2,000 camcorder and $6,000 worth of dance costumes. She lent money to friends. She spent a lot on cocaine.

Then the money was gone.

Then the reverses began. She returned from a gig in New York with no paycheck; she'd spent all the money on a coke binge. Her next show was in early May, in Canada. The off-duty cop hired to bring her through customs gave her a choice: Lose the stash or remain in the States. She opted for the drugs. A few weeks later, in Pompano Beach, Florida, she got into a fistfight with her makeup man, Skip. They were dismissed. Again, no pay.

Savannah was becoming increasingly erratic. Where heroin helped her forget her problems, alcohol and cocaine made her crazy, stirred up the deep demons that had been so long on the nod. At a boxing match at the Forum that she attended with Danny Boy, Savannah punched a guy in the mouth after he called her "porno bitch." Another night, at a club with Julie—they'd made up, despite the outstanding loan—Savannah punched a guy and a brawl ensued. The girls were thrown out.

By now, Savannah was getting third notices from the landlord. She was depressed, but that was nothing new. She talked about killing herself, but that was nothing new either. "When the pressure gets too much, just push your finger here," she'd trill, making a gun with her thumb and forefinger, pointing to her temple.

"Just hold on," Nancy kept telling her. "You'll do the next gig and you'll have money again."

And so it was, on this Saturday night, July 9, a few days before she was due to fly to New York City to dance, that Savannah decided she needed some fun. Her friends all had plans. Her latest crush, Danny Boy, had left the country without telling her. Jason and his Hollywood homeboys would have to do.

"Well," said Jason to the assembled at Danny Boy's, "I guess we should roll."

"I need to take my dog home first," said Savannah. "Want to cruise with me, Jason?"

She had a really cool house, kind of *Miami Vice*, a little more hip, not cheesy. There were naked pictures of her everywhere, some of them six feet high. Jason was kind of on a shy tip, you know, looking but not looking. Savannah giggled at him. "You're so cute! You're blushing!" She stroked his cheek, then all of a sudden raised her shirt, proffered a boob. "I just had my second operation!" Jason was astounded.

Savannah proceeded to show him everything she owned. She pointed to every picture: "My boobs look pretty good here"; "That's when I shaved for a film." She showed him her cats, Willie and Winnie, the place where her tropical-fish tank had been before the earthquake. She took him into her spare bedroom, devoted to dance costumes: her police uniform, her sailor uniform, her thigh-high spangled boots, her racks of boas and bras and G-strings.

She showed him her kitchen, her plates, her pots and pans, her refrigerator, her cupboards, filled with gourmet food from Williams-Sonoma, boxes of Kraft Macaroni and Cheese. She showed him her bedroom, her bathrooms, her view, her walk-through closet, her designer clothes and shoes and sunglasses and hats.

They landed in her living room, her black leather sofas, her glass coffee table. She poured wine and lit the dozens of candles set all around the room. She played deejay, poured wax over this plastic skull, poured wax on Jason's arm, just to fuck with him and stuff. It was cool. They were just laughing and hitting it off, exchanging gossip about stars and people they knew, just friendly, nothing sexual. They switched to some liquor that tasted like cinnamon.

At about four in the morning, Savannah stood up. "I wouldn't mind you sleeping over, but it's like our first night we've actually hung out," she said. "I don't think it would be a good idea. People get the wrong idea."

"That's cool," said Jason, forever amenable.

"I'll drive you home," said Savannah, giving him one more copy of *Sinderella*.

At 10 P.M. the next night, Jason answered the phone.

"Heeeloo-ooo, it's meee-eee!"

It was Sunday, club night for professionals like Jason, who left Saturdays to the weekend warriors. As was their custom, he and a few friends had pooled for a stretch limo. It beat the cost of DUIs.

Savannah arrived in a leather mini, black stockings, high heels, a skimpy top. Jason was like "Oh, my God! Shit!" She was drinking white wine straight from the bottle.

Club Renaissance was dead, so they went back to Danny Boy's and put on some tunes. Savannah talked a lot about Danny Boy. She also told Jason he was cool. "Some of the guys I go out with, you know, friends of people, they always try to get on me and stuff," she said. "It's cool that you're a gentleman. You don't treat me like a porno star."

At 12:30, Savannah suggested they go to her house. They took the Corvette. She drove like a maniac. Jason was screaming, *Slow down! Slow down! Boom!* She hit the tree.

It was only a few hundred yards from her house, just around a curve. The Corvette was fucked. Pieces of the fence poked through the radiator. Steam rose into the starry night.

Savannah was freaking. They managed to drive the car up the hill, into her garage. Jason had slammed his knee but was okay. Savannah had hit the windshield and the roof. They went to her bathroom. Blood and snot were running out of her nose, tears out of her eyes; it was really fucked up, the mascara leaving black streams, mingling with everything else, and she was hysterical. Her head was bleeding from the scalp. "Oh, God, oh, God, oh, God," she chanted, standing in front of her three-way mirror, dabbing at the blood with a washcloth. "I think my nose is broken," she said. She fainted, slid down the bathroom wall.

He threw some water in her face. She sputtered, woke up. Jason said he was going to call a doctor, but Savannah said no. She began to cry again. "My face! It's ruined! How am I going to do my show?"

"Come on," said Jason. "Get up. Why don't you take a Jacuzzi?"

Suddenly, Savannah popped up from the floor. "I have to call Nancy," she said, utterly composed. "Can you please go and take Daisy out and check the accident?"

When Jason returned, he couldn't find her. He went into the bathroom. The Jacuzzi was filling, bubbles rising. The candles were lit. Where was she? He went to the kitchen, then to the bedroom. He called out her names: "Shannon? Savannah?"

He walked through the closet, stuck his head out the doorway into the garage. She was sitting on the concrete floor, crying, rocking back and forth. "My car, my car is ruined," she moaned.

"Don't worry," said Jason. "You have insurance. You can get another one."

"But I was going to go look at Vipers with Danny Boy!"

Jason walked into the garage, knelt down, hugged her, kissed the top of her head, avoiding the blood. She didn't react.

"Listen," said Jason. "I'm gonna go turn off the Jacuzzi so it doesn't flood. I'll be right back, okay?"

Silence.

He came back, poked his head through the door. "Everything okay?"

Savannah looked up at him. "I'm so sorry," she said, and a tear rolled down her cheek, mingled with the blood. From behind her she pulled her blue steel .40-caliber semiautomatic Beretta.

She raised it to her head. *When the pressure gets too much . . .*

Bang!

Jason slammed the door shut, slumped back against it. His soft brown eyes were saucered with panic; his lightly muscled chest was pumping air. "She did *not* just do that," he groaned.

The rescue squad couldn't find the house; Nancy passed them on the way over, found Jason throwing up on the front lawn, went back down the hill and led them to Savannah. The exit wound looked like a tropical flower in her hair.

At 11 A.M., her dad ordered her life-support system unplugged. It was the first he'd seen her in four years. She took a last breath and died.

The expected ensued: "Death of a Porno Queen." The story had sex and drugs and rock and roll. The media scrambled, and millions across America received a guilty teletronic kick in the thalamus, a shot of human urge. Nancy cooperated with everyone. "Savvy would have wanted a Marilyn Monroe funeral. Zillions of flowers, writing in the sky, lying in state at Forest Lawn."

Her father had her cremated. Savannah would have hated the tacky ceramic jar. He keeps it on a table in the living room, surrounded by pictures of his daughter.

Savannah's colleagues and acquaintances scrambled as well, for bragging rights and film rights, for status as best friend, biggest victim, most-wronged. Some indicted the industry, called for hot lines for troubled starlets. Many ducked for cover. Others said the industry was blameless, that Savannah's story was one of decline and fall, that there had never been a rise. The girl was doomed from conception, on a cool January night in Mission Viejo.

"DING DONG THE BITCH IS DEAD" was the headline in *Screw*. "Everyone knew that she was an airhead, and now she's got the hole in her dome to prove it," the item read. At the bottom of the page—which included a picture of Savannah with Xs drawn over her eyes— was a coupon to clip and mail: "I'm not brain-dead! I'll subscribe!"

Jason Swing told the police he was out walking Daisy when Savannah shot herself. He had lied, he says now, because he didn't want everyone saying he should have stopped her. What could he have done? Like, there was a blur, then a shot. When the media started blitzing, he found refuge in the offices of StormyLife Productions, working with producer Bruce Thabit and screenwriter Billy Milligan on the production of *Outside Eden*, a science-fiction action-thriller about a future encounter with aliens.

A superstar comes along only every three years or so in the porno industry. Tori Welles was the girl before Savannah. At 13, she gave a guy a blow job in exchange for a ride to Hollywood. By nightfall she had a pimp named T. He wore a hat.

Today, Tori Welles lives in a comfortable house in Topanga Canyon, with her two babies and a nanny. She has a nice Jewish husband, a former porn actor turned director. She commands $15,000 a week dancing in strip clubs across the country.

"You know," says Tori, "I get so pissed off at these talk shows: 'Victim, victim, victim; abuse, abuse, abuse.' They use it to explain away everything. The real abuse comes when you let it rule your life. You just have to work through it. You have to help yourself however you can."

Sitting there on the garage floor, her nose broken, her car totaled, Shannon may have helped herself the only way she could. She acted ditsy, but she wasn't stupid. She was a porno queen; she earned her living having sex on film. That is what defined her, what her entire existence was about.

Shannon had no family and no past. No friends, no lover, no one who cared for her for purely unselfish reasons. Her life was a shambles; it had been that way from the very beginning. No doubt she thought it always would be.

When things got bad for Shannon, this was her usual reaction: curling into a ball, letting the events flood, waiting to see where she washed up.

Perhaps, on that warm July night, in a garage just over the hill from Hollywood, Shannon Wilsey committed the most willful act of her little life.

(1994)

The Final Days of Gary Condit

Gary Condit had never lost an election. Then a young intern named Chandra Ann Levy went missing.

Four people in a white Dodge Durango, waiting by the side of a country road. It was five-thirty in the evening on the first Monday in March 2002, an almond orchard on the outskirts of Modesto, California. The sun hung low over the distant mountains, illuminating the clouds, casting golden light across the flat, fertile valley. In thirteen hours or so, the polls would be opening; the voters of the 18th Congressional District would finally have their say. A flurry of white blossoms danced in the air, collected on the windshield like snowflakes.

The engine idled. Elvis played on the radio. A succession of vehicles Dopplered past, whooshing down the dual-lane blacktop, kicking up dust and blossoms. A news van . . . a microwave truck . . . a muscular six-wheeler, belching diesel, satellite dish mounted on top. . . .

"There goes CNN," said Gary Condit. He was sitting in the shotgun seat of the Durango, his personal auto, toggled back into a deep recline. There is a slight, soothing Okie twang to his voice; the tone was mildly sardonic—the fox in his redoubt, watching the hounds run by, resigned to persecution, still game. His wiry salt-and-ginger hair, scissor-cut and towel-dried, stood in perfect order around his head. His thick eyebrows were trimmed to a stubble. His cornflower-blue eyes, once known for their Condit twinkle, may forever be remembered for their deer-in-the-headlights glare. "I have not been a perfect man," he'd stammered. That he had not said more had been his undoing.

"There goes ABC," said Cadee Condit, sitting behind Gary, pointing to a Chevy Suburban. Twenty-six years old, dress size zero, she has the same blue eyes as her father, whom she calls Gary or Gar or sometimes the Congressman, but almost never Dad, at least not in public. A former high school

cheerleader, deceptively spunky, she was most recently employed as the personal scheduler for Gray Davis, the governor of California, having worked
her way up from the mail room to his inner office. Since last August, she'd
been living in the modest rancher on Acorn Lane where she grew up, sharing
the place with her parents, her older brother, Chad, and his wife and three
boys—three generations of Condits under one roof, with Gary's parents only
a few blocks away. The wagons were circled. It was a family campaign, just
like the old days.

Cadee looked out the window. Long ago, when Gary was just a fledgling
state legislator, he used to bring Cadee with him to Sacramento. She'd
wander the hallways of the Capitol with his business card pinned to her
shirt. At lunchtime, they'd sneak up a back staircase to the domed roof and
share a peanut-butter sandwich. Through the years, in secret dreams, Cadee
had pictured Gary one day running for president. Never had she imagined
anything like this. She tucked an errant string of flaxen hair behind her ear,
and then her hand came to rest on the gold cross nestled in the cleft of her
collarbone. *Give it to God*, her PawPaw always preached. *Take your pain and your
worries and give it to God.*

Another news van whooshed past. It was fitted with a telescoping metal
tower, a microwave transmitter. "There goes Channel 13," announced Mike
Dayton, the wheelman.

The son of a pharmacist and gentleman farmer, Dayton was born in
nearby Oakdale, known hereabouts as the Cowboy Capital of the World. He
first met Gary and Chad when he was sixteen, at a charity golf outing. Later,
having washed out of college, Dayton volunteered to work on Gary's first
U.S. congressional campaign, a special election to replace the previous office-
holder, Tony Coelho, a six-term Democrat and majority whip who'd resigned
following a junk-bond scandal.

Thirty-one, with twelve years of service under his belt, Dayton is the legislative director of Gary's Washington office. Lanky and bespectacled, he
commutes by bicycle from his house in Virginia to his office on Capitol Hill.
Last summer, he was often seen on television with microphones in his face,
issuing firm denials. Another Chevy Suburban whooshed past, followed by
another van. "There goes Fox," Dayton said grimly. "Looks like we're in for
another clusterfuck."

Cadee did a double take. She gave a look of mock horror. "What did you
say, Dayton?"

"Cluster what?" teased Gary.

Dayton sputtered, a bit embarrassed, a bit indignant, and everyone dissolved into giggles, great peals of nervous laughter that echoed around the inside of the truck, then slowly died, giving way again to silence, to the song on the radio, Waylon and Willie. Dayton tapped his fingers on the steering wheel. Gary sang along under his breath. Cadee pulled her cell phone from her Louis Vuitton handbag, checked to see if she was still in range. Chad would be calling at any moment. He was headed this way in Aunt Leona's '89 Coupe DeVille.

Their final destination was a few more miles down the road, a small local television station, KAZV, owned by a man named Azevedo. Headquartered in a converted farmhouse in the middle of a vast almond orchard, the channel was not available in the local cable lineup—something Gary had been trying to help correct. As a favor to his old friend, Gary had committed to this appearance, a softball interview with the host of a regularly scheduled farm show called *Ag 'n More*.

And that, of course, was the reason for the parade of news trucks down this lonely stretch of Iowa Avenue. On the night before the Democratic primary, with Gary facing a crowded field of challengers, the international press corps had once again descended upon the Central Valley. The appearance at KAZV was tonight's must-have media get: Gary Condit on the eve of judgment day.

Time dragged. More trucks and vans rushed past. At length, the fourth occupant of the Durango spoke up. "What's your favorite story about the press?" I asked.

"Dayton here probably has as gooda stories as anybody," Gary offered.

"I don't know. . . ." Dayton said modestly.

"How about the red car?" prompted Gary. There is a humble, good-natured quality about him: easy to laugh, eager to please, nurturing, almost ministerial. He rested his hand encouragingly on Dayton's shoulder.

"Why don't *you* tell it?" said Dayton.

Gary shrugged and twisted his body around a bit to face his audience. He was dressed in faded jeans, a fleece pullover, and a scuffed pair of brown leather slip-on boots, a crust of mud on one heel. His hands—preternaturally pale, oversized in comparison with his slight, buff frame—were clasped prayerfully in his lap. The skin and meat along the top of his thumb and index finger were bitten and chewed. It looked raw and painful.

"The first time the media really staked out my condo—this was in D. C., right in the beginning—I mean, there were like thirty or forty of them. It was midafternoon, and they were all laying around in those lawn chairs like they do when they stake you out. And I had to get out of there. I had to get to Capitol Hill and go vote.

"So I called up Dayton and I said, 'Pick me up at three, but drive the Escort.' See, he used to have this little red Escort, and then he got a new truck and a guy in the office took over the Escort, and it has sort of rotated around since then. It's about a ten-year-old car, right?"

"Yep," confirmed Dayton. "It's sorta faded to a maroon color. You know how they get."

"Um-hum," said Gary. "So he pulls up right in front of my apartment in the Escort, and he just sets there. And the whole press is just settin' there on their lawn chairs, not doing nothin'. And then all of a sudden, I open the door of the condo and come walking out. I get into the Escort. We pull away. . . . *And you woulda thought they missed Santy Claus!* They went crazy! They were stepping all over each other, falling down, yelling and screaming. I wish somebody had been filming *that!*" He slapped his thigh, threw his head back. Haw-haw-*haw!*

"That was the greatest!" Dayton enthused. He tapped out a drumroll on the steering wheel.

They sat for a moment, and then Dayton took a serious tone. "I always wonder: What do they think you're gonna say, anyway?" For almost a year, since the disappearance of Chandra Ann Levy, Gary and his family and his staff had been subjected to intense public scrutiny, to say the least. They'd been hunted by the press, staked out at home and at work, followed in their cars, photographed while sunbathing in the backyard. They'd been interrogated by the police and the FBI; they'd had to hire lawyers; Gary had submitted a DNA sample, had taken a polygraph test. They'd received hate mail and credible death threats. They'd turned on the television at any time of the day or night to hear people who'd never even met Gary calling him a liar, an obfuscator, a pervert, a hypocrite, an adulterer . . . even a cold-blooded murderer.

"I know what they *want* me to say," Gary answered. He turned his head, looked out the window—row upon row of almond trees, evenly spaced, dark and spindly branches covered with fine white blossoms. He ran his right hand through his thick, bristly hair. He spoke quietly. "They want me to say that I did her."

A shocked silence filled the vehicle. Gary turned back toward the others.

"Not gonna do it," he said, his voice rising in volume, his face rearranging itself into a comic mask, a send-up of an old skit from *Saturday Night Live*—a thin-lipped, nasal, rodent-eyed impersonation of former president George H. W. Bush.

"Not gonna do it!" said Gary Condit "*Not* gonna do it!"

The *Ag 'n More* interview having concluded without incident—the affable host limiting the questions to politics and policy—Gary and his party collected themselves inside the KAZV studio.

"You did good," Chad said to his father. He is a bit taller than Gary, with the same small but athletic frame, the same flat behind, a slightly different kind of gentle twang, a version indigenous to Modesto.

"Real good," Cadee agreed.

Gary smiled earnestly. "I felt pretty good."

"You ready?" asked Chad. He had the tight look of a cornerman, working a wad of gum.

Gary nodded. "Let's get this over with," he said. His Adam's apple bobbed.

"How many you think are out there?" Dayton asked.

"Fifty?" Chad ventured. "I don't know, maybe seventy-five—a shitload."

Chad was sporting a day-old stubble, a leather jacket, and hip Nike slip-on shoes; at home he is known to wear a nylon do-rag and baggy hoops wear, a predilection he shares with his sons. Chad was married at twenty-one to a half-Mexican, half-Italian named Helen, the prettiest girl at Ceres High. A Navy veteran (he joined during the Gulf war in a fit of patriotism, without telling his parents), a three-sport little-league coach, he'd worked for several years as a night security guard at a trailer park. People in the valley say Chad has his father's gift for connecting with people. Senior citizens find him respectful and cuddly. Farmers find him folksy. Businessmen find him comfortable at an expensive lunch. Even the media enjoyed his wry sense of humor, his gum-chewing, wisecracking version of the Condit twinkle—especially the females, a grizzled lot with whom he chastely flirted.

Not very long ago, Chad, thirty-four, had been a young man with a bright future. He'd been working as a top aide to Gray Davis, the governor's main man in the Central Valley, $110,000 a year plus benefits. Two months before Chandra Levy went missing, Chad had been tapped by state Democrats for his first try at political office—a run for the California General Assembly.

All of that was history now. The future was unfathomable. He was doing his best to live in the present—running this campaign, dealing with the press, trying to salvage his father's career and his family's name—while living in a three-bedroom rancher with seven other people and two large dogs, paying his bills out of the dwindling proceeds from the sale of his house. Private school wasn't cheap, but he knew better than to argue with Helen. Dark-eyed and olive-skinned, a stark contrast to the peaches-and-cream Condits, she does all the cooking for the extended family. They call her Sugar because she's so sweet, the nickname bestowed by her mother-in-law, Carolyn Condit, the undisputed matriarch of the household.

"Okay, Gary," Chad said. "We're giving a short statement, then we'll take a few questions, then we're outta here. We're stressing your experience, your record, your thirty years of public service."

"And remember to smile!" Cadee said. She cocked her head and beamed up at him—her own thousand-watt version of the Condit twinkle.

Fifty-four years old, Gary Adrian Condit has held public office since the year he graduated from college, working his way up the political ladder from city council to mayor to county board of supervisors to California General Assembly to the U. S. House of Representatives. He was born in Locust Grove, Oklahoma, the son of a Free Will Baptist minister, the great-grandson of a sharecropper. A mix of German, Irish and American Indian, he is a registered member of the Cherokee nation. At nineteen, married to a Catholic girl from the better side of town, with an infant son born six months after their elopement, Gary came to California to attend junior college. Four years later, in 1972, while the other kids his age were marching and burning draft cards, Gary was finishing his B.A. degree, selling paint at Montgomery Ward, going door to door on nights and weekends in the small town of Ceres, population eight thousand, wearing a short-sleeved business shirt and a tie, mounting his first political campaign.

Over the years, in a heavily Republican district, Gary never lost an election. In 1994, in the November of Newt Gingrich's Republican revolution, with the Democrats taking heavy losses nationwide, Gary won his own seat with 66 percent of the vote. A savvy, effective, elbow-swinging inside player, he had a detailed command of the difficult issues important to his district— air and water, agriculture and trade, immigration and Social Security, veterans' affairs. Never much of a floor speech-maker, he stayed below the radar; he often fixed it so colleagues shared his credit. He never pandered to the leadership, choosing instead to navigate his own path, the one that best suited the needs of his electorate. He pissed people off sometimes, but they were mostly other politicians. Like the time in Sacramento when he and four other young legislators tried unsuccessfully to unseat a powerful Willie Brown from the speakership. In the aftermath of the failed coup, Gary was stripped of all his committee assignments. But Gary's comeuppance in Sacramento actually played well among the voters, an example of his resolve to do right by them, regardless of personal political cost. Next election, they made him their congressman.

During his thirty years as an elected official—twelve in the House—Gary became known for his tireless constituent service. A hands-on congressman, a voracious cross-country commuter, he spent at least three days a week at home, where his family had chosen to remain after his election to Congress. He was beloved by his electorate, the residents of a conservative, racially and ethnically diverse, agrarian district in the Central Valley of California, the place portrayed in the movie *American Graffiti*. In real life, they called it Condit Country: You couldn't throw a peach pit without hitting someone whom Gary or his family or staff had helped through a personal crisis.

In time, Gary became one of the most powerful men in California, even the nation: the second-ranking Democrat on the House Agriculture Committee, the leader of a conservative Democratic congressional coalition called the Blue Dogs, a close confidant of Governor Davis's, considered for a spot in George W. Bush's cabinet. On May 2, 2001, his hometown newspaper, the *Modesto Bee*, lauded Gary for his bold bipartisan work with President Bush. "Other leaders could learn from his example," glowed an editorial.

Just about the time that piece was being written, in the early afternoon of May 1, Chandra Levy disappeared. Gary had met the twenty-four-year-old in Washington the previous October—a graduate student, an intern with the Federal Bureau of Prisons, a petite and vivacious young woman from his district with a history of attractions to older, married men. In his own carefully chosen words, he and Chandra "became very close." When pressed by Connie Chung, in his first public interview on the matter, about a hundred days after Chandra's disappearance, Gary told a television audience of twenty-four million: "We had a close relationship. I liked her very much."

Though D.C. authorities publicly chided Gary for waiting until a third interview with police to admit the true nature of that relationship, they also said repeatedly that Gary was not a suspect in her disappearance. It should also be noted, for the record, that the notion of a link between Chandra and Gary was leaked to the press by unnamed police sources following their first interview with Gary. For his part, Gary asserted, "I answered every question that the law enforcement asked me."

No matter—the damage was done. There were countless articles, endless deconstruction by pundits, boundless gossip among ordinary citizens. One by one, most of Gary's friends and colleagues from both parties denounced and deserted him. The *Modesto Bee* urged him not to run for another term. Even Governor Davis—who many said owed his election to Gary—lined up and took a shot. Chad was informed of Davis's public statements by Larry King at the top of a live interview. The next day, Chad and Cadee resigned their jobs.

All the while, Gary maintained a stubborn public silence, refusing to disclose any details of his relations with Chandra Levy. He insisted repeatedly that he was taking what he believed to be the proper legal and moral steps—posting a reward, telling the authorities what he knew, asking forgiveness from his God and his family (though he would never say for what), carrying on with his duties as a lawmaker, praying for Chandra every night. It was not his obligation to unburden himself to the press, he insisted: The media was not his father confessor. His own father, the Reverend Adrian Condit, concurred: "Let he who is without sin cast the first stone," he told a radio audience, relating the story of Jesus, the prostitute and the mob.

But the longer Gary kept silent, the worse it became. Shut out, the media laid siege. Inside the castle, desperation led to bad decisions, worse results. A flight attendant surfaced, and then a hastily discarded watch box, a couple of comely former staffers, a special answering machine that played romantic music, a wellspring of lurid rumors—leather chaps and a studded harness, knotted neckties under the bed, Arab slave traders, Hells Angels, a possible pregnancy. In short order, a man who was once seen as the ideal grassroots legislator, a true man of the people—the man you could call to get a pothole fixed, your aunt's *problema con la Migra* cleared up, your lost VA check reissued—that man was no more. He had become instead the nation's most reviled figure.

Now Chad opened the door of the KAZV studio. Gary and his entourage stepped outside.

Immediately, spontaneously, totally . . . they were enveloped by the press. Wielding microphones and metal sound booms with furry covers, whining motor drives with stroboscopic flashes and phallic telephoto lenses, shoulder-mounted video cams and handheld microcassette recorders, the odd pad and pen, reporters mobbed the Condit party like so many white blood cells attacking a microorganism, surging and bumping and jostling, shouting hysterically, for they were hungry and tired; they'd been standing in the chill of the almond orchard for hours, watching the sun go down, looking at their watches, considering their deadlines, needing something from Gary, some usable footage, some live quote, some tasty new morsel they could carry home and drop at the feet of their editors, who in turn would feed it to the masses. "Gary! Congressman! Mr. Condit!"

"Could y'all stand back?" Chad pleaded.

Dayton gritted his teeth and leaned against the newspeople, doing his best to clear a lane, fighting his Oakdale instinct to swing his elbows. Cadee held firmly onto the crook of her father's arm as they were tossed by the crowd like castaways on a leaky lifeboat in a storm, a perfect storm, the perfect news story, sex and power and murder and mystery all rolled into one. Cadee hated these crowds. You never knew what to expect. In the back of her mind, she always imagined a crazy man lurking in the seething throng, a crazy man with a gun.

Gary held his ground the best he could, trying to maintain his composure, his balance. In his blue eyes—a beautiful shade of blue, really, the blue of a semiprecious turquoise bolo necktie—you could see that familiar look, that combination of fear and pluck, of cluelessness and determination: that deer-in-the-headlights glare he'd shown to Connie Chung.

People who saw that interview, people who knew Gary, his friends, said that the man who'd appeared on TV that night was not the Gary Condit they knew. In fact, Gary did the interview against his better instincts; his lawyers put him up to it, he says. They'd figured he'd get in front of the cameras and be moved to say a little more than he wanted to, maybe bow to public pressure and admit some kind of fault, ask for some kind of forgiveness. If he did, they'd figured, maybe it would take some of the heat off. If he admitted to being an adulterer, maybe the press and public would be less inclined to think the unthinkable—that Gary had killed Chandra, or at least ordered her death. But once he got out there before the cameras, it all went horribly wrong. "I felt like I'd been put in front of the firing squad," Gary says.

In Gary's mind, the Chung interview boiled down to this: "It was one thing for people to ask me questions about the incident. But they have to respect the answers. You and I may not agree, but you need to respect my answers." About the time she asked Gary the second question—"Did you have anything to do with her disappearance?"—Gary said to himself, *I can see where this interview is going. I'm putting a stop to this now.* Right then and there, he would tell me later, "Connie Chung became President Putin to me. She wasn't gettin' anything out of me; she wasn't going to break me, no way." He told himself, *I just gotta sit here and bear you, but that's it.*

"It's mean, but screw her, you know?" Gary says. "To be honest, if people look closely at that interview, if anybody bothers in history to watch the tape, they'll see where she went into a daze—she just lost it. I mean, I knew I wasn't going to say anything. She just went blank on me at some point. She had no place to go. She had this yellow legal pad. She just kept looking down at her pad. And she asked the one question like ten times, maybe twenty times. I knew this was not going over well. I came very close to saying, 'Hey, Connie, do you got any other questions besides the ones on that yellow pad?' "

And now, on the night before the Democratic primary, in an almond orchard outside Modesto, accosted once again by the media—Lord, how sick of them he had become—he had to reach down deep and gut it out again. He was running for his seat in Congress because there was no reason for him not to run, absolutely no reason at all. Do you think Gary Condit is a quitter? He's not a quitter. He would never quit. He'd never quit. He'd *never* quit. So what if his protégé, practically an adopted son, was running against him? So what if the members of his own party had redistricted his beloved 18th, removing much of Condit Country, adding the inner city of Stockton? So what if he had to sink the entire profits from the sale of his Washington condo, $50,000, into his campaign? So what if many people in America thought he killed Chandra Levy? There was no reason not to run.

He'd been an effective congressman. He had a great record in public service. He had learned his trade; he knew what he was doing. He hadn't gone to Washington to serve the leadership or the president or the boys in the back room. He'd gone to serve the people in his district—so let them decide. If the voters were going to say that they didn't want Gary Condit to represent them, fine, he would go quietly. But he wasn't going to bow out of the race because of what the press said, because of what the pundits said. As he told Connie Chung: He did not kill Chandra Levy. The press had taken a missing-persons case and turned it into a romance novel. He wasn't even a suspect: The police had said so clearly. The only evidence against him was a bunch of lies and innuendo and hearsay, stuff dredged up by the press, stuff they kept repeating on television again and again.

Gary stepped forward, alone, into the klieg lights. The crowd of reporters formed a tense and expectant semicircle around him. He spoke into the garden of microphones swaying before him like so many colorful tulips. He invoked his campaign themes: his thirty years of public service, his record of effectiveness, his loyalty to his constituents. And then Chad opened the floor to questions.

Everyone shouted at once. The loudest guy had a British accent. "What do you believe happened to Chandra Levy?"

"Where are you from?" snapped Gary. His hands were clasped prayerfully at his waist.

"The BBC," said the man.

"Where do you live?"

"Los Angeles."

"I don't have any idea," Gary said.

"Congressman! Gary! Mr. Condit!"

"You," Gary said, pointing.

"If the polls are right and you lose tomorrow—"

"Whose polls are you citing?" Gary interrupted.

"Well, ah—"

"You have to identify your polls. Where are you from?"

"Inside Edition."

"Oh, God!" Gary groaned and rolled his eyes heavenward, half serious, half goofing around, the Gary that few people ever see. It was a spontaneous reaction, a real human moment. It elicited a good laugh from the assembled press, and with that, something turned; you could feel it in the crowd. The edge came off; everyone seemed to calm down a bit. The press was getting its footage. Gary was surviving another clusterfuck, even doing well, connecting, trying a little something new, a new tack here in the late going, a technique he'd arrived at rather spontaneously: a game called Question the Questioners. It seemed to be working. The twinkle had returned to his eyes. For once, facing the media, he seemed to be ahead in the count. "Ask your question," Gary said magnanimously to the man from *Inside Edition.*

"If the polls are right and you do lose tomorrow, is there one thing you will blame for your loss, or one person?"

"I'm not blaming anyone, no," said Gary. "You're not gonna hear me whine and blame. That is not Gary Condit. This is not a blame game. I'm out here doing what I'm supposed to do. I'm out here fighting till the end to win the election. I've tried to be a gentleman. I've tried to be dignified. I've tried to focus on what's important—and you guys have had to decide how to respond. If you think your response has been dignified, like gentlemen and ladies, you'll decide that for yourself. Time will tell if you were right . . ."

It continued in this vein for fifteen minutes or so, portentous questions from the national folks, issue-oriented ones from the locals, the normal give-and-take of a political campaign. Then Chad stepped forward. "One more question," he said. He pointed to a woman in the crowd.

"What do you want to tell the people of this district, given your affair with Chandra Levy?"

Gary's blue eyes saucered; his pearly smile disappeared. He grimaced, a look of maximum distaste. Wherever he went, every single time, every interview he gave, impromptu or prearranged, it was always the same. He never knew exactly what form it would take or when it would come, but it always did. As if every single one of them—from the London *Sunday Observer* to NPR to *Inside Edition* to *Good Morning America*—entertained the fantasy that he or she was somehow going to be the anointed one, the one who managed where all the rest had failed, the one reporter in the entire world who was going to trick Gary Condit into confessing that he'd done it with Chandra Levy.

The deer-in-the-headlights glare returned. He raised his right hand and pointed with his index finger—the knuckles up, the thumb tucked, the finger raw and bitten, quaking with rage—intent on making one thing perfectly clear. "I am not going to acknowledge that," he said through clenched teeth. "You're citing hearsay, rumor, and innuendo."

And that was it. The sound bite they ran on the news.

Gary's house on Acorn Lane has beige siding and brick trim, a shake-shingle roof, a cherry tree in the front yard covered with delicate pink blossoms. At the rear property line, a row of cypress trees rises thirty feet, dwarfing the cookie-cut tract home, giving it the appearance of a dollhouse. The cypress is Gary's favorite tree, known to bend but not break in high winds. Many had been the times that he'd brought a troubled person outside and pointed up at the towering row of evergreens. "You gotta be like them trees," he'd say.

It was ten o'clock in the evening, the first Tuesday in March, Election Day. The polls had been closed for two hours. Outside the house, the media buzzed and swarmed in the odd, shadowless white light cast by the kliegs. News vehicles lined the block on both sides, engines running. The smell of exhaust mixed in the air with the smells of woodsmoke and tree pollen and holstein manure, the Central Valley being the largest milk-producing district in the world.

Last summer, after Chandra disappeared, Modesto was lousy with press. With Congress in recess, the media staked out Gary's office in Modesto and his house in Ceres, seven miles south, grown now to a thriving town of thirty-five thousand. At one point, Chad was accused of attempting to run over a newsman with a white Ford pickup. At another, Cadee was sitting by the pool with a girlfriend when two cameramen came over the back fence. In both cases, police were summoned. According to the *Modesto Bee*, news organizations spent more than $1 million locally before pulling up stakes after September 11.

But they were back again now, in force; the smell of political death was in the air, too. They milled about, swapping tall tales and restaurant reviews, drinking Starbucks, talking on their cell phones, monitoring the network feeds, littering the street with wrappers from the fast-food joints that lined nearby Hatch Road, the nearest exit onto Highway 99, the main artery through the valley.

Inside Gary's house, about fifty friends and family, the inner circle, had gathered to await the results. A grim sort of siege atmosphere prevailed, albeit one masquerading as a potluck supper. Supporters and media were also gathered at three other locations around the district. Though they had no money to pay for polls, the Condits' collective gut feeling was this: During the last weeks of the campaign, they'd started gathering momentum. Maybe Gary could pull this out. That's what Carolyn and Cadee believed; they were the ones who'd insisted Gary run in the first place. At a family meeting held in the living room on the afternoon of the filing deadline, last December 7, Chad had voted no. He'd been out there collecting signatures for Gary. They'd come up short. For the first time in thirty years, they'd had to pay the filing fee to run.

But Gary had decided to run anyway. First, because he had no reason not to run. And second, because if he didn't, Chad would. He had his own papers ready to file, a try for the General Assembly, sure political suicide. "It's better I get clobbered than my son get clobbered," Gary told a trusted friend. The friend had just finished telling him: "Your problem politically is not that people think you killed Chandra Levy; it's that people think you're a fuckin' jerk."

Along with his 2001 Dodge Durango, Gary's house is his most valuable asset, estimated at slightly more than $200,000. The Condits have lived there for twenty-two years; it's the only house they've ever owned. The front door leads into an entryway. To the left is a small eat-in kitchen and the living room, with sliding glass doors that open onto a small swimming pool, the line of cypress trees beyond. To the right, down the hall, are the bedrooms. A few years back, in the mode of empty nesters, the Condits upgraded their master suite and reconfigured the third bedroom, creating two small rooms: a den/gym for Gary and a reading nook for Carolyn. These days, with the consolidated households, the boys' upright piano was shoved into the nook. The gym was now the boys' dorm; there were GI Joes everywhere. In the name of kidproofing, Carolyn had boxed all of her nice things—the crystal pieces and candlesticks, the knicknacks collected carefully over the years—giving the place the barren feel of a furnished rental.

Here tonight, as always, were Gary's folks, the Reverend Adrian and Velma Jean Condit, known to all as PawPaw and MaMaw. Gary's little sister, Dovie—an attractive, fortyish grandmother—used to work for Dennis Cardoza, Gary's chief rival in the congressional race. Everyone in the Valley agreed that Cardoza owed his career to Gary. Cardoza's election party—complete with a band and a full bar—was being held tonight in Modesto, in the main ballroom of the convention center at the DoubleTree. Flush with Washington money, he'd out-spent Gary more than six to one.

Burl Condit, Gary's older brother, is a beefy man with a flattop haircut, a retired Modesto police sergeant, a former lieutenant who made a couple of missteps along the way. Burl's two boys, a deputy sheriff and a firefighter, were sitting around the kitchen table with their wives, one of whom was very pregnant. With them was Dovie's boy, also a firefighter, and his wife. Gary's younger brother, Darrell Wayne, known as Hoppy, was not there. He has a history of troubles with methamphetamine and the law.

Meanwhile, in the kitchen, the Condit women—Carolyn, Cadee, Helen and Velma Jean—busied themselves dishing out MaMaw's famous chicken enchiladas and peach popovers. Other women busied themselves trying to convince the Condit women to sit down and allow them to do the work. It was hot and overcrowded in the small space; the phone on the wall was ringing and ringing. In some ways, over the last three decades, very little had changed.

Carol and Gar, as they call each other, met when they were both fifteen, sophomores at Nathan Hale Senior High in Tulsa. He was really darling—a little bit pious, a little bit wild: typical preacher's kid. She was a mirror of Cadee—just gorgeous, a real good person, too, from a real good family. They were married after their senior year; they followed his parents to Ceres when Chad was just an infant, making the journey west in Gary's '63 Chevy, her little Corvair in tow. Gar wanted to go to junior college: School was cheaper and better in California. It was a big move for Carol. She had never been away from home. She was lonely for her brother and her two sisters, and for her parents, Big Mom and Big Pop, who owned a chain of discount clothing stores, one of the first to specialize in factory seconds. Often, Burl would tease Carol about being so homesick; MaMaw would have to tell him to hush. After almost four full years in Ceres, Carol still hadn't unpacked most of her things. She was ready to move back to Tulsa as soon as Gar finished school.

But then one night during his senior year at Stanislaus State, Gar came home and told her, "Carol, I think I'm gonna run for Ceres City Council." She just looked at him. "I didn't even know what a Ceres City Council was," Carol says. "The only thing I knew about politics is you got an ice cream cone when your parents voted."

At first, Gar started campaigning by himself, just going house to house. He told Carol, "I think this is what I'm supposed to do." Then one day he said, "People think I'm running for student council. I need a picture of you and Chad and me." They took a Polaroid; the print shop made it into a flyer. Soon, others hopped on the bandwagon—old folks from their block, college friends, young couples from church. Every Saturday, while MaMaw and PawPaw minded the kids, the volunteers walked precincts. After dark, they'd gather for a big spaghetti dinner.

So it went until Election Night, the first Tuesday in November 1972. As Carol likes to tell the story, she and Chad were alone in the little rented house on K Street, waiting for Gary to come back from campaigning. "I was glad I'd just picked up the house, because at about six-thirty, people started knocking on the door."

Of course she invited them in. Before she knew it, she was having a party. The phone was ringing off the hook. When he'd left that morning, Gar had predicted he'd come in fourth. But the television was saying otherwise: It looked like he was going to win!

Carol was so excited. When she heard him turning the corner toward the house—the little Datsun needed a muffler—she went running outside to meet him. She felt just like a little girl at Christmas. *Oh, my God! Look!* And when Gary came into the house and saw all the people, tears welled in his eyes. He took Carol's hand and squeezed. It was amazing: all these folks here supporting them, just so excited that they'd had a part in this, that they'd actually pulled this off, that they'd actually won.

The next day, Carol unpacked all her things.

And now, thirty years later, at about ten-fifteen on the first Tuesday in March 2002, many of the same people were in attendance. The party was going on and the phone was ringing; the results were being broadcast on TV. This time, however, things didn't look so good. With 43 percent of the precincts reporting, Gary was up a hundred votes in Stanislaus County—his home territory—and down a thousand in Merced, Cardoza's hometown. In the new part of the district, they were losing two to one. Down the hall, the door to the back bedroom slowly opened. For the first time all evening, Gary appeared.

Chin high, smelling of soap, he strode down the hallway, easing past the capacity crowd watching the returns in the den, touching shoulders and shaking hands, moving toward the front door. He paused just outside the kitchen. He was joined by Chad and Cadee and Carol.

Everyone gathered around. *This is just an election,* Gary told himself. This is the way democracy goes. Don't make more of it than you should. No matter what happened, he was going back to Washington: He still had a term to finish. *You just keep on clicking, man, you just keep moving, you walk, you put one foot ahead of the other and you just keep going. That's all you can do.*

"Everybody in the house, listen up," Chad said. His voice was thin and strained. Ever since he could remember, he'd been active in his father's campaigns. He'd gone to the parades, worn the T-shirts, handed out the flyers. His father was the center of everything, and it made him proud. This was the very first election that Gary had ever lost. "In one minute, Gary's gonna walk outside. I want everyone here to follow him out and stand behind him in the yard. He's gonna make a statement, and then we go from there, okay? Can everybody handle that?"

"Yeah," came the desultory response.

Chad cupped his hand to his ear. "I can't hear you!" he sang.

"Yeaaahhh!" everyone cheered, louder this time, Cadee the loudest. She thrust a fist into the air like a cheerleader.

"No tears, people," Gary said. He clapped his hands together a couple of times, like a little-league coach on the wrong side of a victory. He scanned the crowd around him. He smiled: the Condit twinkle. If there was an upside to this whole ordeal, it was standing around him right now. His friends, his family—you go through something like this, you learn a lot about loyalty and love. Carol was, quite possibly, an angel in disguise. And the kids: The way they stood behind him, there was nothing more precious than that. People will think this sounds hokey, but the Condits had been through a war together; it is something they will always have, something they will always cherish as a family.

"No tears!" Cadee repeated, dabbing at her eye with her knuckle, trying to keep her mascara from running.

"Okay, here we go," said Gary, opening the front door. "Everybody smile!"

On a warm afternoon in the middle of March, a couple of weeks after the primary, Carolyn Condit was sitting on the love seat in her living room. All was quiet in the house: You could hear the kitchen clock ticking. Cadee was in a back bedroom, recovering from some surgery she'd been putting off during the campaign. The boys were in school; Helen was food shopping with the baby. Gary was in his office in Modesto, having just returned from Washington. Earlier, as he was leaving the house, Carol reached up and took his far cheek in her palm, then pulled him close, kissed him gently on the near cheek—the casual, intimate gesture of a loving wife. Chad was sitting next to his mom. She was visibly nervous; this was her first interview with the press in many years.

"I wouldn't wish this on anyone," Carol was saying. Petite and attractive, with a sweet, lilting voice, she was wearing a pair of her daughter's jeans. She tucked an errant string of flaxen hair behind her ear, and then her hand came to rest on the gold cross nestled in the cleft of her collarbone. "It just gives me goose bumps to think about it. The helicopters. The lie-detector test. The searching of our apartment. I mean, we stood right there while they were searching. And they just glared in your eyes and ripped open our closets like they were gonna find just horrid stuff. And they even hooked this gadget up to our sink. It was just so invasive. They were so vindictive. It was just like: How can you do this to a guy who wouldn't even hurt a flea?

"I never felt, for one minute, that Gary did this or that. Never once. And I don't think I'm naïve. I don't think I have a cover over my head. Everybody else has said—the out-there people—they have said that Gar has had an affair. And it's all just ludicrous. It's just so blown up. It's like they're talking about two people that aren't even us. I mean, Gar and I were kids together. We grew up together. There's not anything better that anybody would like than for me to pack a bag and walk out, so they can write another story. But to me, it just seems like they took this healthy, gorgeous man and put an IV in him and drained him of everything, just took his heart out and stomped it. They tried to ruin something really good."

A little more than a year after her disappearance, a man walking his dog—it was said he was hunting for turtles—found the remains of Chandra Ann

Levy at the bottom of a steep, overgrown slope in a secluded area of Rock Creek Park in Washington, D.C. Both Levy's and Condit's apartments, about a mile apart, were convenient to the woodsy, seventeen-hundred-acre park. Friends and family say that Levy, a smalltown girl who aspired to a career in law enforcement, tended to avoid the park; she preferred to jog on a treadmill at her health club. Around the time of her disappearance, at least two female joggers had been victims of armed assaults in the park. Their assailant is currently serving a ten-year sentence. More than thirty bodies have been recovered in the park over the last twenty-five years.

Along with her skeletal remains, police found a Walkman-type radio, a jogging bra, panties, a USC sweatshirt, a lipstick, and a pair of stretch pants that had been tied in a knot—possibly to restrain her. Still missing, according to police, are Levy's keys, her ring and the bracelet allegedly given to her by Gary Condit, the identical twin to a bracelet given to the airline attendant who allegedly was having an affair with Condit at the same time.

Police have officially ruled Levy's death a homicide. They have been unable to determine a cause. As of this writing, in early July, detectives are examining several scenarios: that Levy was killed elsewhere and her body was dumped in the park; that she was attacked while jogging in the park; that she was lured to the park by someone and killed there.

Police have repeatedly said that there is no evidence linking Condit to Levy's disappearance or homicide. However, a grand jury has been looking into allegations that Condit obstructed justice by trying to persuade the flight attendant to lie to investigators about their alleged affair, and also by trying to discard a watch box—given to him by another alleged former girlfriend—several hours before investigators searched his D.C. apartment. Condit appeared before the grand jury in mid-April. A source close to Condit told *Esquire* that he invoked his Fifth Amendment right not to incriminate himself.

For a U.S. congressman, a lifelong politician, Gary Condit seems like a pretty regular guy. He has a decent sense of humor, a healthy appreciation for a nice ass walking down the street in a pair of jeans, a determined first step to the seven-foot hoop, especially when the game is on the line. In my time with him—a month in the Valley, five months overall on this story— he evinced an impressive command of the issues, an almost ministerial commitment to the people of his district. No matter what his political stripe, it is clear that Condit is gifted at his chosen profession—part power broker, part man of the people: the ideal grassroots legislator.

But then there are the women. On the one hand, Condit plays the role of a dedicated family man; he *is* a dedicated family man. On the other hand, the preponderance of evidence says that he's a serial adulterer. It is something good family men don't do. Does it matter? Is it any of our business? Should it ruin him?

Perhaps this whole situation could be explained away. Like the plot of a TV drama, maybe this was a case in which a husband—panicked, trying to cover up an affair, terrified of being caught by his wife—starts telling half-truths and making disastrous missteps. In time, everyone comes to believe he is guilty of murder.

Having spent time with Condit, I have to say it seems impossible that he could have killed someone. But isn't that what the friends and neighbors always say? It also seems improbable that he contracted a killer—though certainly, with his thirty years of public service in the roughneck Central Valley, he must know a few shady characters who could do the job. According to Levy's aunt, Linda Zamsky, who has given the fullest public account of the alleged affair to date, Levy was becoming increasingly impatient with her role as a mistress. There was even a five-year plan, the aunt said. Could Levy have pushed a little too hard? A twenty-four-year-old can be a dangerous loose cannon, especially to an older man who's been married for nearly thirty-five years to his best friend.

But really, now. Could Condit and his accomplices have been so diabolically shrewd? Could the man who lost a face-off against Connie Chung really mastermind the perfect crime?

Still, of the 233 murders reported in Washington last year, only three were of white women. So why Chandra Levy? How can people not be suspicious of Gary Condit? In the end, I put it to him bluntly: "Gary, either you are guilty, or you are truly the most unlucky man who ever lived."

He answered without hesitation: "It was obviously unlucky. I mean, that's obvious, it was. But I do think there is a fundamental problem here. I might not have gotten it across very well, but for the last year, I have been fighting for a principle. A lot of people in history have stood on principle, and sometimes the country was with them, and sometimes they went against the grain. The thing is, you have to be bold enough and brave enough to stand up, no matter what the cost.

"To be honest with you, it's gonna sound immodest on my part, but if you track my career, I'm always ahead of the curve. Political people and other people in public life, sooner or later, they'll have to get where I'm at now. If they don't, you'll have no privacy. At the first sign of a personal tragedy, you'll be gobbled up for frivolous entertainment value. Any person, any family, any individual at any moment who gets themselves into a situation that they can't explain, or that they don't have answers for, and the press puts a camera on it—they could end up having their life destroyed. Freedom of the press is one thing, but I have rights too. All I could do was draw a line and say, 'I'm not crossing that line.' History will be my judge.

"I don't think that anyone outside of my district, outside of my people, my family, really knows who Gary Condit is. And I don't know that I can ever get them to think of me as who I really am. I've been portrayed by the press the way they wanted to portray me. I don't think anything anybody could ever do can redeem my name. The damage has been done. I can't get anything back. And I'm not going to go around trying to change that. That's not me. That's not Gary Condit. I know who I am. I know what I'm about. I know what happened and what didn't happen.

"What more can I say?"

(2002)

The Martyrdom of Veronica Guerin

As the star crime reporter for Ireland's biggest newspaper, Veronica Guerin maneuvered fearlessly around Dublin's underworld. Maybe she should have been afraid.

Eyes sparkling, Veronica walked at her usual clip toward the back door, a cordless telephone cradled to her ear, her Irish brogue lilting with delicious gossip about her favorite footballer, Eric Cantona of Manchester United. Though she wasn't the sort to give in to crushes—she was, after all, a good Catholic girl from the North Side of Dublin, and a married one at that—Cantona was the player she absolutely loved more than anybody else. "My Eric," she called him. He was the mortar in her relationships with friends and colleagues, the icebreaker in her encounters with strangers and sources. Her devotion, she insisted, was not to his dark, French good looks—or maybe it was, a wee bit. Truly, Cantona was a legitimate superstar, the Michael Jordan of English soccer. Veronica knew the game well; she had been a scrappy center forward on the Irish women's international team. Once, in the Manchester airport after a game, she accidentally spent a five-pound note Cantona had autographed. Realizing her mistake, she hunted the bill doggedly, questioning more than 200 people. She found it.

"Just a minute," said Veronica Guerin into the phone, at home on this Monday evening, January 30, 1995. The heels of her sensible pumps clicked across the distressed plank floor of the pub her husband had built as part of the addition to their hundred-year-old cottage in rural Cloghran, twenty minutes from downtown Dublin. Complete with a tap and a twelve-stool bar, it was a gathering place for all manner of friends and acquaintances who had liberty to call without invitation. Her husband, Graham Turley, was a lad's lad. He played Rugby, wore a baseball cap, liked his lager. Veronica rarely drank but found great sport indulging others. "Have another," she'd say, grinning slyly, pushing a pint across the hand-polished surface of the bar. "It looks like you need it."

Reaching the back door, Veronica paused a moment, pushed the hold button on the cordless. The phone was a Japanese product, something that hadn't been available here ten years ago, before the formation of the European Union (EU) brought Ireland into the modern age, for better or worse. Nowadays this isle of poets and pubs is known to smugglers worldwide for its unpatrolled coastline; it has become a key transshipment point for all varieties of drugs, giving rise to a new culture of gangs and violence that is ripping the woolen fabric of Irish society. In the past few years, an unprecedented eleven gangland hits had been carried out by contract assassins. None of the murders had been solved.

The cordless phone Veronica was carrying was linked to one of three land lines installed in the house. On the kitchen counter were her two cellular phones. Down the hall, she had yet another line in her office, a fax machine set upon a desk strewn with the revealing clutter of her life: a Frank Sinatra tape, several bread recipes, a child's mitten, a shopping bag from a smart San Francisco jeweler, travel brochures and programs from soccer matches.

Until a moment ago, Veronica had been talking on three different lines at once. Her dexterity with telephone and tongue was the butt of endless *craic* from her colleagues at the newspaper, who marveled at the way she could carry on a conversation while driving her sporty red Opel Calibra at high speed across the countryside, running down a hot tip. She was, as you might expect, well-known to local gardai, as the Irish police are called.

Once, Graham had received a message that Veronica had gone to the garda station with Cathal (pronounced Ka-*haul*), their 6-year-old son. Upon his arrival, Graham discovered they'd locked her up for accumulated parking fines. Cathal, of course, had demanded to be locked up with his mum. Graham will never forget entering the jail and hearing the laughter—mother and son, she in a pastel business suit and he in sneakers, both with the same twinkling cornflower blue eyes, playing cops and crims inside a jail cell. Standing watch was a complicitous garda. Veronica had found his soft spot—he was a Leeds supporter, a fan of one of Manchester United's rivals.

Graham's wife was an incredible woman. He called her Ronnie; she was his best pal. Sparky and tough, impatient but genial, she was a combination of type A and salt-of-the-earth; she had to be first at everything she did, but she had to do it fair and square.

At 35 Veronica had already worked as an accountant, a public-relations consultant and a political-party operative. Now in her fifth year in the newspaper business, she had found her niche as an investigative reporter, working for the 252,000-circulation *Sunday Independent* (known as the *"Sindo"*), the largest and most read newspaper in a nation that published five Sundays and eight dailies.

Known to her opinionated, newsaholic countrymen by her first name, Veronica had countless friends and acquaintances, contacts and sources. She had a way of bringing them out, of creating intimacy. She was never judgmental, in person or in print. She was an arduous investigator, with an accountant's eye for documentation and detail; never did she publish a word about which she wasn't positive. She was passionate but not philosophical. She swore like a sailor: "Don't give me that shite! Would ye ever go and fuck off!"

In the short course of her newspaper career, Veronica's drive and energy had already become legend. She'd take off spontaneously to investigate a hot lead and return three days later, not having slept a wink. Similarly, she'd make fourteen phone calls to get a colleague a discount on a vacation she thought he needed. "It was like she was fitted with a turbo," Graham would later say, "just the bubbliest, warmest, most energetic person you ever could meet."

Now, at a little before 6:30 on this January evening, Veronica opened the back door of her house and stepped outside. She looked left and right. Odd. Nobody there. She heard the knocking again and realized it was coming from the front. No one ever used that door. She punched the hold button. "Flip it, Lise," she told her caller. "I'd better answer this. I'll see you tonight."

Customarily, Veronica's Monday nights were dedicated to languor. By this hour, she was ordinarily beached in front of the TV with Graham and Cathal, eating carryout, watching the news and the soccer roundup, waiting expectantly for the soaps and her favorite public-interest show, *Questions and Answers*, to be followed by a long, hot bath.

Tonight, however, was not to be a usual Monday. Though it was the end of January, her colleagues from the *Sindo* were having their office Christmas party. And before the party, Veronica was scheduled to appear on the popular *Gerry Ryan Tonight* show.

Since coming to the *Sindo*, Veronica had created a beat for herself by concentrating on the dangerous new world of gangs and drugs that was plaguing Ireland. In the last year, according to the Department of Health, ecstasy use had risen 1,000 percent in Ireland. Use of LSD and heroin (which had dropped in price by almost one-third) was up almost 300 percent. Seventy-five percent of the prisoners in Dublin's Mountjoy prison were serving time for drug-related offenses, ranging from possession to armed robbery. Murders were at an all-time high. And while the unemployment rate hovered near 20 percent—the highest in the EU—Irish drug barons were living flamboyant lifestyles, spending scores of thousands of pounds on gambling and entertaining each week, sporting cellular phones with built-in scramblers costing upwards of £11,000. Between the weak national police force and criminal laws that favored the accused—a legacy of centuries of subjugation—the drug barons, suggested one politician, "are almost immune from the criminal law; they are able to distance themselves from the evidence and buy their way out."

It was these barons whom Veronica had targeted. Unlike traditional Irish crime reporters, who relied on garda information and remained at arm's length from the crims, Veronica had pioneered a new approach, getting up close and personal with the most notorious thugs in Ireland. The public was riveted by her weekly dispatches from the Irish underbelly. "Crime is an evil subculture existing within our culture, and to me, exposing it is what journalism is about," Veronica said in an interview. "I suppose that's why I do it. It is a story that has to be told."

Five days earlier, on Wednesday, January 25, an armed gang had stolen £3 million in cash from a Brinks Allied Security van depot in Dublin. Gardai told reporters the robbers were led by a young crim nicknamed the Monk, one of five or six minor dons who were jockeying for control of the underworld following the assassination of their godfather, a man known as the General.

On Sunday, bannered across the *Sindo*, was Veronica's latest scoop, an interview with the Monk, the "most unlikely criminal mastermind I could imagine . . . an anonymous figure in blue jeans and white shirt, a pleasant smiling man looking younger than his 31 years. He could have passed for anyone if he hadn't possessed the most penetrating, disconcerting stare I had ever seen," Veronica wrote of her encounter.

Although Irish libel laws prohibited her from revealing his identity, it didn't matter. Ireland is a homogeneous nation of only 5 million; the world's largest village, it's called. Everyone, from publicans to housewives, knew the Monk's real name. "He hated the limelight and considered my interest an invasion of his privacy," Veronica wrote. "When I tried to question him about suspicions that he was the city's major heroin dealer, he refused to reply."

Veronica reported that the Monk was first arrested for larceny at age 8. His case history was a classic Dublin inner-city tale—thirty court dates over the next fourteen years, jail sentences for burglary, assault, vehicle theft and grand larceny. The Monk was freed from prison for the last time in 1985; "his activities are now covered by a respectable lifestyle," Veronica wrote, adding that he was a devoted husband and father of five children, all of whom attended expensive boarding schools.

Toward the end of the story came revelations concerning the Monk's private, possibly illegal financial dealings: "This man, the chief suspect in a £3 million cash robbery, took advantage of the 1993 tax amnesty to declare himself a financially legitimate citizen."

A brash, damaging, carefully researched story, it had a nation of gossips clacking their tongues. Politicians and garda were red faced. Criminals were both jealous and embarrassed. The source for much of the story was one of their own.

Over the last year, John Traynor, known as the Coach (as in trainer), had become Veronica's deepest well. It was the Coach who had supplied the information for her first great crim story, the one that had launched this phase of her career, about the now departed General and his unusual relationship with his wife and her sisters. The article began:

> That the arrangement worked is now indisputable fact. Mourners at the funeral of Martin Cahill, more infamously known . . . as the General, saw the evidence for themselves. Three women, clutching each other in shared grief as the murdered remains of the man they loved were lowered into the earth. Three sisters, still united in their love for one man. . . .
>
> I found out there was another side to the General. The man the public came to know as the flamboyant gangster—taunting the guards, wrapping his iron grip around south Dublin—had another side. . . . He was fiercely loyal, I was told, a loving, caring and affectionate man. His expansive abilities in crime extended to love, and he had more than enough affection and devotion to share between his lovers. . . . Cahill had 10 children by the three Lawless sisters, Frances, Tina and Anna.

The General was portrayed as an evil genius who once "ironed out a few problems" with a gentleman by pressing his face with a hot steam iron. For amusement, the General regularly let himself into garda archives with a purloined key, stealing hundreds of confidential files and crippling scores of investigations. The General delighted in taunting the gardai who kept him under surveillance, appearing at times in public wearing an IRA-type ski mask and his pants pulled down to his ankles, revealing Mickey Mouse boxer shorts.

It was said in the underworld that associates of the General were furious about the story; their ire was focused especially on the Coach, a boastful, well-coiffed man who, it would later be reported, owned a brothel and had several gardai on his payroll. Other criminals had a different take on the Coach's canary act: He was feeding Veronica self-serving bollocks, altering the political landscape of the underworld for his own purposes, pulling her unwitting strings.

So it was a great surprise to everyone when, eight days earlier, on Sunday, January 22, another exclusive article appeared in the *Sindo*: THE COACH WHO'S TAKEN THEM ALL FOR A MULTI-MILLION RIDE.

Illustrated with a fanciful drawing of the Coach smoking a big cigar, the piece opened:

> His mind's eye holds a vivid picture, an image of a man in a Swiss hotel room, running greedy fingers through a fortune. He has good reason to remember the scene, for the man in the picture is himself, and the cash in his hands is almost one million pounds. In his mind, the memory will never fade, because the man they call The Coach is addicted to the sweet smell of money. . . .
>
> "I'm the best in the country at fraud," he told me, "and if I didn't live such an extravagant lifestyle, I'd be a millionaire."

Veronica's source, a 43-year-old Southsider, had a record of convictions in Britain and Ireland for crimes that included grand larceny and possession of firearms with intent to harm. She reported that he owned pubs and shops in Dublin and county Kildare, had extensive real estate investments, three racing cars, a BMW and a £200,000 yacht and kept a suite of rooms at a luxury hotel. "His lifestyle has given rise to accusations . . . that The Coach is involved in the heroin trade, a claim he vehemently denies," Veronica wrote. She linked the Coach with a kidnapping and several robberies and burglaries and reported in detail a "scam that defrauded the Irish Collector General of £2.75 million."

On this Monday evening in late January, therefore, much of Dublin was talking about Veronica's stories. Though she had an endearing way of deflecting praise back upon its giver, she was clearly pleased with the buzz she'd created: the phone calls, the radio and TV interviews, the banner headlines. Oddly, she seemed unconcerned about her safety—even after an unknown assailant had shot a .45-caliber bullet through a window of her house four months earlier as she was putting Cathal to bed. "I don't think I have ever thought, I am in danger," Veronica told an interviewer. "There is a human side to everybody. Even to the most dangerous hardened criminal. Very often it is because they have families and they have children. If they have a wife and kids, it makes them a little more humane."

Now, reaching the front door of her house, Veronica flipped on the outside light and turned the latch.

Someone shoved hard, and the door burst open, knocking her backward into the hallway, onto the floor. A man dressed in black stepped inside. He closed the door behind him.

"My clearest memory is of the gun," Veronica would write.

> My eyes were just fixed on it. It was long, grey, steely, shiny and was pointed directly at me. His gloved hand, which appeared massive, lifted the gun up to my face. I shifted my eyes up to his, I think maybe to appeal to him, but he had no eyes, just a black motorcycle helmet. . . . My eyes went back to the steely gun. . . . I saw the narrow barrel with a little lump at the top of the tip. . . . I put my hands up to cover my head and I curled myself up into a "foetus-like" position. . . .
>
> My roars came from the pit of my stomach and I can remember them, coupled with the noise of the shot, it wasn't a bang, more like a roll of thunder. . . . My next memory is of his footsteps running away, loud thumping footsteps on the wooden hallway floor. I said aloud: "I've been shot. Jesus help me, I've been shot." I touched my head. My leg was stinging. I saw little blood, but there was a neat round hole in my leg. I realised I had to get to the phone.

Early on the dew-drenched morning of September 14, 1995, Veronica was speeding through county Kildare when suddenly it occurred to her: John Gilligan! Doesn't he live round here?

If ever a journalist worked by feel, it was Veronica. So many irons did she have in the fire, so many people did she speak with every day, so many plans and dates and rendezvous did she make and break and reschedule that she seemed to be in constant motion, never quite sure where she was going or where she would end up. She did her best thinking in the car with the window down, wind tousling her pixieish haircut, cellular phone cradled to her ear. Similarly, she'd pass hours or days in the Opel on a stakeout, her seat partially reclined, sipping coffee, watching and waiting. Graham would drop by occasionally with fresh cell-phone batteries and a picnic basket. Sometimes he'd bring Cathal. They'd make it a family outing: eating lunch, spying on crims.

Veronica had a near photographic memory, an extensive mental Rolodex. Now, in the car, she pulled up Gilligan's address, plotted a course in her mind. She wheeled right, toward the Jessbrook Equestrian Centre in Enfield.

Exactly one week earlier, Veronica had written a letter to John Gilligan, saying she was researching an article about him and wished to meet. He hadn't replied.

Known as the Warehouseman, Gilligan was a gray-haired 44-year-old career crim, recently out of the slammer. A specialist in warehouse robberies, he had recently, Veronica believed, become a major dealer. Gilligan's official records listed him as a resident of Dublin council housing. His two adult children were on the dole; he had gotten off two years earlier. His wife, Geraldine, was the owner of record of Jessbrook, a £4 million estate and equestrian center with a 5,000-seat arena under construction. The horsey locals had been impressed by a recent event at Jessbrook, particularly by the graciousness of their hostess, though it was whispered that she put on airs, tried a bit too hard to mix. When Gilligan turned up, he was noticeable from a distance, a man in a tracksuit in a crowd of crombie coats and trilby hats.

Gilligan claimed on his tax returns that his income derived from gambling. In the past year, he had paid £80,000 in taxes. However, as a result of her research, Veronica believed that millions were being laundered through Jessbrook. Conveniently, the equipment and materials needed for the equestrian center were available in Amsterdam, where drugs were plentiful and where Gilligan frequently traveled.

Veronica entered the gates of the 300-acre property just before 9 A.M. A woman at the equestrian center's office gave polite directions to Gilligan's house, and Veronica drove down a narrow road to a gate. Standing beneath surveillance cameras, she pressed the intercom switch.

In time a buzz sounded, and the electric gate swung open. A driveway led to the big house. Gilligan's Land Rover was parked outside. Veronica knocked at the front door.

She recognized Gilligan from his mug shot. He was wearing a silk dressing gown and soft slippers. "Yeah?" he said, scratching his stubble.

"Mr. Gilligan?"

"That's right."

"I'm Veronica Guerin from the *Sunday Indo*. I'd like to ask you some questions."

By now these words were all too familiar in certain circles, and John Gilligan's immediate reaction was to retreat a step. Frozen, he focused on the woman before him.

Since the shooting nine months before, Veronica had been elevated to the status of folk hero in Ireland, both subject and storyteller rolled into one, the sensational events of her life duly reported each Sunday in the *Sindo*. "What's on with Veronica now?" asked sleepy husbands on their way to tea kettles all across the nation.

Veronica's entire life, it seemed, was the stuff of high drama. Not only had she been shot but the assailant's bullet had shaved the major artery in her thigh. The surgeon's report contained the word *miraculous* in four different places. The day after the bullet was removed—a .45 that she kept as a souvenir—she snuck out of the hospital. With Graham driving, she traversed Dublin, searching out every crim who she suspected had connections to her shooting. En route, sick with fear, she vomited. Still, she carried on, hobbling on her crutches up to front doors, into garages and pubs, leaving a letter for each crim, putting them on notice that she was not afraid. Her main suspect was the Monk. She invited him to her house for tea, and they visited for six hours, during which time he persuaded her that he was not responsible. She was convinced that one of her other good crim sources was instead.

Part Bob Woodward, part lass-next-door, Veronica stood for everything good about Ireland and its people. She even went to Mass every Sunday. Her parish was known as Our Lady of the Airport, situated as it was just across an access ramp from the departure terminal at Dublin's airport.

Raised in a two-story, semidetached house in blue-collar Artane, in north Dublin, Veronica was the fifth of six children born to an accountant and his wife. Throughout her life, she maintained a strong allegiance to the North Side; she walked and talked like a Dub, and she was proud of it. In a nation where identity derives from one's village or town or county of origin, Northsiders are known for being boisterous, hardworking, lower-middle-class, poor but honest. They are constitutional republicans, staunch Catholics, believers in an Irish dream of self-betterment and upward mobility, great criers and singers and drinkers and sports fans.

Veronica's father, the son of a laborer, had elected to live in a nicer part of Artane, but still in Artane. He sent his three daughters to convent schools run by the Holy Faith sisters. Veronica was a daddy's girl, a tomboy, and at a sinewy five feet eight, a standout in basketball and soccer. From her "da" she acquired her competitive drive and perhaps her penchant for salty speech, and certainly her love for sports and populist politics. At an early age, she joined the youth wing of Fianna Fáil, the political party that received 40 percent of the vote in the last election. FF activities led to a fast friendship with the sons of then prime minister Charles Haughey and with Haughey himself. Often this daughter of the working class found herself romping on Haughey's 300-acre estate or on his yacht, *Celtic Mist*, or on his private island. Through the Haugheys, Veronica would also meet her husband—a working-class boy from the next town over. Graham served as best man at the wedding of the youngest Haughey brother, Sean, who would later be elected lord mayor of Dublin and then a national legislator.

Veronica studied accounting at Trinity College, then went to work in her father's small firm. Upon his death, she opened a public-relations agency, then returned to school for a degree in marketing. Later she became a personal assistant to Charles Haughey; her close relationship with the former prime minister was reflected in her choice of a name for her son. Cathal is the Gaelic form of Charles, Veronica's bow to the Irish-pride movement.

Veronica became pregnant at age 28. Doctors followed the good news with the bad: She had cancer. For the safety of the baby, she elected to forgo treatment.

In the fall of 1990, with her cancer in apparent remission and her baby healthy, she decided to become a journalist. A voracious, lifelong reader of newspapers, she targeted *The Sunday Business Post*, figuring that the fledgling publication would be open to new freelancers. In a meeting that she landed with the two top editors, Veronica offered several story ideas, most of them involving the travel industry, with which she'd become familiar while working in PR. Impressed with her résumé and taken with her personality, the editors told her, "Go off and see what you come up with."

Four months later, Veronica's first major investigative scoop was published. Working the vast network she'd assembled during her years in business and politics, applying her accountancy skills and her natural curiosity, relentlessly pursuing sources and details, she uncovered a financial crisis inside a subsidiary of the government-owned airline, Aer Lingus. At one point in her investigation, she persuaded a disgruntled creditor to nominate her as his accountant so she could gain legal entry to a high-level, confidential company meeting on the Isle of Man. When she walked into the room, top executives of the company were dumbstruck.

In September 1992, Veronica came into the office vibrating with smug excitement. Somehow she had managed to obtain tapes of four intercepted telephone conversations between high-ranking members of rival party Fine Gael concerning illegal telephone taps on politicos and journalists throughout Ireland. The tapes were outrageously incriminating, brought to light at a time when a public debate was raging on the very subject of phone taps. *The Business Post* rushed the story into print, accompanied by transcripts. Veronica and her editor were arrested and charged with reproducing the contents of illegally taped calls. They pleaded guilty and paid a £1,000 fine.

Though she was a natural reporter, Veronica had trouble at first with writing. She would come to the office on deadline day with a disk full of disorganized facts and back story, a 5,000- to 7,000-word rough draft that editors would carve into an article of 700 to 1,500 words. No one complained, however, since her stories were always hard-hitting and dead-on, substantiated by a box full of documents.

For her efforts, Veronica was paid £200 to £300 per article, "32 pence an hour," she liked to joke, overlooking the additional costs of entertainment and travel—even a trip to South Africa—that she paid for herself. Though *The Business Post* eventually offered her a staff job, she preferred being under contract, free to set her own hours and agenda. Clearly, money was not important to her. She and Graham were comfortable but not well-off. He was a skilled carpenter and contractor who specialized in house restorations, largely for Irish yuppies. As it was, Veronica wanted for nothing. She was a woman of mostly simple tastes, forever a Dub. Though she never discussed her illness, Veronica's bout with cancer seemed to have imbued her with special strengths and new priorities, a singularity of purpose. Having faced down her disease, she seemed to be living her life at high rpms, never wasting a moment.

In mid-1993, Veronica left *The Sunday Business Post* for the harder-hitting *Sunday Tribune.* Many believed the move was hastened by an unwillingness on the part of the financially shaky *Business Post* to risk running Veronica's scoops. Unlike American laws, Irish defamation statutes have a distinct antimedia bias; the burden of proof is placed upon the newspaper. "We find ourselves in the position, effectively, that everything printed in the newspaper is presumed to be false until the contrary is shown in court," says a prominent Irish solicitor. "There is a constant friction between editorial and management. Most of her stories were potentially very costly. Some people didn't want to be taking those kinds of chances."

At the *Trib*, Veronica had full backing, and she scored almost immediately with her biggest story to date: an exclusive interview with a Catholic bishop who had fled to Ecuador after revelations that he'd fathered a son by an American divorcée.

Veronica spoke with the exiled bishop of Galway, Eamonn Casey, for five hours, beginning with the subject of Eric Cantona. But she did not file a story. She decided instead to wait, stay in touch, build a relationship. Won over by Veronica's humanity—by a personal, genuine approach not often employed by the members of the media—Casey consented to sit for several in-depth interviews.

The result was a spectacular series of revealing pieces that ran over three Sundays. In them the bishop spoke about his infatuation with Annie Murphy, their sexual relationship, their 18-year-old son, Peter, and his "humiliation" and "sense of shame." The *Tribune's* circulation soared to 120,000, 40 percent above normal.

In private Veronica would later say that the Casey story was the most disappointing of her career. Shortly before the sessions were to be held, Vincent Browne, a well-known journalist who was the chief editor of the *Trib*, announced to Veronica that he would be leading the interviews. Veronica protested vehemently, but in the end, Browne did sit in.

In early 1994, Veronica switched to the *Sunday Independent* and began producing her sensational stories about the General, the Monk and the Coach. (Vincent Browne would subsequently be dismissed by the newspaper's board, partially for losing Veronica.)

After she was shot, the *Sindo* paid for the installation of a £25,000 security system at her house. The gardai assigned bodyguards, but she dismissed them within a day. "You can do fuck-all if you're trying to be a crime reporter and you've two guards walking around with you," Veronica explained. Worried, Graham sat his wife down for a talk. "Are you sure you want to keep this up?" he asked.

"I love this" was all Veronica would say. "I just love this."

She elaborated in a taped interview: "I don't think about being shot. That's how I deal with it. I'd lose a lot if I was to give in to that, remembering, feeling fear. That would mean they have won. But they can't win. I really and truly believe that. I really do think that as journalists we are serving a purpose. It puts pressure on the legislature, and they'll have to give the resources to the gardai to tackle them. These guys hate being tackled."

For Graham that was enough. And, really, it didn't matter. Trying to talk

Veronica out of anything was impossible. She'd always gone her own way. It appeared to Graham that she was in control, and resourceful enough to improvise her way through any situation. Once, when his cement mixer was stolen from a job site, Veronica made a few phone calls. By nightfall it was returned.

Now, eight months after the shooting, Veronica was getting ready to tackle her latest quarry, standing eyeball to eyeball with the Warehouseman, John Gilligan, at the front door of his house at the Jessbrook Equestrian Centre. In an affidavit she later filed with the gardai, she remembered what followed.

A menacing silence hung in the air between them. Gilligan's eyes bugged. He lunged for the startled journalist, grabbing a fistful of her suit lapel with his left hand, punching her in the head and face with his right. "If you write one word about me, I will fucking kill you, your husband, your fucking son, your family, everyone belonging to you, even your fucking neighbours!" Gilligan roared, raining blows, practically lifting her off her feet, driving her backward across the lawn toward her car.

Gilligan threw her across the hood of the Opel. Her head hit the metal. Using both fists, he punched her rapidly in the head, face, breasts, stomach. He ripped open her blouse. "Where's the wire?" he bellowed. "Where's the bleedin' tape?"

"I have none," sobbed Veronica, sliding down the fender, crumpling to the ground.

He stood over her in his silk dressing gown and soft slippers, sucking wind. "Get the fuck out of here!"

Gilligan denies the entire incident.

"I beat it!" said Veronica, laughing delightedly into her mobile phone. She was driving at the posted speed limit on the Naas dual carriageway, headed from the Naas Courthouse to the downtown offices of the *Sindo*. "They let me off with a £120 fine!"

"I can't believe you," said Lise Hand, at her desk at the *Sindo*. "How fast were ya goin'?"

"One hundred and two in a sixty-mile zone," said Veronica. "I thought for sure they were goin' to take me license this time."

"What did you tell 'im?"

"I asked for leniency, seein' as how I'd been behavin' meself."

"Behavin'? You call 102 behavin'?"

"Sure. Last time they got me for 103!"

The women had a great laugh, then Veronica hung up. It was nearing I P.M. on Wednesday, June 19, 1996. Up ahead the traffic light was yellow. She geared down and braked to a stop in the far left lane just as the light blinked red. A Ford Escort pulled up next to her. She punched some numbers into her phone.

Nine months after her run-in with Gilligan, Veronica was still on her crusade, though she'd lately become a bit ambivalent. The beating, she told friends, had shaken her more than the shooting, though its physical effects were not nearly as lingering: She still walked with a slight limp from the leg wound.

She'd been thinking about returning to political or business stories. Her friends thought she looked tired; for the first time in her career, she complained about being overworked. Complicating things were controversial staff and budget cuts at the prosperous *Sindo.* Veronica was the franchise: She was writing three stories a week, was being featured in the *Sindo's* ad campaign. And there were the increased responsibilities of her public profile— chat shows, current-affairs forums, union meetings, awards dinners. In December 1995, she had won the International Press Freedom Award from the Committee to Protect Journalists. Characteristically, she was embarrassed to be singled out for recognition. The previous year's award had been given posthumously to the entire staff of a newspaper in Tajikistan.

In early June, however, Veronica's fight against crime gained new momentum. Using his parliamentary privilege, a maverick representative from drug-scarred central Dublin had stood on the floor of the Irish legislature and revealed the identities of two drug dealers. The Boxer, he stated for the public record, was a 25-year-old millionaire named Tommy Mullen. His partner, the Penguin, was George Mitchell.

Veronica went immediately to her editors and lobbied to follow the legislator's lead. She was tired of dancing around. She too wanted to name names, to see results. After a heated conference, it was decided that if Veronica approached suspected criminals and asked them to explain the sources of their wealth, then she could print their real names and their answers. Readers could draw their own conclusions.

THE MAN THEY CALL THE BOXER was the headline on June 16. The story told of Tommy Mullen's "endless supplies of cash and an expensive lifestyle, everyone's idea of a Lotto winner's dream." When asked how he had managed to accumulate such a large amount of cash, Mullen said he'd worked since age 15 as a roofer and done very well. About his frequent run-ins with gardai: "Oh, that was drug searches, but they never questioned me about anything." About allegations by dealers that he was part of the drug business: "Sure they'll say anything if you pay them." About how he made his money: "Me own business." About threats to his life by IRA vigilantes: "No comment."

The following day, gardai raided the Boxer's house.

Encouraged, Veronica set her sights on her next target. They sat down together in a hotel coffee shop, as they had so many times before.

"I think you are going into the paper," Veronica began.

The Coach, John Traynor, listened in silence as Veronica said what she'd come to say: Her editor had received, anonymously, a garda report naming the Coach as a heroin dealer. She had evidence that he was connected with the Boxer and other crims. She had evidence that three men from Liverpool had been arrested in Dublin with a shipment of drugs bound for delivery to the Coach. And, Veronica said, she had evidence of gardai on his payroll. Evidence of his ownership of a house of prostitution. Evidence of his bisexuality. "My editor is wondering what's going on between you and me, why I am not using your name when I am using others," Veronica said. Her allegations would later be repeated in a court affidavit.

The Coach flew into a rage. He left the coffee shop and drove immediately to his solicitor's office. Petition was made to the High Court in Dublin for an injunction prohibiting Veronica and the *Sindo* from running a story about him.

And so it was, on this afternoon of June 19, that things were pretty much status quo in the life of Veronica Guerin. The Coach, the Boxer and the Warehouseman were, to say the least, very angry at her. On the other hand, she had just managed, by the sheer force of her personality, to persuade a traffic-court judge not to take her license away for speeding. She was headed now to the offices of the *Sindo* to discuss the newspaper's strategy against the Coach's court action. She sat in her red Opel in the far left lane at the intersection of Naas and Boot Roads, waiting for the light to change.

Meanwhile, not too far away, at Mondello racetrack, the Coach was making a rare public appearance, having decided to take a spin in one of his race cars.

In Buckingham Street, in north central Dublin, the Monk and two of his brothers were seen "acting ostentatiously, as though they wanted to draw attention to themselves," according to gardai.

All over the city, in fact, on this brilliantly sunny day at a little before one in the afternoon, well-known crims were making noisy appearances in public places.

Veronica called Graham on her cell phone, then hung up and called a garda detective, an old friend. He'd been razzing her mercilessly about her speeding ticket, predicting she'd lose her license, that she'd be riding her bicycle to interviews. She got his answering machine. She listened patiently to the greeting, smiling to herself, planning her retort, waiting for the sound of the tone.

From behind her now came a powerful white motorcycle, working its way between the rows of idling cars. There were two men on board. Both were overweight, in their thirties, wearing black leather jackets and white helmets.

The garda's answering machine beeped.

The motorcycle drew even with Veronica's window. The pillion passenger dismounted, raised the visor of his helmet. He had blue eyes, a fair complexion, a mustache. He pulled a .357 magnum from inside his coat.

"Ha, ha, ha," Veronica said into the phone. "You didn't get me!"

Five shots rang out.

"How are things?" asked Graham Turley, Veronica's husband, sitting down in a chair in the parlor of his mum's house. Father Declan Doyle, pastor of the airport church, stood to one side, hat in hand.

"Grand, Dad," sang Cathal. The 7-year-old was playing with a big box of Legos a neighbor had dropped by. The television set was unplugged.

"You remember the last time Mum was shot?" asked Graham.

"Yes."

"Well, it's happened again."

Cathal fitted another Lego onto the stack. "Where was she shot this time?" he asked absently.

Graham hesitated a moment. "In the heart."

Cathal looked up at Graham. It was apparent that his *da* was upset. The boy sauntered over, climbed into Graham's lap.

Father Doyle put a hand on the boy's head, ruffled his hair. "Cathal, can you make a courthouse with the Legos? Let us show you what happened."

The men eased down onto the floor with the boy, and together they built the Naas Courthouse, two cars, a motorcycle.

When they were done, Cathal sat in silence. Then he asked, "Is Mum coming home?"

"No," said Graham. "Remember we talked about this before?"

Cathal thought for a moment. "Oh, I got it. She's with God now, and she'll be looking down at me and everything I do from now on."

"She'll never leave us," said Graham, gathering up his boy.

• • •

From the moment of her instant death—two bullets in the head, three in a group near her heart—Veronica has had a profound impact on life in Ireland. She was the first Irish reporter ever killed in the line of duty, and her sainthood was now complete; people can tell you exactly where they were when they heard the news of her martyrdom on Radio One.

One week later, at I P.M., the time she was shot, tens of thousands across Ireland observed a minute's silence in memory of Veronica. Well-wishers outside the Irish parliament building left hundreds of cards and bouquets. Czech president Václav Havel joined a throng at the *Sindo*. The funeral was attended by a capacity crowd of friends and political luminaries—including the president and the prime minister of Ireland. Minister for Justice Nora Owen wept openly as Cathal brought forward Veronica's prize possession and laid it by her casket: an autographed picture of herself with Eric Cantona, taken at Manchester's home field, Old Trafford. Graham paid moving tribute to his wife, speaking of her love for "Sunday papers, football and family. . . . We promised each other we'd have great fun, and we really did," he said, his voice faltering. "Believe you me, we had great fun."

Conspicuously absent from her service were the crims. What Veronica could not manage in life, she had achieved in death: Directly following her murder, many of Dublin's major crims fled the country.

On July 5, Veronica's thirty-seventh birthday, the Irish legislature announced the enactment of a £54 million crime bill to combat the drug barons. The bill mandated more prison beds, an evaluation of the efficiency of the gardai, the creation of an authority to freeze assets of suspected drug dealers, a change in bail laws to allow judges to bind over suspects in serious crimes and curbs on an accused's right to silence.

By January 1997, gardai had arrested and questioned 131 people in connection with the murder, carried out 276 searches and seized large quantities of drugs and cash. The massive heat by the gardai had disrupted crime-as-usual in Ireland. A rent-a-gun operation was squashed, and the supply of cannabis had all but dried up, though heroin was still as cheap, pure and plentiful as before. Gardai also arrested one of their own, a detective from southwest Dublin, on charges of accepting a bribe and perverting the course of justice. In addition detectives say that they have evidence of at least fifteen other gardai who they suspect took payments of up to £500 a week from drug barons. One of these fifteen gardai is believed to have received £3,000 for signing passport forms for gang members fleeing the country after the shooting.

Though the Monk, the Boxer and the Coach are scattered around Europe, the gardai succeeded in squashing John Gilligan's gang. Its money-collecting and money-laundering system was exposed and destroyed, and Gilligan's lieutenants fled the island. Gilligan, who has said in interviews that he believes he is the prime suspect in the murder, was arrested by British authorities, picked up at Heathrow Airport on his way to the Netherlands with a suitcase containing £300,000 in cash. He is currently being held in a high-security prison in London on charges of money laundering. Following his arrest, officials of the newly formed Irish Criminal Assets Bureau, as their first order of business, raided the Jessbrook Equestrian Centre, seizing ten horses, two jeeps, furniture, trailers, machinery, televisions and video recorders.

On February 4, 1997, gardai charged Paul Ward, 32, who they believe had connections to the drug trade, with Veronica's murder. In a home video shown on *60 Minutes*, Ward was seen living it up at a Caribbean retreat hosted by John Gilligan in early 1996. When charged, Ward was already being held in Dublin's Mountjoy Prison for conspiracy and accessory to murder in connection with Veronica's death. In January, Ward was one of five inmates who took four prison guards hostage for several days, demanding better conditions; Ward also demanded that his innocence be recognized. The situation was defused by authorities. Because of Irish gag laws, further details on Ward's involvement in the murder will not be released by gardai until trial. At press time, a trial date had not yet been scheduled.

Veronica's martyrdom has not been in vain. Her death was a wake-up call that has inspired citizens to action. Community organizations and vigilante groups have regularly marched into drug-infested areas. People countrywide have been putting pressure on the government to empower the gardai and the courts even further. Never in the history of Ireland has legislation been enacted as swiftly as the crime bill was.

"Veronica always said it was our job as journalists to bring corruption to light, to inspire the people and put pressure on the legislature to make Ireland a better place," says Lise Hand, who was Veronica's best friend at the *Sindo*.

"I think everybody lost a bit of innocence when Veronica died. Maybe she was a bit naive; she wasn't as hard-bitten as some others of us hacks. She basically had the same feelings about crime as your ordinary Joe Sober, except the difference was that instead of sitting in a pub with a pint giving out the state of the nation, Veronica got off her arse and did something about it. That's what it takes to be a hero: a little gem of innocence inside you that makes you want to believe that there still exists a right and a wrong, that decency will somehow triumph in the end."

(1997)

Janet's World

Janet Cooke caused the biggest scandal in the history of journalism when her Pulitzer Prize–winning article about an eight-year-old heroin addict turned out to be a fake.

She sashayed into the acre-square newsroom of *The Washington Post* on the third day of 1980, wearing a red wool suit over a white silk shirt, the neck opened casually to the second button, exposing a thin gold chain, a teasing glimpse of lingerie, the slight swell of a milk-chocolate breast. Her long acrylic nails gleaming in the hard fluorescent light, she made her way down a long aisle between the desk pods of the Metro section toward the Weekly.

As she passed, heads turned, eyes bugged. People swiveled around and watched the pleasing sway of her hips, the jaunty bounce of her Marie Antoinette ringlets, a mass of dark, lacquered curls that trailed past her shoulder blades. For years the customary greeting in the newsroom had been "What's the gossip?" At the moment, this clearly was it.

Her name was Janet Cooke. Six months earlier, when her letter and CV had crossed *Post* executive editor Ben Bradlee's desk—on one of those slow afternoons when he would occupy himself reading unsolicited applications from reporters around the world—the brass-balled legend had sat up abruptly in his chair. Before him, as he might have said, was a fuckin' wet dream: 25 years old, Phi Beta Kappa from Vassar, master's in literature, fluent in two foreign languages, television experience, one writing award in two years at the Toledo *Blade*, member of the National Association of Black Journalists.

Bradlee took up a red grease pencil, circled "Phi Beta Kappa," "Vassar" and "Black Journalists." At a time when papers were just beginning their perilous journey toward "newsroom diversity," here was the ideal candidate—an Ivy League twofer with a résumé of gold. He sent Janet's letter along to Metro Editor Bob Woodward, noting that she should be recruited before *The New York Times* or the networks scooped her up.

Now it was her first day, and she was almost two hours late, having lost her way walking three blocks from her hotel. Over the coming weeks and months, the layout of the capital city would elude her dramatically. Driving four blocks to a grocery store, she'd end up in Maryland. The two-mile commute from her apartment to work routinely took an hour. On assignment she'd struggle through the streets in her Datsun 240Z. She'd pull over, cry a little, read her map, set out again. Finally, magically, she'd arrive at the place she'd been searching for, and her work could begin. That was another drama for a woman whose father had instilled in her, from the earliest age, one great and overriding philosophy: *Because you're a girl, because you're black, you must do everything twice as well as anybody else. There is no room for screwing up. There is no slack.*

As Janet strolled so erect and proud and seemingly in control down the long aisle toward the Weekly, she had no idea she was causing such a stir. In fact, so constant was the turmoil of self-doubt inside her head that she rarely knew what was happening around her. Had she been able, she would have noticed that she was getting just the kind of reaction she had always worked for and wished for and dreamed about. But inside she was terrified. What if I'm not good enough? she agonized.

Janet carried on, plying the industrial carpet in her sensible black pumps, holding her chin high, hooding her large almond eyes, aiming them straight ahead. She concentrated on an old favorite song, "I Whistle A Happy Tune," from *The King and I*. "That's my anthem," she would joke, eyelids fluttering, full lips curling upward into a mischievous grin, the *m* in *anthem* beginning to resonate, gathering harmonics in her throat, transposing into a low, coy, sultry, devilish giggle, her trademark, her smoke screen.

At last Janet arrived at the Weekly. She was met by Stan Hinden, editor of the three zoned editions that made up the section. Launched in reaction to the recent boom of "neighbor papers" across the nation, the Weeklies featured good-news stories, roadwork listings and a commuter columnist called Dr. Gridlock.

The Weeklies were considered the *Post*'s boot camp, peopled with interns and probationers, most of them minority or female. Almost from the beginning, Janet noticed the difference between the Weeklies and the rest of the paper. She called her section "the ghetto," liked to joke that her parents had spent lots of money trying to keep her out of such circumstances. If she was good enough to be hired by the *Post*, she wondered privately, why wasn't she good enough to be part of the "real" staff? What was wrong with her?

Stan Hinden took Janet's coat, then led her to her new editor, Vivian Aplin-Brownlee, a light-skinned black woman from Texas who was known for her prickly tongue and her skill in office politics. Though Vivian, 34, carried a big stick, she also had a finely honed editor's pencil. Many likened her to a drill sergeant, someone who fondly, ruthlessly tore you down in order to build you back up—Lou Gossett with a short Afro, dangling earrings and oversize glasses.

Like most of the black staffers at the time, Vivian was equally fluent in the King's English and in jive, the first used with whites, the second only with other blacks. Janet had never encountered a place like the *Post*, had never met black people like those in Washington. Here, it seemed, race permeated every issue; Janet did not speak jive.

During her first job interview at the *Post*, Janet had met Dorothy Gilliam, the grande dame of black female columnists. Gilliam asked what Janet thought the role of a black reporter should be. Janet was shocked by the question. She had never dated a black man. She had never had a black girlfriend. On the bus home one day during her sophomore year, two of the black boys from her high school doused her with baby powder so she would look the color she acted. As a child, before bed each night, she would pray on her knees: "Please, God, let me wake up blonde."

To Gilliam's question, Janet responded that the first thing a black reporter should do is not think of herself as black. She should just go out, find the story, come back and write it.

Gilliam looked stunned. "Why, you poor silly little girl."

Thankfully, Janet's answer had not counted against her. She was here now, hired, standing in the Weekly on her first day of work. After many introductions, there was a lull.

"Um, where do I sit?" ventured Janet.

Hinden scratched his head of white hair.

Seconds ticked by. Janet began to roil. Great, she thought. This is the beginning.

Hinden led a little tour, walking from desk to desk, trying to find a suitable space for his new prize. Janet followed two steps behind, mortified, the voice inside her head growing more sarcastic, more hysterical: Jesus Christ, this is the *Washington fucking Post*. Can't they find me a desk?

"I want my life back," says Janet Cooke, sitting on a bench at the Crossroads shopping mall, near Kalamazoo, Michigan, sixteen years after her first day at the *Post*. The temperature outside hunkers cruelly below zero; the light is thin and bleak.

Though Janet has gained a few pounds and now favors black clothes over dramatic reds, her hair is still long and luxuriant, and her air is still confident, intelligent, commanding and playfully sexual. In a few minutes, she will sigh and head toward Hudson's department store for her $6-an-hour shift in the midmarket-women's-wear Liz Claiborne boutique.

On September 28, 1980, nine months and fifty-two bylines into her tenure at the *Post*, Janet caused a firestorm with her front-page story about "Jimmy," an 8-year-old heroin addict. On April 13, 1981—after the Pulitzer committee, enthusiastic about both her writing and her status as a black female, juggled her entry from the local-news to the features category in order to assure her a prize—Janet was awarded a Pulitzer. Two days later, Janet confessed that "Jimmy's World" was fiction. The *Post* returned the Pulitzer. Janet resigned.

Since then Janet Cooke has become one of the most infamous figures in journalism. Databases list thousands of entries under her name; her case has come to symbolize such diverse issues as plagiarism and fabrication, anonymity and unnamed sources, minority recruitment, newsroom ethics, résumé fraud, the precarious practice of New Journalism. Universally vilified from the moment her transgression was revealed, constantly dogged by the press, Janet has spent her life on the run: first as the wife of an American diplomat in Paris, more recently as a divorced, nearly destitute part-time retail clerk in Toledo; Ann Arbor, Michigan; and Kalamazoo.

Except for a short interview with Phil Donahue on the *Today* show about a year after her debacle, Janet has never spoken out. Recently, she asked me to write her story, fearing that a first-person account would sound too self-serving. Her objectives: a renewed writing career and, more important, the retrieval of her name from the files of infamy.

This is Janet's exclusive story. Though I was picked as a sympathetic author, I will try my best to convey the incidents faithfully. I was close to her for much of the time she was at the *Post*. We became friends soon after her arrival. By the end of February, we had begun a love affair. It ended officially in June, but it hung on—a painful, exhilarating psychodrama, complete with pills, scenes, stalking, dead roses, incredible tales and ripped bodices—for another year.

Janet was beautiful. She was as smart as any woman I have ever known: She had a deft command of language, humor, irony and detail; she could trade barbs and insights and stories with the best. She was passionate; she was vulnerable and needy; she brought out the best and worst in a man. She liked to leave little notes in odd places, to buy little gifts. She could find, in a cobwebbed larder, the ingredients for a midnight snack. She made cookies with Godiva chocolate. She was formidable.

And, as much as it pains me to say it, she was a liar. It was her lying that killed my love, my trust, our relationship. There were small white lies and large, ornate fabrications. In the years following our breakup, every now and then I would encounter a piece of information I had always thought was fact, only to remember that Janet had been the source.

After the Pulitzer was returned, I was suspected of collaborating on "Jimmy," my name having been found on the "edit trail" of the *Post's* computer system. Bob Woodward grilled me twice over two days. He is, I discovered, as good as they say. Had I something to confess, I surely would have.

Janet's mental state between August and April was such that I found myself, just before the announcement of the Pulitzers, on a jet to Europe. Twenty-four years old, I was out of my league in a very grown-up game. We called what we shared a "special friendship." There is, she helped me learn, no such thing.

I read about Janet's award on a ferry between Dover and Calais. In the train station, I sent her a telegram: "Standing ovations." Two days later, walking down the Champs-Elysées, I saw the headline: REPORTER CONFESSES STORY SUBJECT FAKED. I became dizzy and disoriented. I crumpled to a seat on the curb, feet in the gutter, as cars and people whizzed by.

The day "Jimmy's World" had run, all those months before, I'd had burgers at the Post Pub with Pat Tyler and Joe Pichirallo, both respected investigative reporters on Metro. I think, like a good journalist, I wanted to get my thoughts on the record. "Jimmy's World," I predicted, would win the Pulitzer. Then it would be revealed as a fake.

I didn't know how I knew this. Indeed, I wasn't sure my feelings weren't just jealousy. But the story didn't feel right. The dialogue, for instance, sounded like a white person imitating jive. Blacks in D.C.'s ghettos didn't say, "I be goin'." They said, "I goin'." And the appointments in the shooting gallery—matching chrome-and-glass tables? Could Janet, with her terrible sense of direction, even have found Jimmy's house at night?

I had no evidence, just instinct. Because I was a friend, I never asked. I didn't want to know.

Despite the reams of commentary and discussion that have accumulated in the interim, I have always felt that no one has ever understood this whole sorry mess. For all the attempts to render Janet's transgressions into civic and journalistic lessons, her actions, from where I sat, had nothing to do with social, political or philosophical issues. They had nothing to do with newspaper ethics or the Fifth Amendment. Writing "Jimmy" was a highly personal act in a highly personal drama, a choice of action best explained, perhaps, as a damaged person's attempt to right the wrongs of her past, to overcome the paralyzing condition of self-loathing and self-doubt.

The truth is, Janet wasn't trying to win a Pulitzer. She wasn't out for fame and glory. New to the business and to the big time, she had no idea how hard a story like "Jimmy" could hit. Janet never considered the ramifications of lying to Ben Bradlee, Bob Woodward, 1 million Post readers and millions more worldwide.

"A Pulitzer was not her endgame," says Vivian Aplin-Brownlee today. "She just wanted to get out of the Weekly, away from me."

Simply put: Janet needed a story to turn in.

She wrote one.

"What I did was wrong," she admits, her head and eyes lowering. "I regret that I did it. I was guilty. I did it, and I'm sorry that I did it. I'm ashamed that I did it."

She also says this: "What I did was horrible; believe me, I think that. But I don't think that in this particular case the punishment has fit the crime. I've lost my voice. I've lost half of my life. I'm in a situation where cereal has become a viable dinner choice. It is my fault that I've never spoken up. But I'm a 41-year-old woman now, and I'm starting to understand some things about life, about my life. If people only understood why this really happened, maybe they'd have a different take on things. Maybe they'd think I wasn't so evil."

Janet Leslie Cooke was born in the tenth year of a stormy, four-decade marriage between Loretta and Stratman Cooke.

Her father, the eldest of five boys, attended the Tuskegee Institute, served as one of the black Airmen. Her mother was the eldest of nine children. She was in high school when Stratman came to town; she picked him out as a boy who was going places. The pair eloped, then settled in Toledo, where Stratman finished his engineering degree. She worked in a local ordnance plant.

Upon graduation Stratman found a job as an air-conditioning repairman for Toledo Edison. Cooke family lore recalls Stratman encountering the company's president one day. They spoke; the big man was impressed. "You got a suit, boy?" he asked.

In the ensuing years, Stratman studied law and opened a private practice, meanwhile continuing his rise at Toledo Edison. He retired recently as corporate secretary. He refused to be interviewed for this story. Loretta Cooke also declined. For the last fifteen years, she has been the only press contact for Janet. Now that Janet's finally ready, says Loretta Cooke, she can speak for herself.

Her father, Janet remembers, "was very smart, very handsome, very mean, very rigid." He still lives in the house where Janet was raised, a big, old converted duplex right at the edge of the inner city, in a black district that is neither ghetto nor historic. When Janet was young, the lawn and the garden were showpieces. The grass had to be trimmed precisely a quarter of an inch from the concrete.

The interior of the house was in the throes of constant renovation, the excuse the Cooke females used for not inviting people inside. Janet and her younger sister, Nancy, weren't allowed outside their yard, weren't allowed to get dirty, to make noise or to make friends. They were allowed to study, play piano, attend their Catholic church, listen to their parents' extensive collection of classical and opera records, buy and read as many books as they wished. The few fond memories Janet has of her dad have to do with books and the written word. Every Sunday they'd go to the fountain at the drugstore and read *The New York Times* together. Before she got her malt, Janet had to impress the soda jerk by reading a few paragraphs out loud.

When she started school at the public elementary, Janet remembers, she was "appalled" that none of the other kids—all of them black—were able to read. Her father explained, "These children really can't be your playmates. They are not intellectual enough or well-bred enough for you."

"Everyone in town knew my father, but no one knew what was really going on inside that house," says Janet. "Our family had no relations with any other family on the block. I never could figure out why he wanted to live in an all-black neighborhood if we couldn't talk to anyone. That's the kind of mixed message I grew up with."

From an early age, Janet was drilled for excellence. Summers, there were reading lists, book reports, assignments. In second grade, a teacher called to say that Janet was having problems with writing. She frequently reversed her *b*'s and *d*'s, was making other little mistakes that would later be seen as signs of dyslexia. Stratman sat Janet down with a number-two pencil at the big dining-room table, kept her there until the early hours, pacing back and forth, calling out like a drill sergeant: "Now make a *b*. Now make a *d*. Write the word *saw*. Write the word *was*."

When her mother finally came downstairs to protest, a huge row ensued. Janet fled to her room. Why am I so stupid? she asked herself as her parents battled downstairs. A few years later, lying in bed at night, her parents fighting, she would dream of moving to Paris, land of Josephine Baker and James Baldwin. Trying to block the noise, she'd conjugate French verbs out loud, concentrating on her accent, knowing that someday she'd get to France.

By third grade, Janet was enrolled with the children of Toledo's elite in the Maumee Valley Country Day School, one of two black students in her graduating class of forty-three. "I guess it was at Maumee that I first started having this overriding fear that I would never be good enough to do anything. I had fabulous grades, I was a cheerleader, I was a Merit scholar, but I always felt like I was falling just short of the mark. No matter how many Peter Pan collars and kneesocks I wore, I knew I was never going to fit in."

Stratman's iron fist created a family that was highly skilled in subversion and deceit. Janet learned from an early age that a well-placed lie could save a lot of trouble. "He had absolute control over the lock on the door," says Janet. "To get out, you had to say where you were going. You couldn't say you were going out with friends or to the movies or to a department store, but you could say you were going to the library or a museum or the grocery store. You couldn't buy so much as a skirt or underwear without his approval. My mother and sister and I would buy things and leave them in the trunk of the car until he was gone. One of us girls had to be home before Dad to get the mail. He'd say, 'Has anyone seen the Lion's bill?' And we would all chime in, 'No, Daddy.' Of course, it was in Mother's purse. We used to tease her that she couldn't even go to the bathroom without the thing. Later, after she went into the hospital and my father found out everything, she got herself a P.O. box.

"I've thought about this a lot in the last couple of years," says Janet, sitting on the bench in the mall, checking her watch. "I've thought about lying and how it relates to me, and when I started doing it and why I started doing it, and why, for a long time, it has not been the red flag for me that it is for most people. The conclusion I've come to is that lying, from a very early age, was the best survival mechanism available. And I became very good at it. It was like, do you unleash the wrath of Dad's temper, or do you tell something that is not exactly true and be done with it?

"It is a very twisted way of thinking, I know. Believe me, I know. The problem becomes, what do you do when your worldview is based on such a twisted proposition? What becomes of you?"

She cocks her head coquettishly, throws up her arms, palms high. "Well, I think we know just what becomes of you, now don't we?" says Janet, smiling sadly, her words trailing into a low, sultry, devilish laugh, her trademark, her smoke screen.

Early in her junior year, in the hallway at school, Janet spotted her English teacher headed briskly her way. The class had just completed a big essay. Oh God, thought Janet. What did I do?

"Your paper," said the teacher breathlessly. "It's marvelous! Have you considered going into journalism?" For years it had been assumed that Janet's career path would take her to an Ivy League college, a prestigious law school (preferably Harvard) and eventually a place beside her father in his law practice. "It had always been hanging over me, like some kind of eternal damnation, an adulthood working for Daddy."

About this time, *Ms.* magazine was founded by Toledo native Gloria Steinem. Janet idolized the feminist icon. "That this girl could come out of Toledo and say, 'You don't always have to do what your father or your husband says.' You can't understand the impact. Suddenly, there was light at the end of the tunnel."

Slowly Janet began to rebel. She began to think, Fuck it, Daddy. I'm going to open the front door. I'm going out with friends. I'm inviting them home. She began asking the hard questions. "Why do the lights have to be out at a certain hour? Who said we can't go shopping?" The two fought bitterly and often.

Feeling as strong as she ever had, Janet went off to college at Vassar. She hated it immediately. "It was very snotty, very white, very isolated. It was like I'd stumbled into some horrible sorority meeting. I was constipated for the first six weeks—I wasn't going in a bathroom with twenty-five other people. And the food. I lost fifteen pounds.

"Socially, I was lost. The races were very polarized. There was the black dorm and the black dining table, and if you didn't participate—and I didn't, I thought it was ludicrous—then all the blacks hated you. I hung out with a group of hippie intellectuals on my floor. We did things together, but I couldn't go places with them; I didn't have any money. My dad refused to give me an allowance. And as a freshman, you couldn't get a job. So, literally, the only money I had was the $10 my mother would sneak into a letter now and then. I couldn't tell people that. This one girl had a mink coat. So I just made up excuses, you know. I lied."

That summer of 1973, Janet landed her first newspaper job, an internship at *The Blade*. She was assigned to the consumer affairs column, the Zip Line. People would write in and complain about being wronged, and Janet would check it out.

"I hunted down the facts and chewed on them until I knew exactly what the situation was. Wow, I thought. So this is the power of the press. For once in my life, *I* was in control."

In the fall, Janet quietly enrolled as a sophomore in the honors program at the University of Toledo. After her graduation from U.T., she took a job at the local public-TV station, but what she really wanted was to get back to writing, to *The Blade*. She would call every week and ask if a slot had opened up yet. After about a year, in the fall of '77, Janet went to work as a full-fledged reporter in the Living Today section.

Janet's clips from *The Blade* show a precocious if untrained talent. The beat she carved out for herself involved subjects of personal interest: spousal and child abuse, sexual abuse, women in the workplace. Some stories relied upon composite or anonymous sources. "It was great. I was writing every day, getting paid for it. I'd be in the grocery store writing a check and people would recognize my name from my byline. They'd say, 'Oh, I read your story in Sunday's paper.' And I was like, 'You did?' You can't imagine how important that was. People thought I was really good."

In the spring of 1979, a few months before her birthday, Janet began to panic. My God! she thought. I'm almost 25. Am I going to stay in Toledo till I die?

Janet decided it was time to move on and up. She set her sights on *The Washington Post*. She began reading the *Post* every day, studied the paper's history. She made a list of reporters' bylines that appeared most frequently; she investigated their backgrounds and credentials.

It didn't take long for Janet to realize that her education and experience level wouldn't pass muster. She went into a funk.

Three days after her twenty-fifth birthday, on July 26, 1980, a broken romance freshly behind her, a new sense of purpose welling inside, Janet sat down at her typewriter.

"My goal," she says, "was to create Supernigger."

The meal was served on fine white linen: two salads, two soups, two Cokes.

In one chair was Vivian Aplin-Brownlee. On the edge of the other was Janet Cooke. It was time for her six-month review.

To all appearances, Janet was doing very well. By mid-February she had scored her first big piece, a much discussed takeout on the mood in the 14th Street drug corridor following the assassination of a policeman. Janet sent me a note about the reaction: "You should have been here. It was terrific. Graham, Bradlee, flowers, phone calls . . . the works. You are right. I AM spoiled. And if you thought it was bad before . . . By the way, I couldn't get a hotel room in Key West, so I have to go to Nassau (poor me)."

Janet had made a few girlfriends, all of them white, from the paper's large pool of support staff. As for the white men, well, though Janet considered them rude and awkward and poorly dressed, they were clearly taken with her, tending to babble in her presence. Beauty, elegance, an appearance of chic composure, a sense of humor with a salacious bent—these were not the normal attributes of a modern newspaperwoman. With Janet in residence, the Weekly section began seeing a host of new visitors. Publisher Don Graham bounded through on his way to the company softball game. Ben Bradlee puffed up his chest, paused long enough to launch a few jaunty bons mots, usually in French. Woodward would stand there looking lost, chewing his Beech-Nut furiously. "How are ya?" he'd ask, in his nasal Illinois accent.

Janet's worst problems at the *Post* came under the heading of race relations. None of the blacks much liked her, and the feeling was mutual. Janet's musical tastes tended toward the Rolling Stones, the Who, Steely Dan, opera and classical. She loathed dancing. She dressed like a preppy. She wore hair extensions and falls. Once, when black city editor Milton Coleman called her at home on a Sunday, he heard strange noises in the background and asked who was screaming. "That's *Carmen*, Milt," said Janet, her voice dripping. "I'll go turn her down." When Janet was assigned to cover a Kool and the Gang concert, she bugged her eyes like Pigmeat Markham and said, with the appropriate accent, only half-jokingly, "Da who and da who? Is dat be sum sorta new colored Mafia?"

Perhaps the oddest aspect of Janet's work was her beat. This shy, sheltered girl from Toledo was haunting the seedy underbelly of the 14th Street strip, a twenty-four-hour drug bazaar about one mile from the White House. On one of her first trips to the ghetto, a kid looked her up and down and asked, "What kinda nigger are you?"

Janet didn't hesitate a beat. "The kind you've never met in your life, young man."

This lunch was Janet's fourth with Vivian. The first had included Stan Hinden; the second two, Milt Coleman. Coleman was a tall, very dark, very down member of Washington's young and elite black middle class, the true movers and shakers in a town known to its majority residents as the District of Chocolate. Coleman had cut his teeth in the civil rights movement; he had covered Marion Barry when the mayor was still wearing dashikis. Later he became the Metro editor and the reigning black conscience of the newspaper. In time Coleman fulfilled his allegiance to the *Post*, revealing that his friend Jesse Jackson, during a private conversation, had referred to New York City as "Hymietown."

Now, at lunch with Vivian, Janet was relieved that Coleman wasn't around. Like most big black men, he made her nervous. At the same time, she was none too comfortable with Vivian: Relations between the two had never been good. In a sense, Vivian had become the new Stratman in Janet's life, perhaps even more powerful, since she doled out praise as often as she did harsh criticism. As with her father, Janet felt that nothing she did would ever please her boss.

From the moment she'd met Janet, Vivian didn't like her. "I thought her appearance was off-putting—a whole lot of glamour and flash, as opposed to substance," Vivian said recently from her home in Washington, D.C., where she has lived since quitting journalism to raise a family fourteen years ago. "I would look at her preening at her desk, getting ready to go out in the street and talk to the people. She didn't speak the language. She was hardly useful to me at all."

Vivian speared a forkful of salad and crisply began the evaluation. First, she said, three black male reporters had complained of riding five floors in the elevator with Janet and not hearing so much as "hello." Vivian warned her that she should be nice to these men because they had access to Bradlee, who loved to gossip. If Bradlee should ask the men about Janet, it was in her best interest to make sure they had something interesting to say.

Vivian laid into Janet's habit of resting her feet on the desktop—"What kind of a lady is that?"—then segued to the subject of her economy-sized bottle of Maalox, advising her to hide it in a drawer. She further advised that making a few black friends around the newsroom might ease the pains in Janet's stomach. "You know, they call you the Ice Princess," said Vivian.

Dumbfounded, Janet pushed away her salad. "What about my work?"

"It's fine. Great. But you need to remember two things. First, no matter how good your last story was, people around here want to know, 'What are you going to do for me today?' Second, no matter how good a writer you think you are, you're nothing without me. I've made you what you are, honey pie. I can unmake you just as fast."

"I can't keep running all the way back there," I said into the phone, standing behind my desk in the front row, spying her clear across the newsroom at yet another borrowed desk. She waggled her fingers in my direction: a limp, needy, self-deprecating hello.

Already, over the past two hours of this mid-September morning, I'd been summoned to her screen four times. "Why don't you just transfer it to my terminal," I said.

The night before, Janet had called me at home at the stroke of twelve. She was hysterical. She'd found the boy, she said.

Details flowing like tears, tears like details, she poured out her tale. His name was Tyrone. He lived in a dreadful part of town. She interviewed the boy and his mom. Toward the end of the evening, she'd watched Ron—the dealer, the mom's boyfriend—give the boy his shot of heroin. Such a beautiful little kid. It was interesting, she paused to note, how smoothly a needle could pierce the skin, sliding in so easily, like a straw into the center of a freshly baked cake.

The boy nodded out. Ron picked up a butcher knife: "If I see any police, Miss Lady, me and my knife will be around to see you." Janet fled the house and vomited, she said.

Now, on the phone, she broke down in earnest—a wailing, strangled cry, afraid and alone. I tried to comfort her.

In time Janet settled down a bit, switched gears. She read me some quotes, solicited advice on structure. As she chattered on, I kept thinking, Didn't I see her car when I drove past her apartment two hours ago?

After forty-five minutes, Janet began to sob again. "I'm so scared. Do you think, well—"

"You want me to come over."

"Just for a little while?"

Now, at noon the next day in the newsroom, I was committed to seeing her through the writing of this story, something that usually took weeks. Back in February, when she'd written the note to me about her 14th Street piece, there was another paragraph: "Listen, thanks for letting me bother you. . . . I probably never would have finished the story if you hadn't been around."

That, I must admit, was the root of our relationship. I was her boyfriend, her lover, her friend, her enemy. But most of all, I think, I was her editor.

I worked the night shift, seven to three. Roaming the nearly empty newsroom, waiting for a disaster to drop, I would come at last to Janet, sitting alone in the back of the room, bathed in the sickly light of the terminal. I began offering suggestions. From there, I guess, I penciled my way into her affections.

In late July, Janet started researching a story about a new type of heroin that caused the skin to ulcerate. Because it was a big story, and because Vivian had slated all of August for vacation, Janet was assigned to Coleman and the Metro desk for the duration. Janet was overjoyed.

"I would have done anything to get away from her," says Janet. "If they would have said, 'We'll get you away from Vivian, but you're going to have to sit out on 15th Street,' I would have said, 'Can I start tomorrow?' Things were just vicious with her, and I never knew why. I didn't want her job. I didn't want her man. I didn't want her life. Why did she hate me so?" With a little luck, Janet figured, she could make a big hit with this story and effect a transfer to Metro.

In the course of her typically exhaustive reporting, Janet landed an interview with Dr. Alyce Gullattee, the head of Howard University's drug-abuse program. Sitting in were two of Gullattee's outreach workers.

During the interview, while Gullattee was out of the room, the subject turned to the ages of the addicts. "There's even an 8-year-old who's being treated at RAP [a residential drug-treatment facility]," said one of the workers.

Janet's ears pricked up, but she acted cool, continuing the general interview, doubling back now and then to the boy. They weren't going for it. They wouldn't tell who he was.

When Janet got back to the newsroom, Coleman was ecstatic. "That's a fuckin' front-page story!" he said. "You've got to find that kid!"

Janet called RAP. The director said he had no such patient.

So began almost eight weeks of frantic searching. At one point, when Janet spoke to an administrator in Southeast D.C., it seemed as if there really was an 8-year-old heroin addict. But he refused to help.

Janet went to Coleman and explained she couldn't find the kid, that the administrator wouldn't divulge his identity. Coleman went to the *Post*'s managing editor, Howard Simons, then came back to Janet. "OK, it's set. Tell him we don't need to know their names," said Coleman.

The administrator stopped taking her calls.

Vivian returned after Labor Day. She summoned Janet. In a rare moment of public weakness, Janet said she didn't think she'd ever find the boy. "Well, find another boy," Vivian said. "It's make or break, girlfriend."

Janet sat down at her desk, pretended to make a call. She felt like an utter failure. Now she'd never get away from Vivian, never get to Metro. She'd be a laughingstock. She'd be fired.

Meanwhile, in the back of her mind, "I kept hearing Milton telling me to offer total anonymity. At some point, it dawned on me that I could simply make it all up. I just sat down and wrote it."

And so it was that Janet called me at midnight, apparently to test out her story. Then, early the next morning, she told Coleman. He told her to write it strong, like a Coltrane song, sent her to her keyboard.

Now, at noon in the newsroom, Janet was already finished with her piece, another odd development I let slide. She transferred it to my terminal.

> Jimmy is 8 years old and a third generation heroin addict, a precocious little boy with sandy hair, velvety brown eyes and needle marks freckling the baby-smooth skin of his thin brown arms.
>
> He nestles in a large, beige reclining chair in the living room of his comfortably furnished home in Southeast Washington. There is an almost cherubic expression on his small, round face as he talks about life—clothes, money, the Baltimore Orioles.

The story continues for 2,000 words. Jimmy begins twisting uncomfortably in his chair, needing his fix. Ron enters with a syringe, calls the boy over.

> He grabs Jimmy's left arm just above the elbow, his massive hand tightly encircling the child's small limb. The needle slides into the boy's soft skin like a straw pushed into the center of a freshly baked cake. Liquid ebbs out of the syringe, replaced by bright red blood. The blood is then reinjected into the child. . . .
>
> "Pretty soon, man," Ron says, "you got to learn how to do this for yourself."

I made a few changes, transferred it back to Janet. Then I called her extension.

"I think you may have just won yourself a Pulitzer, Miss Cooke."

"Maybe now they'll find me a desk," she said, laughing.

• • •

The presses began rolling at 9:54 P.M., Saturday. By the next morning, wrote *Post* ombudsman Bill Green, in an 18,000-word investigation published by the paper after its disgrace, "the switchboard lit up like a space-launch control room."

To a journalist, "Jimmy" was what Woodward would call a "Holy shit!" story, the most precious coin of the realm. But to readers, "Jimmy" was a clear example of exploitation, of headlines being put before humanity. How could this great liberal enterprise that had brought down a president write about this poor child and then keep him hidden? On Monday morning, D.C. police launched a massive, citywide search. On Tuesday Mayor Barry announced that officials knew who Jimmy was and that he was in treatment. Then Barry's office retracted his statement. Later the police would halt the search, calling "Jimmy" a hoax. By the following weekend, Green wrote, city editor Milton Coleman was beginning to feel uneasy. At first he had bought Janet's story without question. The details, he concluded, were solid. Those parts about the needle: like a straw into a freshly baked cake. How could an innocent Oreo from Toledo make that up?

Likewise, Bob Woodward had signed off on the piece. The Watergate hero told Green, "The story was so well written and tied together that my alarm bells simply didn't go off. My skepticism left me."

One vocal doubter was the streetwise black reporter Courtland Milloy. He was teamed with Janet on a follow-up story, and they drove around Jimmy's neighborhood together. Milloy told Green, "It didn't take long to see that she didn't know the area."

Vivian was also skeptical. She told Green: "I never believed it, and I told Milton that. . . . In her eagerness to make a name for herself, she would often write farther than the truth would allow. When challenged on facts in other stories, Janet would reverse herself, but without dismay or consternation. I knew she would be tremendously out of place in a shooting gallery. I didn't believe she could get access."

As can be imagined, Janet was in a state: "I was astonished by the attention I got. It just hadn't occurred to me that I'd make such big waves. I just wanted it to go away."

We were at a rock concert at the Warner Theatre, sitting in the balcony.

Midway into the show, the lead guitarist jumped off the stage, commenced a Chuck Berry duckwalk up the center aisle. Rockets burst. Lasers strafed the crowd.

"I deserve more attention from you," Janet said.

"But we broke up seven months ago," I said. "I'm just a friend, remember?"

The guitar wailed. Janet began to cry.

"Jesus Christ," I hollered over the noise. "What do you want?"

The song crescendoed. The audience rose, cheering, a standing ovation.

Janet stood, too. She stretched her arms out over the applause, as if to catch it, a lover in a field of daisies. "This," she said. "I want this." The look on her face was blissful.

This was Janet's world between October and April. She lived on a diet of Dexatrim, vitamins, Coca-Cola and chocolate. She stopped opening her mail, answering the door. Her apartment was a mess, old newspapers and balled-up clothes strewn about. She would become frightened when the telephone rang. She developed insomnia. As a tonic, she drank Jack Daniel's or Dewar's. She called me one night to say she'd swallowed a whole bottle of Valium. When I got there, she confessed she'd lied. She called another night to say she was about to bleach her hair blonde. She drove over and looked in my window, braving a dark back alley and a set of basement stairs to see into my bedroom. She called from a pay phone, asking, "Are you done with that slut yet?"

She said she was going to a shrink; at the appointed hour, she'd be spotted at Bloomingdale's. She was always late but always had an elaborate excuse. Once, after missing Thanksgiving dinner, she said she'd been walking down her hallway on the way to her car when she heard something scratching on a door. She opened it and found a man lying on the floor, having a heart attack. She administered CPR until the ambulance came.

Though she was making about $27,000 a year, Janet's finances were a disaster. She was maxed out on her gas card, close to the edge on the others. In December, realizing she could no longer afford her own apartment, she moved into the exclusive Ontario Apartments, the setting for Nora Ephron's book *Heartburn*. Her roommate was Elsa Walsh, a young reporter who'd recently begun dating Woodward.

At work the pressure to come up with another fabulous tale led Janet to the story of a 14-year-old prostitute. This time Coleman insisted on meeting the girl. Lunches with the prostitute and her pimp were scheduled, rescheduled, canceled. The story didn't run. Some editors asked why. Did this mean Coleman didn't believe Janet? Did he now think that "Jimmy" was a hoax? If so, why had the story been nominated for a Pulitzer?

"I had huge phone bills," says Janet. "I'd call my mother and just cry on the phone for an hour. And she was like, 'Sweetie, you have every reason to be happy. You have a beautiful apartment, a great job, a nice roommate. You've been nominated for a Pulitzer Prize, for Heaven's sake!'

"I couldn't say, 'I'm drowning here. I'm lonesome. I've really fucked up bad.' I mean, for the first time in my life, my father acted like he was actually proud of me. How could I tell them what had happened?"

"Say two words in Portuguese," challenged Ben Bradlee.

Janet shrugged.

"Do you have any Italian?"

"No."

"If you had to speak French to me right now to save your job," said Bradlee, sighing heavily, "what would you say?"

Janet could speak French. All those nights as a girl, lying in bed, conjugating verbs, dreaming of Paris. But as she stood before Bradlee, seated in his big chair, something just came over Janet, and she dug in her heels. Four French words echoed in her mind. They translated, "Go fuck yourself."

In the end, it was the résumé that got her. Supernigger fell to earth.

The Pulitzers were announced publicly on April 13. *The Blade*, proud of its former employee, prepared a story. It went to press at 8 A.M.

Later that morning, Ombudsman Green wrote, *Blade* editors read the biographical sketches of the Pulitzer winners that moved over the AP wire. The sketches were based on the résumé submitted with the entries. *The Blade*'s bio for Janet, taken from its personnel records, differed considerably. *Blade* editors alerted the wire service.

By afternoon an AP reporter called Janet. She stood by her Pulitzer bio. What no one had yet realized was that her Pulitzer bio differed from her first fake résumé, the one she had created when applying to the *Post*. For the Pulitzers, she had added two more languages, a year at the Sorbonne and six more writing awards.

Sometime after three, Ben Bradlee and managing editor Howard Simons received simultaneous phone calls. An AP editor wanted Simons. The assistant to the president of Vassar wanted Bradlee. Both callers were asking about Janet's résumé.

For the next eleven hours, Janet was interrogated, cajoled, comforted, pressured, flattered, put on the spot. One by one, Janet admitted to the false résumé items.

She drew the line at Jimmy.

At 11:30 P.M., according to Green, Coleman and Janet joined Woodward; David Maraniss, Woodward's deputy; and Tom Wilkinson, the assistant managing editor for personnel, in the fifth-floor conference room. Janet says she has little recollection of the events. The quotes that follow come from Green.

David Maraniss was cast as the good cop, as he was every day. He was known to his staff as "a real human being." Janet loved David. Everyone loved David. He had soulful, droopy eyes; he listened; he really seemed to care.

Woodward played the bad cop, also as usual. "You've got to come clean," he said. "Your notes show us the story is wrong. We can show you point by point how you concocted it. . . ."

"This is getting too cruel," said Janet, sobbing. "All I have left is my story."

"Give up the Pulitzer, and you can have yourself back," said Maraniss.

"If a just God were looking down," said Woodward, "what would he say is the truth?"

"I don't know what you mean," said Janet coldly.

Eventually, Woodward gave up. He, Coleman and Wilkinson left the room. Maraniss took a seat next to Janet. They both began to weep.

"I was afraid I was going to be left alone with you," she said. "I could never lie to you. . . . Why are you smiling?"

"Because I had a tremendous surge of empathy for you, refusing to submit to the institution in an absurd situation. . . ."

"Oh, David," sighed Janet. "What am I going to do?"

They talked for a while, exchanging intimacies. Then, at 1:45 A.M., Maraniss told Green, he said to Janet, "You don't have to say anything to the others. I'll do it for you. What do I tell them?"

Janet swallowed. "There is no Jimmy and no family. It was a fabrication. I want to give the prize back."

A few days later, I returned from Europe. On Saturday afternoon, my doorbell rang. It was Janet.

She seemed sedate and as light as a feather. Clearly, a burden had been lifted. She was wearing a short Afro and baggy clothes. She told me how things had gone down at the *Post*. "Be careful," she warned. "They're trying to pin this on you, too."

I thanked her. We had a good cry, a lingering hug. We said farewell.

Back at the Ontario, dozens of news crews were camped on the grass outside her first-floor apartment. Loretta Cooke taped garbage bags to the windows for privacy. Stratman set about untangling Janet's finances. He wrote checks for all her debts but refused to sign them until Janet took a scissors to her credit cards. Janet was taking twenty milligrams of Valium every four hours. She complied with her father's request.

In time the reporters went away; Elsa Walsh moved out. Janet took a smaller apartment and began dating another resident of the Ontario, a Jewish lawyer from Toledo named Joe Phillips. They were married in Washington—big dress, big cake, big bill. Her father paid but refused to attend. After the wedding, Loretta Cooke filed for divorce. Joe's parents were present but not happy.

Janet and Joe settled into a condo in the Maryland suburbs. At first she tried working on her memoirs. It was also reported that a publishing house had advanced her $50,000 to try her hand at fiction, but no contract was ever signed. She wrote a few stories for *Cosmopolitan*, but none ran. One story for *Washingtonian* about escort services began, "Call her Samantha. . . ."

After about a year, needing something to do, Janet went to work behind the jewelry counter at Bloomingdale's. When a news crew showed up, acting on a tip, she finished out the week and quit.

Janet and Joe had gone to France on their honeymoon, and once she was there, she knew for sure that this was the place she was meant to live. By coincidence a diplomatic job soon opened up. They moved to Paris in 1985. Living in Paris was just as she'd always imagined. They had a beautiful flat on the avenue du Président-Kennedy in the sixteenth arrondissement with a view of the Eiffel Tower.

Because France has always been a haven for expats and exiles, because the French have always had a special love for writers and writing, Janet found herself in a most agreeable atmosphere. The French, she says, tended to look upon her transgression as an *erreur de jeunesse*, a childish mistake. Everyone she met urged her to get back to her writing.

Less pleasing was her marriage, which became, in stages, unhappy, lonely and then stormy. After more than a decade, she petitioned for divorce. She did not fare well against an American attorney with diplomatic protection in a French court.

Finally, about two years ago, having gone through an entire winter with no electricity, Janet called home, asked her mom for a plane ticket.

Walking to the gate at Charles de Gaulle airport, she noticed a man following her with a camera. She stopped, turned, grabbed his long lens in her large palm.

He was on assignment for *People* magazine's twenty-fifth anniversary issue, the "Where Are They Now?" feature.

"A pitiful tale, is it not?" says Janet, dissolving into her trademark laugh. She is sitting on the bench in the Crossroads mall, outside Hudson's department store, due shortly to begin her shift at Liz Claiborne. It is, of course, a different day, though the only indication is the date on the calendar—the weather and the landscape remain unchanged.

"No, no, no," Janet points out, a devilish grin on her face. "Something *has* changed!" She rummages through her oversize purse and pulls out a pay stub. "See that? Six dollars and fifteen cents. I got a 15-cent raise! Which island should we buy?"

Since her return from Europe, says Janet, "I've learned a lot of things about how most people probably live. And lemme tell you, it ain't pretty."

In Toledo, Janet worked at the Limited Express for $4.85 an hour. With no car and cuts in local bus service, she was forced to walk miles home some nights. One frigid evening, icicles formed on her long eyelashes. For some reason, her mother would not let her borrow the car. Before she went in the hospital for surgery, Loretta Cooke bought the Club for the steering wheel and hid the key.

Hence Kalamazoo. Some friends, a job, anonymity, a quiet struggle.

These days, when Janet goes food shopping, she makes hard choices. Vegetables or chicken? Fish or potatoes? She might want Quaker Oats, but she settles for generic. She understands now why poor people are often fat.

Janet has bad asthma, but she can't afford a doctor. Because her job isn't quite full-time, she doesn't receive benefits. Certainly, she is a valued employee. Ever the overachiever, she was hesitant even to take time off for this interview. Currently, she's two months behind on her car payments because of an illness in January. To cut costs, Janet has to keep the heat low, which is bad for her breathing. She has a terrible cough. She can't afford to have drinks with the girls after work. Even if she has a few extra dollars, she has to weigh the mileage, the cost of gas. Dry cleaning is out. Her bathroom looks like a Chinese laundry.

"Even if you excluded everything that might be remotely considered extravagant, you still—I mean, if one thing goes wrong, you're screwed. And something always goes wrong when you're poor."

In the course of this story, Janet has been portrayed as an unhappy child, an alienated young woman, a talented reporter, an infamous liar, a compromised exile, a nearly destitute shop clerk. A woman who was damaged by a bitter parent, who was himself damaged by the ugly history of race relations in this country. A woman who learned deceit as a means of survival at an early age; who never had a clear view of her capabilities or her place in the world; who has lived her entire life on the verge of a nervous breakdown. The startling beauty who sashayed into the acre-square newsroom that January day has been reduced, in stages, to a 41-year-old divorced department-store worker sitting at the kitchen table with a bowl of cereal at her elbow, chewing her nails (real now—acrylic is too expensive), brow knitted over her checkbook, trying to decide whether to pay her rent or her car note this month.

It is not a pretty picture, but it's the un-embroidered truth.

Had Janet committed her indiscretion more recently, perhaps her life would be different. Back in '81, when the press staked out her apartment at the Ontario, there were no cameras in the bushes, no guerrilla assaults on the building. While under siege, Janet was able to come and go at will, using a back entrance. Nowadays that door would be covered.

But while the media have become more voracious over the years, they have also taken on new and different roles, one of which is Father Confessor. People today know well that the surest route back to grace is a massive public appeal. You transgress; you confess; you are forgiven.

Having been away from home for so long, Janet missed much of this change. She doesn't think this article will automatically redeem her. She doesn't know what will happen exactly, though she knows things can't get worse. What she is hoping most is that people will understand what happened. She wasn't trying to chip away at the foundations of the First Amendment. She wasn't trying to pull off a massive hoax that would bring her fame. She was desperate; she was damaged. She did what she knew how to do.

Now, at last, she has done something else, something she has learned in her later life, in the years since "Jimmy." She has told the truth. It is a beginning.

(1996)

Requiem for a Gangsta

Eric "Easy E" Wright helped pioneer gangsta rap. In the end, it wasn't guns or rivals that got him.

The bass beat faded, the video screen turned to snow. The CEO of Ruthless Records thumbed the remote, tilted back in his leather chair, adjusted his wraparound shades, inhaled deeply on a fragrant blunt. The next move was his.

He regarded the gentlemen before him, then regarded them some more. At 30, Eazy-E was the founder, owner and president, as well as chief executive, of Ruthless Records. He said sometimes that the *E* stood for Eric; his full name was Eric Wright. Other times he said it stood for Encino, though the significance of a nowhere valley town to a guy raised in Compton, the heart of gang turf in South Central Los Angeles, was left unexplained. He was also heard to declare, in his sly, trademark, high-pitched voice, that the *E* was for entrepreneur. Eazy was always angling to make money. As a kid, he bicycled a paper route, mowed lawns. Later he graduated to burglary, selling rock cocaine. For the past nine years, he'd been a music mogul.

Eazy fingered the ends of his sparse mustache. It was a spring afternoon in 1994; his gold-and-diamond ID bracelet glowed in the midday light filtering through the tinted windows of his office suite. With his eyes shielded by dark green locs, his milk-chocolate face totally void of expression, you could never tell where you stood in negotiations with Eazy. He would read a magazine during a meeting, chew paper, toss spitballs. When you pitched him, you wound up and threw, then dangled there, hanging off balance at the edge of the mound, waiting for a call, waiting a little longer.

Eazy eyeballed the group fidgeting before him, some Mexican rappers called Brownside. He sucked his teeth. His Ebel watch ticked off the seconds.

What up with this nigga? wondered Toker, the leader of Brownside, seated at the moment across two long, black leather sofas. Toker, Danger, Trigga, Sharp, Junior and Boxer were decked in full Mexican-gangsta regalia—neatly pressed Pendletons buttoned at the neck, white T-shirts beneath, khakis over-sized enough to fold into pleats. Two of them wore hair nets, one a blue do-rag. Their gats were stashed outside, in the trunk of Toker's '64 Impala low-rider. The scent of pomade radiated around them, mingling in the air with Eazy's Jheri Kurl juice and the strong stink of indica bud.

Toker waited him out. He wasn't goin' to say squat. This was Eazy's hood, all uppity-uppity, a place called Woodland Hills, with huge cribs looking like Swiss chalets and mini Taras and shit, lawns like a golf course. Though it was only ten or fifteen miles from where Toker grew up, he'd never heard of the place. Toker and them had rolled all the way here in the right lane of the freeway, worried about missing the exit.

Brownside was up from 49th Street, South Central L.A., Crip country. Back in the day, in the mid-'80s, when Toker was first on the corner, having turned from gang-banging to slinging rock cocaine, everybody had just started listening to rap. You had Ice-T trying to come out hard-core, but mostly there really wasn't nothing that nobody could relate to. The rhymes was wack.

Then Toker heard Eazy on the radio. He was kickin' up songs about what was happening on the street: drive-bys, dope sacks, police wacks. It was what they was living.

Beginning in 1986, with the release of a twelve-inch single, "Boyz-n-the-Hood," and following up two years later with the album *Eazy-Duz-It*, by Eazy, and a year after that with *Straight Outta Compton*, by his seminal group, Niggaz With Attitude (N.W.A.), Eazy-E and Ruthless Records had pioneered what has come to be known as gangsta rap. Along the way, Eazy helped to remake the face of style, entertainment and politics in America.

Like rock and roll in the '50s and soul in the '60s, gangsta rap has become the coin of the creative realm. The form can be seen in everything from the baggy look in fashion to the reality-oriented programming on television. Rap's content of discontent—sanctified by the Rodney King beating, by crime statistics, by a general foment among minorities of every stripe—has contributed to the embattlement of the proverbial "old white men in suits," an assault on the status quo in America that has translated into political upheaval and, recently, to direct attacks on rap by conservatives. To some, rappers like Eazy are the trumpeters of the apocalyptic hordes.

But to guys like Toker, to millions of kids across the country, Eazy's was the ultimate success story. He was an explorer who opened up new territory, created new possibilities. He defied the old rules, made up new ones as he went along. He did megabusiness with a joint between his lips. He released songs with titles like "Fuck tha Police." He made white people sweat. He giggled all the way to the bank.

Soon everyone in the ghetto was aspiring to rap stardom, buying drum machines and eight-track recorders, forming labels, rhyming about 9s and .40s and bitches and hoes. Then the folks in Hollywood discovered gangsta culture and the next thing you knew, white kids in Kansas were wearing falling-down jeans, greeting one another with a hearty "Yo!"

After a few years on the corner, Toker and his homies decided that there oughta be some Mexican rappers, too. They wrote a song called "Gang Related," bought time at a studio. They rented video cameras, hired some white guys to play cops. Then they hired a music lawyer who got them this meeting with Eazy-E.

Now, sitting expectantly on the leather sofas, Toker and his boyz continued to fidget. Eazy said nothing, just kicked it in his executive chair, his chin hiked, giving him the proud effect of a king. He pulled on his blunt—a short cigar hollowed of tobacco and refilled with weed. He adjusted his bracelet. He picked a piece of skin off one knuckle. He liked to keep his hands rough, he told people, in case he had to mix it up. For such a little man—five feet four, maybe 130 pounds—he did have big hands. How many fights he'd actually been in was subject to some question. But it didn't matter. What was strongest about Eazy was his bank. He always had a thick roll of dead presidents in his pocket. He paid for his Mercedes 600 SEL with cash. He told people his company was worth $20 million. His personal fortune, he said, was $60 million.

Finally, Eazy spoke. "Mannn," he said, shaking his head, his moist ringlets tickling the back of his neck. "This is like some cool shit here, man. Who owns you guys?"

"Don't nobody own us, motherfucker," said Toker.

"Who shot the video?" Eazy asked.

"We shot it ourself."

"Man, you bullshittin'," laughed Eazy, slapping his thigh. "Where you guys get the money?"

Toker eyeballed him. "Where you get *your* money when you started?"

Eazy regarded them a moment, refocusing. "Daaamn!" he exclaimed. "It's like that!"

"It's like that, motherfucker," declared Toker. He folded his arms across his chest, raised his own chin a notch.

"So what kinda deal you want?" asked Eazy. "What's up, man? I wanna fuck with you guys. Let's do business."

"Look, homey," said Toker. "We don't want no money up front. We got our own label. All we lookin' for is a motherfucker who wants to fuck with us and give us some kind of distribution deal. We kinda want to get our foot in the door, man."

"Oh, man," said Eazy—a sudden, theatrical frown. "I don't think nobody gonna give you guys no deal like that."

Toker sagged. Back on 49th Street, he said something and it happened. Here in Woodland Hills, his juice was water. He shrugged. "Well, look man," said Toker. "How would you come at us? That's why we came to you, man."

With that, Eazy giggled his smart-ass little giggle and signed yet another rap act. For no money down, on the strength of a handshake, Eazy picked up the option on Brownside's work, present and future, and the option of signing any other group that Toker and Fellon Records wanted to bring in.

In return, Brownside gained a place on an august family tree that had as its roots N.W.A.—featuring Ice Cube, Dr. Dre and MC Ren. Its branches included the D.O.C., Michel'le, Above the Law, all the way up to Snoop Doggy Dogg, Tha Dogg Pound, Hoes With Attitude, Bone Thugs-N-Harmony.

That spring, as Toker and his homies sat before him, Eazy and Ruthless were as hot as a Tec-9 at a drive-by. He had more than thirty groups signed to his label. Demo tapes by the dozens were stashed in the trunk of his gray Mercedes, along with videos, clothing and old containers of carryout food.

His *Ruthless Radio Show*, on KKBT-FM, in L.A., a Saturday-night call-in party show with Eazy on the mike, was being shopped nationally for syndication. A video game featuring Eazy's likeness was due out soon. His movie production company, Broken Chair Flickz, was circulating a screenplay around Hollywood. Another rap record company, catering to children, was also being discussed.

Eazy's recent EP, *It's on (Dr. Dre) 187 um Killa*, had entered the R & B charts at number one. Sales had reached double platinum, 2 million— payback for the loss of face Eazy had suffered at the hands of his old discovery, Dr. Dre, and Dre's new manager, Suge Knight. A two-volume set was nearing completion. *Str.8 Off the Streetz of Muthaphukkin Compton* would feature collaborations with artists ranging from Guns N' Roses guitarist Slash to Naughty by Nature. Also in storage was enough never-before-released music by N.W.A. for a double album. Eazy's dream was a reunion of the group, most of whose members weren't speaking to him anymore. Though it didn't seem likely—they countered with talk of a reunion of N.W.E., "Niggaz Without Eazy"—he was still trying. He told people he'd find a way.

"Ninety-five gonna be our year, man," Eazy told Toker and Brownside, sitting on the sofa. "Ruthless gonna blow the fuck up!"

As it turned out, 1995 was Eazy-E's *last* year.

In February, after checking into L.A.'s Cedars-Sinai Medical Center with chest pains and breathing problems—he thought it was a lingering case of asthmatic bronchitis—Eazy learned he had AIDS. He died a month later, on March 26, of heart failure due to a collapsed lung and AIDS-related pneumonia.

Ten days before his death, his attorney read a statement from Eazy, announcing his illness. The volume of sympathy calls from fans was such that Cedars-Sinai, a hospital long accustomed to celebrity patients, was forced to employ extra operators. Eazy received more calls at the hospital than Lucille Ball had.

Eazy left behind a wife, Tomica Woods, a former assistant at Motown, who declined to be interviewed for this article. Depending upon whom you believe, they'd been married in a hospital room either two days or three weeks before his death. The couple had a young son, Derrek, and a little girl, Daijah Nakia, who was born in September of '95. Tomica and son have so far tested negative for HIV. There are seven other acknowledged children, by six other women.

Also left behind was a new will, reams of litigation, mass confusion. Shortly after Eazy's death, police locked the doors of Ruthless Records to protect tapes and videos, which were beginning to disappear. A lawsuit by Michael Klein, director of business affairs for Ruthless Records, claims 50 percent ownership of Ruthless. The suit questions the validity of the will and of the marriage, which was performed either while Eazy was on heavy medication or the day before he was put on life-support systems. It asks for a determination of company ownership. The suit alleges that Eazy had often said he'd never marry, that in his "debilitated state" he'd been duped into the marriage and the new will. It also alleges that thousands had been diverted from Ruthless bank accounts by Tomica and her attorneys. At this writing, the court has appointed a special administrator to oversee operations at Ruthless Records.

Also before a court is a petition asking the hospital to turn over samples of Eazy's blood for a DNA test. At issue is the paternity of an infant, "Baby M." An attorney representing two other children has also filed a paternity suit. People close to Eazy expect many such suits. Wherever he went, women asked for his phone number. He took theirs instead, jotting them down in a small spiral notebook he always carried. It is said that he often had sex with five different women a day. He told folks he wanted a football team of kids. He lavished clothes and attention upon all his acknowledged children, sent them to expensive private schools, provided nice cars for the moms.

Eazy's death brought to a close what was arguably the most influential career in rap music to date. As of July 1994, the progeny of Eazy-E—rappers he discovered, rappers discovered by people he discovered—had sold more than 28 million albums. Today, with sales increasing exponentially from new groups and old titles, it is probably close to 50 million or more.

"Yo, listen up," said Eazy-E to the homeboys he had assembled, an all-star crew of young rappers standing around a glowing sound board. "What we need is some new shit. That other shit ain't sellin'."

"Well, what you lookin' for?" asked Dr. Dre.

"I don't know," said Eazy. "Something hard. Superhard. Maybe a lot of cussing."

The year was 1986. The place was Donovan Sound Studios, in Torrance. Eazy was 22, the oldest person in the room. A bright kid with loving parents—his mother a Montessori teacher, his father a Postal Service worker—he had turned inexplicably to the gang life. He had dropped out of school in tenth grade, proceeded to step up the ladder of crime.

By now he was rolling a burgundy Suzuki Samurai with a white top, wearing gold chains. How Eazy got the idea to become a rap mogul no one seems to remember, though he did like to go to the clubs and to the rap parties held regularly at Skateland and World on Wheels, near his neighborhood. Maybe in music and musicians he saw a potential for power similar to the kind he wielded in the world of drugs. He knew that dealing wouldn't last forever.

He called his company Ruthless Records, a reflection of his self-perceived style of business. He *was* pretty ruthless. Take the group gathered at Donovan Sound. He'd gone out and stolen them, raiding the best talent from an already existing label, Crew Cut Records, run by a guy named Lonzo. From the group CIA, he took Ice Cube, a young songwriting prodigy. From the World Class Wreckin' Cru came DJ Yella and Dr. Dre.

Dre was the heavyweight on the scene at the time. He was a deejay at a popular club called Dotos. His group was one of L.A.'s first well-known rap acts. Its members wore glitter makeup and lacy clothes, aimed for dirty/funny in their rhymes. At Dre's suggestion, Eazy recruited MC Ren and Arabian Prince (who would later enter rap-trivia annals as the dropped sixth member of the original N.W.A.).

In the spring of '86, when Eazy put his group together at the studio, L.A. rap music was considered imitative and second-rate. The prevailing belief was that hard-edged urban rap could breed only under the close, foul-weather conditions of the East Coast ghetto. Though Ice-T and his crime raps were beginning to emerge, the most popular California acts were jesters like Tone Loc and the L.A. Dream Team. "Our music is different from the East Coast," said one of the Dream Team. "It's more musical, more up-tempo. It's not as hard a life. We do have street violence, but the New York life is harder than that of sunny California and Hollywood."

And so it was that Eazy rented this studio and assembled his little Manhattan Project of rap. After much debate, the time ticking away, Eazy suggested that Cube write about gangs, the whole lifestyle Eazy had been living. They came up with "Boyz-n-the-Hood."

They laid the tracks, Eazy doing most of the rapping. Eazy took the tape to Macola Records, a custom pressing plant on Santa Monica Boulevard. For $7,000 in cash, Eazy got 10,000 twelve-inch vinyl records. He drove them to stores, sold them to dealers at swap meets. He ordered more. By word of mouth alone, the record sold 500,000 copies.

In March of 1987, Eazy met Jerry Heller in the lobby of Macola. Heller had started with promoter Bill Graham at the beginning of the rock era. Heller had been the first to bring Elton John and Pink Floyd to America. Legendary music manager Irving Azoff called Heller his mentor. Heller thought Ruthless was the greatest name for a record company he'd ever heard. Knowing the formula for musical success—the more hated by parents, the more popular with the kids—Heller recognized rap as the next wave.

After playing the demo for a few of his old contacts, who told him he was crazy, Heller went to Priority Records. Priority's marquee act was the California Raisins. The deal Heller cut at Eazy's insistence was unique. All records would be released by the Ruthless label, through Eazy's production company, a privilege and a piece of the action that was usually reserved for only the biggest stars.

In September 1988, Eazy and his group once again went into the studio.

When *Straight Outta Compton* was released by Niggaz With Attitude, featuring its keynote song, "Fuck tha Police," a firestorm erupted. Radio stations and MTV refused to play the cut. The album went gold in weeks.

In Phoenix, midway through a fifty-city tour, things began to go south for N.W.A. The members of the group were feuding with Eazy, questioning their shares of royalties and gate receipts. Eazy gave Jerry Heller a call, and Heller flew down with dubious contracts for all the members to sign, plus signing bonuses of $75,000 each. "He said, 'If you sign the contract, you get the check,' " Ice Cube recalled in a 1990 interview.

"So Heller give me this contract, and I said I wanted a lawyer to see it. Everybody else signed," said Cube. "I just told them, 'I wanna make sure my shit right first.' I remember them niggas jokin'. They say, 'Yo! $75,000! If that shit ain't right, ain't nothin' right!' "

In the end, Cube left the group. Eazy-E kept silent, let Heller speak for him. "The real reason that Ice Cube left N.W.A. was that he was incredibly jealous of the notoriety and success of Eazy-E," Heller has said. "He wanted to be Eazy-E. He was jealous because not only is Eazy a key member of N.W.A. with a successful solo career, he's also the president of his own record company. Eazy-E is a major star and a successful businessman. Ice Cube isn't."

"How can I be jealous of a motherfucker with no talent?" asked Cube in response. "He got money. I'm gonna have talent and money."

N.W.A.'s third album, *Efil4zaggin* ("Niggaz 4 Life" spelled backward), was made without him. It was the first gangsta-rap album to reach number one on *Billboard*'s chart.

Cube went on to a successful solo career. Soon he debuted as an actor, later as a producer. His first role was in the movie *Boyz N the Hood*.

Eazy-E stared up at the man before him, a guy they called Suge (pronounced *Shug*, as in sugar). Six feet three, 320 pounds, a former football star turned bodyguard turned rap manager, Marion "Suge" Knight had a reputation for violence. In the near future, he would be sued by two rappers charging assault. The rappers, two brothers, would allege that Suge pulled a gun, hit one of them on the head with it, forced them both to remove their clothes, then robbed them. Suge was Dr. Dre's new manager. (Knight declined to be interviewed for this article.)

"Where Dre at?" asked Eazy, trying to sound tough. It was an evening in April 1991, at a darkened sound studio at Solar Records. Dre had paged Eazy, asking for a meeting, one-on-one. Now Dre was nowhere to be found.

"We don't need him for this piece of business," said Suge, reaching for his breast pocket. He pulled out some legal documents.

For months, according to a suit filed under federal racketeering statutes in Los Angeles federal court, Suge Knight and his posse had been terrorizing Ruthless Records. It had begun more than a year earlier, when Dr. Dre and Eazy had a falling out, and Dre signed with Suge. Together they formed their own company, Death Row Records.

Known by now as the best producer in the business, Dre took with him the top acts from the Ruthless stable—Michel'le, Kokane, D.O.C. Just as Eazy had robbed Lonzo at Crew Cut Records, Suge and Dre had now ganked Eazy. This time, however, there was a slight problem. The rap business had become more sophisticated. A victor could no longer just take the spoils. He needed a signed, notarized release.

When Eazy refused to release Dre and the others, Suge began a reign of terror. One day, according to court documents, Suge walked straight into Jerry Heller's office at Ruthless and placed his index finger on Heller's gray temple. "I could have blown you away right now," he was alleged to have said.

Heller hired an Israeli security consultant and two bodyguards; he installed surveillance cameras and extra alarms. He ordered that a shotgun be kept under the reception desk at Ruthless. He kept guns in every room of his house, a grand stucco affair in a gated community in Calabasas, two doors down from Eazy. Dre lived one block over.

Eazy fronted off the threats, kept on the move. He had always spent most of his time in his cars anyway. He'd drive around all night thinking, making calls, visiting women. Eazy liked his women short and pretty, feisty, sort of street but with some education.

He wore two pagers on his belt, kept three cellular phones within reach. He seldom drank, though at a nice club he'd order a Midori sour. He liked eating at McDonald's, Benihana, Sizzler or anywhere he could get his favorite dish, fettuccine Alfredo. He often ordered several entrees to pick through. He loved Disney World, other theme parks with rides; he loved visiting his children, though he usually didn't stay long. It seemed like he always had a meeting to make, some work to do, Monday through Sunday, 24-7. He'd show up at Jerry Heller's house at three in the morning with a demo tape someone had handed him in a club.

Eazy rarely stayed in his own lavish house in Calabasas. Having grown up in the friendly, cacophonous atmosphere of the hood, Eazy thought the house, secreted in a canyon a few miles from Malibu, surrounded by rich white people, was isolated and creepy, too quiet. He also had a big house in Westlake with a waterfall out back. He hardly ever went there either. He preferred his house in Norwalk, a short drive from Compton.

The Calabasas house was even bigger and farther away than the Westlake place. In the white marble foyer, there was a neon sign, WELCOME TO EAZY'S PLAYHOUSE. It was a great party house, and that's what he used it for. You'd walk in and find three or four kinds of designer marijuana on the dining room table, plenty of beer and juice and whatnot in the fridge. The living room was done in white shag carpet with cream-colored leather couches, brass-and-glass tables. A huge entertainment room was painted completely black. It sported a projection TV and a state-of-the-art audio system. Scattered around the house were his various collections: pogues, pistols, bottles of designer cologne. His other passion was expensive monster dolls—Freddy Krueger, a $2,500 Chucky. Most of the dolls came from kits, which Eazy paid people to assemble.

The big garages at the houses also served him well. Besides the gray Mercedes, Eazy had a Jeep Cherokee, a couple of BMWs. He owned four vintage Impala low-riders—three from 1964, one from 1963. The cars were stacked: Dayton wide wheels, full hydraulics that could bounce the cars off the pavement like basketballs. The stereo systems ran $15,000.

Now, however, in a darkened sound studio, Eazy was on foot and alone. His best producer and former best friend had left his company, taking with him Ruthless's biggest acts. Suge Knight loomed above him, brandishing legal papers releasing Eazy's artists.

"So, you gonna sign the releases?" asked Suge, according to court documents.

"Fuck you, motherfucker," said Eazy.

"Look G," Suge allegedly said. "I got Jerry Heller stashed in a van."

"Fuck you!" said Eazy.

Then Suge pulled another piece of paper from a pocket, a wrinkled scrap. On it was written an address in Compton. "I know where you mamma stay," said Suge, nodding his head toward a dark corner of the room. Two bodyguards stepped forward, each carrying a lead pipe.

Eazy signed the releases.

Dr. Dre's first album with Death Row Records, *The Chronic*, was released in 1992. The video for the single "Dre Day" went into heavy rotation on MTV.

The guest rapper on the cut was Dre's new discovery, Snoop Doggy Dogg. The video featured an Eazy-E look-alike jumping up and down like a clown. Behind him was a group of rappers portraying minstrel-show types. A pudgy, gray-haired white guy ordered them around. "I work for Sleazy E— I wouldn't have it any other way," the white guy declared, winking. "Just sign your life—I mean your name—on the contract."

The song ended like this: "Oh yeah. And P.S. Fuck Mr. Roarke and Tattoo, a.k.a. Jerry and Eazy."

The record sold 3 million.

Eazy collected a percentage of the royalties, a condition of the contract that Knight and Dre eventually signed in order to legally release Dre's album.

Says a record promoter who worked with Eazy since the Macola days: "I think Suge kinda stole a lot of Eazy's self-esteem, you know, bum-rushin' his office, taking away his groups. Then Dre come out dissin' him on MTV. Daaamn! Suge kinda made him a broken man. Eazy lost a lot of respect behind that. No matter how many lawyers and managers you got, rap is still a contact sport, you know what I'm sayin'? People thought Eazy come off with his tail between his legs like a bitch."

"What did the doctor say?" asked Eazy from his hospital bed in Cedars-Sinai. "What did they tell you?"

"Ummm, he said your T cells are kind of low, and that those are the good ones that fight off the virus and stuff," said Charis Henry, Eazy's former assistant, a homegirl and ex-rapper with a degree from Loyola Marymount.

When Eazy dropped all that weight, then ended up in the hospital, Charis put two and two together and rushed to his side. She had started working for Eazy at her own suggestion. Over the years, they'd become close, but they were never lovers. She knew a different Eazy: boyish, silly, sly, mindful of his language. He always excused himself when he cursed in front of her.

Charis had been with Eazy since before the falling-out with Dre. She was the one who had written the $2,500 check that bought Eazy his seat at a luncheon in Washington, D.C., with 1,400 Republicans and President George Bush, a little joke Eazy played on the White Establishment after he'd found himself on a Republican fund-raising list.

Charis was the one who called up the lawyers when Eazy wanted to get in touch with L.A. police officer Theodore Briseno, one of the defendants in the Rodney King beating. Eazy attended the trial almost daily, sitting near

Briseno. He told the press that Briseno was a Mexican, not a white guy. He said Briseno had tried to stop the beating. Other rappers said Eazy was a sellout, raising the puppet theme once again.

Charis had also been there as Eazy slowly recovered from his loss of face at the hands of Suge and Dr. Dre. Soon after the alleged reign of terror abated—an easing of hostilities that coincided with the filing of the federal racketeering charges against Suge Knight—Eazy began working even harder than before, signing groups, releasing albums, coming up with new ideas. With the release of *It's on (Dr. Dre) 187um Killa,* Eazy was clearly back in the house. " 'Dre Day' was my payday, and Snoop look like an anorectic mutt," Eazy rapped, a dis that made people stand up and go "Daaamn!" Eazy had fought back to respectability.

Recently (under Tomica's influence, many say), Eazy had parted ways with Jerry Heller and with Priority Records. With Heller out of the way, rumors went, chances for an N.W.A. reunion seemed brighter. Eazy was photographed talking with Ice Cube at a New York club, their first major conversation since the Phoenix incident nine years earlier.

Now, in a private hospital room filled with flowers, Charis was trying to put a positive spin on some bad news, chattering nonstop like always. What the doctor had said, precisely, was that Eazy's T-cell count was only five. Charis and Tomica, also present in the room on this March afternoon, had decided that it wasn't necessary to tell him the exact number.

"So what we need to do is build those T cells up," Charis continued cheerfully. "There's teas and things you can take. Don't worry about that. But right now, I want you to continue eating. If you have four bites of fruit today, I want you to have eight tomorrow. If you don't eat—"

Eazy cut his eyes to Charis. He looked annoyed.

"Do you want me to leave?" Charis asked Eazy.

"No," said Eazy, his voice muffled under an oxygen mask. "I want you to be quiet."

"Well, I'll tell you what," said Charis. "You eat five bites of soup, and I'll be quiet."

Eazy perked up, pulled the mask off his face. "Hurry up and give me the soup," he said with a smirk.

They buried Eazy-E in a gold-plated coffin, wearing baggy jeans, a Pendleton shirt, wraparound shades, a Compton hat. Missing from his outfit were his gold-and-diamond bracelet, his Ebel watch, his assortment of gold rings. He lay in state, fingers interlaced, at the foot of the altar in the massive sanctuary of the First African Methodist Episcopal Church, a stately brick monolith with stained-glass windows on a little hill overlooking deepest South Central. Outside, police patrolled every corner for miles. People made their way quietly, reverntly by car and on foot, toward the church from every direction.

As bow-tied Fruit of Islam bodyguards watched closely, more than 3,000 mourners filed past Eazy's body: teenagers and church ladies, homeboys, club girls and neighborhood folk, a number of white record execs, even the mayor of Compton. The city council had proclaimed this Eazy-E Day. For better and for worse, Eazy had put Compton on the world map.

Ten days before he died, Eric "Eazy-E" Wright issued this statement:

> I may not seem like a guy that you'd pick to preach a sermon, but I feel it's now time to "testify" because I do have folks that care about me hearing all kinds of stories about what's up.
>
> Yeah, I was a brother on the streets of Compton doing a lot of things most people look down on, but it did pay off. Then, we started rapping about real stuff that shook up the LAPD and the FBI, but we got our message across big-time and everyone in America started paying attention to the boyz in the hood. Soon our anger and hopes got everyone riled up.
>
> There were great rewards for me personally like fancy cars, gorgeous women and good livin'. Like real non-stop excitement. I'm not religious but wrong or right, that's me. I'm not saying this because I'm looking for a soft cushion wherever I'm heading, I just feel that I've got thousands and thousands of young fans that have to learn about what's real when it comes to AIDS. . . . I would like to turn my own problem into something good that will reach out to all my homeboys and their kin because I want to save their asses before it's too late.

(1995)

"Damn! They Gonna Lynch Us!"

Black motorist Rodney Glenn King's videotaped beating at the hands the LAPD became the most scrutinized police brutality case in history. But what actually happened?

Pooh and Glenn and Freddie G. was kickin' it late that night outside Pooh's house, all three sitting in the car. The stars were out and the radio hummed blues into the cool March air. It was a typical Saturday on the wrong side of Altadena, near the border between the Bloods and the Crips; some homeboys, some reefer, some Old English 800, something ready to go down.

Glenn was behind the wheel of the white Hyundai, a four-door that belonged to his grandma. He stared out the windshield, worrying his sparse mustache. Freddie G. snored at shotgun, his crippled leg snug in a metal brace. Pooh lounged behind Glenn, lids heavy, head angled forward to keep his Jheri curl from getting scrunched. It had been a long night. Sort of a reunion.

Glenn had been trying to hook up with Pooh all week. Tonight, he'd just come on by the house. Pooh was playing with his baby girl, half-watching television.

"What up?" said Glenn. He'd walked over, slid Pooh some skin. He'd known Pooh since Little League. Through the years, they'd lost touch on and off, but that's how it was in the neighborhood. You away a while, you back, you pick right up. Glenn was chatty, like always, pretty funny, built like Baby Huey, six feet three. He liked Snickers bars, Mexican food, Marlboros in a box, the ladies. Twenty-five years old, he was married to his second wife, Crystal. She had two kids. They lived with his relatives in the house where he grew up.

Pooh and Glenn had chilled a while, then hooked up with Freddie G. Helms and drove to the park. Then they rode back to Pooh's house, parked by the curb. Freddie G. rapped a little, fell asleep. Now it was quiet in the car, just the music from the radio, a show called *The Quiet Storm*. Then Glenn started the car and drove off down the hill toward the Foothill Freeway, the 210.

Five hundred miles of freeway in Los Angeles County, a vast sprawling valley of highways, a canopy of stars and darkness, the mountains hunkered just north. A few dollars' worth in the tank, some homeys in the car, a pleasure cruise in a rolling clubhouse—what else is there to do? No apartment, no money, the movie stars got all the Lakers tickets. Concerts are too dangerous. House parties are okay, but you don't go unless it's people you deal with. You never know when you're gonna get caught in someone else's beef, settled with a spray of bullets.

They go to different cities—Monrovia, Duarte, Irvin, Pomona—different patches in the vast racial quilt that covers the San Fernando Valley, over the hill from Hollywood: cookie-cutter residential outposts of strip malls and fast-food joints. In some cities, all the signs are written in Chinese, all the cars are filled with Chinese people. In others, there are Vietnamese, Mexicans, Koreans, Salvadorans, blacks. White people are seen on occasion. Usually they're in black-and-white cars. On the doors, there's a sign written in English, the slogan of the Los Angeles Police Department: "TO PROTECT AND TO SERVE."

So that's what you do on a Saturday evening: Just get out on the freeway, choose an exit, turn right, right again, look around for ladies. Don't stay too long, though: too risky. At home in Altadena, the police get used to you. They don't mess with you if you ain't done nothing wrong. But if you go to a different city, they pull you over just like that, especially if there's a lot of guys with baseball caps in the car. They keep you ten or fifteen minutes. They ask what's going on in the neighborhood. You're like, "I don't know," 'cause you don't stay in that neighborhood. They make you sit on the curb or get down on your stomach. They put their knee in your back. They take your ID and forget to return it. Like Glenn once said, "They consider themselves different humans than we are. They all a family, one big family. And we another family."

The other choice is staying home, but Altadena's no picnic either, not on this side of town. East of Fair Oaks Avenue, that's chamber-of-commerce Altadena: million-dollar houses, Neighborhood Watch, the hundred-year-old deodar pines on Christmas Tree Lane festooned with holiday lights. West of Fair Oaks, down Lincoln Avenue, that's Pooh and Glenn and Freddie G.'s Altadena: cracking paint, brown weeds on the lawn, cars on cinder blocks in driveways, blue collars, brown skins, bandannas, suburban gangs.

Living as he did by the shifting border, Pooh had his days as a Blood. His set was the Playboys. His court file begins at age 15. Bryant Keith Allen, a.k.a. Pooh and Boss, was first arrested for stabbing a man in the stomach. He was sentenced to one year probation, 120 hours of community service. Two years later, he was arrested for swinging a blackjack at a man who was helping children board a school bus. Six months in probation camp, an A.A. meeting once a week. Returning home, Pooh was arrested for staggering along a street, a bottle of beer in his hand. Fifty more hours of community service.

Pooh went down hard two years later, when he was 19. At 8:15 one evening, Pooh and two accomplices, all of them armed with automatic pistols, robbed a liquor store. Two hours later, they hit a McDonald's. They roughed up the cashiers, brained the manager, emptied the cash drawers and the safe. Making their getaway, they encountered cops, who opened fire. Pooh went down, three shotgun pellets embedded in his leg and foot. He gave himself up.

Court records say that Pooh was suspected of pulling three to five other armed robberies that same month. His sentencing report recommended the max: "It seems that defendant is out of control and needs to be removed from society for the protection of us all." Pooh pleaded guilty, got five years.

Back on the block, Pooh was keeping clear, trying to put the gangs behind him. Recently, he'd ended the longest work stint of his life, six months with a paper company at $5.50 an hour.

Now Glenn nosed the Hyundai onto the entrance ramp of the 210. He stared straight ahead, hummed a song to himself. It was a simple life he'd led. His parents were Jehovah's Witnesses. His father was a handyman; on weekends he liked to fish and to drink whiskey. Glenn was in the special-education class in high school. He had trouble reading, often skipped school. By the time his class got to its senior year, Glenn was at least a grade behind. Six months before graduation, he dropped out. After that, Glenn seemed adrift. He was into singing on the corner, hanging out in the park.

Rodney Glenn King entered the system when he was 18, when he was arrested for trying to run down his first wife, Denetta. She chose not to press charges, and Glenn was convicted of reckless driving, sentenced to eighty-four hours of community service. Two months later, Glenn was arrested for stealing $251 worth of auto parts from the Pep Boys in Pasadena. He was found guilty of trespassing, placed on sixty days probation. In 1987, Glenn tried once again to run down Denetta. Once again, she chose not to press charges. Glenn pleaded no contest to misdemeanor battery and was placed in a domestic-violence program. Two years later, he was arrested for soliciting an undercover policewoman. Glenn pleaded guilty and was fined $352.50. When the fine went unpaid, an arrest warrant was issued. Tonight, it remained outstanding.

Glenn's one attempt at a capital crime was a stupendous failure. He was 23, by then divorced from Denetta and married to Crystal, a high-school friend. According to court records, early one evening Glenn got in the Hyundai and drove east, to a Chinese neighborhood called Monterey Park. He entered the 99 Market, bought a single piece of bubble gum, then pulled a two-foot tire iron from beneath his jacket. "Open the cash register," demanded Glenn, who loomed a foot taller than the store owner behind the counter, Tae Suck Baik.

Baik opened up, let Glenn take the cash. Then Glenn reached for two cashier's checks. Baik grabbed Glenn's hand. "You don't need checks," he said.

Glenn stopped a moment, pondering.

Baik reached below the counter, came up with a three-foot metal rod. He grabbed Glenn's jacket and began whipping him with the rod. Glenn staggered, fell, dropped his tire iron. Baik ran around the counter and hit Glenn some more. Glenn reached for an aluminum pole, hit Baik once, then fled the scene with $200 and the cashier's checks. Baik ran out after him and wrote down the license number of the white Hyundai.

Ten days later, Glenn was apprehended, the checks still in his glove compartment. He was sentenced to two years in state prison. Released after one, he returned in December 1990 and went to work renovating concession stands at Dodger Stadium. "He never missed a day, including two weeks when he had car trouble and had to ride the bus to Chinatown and then walk over the bridge to the stadium," says his supervisor. "He was a good man. I think he was sorry when the job ended."

Now, at thirty minutes past midnight, Sunday, March 3, 1991, Glenn followed 210 as it banked gently west, a dark ribbon of asphalt cut through a fairy kingdom of textured hills and craggy mountains. He drove on, hypnotized by the series of glowing lane dots, by his thoughts. Freddie G. was still asleep. Pooh listened to the radio, a station called KKBT-FM, the Beat.

Past Pennsylvania Avenue, past La Tuna Canyon Road, past Sunland Avenue, past a California Highway Patrol car idling by the side of the road. . . .

Inside the cop car, the radar gun shrieked. The deputies were a husband-and-wife team, T.J. and Melanie Singer. Startled, they checked the readout. One hundred and fifteen miles an hour, according to the report they filed later. The Hyundai whooshed past. The Singers peeled out, officers in hot pursuit, Code 2.

Pooh, in the backseat with his eyes closed, all of a sudden felt a little twinge, the kind you feel at a stoplight when someone's staring at you. He opened his eyelids to slits. Red light danced across the seat in front of him. He twisted around, head low, looked out the rear window.

Shit! Police!

Pooh turned toward the front. Freddie G. was still sleeping. Glenn drove on, seemingly unaware of the cops following them.

Why ain't Glenn pulling over? wondered Pooh.

Not far away, in an LAPD patrol car, a bulletin blipped across a computer screen. The terminal was mounted on a dashboard between the two officers. The Mobile Digital Terminal looks like a word processor. It is the latest hardware in the modern war on crime, linked by computer relay to the police department's NASA-developed command-and-control center, located in downtown LA, five floors below ground in a hardened bunker.

It was against policy to send personal messages via the MDT, but on this night, Officer Larry Powell, riding with his partner, Timothy Wind, was taking the liberty to chitchat.

"What are you up to?" typed Officer Corina Smith. She and Powell were dating. "We are up on the rock on top of some abandon house with narco and BFMV [burglary from a motor vehicle] suspects in it. We are waiting for them to hit some places."

"Sounds almost like our last call," typed Powell. "It was right out of Gorillas in the Mist."

"HaHaHaHa," typed Smith. "Let me guess who be the parties."

"Good guess," responded Powell.

Powell, 28, looked like a cop on the beat. Pug-nosed and thick-jowled, Irish worry knitting his brow, he was a three-year veteran. His father, Edwin, was a Los Angeles County marshal. Former neighbors remember the boy as quiet, hardworking, responsible. If you ever needed a hand, you could ask him. After high school, Larry went to Cal State for two years, then joined the force. With their youngest gone, his mother and father had opened their empty nest to a series of babies born to drug-addicted mothers.

Before going on patrol tonight, Powell and other officers had trained with their PR-24 batons, two-foot metal-alloy nightsticks. Powell was judged weak and ineffective, ordered to drill a second time, concentrating on baton chops to the shoulder blades, elbows, wrists, knees and ankles.

Powell's partner was a 30-year-old rookie who had graduated from the academy in November. He too had taken training tonight, to far better reviews. "He demonstrated excellent technique and made contact in all the right places on the practice board," his supervisor had noted.

Tall and skinny, with an overbite, Tim Wind had come to Foothill Division from Shawnee, Kansas, where he'd served on the fifty-four-member force in the suburb of Kansas City. Wind was married, the father of a toddler son. He was still on department probation.

Wind's move from Kansas was the law-enforcement opportunity of a lifetime. The LAPD, most cops will agree, is the nation's showcase force. Starting with *Dragnet, The Mod Squad, Adam-12* and *S.W.A.T.*, up through *21 Jump Street*, fact and fantasy had begun to blur where California cops were concerned. The 8,300 very real men and women of the LAPD had become something of a legend, their chief looked upon as kind of a four-star general of local crime fighting. The LAPD had a reputation as being a closed society—a clean-cut paramilitary organization that dealt in only the finest: training, equipment, commanders, men.

Just then, at 12:47 A.M., a message from headquarters interrupted Smith and Powell: "To all units: CHP advises their officers are in pursuit of a vehicle failing to yield, white Hyundai, license 2KFM102, now approaching Glenoaks. . . ."

Powell and Wind took off.

Back in the Hyundai, Pooh swiveled, checked the rear. The police were gaining. Why Glenn acting like this? he wondered. To Pooh, Glenn was usually one of the smart ones. He wasn't no gang banger; he was always the one sayin' you shouldn't do this or that. But now Glenn was behind the wheel, and it was like he wasn't there. Who knows where he was? Maybe thinking about getting caught and violating his parole. Maybe thinking about that old bench warrant; the cops could take him right off the street. Maybe, says a friend, Glenn was off in a faraway place he sometimes goes. It's a defense mechanism or something, an escape route. Just now, with the police in pursuit, it was as if he'd had a glitch. Something in his brain that said, This isn't really happening. It's gonna go away.

Glenn pulled off the freeway at the Paxton Street exit and rolled through a stop sign at the bottom of the off-ramp at about fifty miles per hour, according to police.

Pooh was getting scared. The cops were closing in. Glenn stopped for a red light, then gassed it. Sirens now, more cars, Powell and Wind, others, Code 3. A helicopter beat the air overhead. Pooh thought to himself, The next stop that come, I'm gonna jump out the car! Then he thought better: No, I can't do that. The police might think I got something. Then he realized: Shit! These motherfuckers could start shooting!

Pooh swiveled, raised his palms high, surrendering out the rear window. "Glenn! Glenn!" he hollered. "Pull over! Stop!"

Fifty years ago, had there been a balcony where George Holliday's now stands, the view of Hansen Dam would have been breathtaking. Shimmering in the undulating foothills, Holiday Lake stretched 130 blue acres, 30 feet deep, a huge park built by the county in 1949. Rimmed with trucked-in sand, there was a shallow section for swimmers, barbecue pits on a wide grassy knoll for lazy Sunday afternoons. On weekends, the parking lot was jammed with colorful cars with big metal fins, filled with postwar Americans hard at work developing the concept of leisure time.

Years went by. Heavy rains and forest fires caused erosion, and silt from the San Gabriel Mountains and the Angeles Forest filled the lake. By 1982, the water was declared stagnant and unhealthy. Today, heavy machinery rumbles in a big pit, scooping up the 30 million tons of rock and sand and silt in what was once Holiday Lake. Homeless men wander the hills, picking through Dumpsters. The parking lot is now a city street, a scene out of urban South Central, plucked up somehow by providence and landed amid green landscape. Black men stand in clusters, drinking from paper cups; money and drugs change hands. Two rusty motor homes are parked semipermanently. People knock, enter, the doors bang shut.

Though the lake died a premature death, the Foothill District, as it is known to the LAPD, would begin to flourish. In the past ten years, due mostly to Asian and Hispanic immigration, California's population has grown twice as fast as the rest of the country's. Foothill has absorbed much of the new burden: Nestled into the mountains, twenty minutes from downtown, it is the fastest-growing community in L. A. County.

Sixty percent Hispanic, ten percent black, thirty percent Asian and Anglo, as Caucasians have come to be termed on the California census, it is a demographic picture of America's future. The area is plagued with the most drunk drivers, heroin addicts and car thefts in the San Fernando Valley, a bubbling pepper pot of towns and colors and trouble.

The statistics don't lie, but they don't tell the whole truth about Foothill, either. If you're not a person of color, if you're not poor or illiterate or unemployed, if you don't know anybody who breaks any laws, Foothill is a middle-class exurbia. Affordable condos, picket fences—this is the place where George Holliday moved three years ago, a pit stop on the road to what people used to know as the American Dream.

Born in Toronto, George lived most of his life in Indonesia and Argentina. Six years ago, at 26, he decided to come to America. George arrived at LAX with $700 in his pocket and a suitcase in each hand, a strapping, freckled, sandy-haired rugby player with an itch to succeed. By lunchtime the next day, he was cooking burgers in a fast-food place. He worked there for about two weeks, until he found a job as a plumber.

Today, George is the general manager of a local office of a national plumbing concern called Rescue Rooter. He recently married his Argentine girlfriend, Eugenia. They'd moved to Mountainback three years ago, a tidy development of neo-Tudor garden apartments, up a hill and behind an iron fence from Foothill Boulevard.

When they first had moved in, the neighborhood wasn't great. It seemed that every day, park rangers and police were rounding up drug dealers across the street at Hansen Dam. It was a bit of a nuisance and a little scary, considering the way they talked about it so much on the news. But when you came right down to it, none of it really touched George and Eugenia. "The cops, you're not really aware of them," says George. "You need them, you call them. The rest of the time you live your life."

And a good life it was. George had his work, Eugenia stayed home, met him often for lunch. A few months before, the couple had decided to buy a camcorder. George brought it home on Valentine's Day, a Sony CCD-F77. On Saturday night, March 2, George loaded film into the camera, plugged the battery pack into the recharger. The next day was the Los Angeles Marathon. He was sponsoring one of his employees in the race. He went to bed early, setting his alarm for 6 A.M.

Over the years, George had become accustomed to the night sounds of police sirens screaming down Foothill Boulevard. Usually, he slept right through it. But this night, at about 12:50 A.M., George woke with a start. Something was peculiar. The sirens wailed in the distance, as always, but this time they crescendoed and died with a screech of rubber outside his bedroom window. George jumped up, naked, from the bed and pulled back the window shade.

Across the boulevard, a hundred yards away, a white Hyundai was pulling to the curb. A half-dozen police cars pulled up around it.

George watched a second, then flashed. Hey, he thought, let's get the camera!

"DRIVER! PUT YOUR HANDS OUT THE WINDOW. TAKE YOUR LEFT HAND, UNLOCK THE DOOR, AND STEP OUT!"

Inside the white Hyundai, Freddie G. awoke with a start. When last he'd been conscious, he was chillin' in the car outside Pooh's house, in Altadena. Pooh, in the back, had his hands up, palms high in surrender. Glenn, legally drunk, struggled to execute the commands issuing from the PA. He blinked his eyes, tried to focus. He took his left hand off the steering wheel, rolled down the window, stuck his arm out. Then he took his right hand off the wheel. He reached across his chest.

Pooh peered out into the darkness. There was a grassy knoll, some high trees, white police everywhere. Damn! he thought. They gonna lynch us or somethin'!

If you're black or brown or yellow and you live in Los Angeles in the year 1991, there are some things you just know. One is that two thirds of the county's population are people of color like you, and that the rest of the United States' cities are headed quickly in that direction. Another thing is this: white people are still in charge, and they generally make that clear.

How differently the police can be perceived:

"They consider themselves different humans than we are," Rodney Glenn King had said. "They all a family, one big family. And we another family."

"The cops, you're not really aware of them," George Holliday had said. "You need them, you call them. The rest of the time you live your life."

"There has existed for many years a simmering—sometimes boiling—relationship of mistrust and animosity between the LAPD and Los Angeles's minority communities," the Southern California Chapter of the American Civil Liberties Union said recently. "This is fueled and maintained by abuse directed toward those communities [by the police] . . . who have shown a historic tolerance toward prejudice and abusive behavior within its own ranks."

In 1980, Los Angeles paid out slightly less than $1 million to resolve lawsuits alleging police misconduct. In 1989, the outlays had risen to $9.1 million. Last year, a record $11.3 million was paid to victims and families, more than in any other city in the nation except Detroit, which has 4,000 fewer officers than the LAPD.

The 1990 totals include suits alleging excessive force, false arrests, wrongful deaths, civil-rights violations, negligence, misconduct. Of the thirty-two cases settled, eight involved police shootings, thirteen involved physical abuse. Between 1987 and 1990, 4,400 misconduct complaints were filed against the LAPD. Forty-one percent of all complaints were filed by blacks, who comprise only 13 percent of the population of L.A.

In one case, police in an armored personnel carrier, mounted with a fourteen-foot battering ram, stormed a suspected crack house. Inside were three small children, two eating ice cream cones. No drugs were found. In a raid on a South Central neighborhood, a force of eighty LAPD officers beat and terrorized occupants of several apartments during a drug search, carried out with crowbars, sledgehammers and axes. Several dozen suspected gang members were taken into custody, seven were booked—none was charged with a crime. In the aftermath, residents of the apartments discovered that one of the cops had spray-painted some graffiti on a living-room wall: "GANG TASK FORCE RULES!"

"There is a culture of violence that has swept the nation's police forces," said Representative John Conyers, of Michigan, a member of the Congressional Black Caucus. Analysts say police brutality has its roots in racism, academy training, group identification, slack departmental discipline, fraternal traditions that encourage a "code of silence" among officers. Police themselves say that they have been conditioned by experience to expect the worst in encounters with the public. "We've seen over and over how seemingly benign situations can result in our own deaths," wrote a female LAPD officer in a *Newsweek* editorial that ran on March 25. "The social conditions within which we operate are complex. So are the range of emotions each cop experiences daily. We never know what to expect. We all want to see tomorrow."

The roots of the LAPD's brutal statistics can be traced to its history. Back in the Twenties, when gangsters and vice lords were hip-deep in politics, the LAPD was known as the palace guard of the city bosses. In 1950, a reform movement was mounted, and the city charter was amended. New rules called for the chief of police to be hired through a civil-service process instead of being appointed by the mayor. The first new man was William H. Parker.

Next to FBI Director J. Edgar Hoover, Parker would become the most celebrated law-enforcement official in history. A former marine, Parker installed a boot camp and stressed chain of command and pride in badge and uniform. It was Parker who coined the phrase "thin blue line" to describe his police force, but he is best remembered for the inauguration of "proactive," offensive policing. Rather than wait for crime to be committed, Parker decided, the police should take the initiative: Go get them before they get us.

Parker's chauffeur and bodyguard back then was a young cop named Daryl Gates. Born in Glendale, in 1926, Gates was the son of an alcoholic plumber and his devout Mormon wife. Gates wanted to be a lawyer but didn't have the funds. He settled for a $290-a-month job with the police department.

Parker died in 1966. Gates worked his way through the ranks, placing first on every exam. In 1978, Gates became chief and since then has become known nationwide for bringing the Parker principle of "proactive," military-style law enforcement into the modern era. He pioneered the SWAT team in America, and the use of the battering ram. One of his favored methods was the "pretext traffic stop," which called for motorists to be pulled over based on their "profile." Wholesale roundups of homeboys were employed in the ghettos, carried out by a special unit called CRASH.

Gates's rise coincided perfectly with the war on drugs; with law and order the Maypole around which politicians danced, his style of policing was an advertisement for government in action, a tonic for suburban fears. He and other local generals operated with virtual carte blanche. "We must do whatever is necessary to deter those who would suppress us at home," he once told an audience of police boosters. "We are not just the first line of defense, ladies and gentlemen, we are the only line. But you can count on us. We will win this war."

Over the years, Gates has told many audiences many things. He told a Latino audience that Latino officers were not being promoted because they were lazy. Once, discussing the controversial "carotid choke hold," Gates suggested that blacks had died because "their veins or arteries do not open up as fast as they do on normal people." He told a U.S. Senate panel that "casual drug users should be shot." When his own son, a heroin addict, was jailed for robbing a pharmacy, Gates said, "He'll get no help from me."

Gates's attitude seemed to trickle down to the rank and file. A random review of MDT transmissions: "Sounds like monkey slapping time." "If you encounter these negroes, shoot first, ask questions later." "Capture him, beat him and treat him like dirt." "Shoot him twice for me."

CHP Officer Melanie Singer approached the white Hyundai with caution.

Behind and all around, twenty-six other officers stepped gingerly out of patrol cars.

"What's your name?" Singer asked the driver.

"Glleeenn," he slurred, exhaling a pungent cloud of malt liquor.

Singer reeled, took a step back. "Get down on the ground, Glenn," she ordered, not unkindly.

Glenn, both hands out the window, looked quizzical, then hoisted himself out of the Hyundai. He seemed slow, a little stiff. He also seemed happy.

Glenn looked up at the helicopter, shielded his eyes from the blinding spotlight. He smiled and waved. He let out a full, deep belly laugh. Then he began to dance, shuffling his feet, a pitter-patter step. He smirked at Singer.

"Get down on the ground!" she commanded.

"Why you want me to get on the ground?" he asked. He danced a few more steps, then stopped.

He reached down with his right hand, fingers moving toward the back pocket of his pants.

"Get your hands away from your butt!" yelled Singer.

Glenn turned, about-face. He bent forward a little from the waist, grabbed a handful of his right buttock, jiggled.

Singer was flabbergasted. She drew her weapon. "Hit the ground!" she ordered.

"No. No!" came a deep voice. Singer cut her eyes right. A sergeant was stepping forward. Sergeant Stacey Koon, LAPD.

Koon was 40, a fifteen-year veteran of the department. Muscular, stern-faced, with a receding hairline, Koon was married to a nurse, the father of five children, a devout member of Our Lady of Perpetual Help Catholic Church. Neighbors remember the time a dog jumped his fence and entered his house. Koon had threatened the pet with his pistol.

Koon took an easy step forward, sized up the perp. He saw a big man, buffed out, very muscular. He appeared disoriented and unbalanced. Koon suspected PCP.

"Get back! We'll handle," rasped Koon to Singer. Then he addressed Glenn: "Get down on the ground!"

Koon pulled his Taser, a device that shoots darts connected by wires to a power source. Once the darts are implanted in skin, a 50,000-volt charge can be dispensed. "If you don't start following orders, I'm going to electrocute you!" he commanded.

Glenn dropped to all fours. To Koon, Glenn looked like a lineman set for the hike. Koon didn't know what this guy was going to do. He might rush an officer, take his weapon, get him in a death grip—anything was possible.

Shit! Now Koon noticed two other suspects in the car. He sensed a setup. He decided gunfire might be necessary. "Powell!" he barked like a platoon leader. "You're the designated shooter!" Then he ordered some other officers to get Pooh and Freddie G. out of the car.

Glenn, meanwhile, was on the ground. He appeared to be doing push-ups. Koon signaled. Cops swarmed. Powell went in with the handcuffs. As Powell tried to cuff him, Glenn rose up, throwing off officers like rag dolls, according to one cop, trying to get away, according to another. In either case, in the shuffle, Glenn bumped against Powell, almost knocking him off his feet. Powell, falling backward, thought this was it. He reached for his gun. . . .

Koon fired the Taser. He scored twice, back and side. Then he hit the hot switch: 50,000 volts.

Glenn screamed for a full five seconds. A witness would later say it sounded like a death wail. A cop would later say "wounded animal." Glenn began crawling, scuttling across the asphalt.

"Anyone else have a Taser?" Koon yelled. Others were yelling now too. "Get down!" "Lie down!" "Put your hands up!" "Put your hands behind your back, nigger!"

One hundred yards away, on the second floor of the Mountainback apartments, George Holliday slid back the balcony door and stepped outside. No shoes, no shirt, it was cold. He tried to hold the camera still. The helicopter circled above, its 30 million-candlepower spotlight bathing everything in a grainy incandescent glow, as if the night had opened and the heavens were peeking through.

George peered through the viewfinder. Glenn was down on all fours, like the starting position in wrestling. Suddenly, he rolled to his right and got to his feet, a sit-out, a three-point escape. He ran one, two, three steps west, toward the back bumper of the Hyundai.

"Powell and Wind," Koon barked. "Batons! Power strokes!"

Powell surged forward and cut off Glenn's angle. Earlier tonight, at baton training, Powell had been admonished for weakness. Now his PR-24 flashed down full stroke and connected with skull and face, crushing the bones around Glenn's eye like an eggshell. Glenn screamed, fell, blood began to flow.

Powell commenced pummeling at will, both hands on his baton, a grip like a baseball bat, a stroke like a golf club, back and forth, back and forth, swinging the two-foot black metal truncheon across Glenn's body. Head, neck, shoulders, back, kidneys, legs, ankles, feet. Ten, twelve, fifteen blows, in rapid succession.

Powell stopped. He stood poised over Glenn, breathing hard, weapon cocked just above his shoulder. For a moment, Glenn lay motionless. Then he groaned, turned his head. Powell wound up . . . a cop grabbed the top of his baton.

"Do you give? Do you give?" It was Koon. He came closer, manipulating the double wires from the Taser like a man trying to untangle the strings of a fallen kite. "Okay," barked Koon. "He gives." Melanie Singer sighed. It was over now. The perp had been subdued. Time to cuff him and get out of there.

Glenn pushed up off his stomach, rose to his knees and leaned back, like a prizefighter trying to get up from the canvas.

Powell commenced pummeling again. Wind started in too. Head, neck, shoulders, the whipsaw action, back and forth, back and forth. Powell was adrenalized. He saw the perp in a tunnel of light, so intent that he didn't even notice that his partner had joined in too. Wind was at Glenn's back, hitting kidneys and shoulder blades. He felt highly excited, transfixed, determined to hold up his side. He was frightened. He thought maybe he wasn't strong enough to hurt the guy. He stroked harder. Glenn's face split open. Blood splattered in a radius of five yards.

Meanwhile, Pooh and Freddie G. were on the other side of the car, on their stomachs in the grass, their heads turned away from the action. Pooh heard bones breaking, loud thumps, gushy sounds.

George Holliday was glued to the scene in his viewfinder. It was like a movie for real; you were riveted. He was just stuck there, thinking that this had to be filmed, just making sure that the camera was going. All he could think was, What did this guy do? What did he do to deserve this?

Beneath his balcony, twenty other residents of Mountainback stood watching. "Oh, my God! They're beating him to death!" cried one woman.

"They're stomping him like a bug!" shouted another.

"He's not even fighting back!"

"All them motherfuckers laughin'!"

In the road, Glenn moaned. "Please stop, please stop."

For ninety full seconds, Powell and Wind beat Glenn with their sticks. They beat a while. They stopped a while. A car drove by slowly, westbound. Glenn was scared for his life. It hurt real bad. Just keep breathing, Glenn, he told himself. The officers continued to pound. Powell was at his head, Wind at his feet, Koon in the center, controlling the wires. Glenn rolled back to front, trying to ward off the blows, lifting an arm here to cover his head, reaching down there to cover his leg, rolling back to front, rolling away, rolling the whole length of the Hyundai, bumper to bumper, trying to get away, crying out in animal anguish, the cops still beating, beating, now on the head, now on the legs, now on the kidneys, whipsawing, kicking with heavy shoes.

Finally it was over. Some of the cops swarmed. They pulled Glenn's arms behind his back, cuffed his wrists, hog-tied him, binding his hands to his feet with a nylon rope. Then a couple of cops hauled him off to the side of the road, pulling him by his ankles, sliding him across the gravel on his chest, head dragging. Other cops stood silent, heads bent. Through his viewfinder, full zoom, George could see the body language of guilt.

Within minutes, Koon was back in his patrol car, headed for the station house, and Larry Powell and Tim Wind were back in theirs, headed for the hospital. Once Glenn had been cuffed, most of the cops sped away. The rest left right after the ambulance crew hefted Glenn onto a stretcher, still hog-tied. As a joke, one of the officers at the scene pulled the sheet over Glenn's head. Glenn wondered, If this is what it is being dead, why do I feel this way?

As the Hyundai was being towed away, Pooh and Freddie G. were told they could go. They asked the cops where they were. The cops laughed. Crip country, they said. Then they drove away. "Shit!" said Freddie G., leaning on his crutch, watching the taillights recede. "They took my ID."

Pooh and Freddie G. walked over to the iron gate at Mountainback. George had stopped filming and gone inside, but several other residents remained. Pooh stuck his face through the fence and asked if they could use a telephone. They were directed to a pay phone at a gas station a few blocks away.

Now, in his car, Koon pulled the MDT in his direction, typed out a message to his watch commander. "You just had a big time use of force. Tased and beat the suspect of CHP pursuit, Big Time."

"Oh well. I'm sure the lizard didn't deserve it. HAHA. I'll let them know OK," typed the watch commander.

"I'm gonna drop by the station for a fresh Taser and darts," typed the sergeant. "Please have one ready at the desk."

T.J. and Melanie Singer walked into County Medical, looking for Glenn.

They found him on a gurney. Wind and Powell were nearby. Both appeared to be snoozing.

"You must be LAPD's designated hitter," T.J. Singer said to Larry Powell.

"I tired myself out hitting that guy," said Powell, nodding in Glenn's direction.

Now Glenn stirred, raised his head a few inches. Though Koon's report would list Glenn's injuries as "several facial cuts due to contact with asphalt, of a minor nature, a split inner lip," Glenn had been hit at least fifty-six times. His facial cuts required twenty-five stitches. One doctor would remark that it looked as if Glenn had been run over by a train. The bones in his cheek and around his eye were shattered. Glenn's leg was broken, there was a huge bruise on his chest, he had wounds on his arms from trying to defend himself. Initial indications suggested some brain damage and possible loss of feeling in his mouth and on the side of his face. He'd been out cold now for a while. Earlier, in the emergency room, he'd leaned over to Koon and said "I love you." Then he'd smiled and clapped.

Glenn stirred, regaining consciousness. "What happened?" he asked.

Powell walked over to Glenn. "We played a little baseball tonight, didn't we?" he said.

"What do you mean?"

"We played a little hardball, and you lost."

There was silence awhile, then T.J. Singer spoke. "Why didn't you stop your car?" he asked Glenn.

"I was trying to get home to my wife, man."

And that was it, at least for the next thirty-six hours or so. The cops noted a minor fracas on their nightly report and went home to get some shut-eye. Glenn dozed in the lockup wing of the county hospital, stitched and plastered, heavily sedated. Glenn's brother Paul called the Foothill Division and said he wanted to file a complaint. The sergeant on duty refused to initiate an investigation. George Holliday took his videocam to the L.A. Marathon, then to a wedding.

On Monday, when the evening news came on, George got to thinking. Maybe somebody might want to see his video. He called Channel 5. They told him to bring it in.

By midnight on Tuesday, March 5, George's answering-machine tape had filled up with messages from the press. And by the next morning, when CNN aired the video and a crowd of reporters and cameras gathered outside

George's balcony, the brutal beating of a motorist by LAPD cops had been broadcast from Austria to Zaire. Over and over and over the tape was played, the most sensational news footage to hit the airwaves since the war in the Persian Gulf. The image of Glenn cowering beneath Powell's and Wind's blows was burned onto America's retina, more powerful than any movie, real-life action drama, brutality so ugly that watching it made you wince.

The outrage was profound. George Bush made a comment. Jesse Jackson made a speech. Al Sharpton led a march. The FBI investigated, knocking on policemen's doors. The U.S. Department of Justice began a nationwide probe. Citizens called for the ouster of Los Angeles Mayor Tom Bradley, a black former cop. Bradley and others called for the resignation of Chief Gates. Gates joined the call for the ouster of Bradley.

Commissions were formed. Panels were seated, investigations and tribunals were convened. Gates was suspended. Gates went to court. Gates was restored. Gates called on the city to pay his legal bills. The city council sided with Gates. The Police Commission sided with Bradley, then sued the city council for money to discharge the powers granted them by the city charter. They went to court. Finally, Gates said he would retire in April 1992.

Experts opined about the psychology of group violence, the wantonness of the American spirit, the relative merits of "proactive" policing, the state of minority relations in the country.

In the meantime, indictments were handed down. Koon, Powell, Wind and another officer, Ted Briseno, seen in the video stomping Glenn once with his boot, were all charged with assault with a deadly weapon and unnecessarily beating a suspect under the color of authority. Koon and Powell were also indicted for filing a false police report, and Koon was additionally charged with acting as an accessory to a cover-up. If convicted, Koon and Powell could be sentenced to a maximum of seven years, eight months in state prison. Wind faces a maximum seven-year prison term. Briseno faces a max of four. Koon, Powell and Briseno were suspended from the force. Wind, a probationer, was fired, as were two L.A. Unified School District cops who happened upon the scene but did not file a report. T.J. and Melanie Singer both received written reprimands, for filing inadequate reports.

George Holliday experienced his fifteen minutes of fame. He appeared on *Geraldo*, in *People*, on a Japanese news show. Strangers wrote to offer free meals. Hollywood showed interest in buying the story of his life. Recently, a team of attorneys has drawn up a federal-copyright-infringement suit on

George's behalf. The target of the suit has not yet been identified; a figure of $7 million has been mentioned.

Freddie G. was killed in a traffic accident involving alcohol. Pooh has been visited by bad dreams, is under psychiatric care, is suing the county. Shortly after the incident, Pooh was picked up for driving under the influence. His case is pending.

Glenn has become known as Rodney to the whole world. He has become something of a folk hero, maybe an antihero. Amid reports of depression, confusion, plastic surgery, counseling, pain, alienation of affection and a long road to recovery, Glenn was stopped once by police for driving with an expired registration and no driver's license. He encountered the LAPD yet again, in an alley near the Sunset Strip, where he was receiving favors from a transvestite hooker in the front seat of his new Chevy Blazer. When undercover cops approached his truck, Glenn sped off, almost hitting one of them. The police insisted that they had been tailing the hooker. Glenn's attorney insisted that police were attempting to gather discrediting evidence for the $83 million lawsuit Glenn has filed against the county.

Except for a brief press conference, following his release from the hospital, Glenn has declined to speak in public. What he was thinking that night, why he didn't just stop when T.J. and Melanie Singer first gave chase, remains a mystery, even to Glenn himself, say friends.

In the end, perhaps, it doesn't matter what Glenn was thinking, or even what Koon, Powell, Wind and the rest of the police officers were thinking. On a March night, on a lonely road in Los Angeles County, in the year 1991, certain ugly human truths were uncovered. Three minutes of 8-mm. videotape confirmed what many in America definitely knew, what many more in America probably knew but wanted to disbelieve.

Of all the millions of words that have been printed about the Rodney King Incident, as it has come to be known, several hundred came to the *Los Angeles Times* from a man named Thich Nhat Hahn. This is some of what he said:

> People everywhere on the planet have seen the image of the policemen beating the young driver. The moment I first saw it, I saw myself as the one who was beaten, and I suffered. We were all beaten at the same time, we were all the victims of violence, anger, lack of understanding, lack of respect for our human dignity.

But looking more deeply, I was able to see that the policemen were also myself. Our society is full of hatred and violence. Everything is like a bomb ready to explode, and we are part of that bomb. If we are not mindful, then one day our child will be the one who is beaten, or the one doing the beating. It is our affair. We are not observers. We are participants.

(1991)

The Rise and Fall of a Super Freak

Rick James, once known as the King of Funk, was one of the biggest names in the music industry. Then he discovered freebase cocaine.

It must have been very late, around the time that night begins to turn on an imperceptible pivot and 2 o'clock becomes 6 in the morning. The place, if hazy memories serve, was the Red Parrot in New York City. The year was 1981. Or maybe it was '82. Definitely one of those, '81 or '82, toward the end of the Disco Era, a jangled, fuzzy, grandiose time when sex partners were changed more often then bed sheets and brain cells were slaughtered by the hundreds of millions. At clubs like Studio 54 and Xenon—the Studio for the Warhol Crowd, Xenon for the Eurotrash—beautiful people with pin-hole pupils were doing the Hustle and even the wild thing on strobe-lit dance floors, snorting crystalline cocaine out of little plastic bullets, gulping Quaaludes and champagne to dull the edge. What month? What year? Who the fuck can remember? The pace hadn't slowed since 1974. If you can remember exactly, you weren't there.

Rick James was there. His first rock and roll band had included Nick St. Nicholas, later of Steppenwolf. His second included Neil Young. He was a staff writer/producer for Motown when the Jackson parents brought their five sons through the door. Prince was once his opening act. James's trademark song, "Super Freak," sold more than 40 million copies in 1981. Later, a rapper named MC Hammer would cop the bass line of Super Freak for "U Can't Touch This." It sold millions more internationally.

By the time this night had come, Rick James was known around the world as the King of Funk, one of the biggest names in the music business. He had written and produced songs or albums for Stevie Wonder, Smokey Robinson, the Temptations, Teena Marie, Chaka Kahn, the Stone City Band, Eddie Murphy, many more. His live shows were legendary. His long braids dusted with glitter, he strode the stage in thigh-high boots and spandex, crouching to accept joints and kisses from his adoring fans.

"Between Parliament and Prince, Rick James carried the banner of black pop over that fertile territory known as funk," wrote critic David Ritz. "As the seventies melted into the eighties, Rick was bad, superbad, the baddest of the bad. His orchestrations were brilliant, his shows spectacular. He worked in the celebrated R&B instrumental tradition—percussive guitar riffs, busy bass lines, syncopated horn punches—extending from Louis Jordan, Ray Charles, Ike Turner, James Brown, Sly Stone and George Clinton . . . His funk was high and mighty while his attitude stayed down and dirty. His eroticism was raw. He was an early gangsta of love, outrageous, unmanageable, both benefactor and victim of his own inexhaustible energy."

So it must have been sometime in 1981, because James was at the height of his powers. He was in New York to celebrate the conclusion of a long national tour to support sales of *Street Songs*, the album that launched "Super Freak," as well as "Give It to Me Baby," "Ghetto Life," and "Fire and Desire." Sitting with him around the table at the Red Parrot—drinking Courvoisier and Perrier-Jouet, chatting up a seemingly endless stream of women—was James' usual coterie: seven or eight or nine of the boys in his Stone City Band, each one, like James himself, a black man standing over six feet tall, wearing long extension braids, leather pants, a rhinestone belt, a parachute-silk shirt and python cowboy boots. They didn't call it a crew back then, but Rick James had one; he never went anywhere without the boys in his band. They were somewhere between a family and a musical commune.

For a while, they'd all lived together in the Hearst Mansion in Beverly Hills. Then James bought a ranch in Buffalo, and they all moved in together there. They rode James's Arabian horses (his favorite black stallion was named Punk), raced his ten snowmobiles, swam in the indoor pool, meditated amidst the jade sculpture and banzai trees in the "Oriental Room," played full court basketball or marathon games of Bid Whist, recorded in the basement studio, did drugs, lots of drugs, all the time. Rick James believed in drugs. As he'd said to the crew when he'd first assembled them: "Look at my lyrics to my songs. All of the songs are about drugs. They're about women and about drugs, and they're one and the same. That is the persona of this band."

When it started feeling a little crowded in the 28-room "ranch house," James bought the house next door, let everyone live there. He took care of his crew. If someone's momma had a medical bill, he'd give them the down payment. He never let a birthday pass without a catered party, though none bested the one he gave for the comedian Eddie Murphy, with hundreds of guests and a different kind of food in each of the themed rooms of the house.

James also let the crew drive his cars—he had more than a dozen, from Jeeps and Mercedes to an Excaliber and a vintage Rolls. Often, he'd give them upwards of $80,000 in cash to go shopping. He loved shopping. He'd stand in the middle of a store and point. Thirty pairs of cowboy boots. A half-dozen Cartier tank watches as gifts for different women. Ten exotic hides—including a lion, a bear, a zebra—for his "African Room." Intricately carved wooden furniture for his "Sausalito Room." Three hundred and sixty-five suits, one for every day of the year, even though he never wore suits, seemed to live in the same old pair of leather pants. He'd go to Bloomingdale's, in Manhattan, just to cause trouble. He'd walk through the store. A riot would ensue as women rushed for his autograph. One trip through Bloomies brought him face to face with Linda Blair, grown up considerably since her role in *The Exorcist.* Though he never talked about any of his women, other than to say how sweet or beautiful or thoughtful they were (he was known in private as a romantic), he did allude once to Linda's talents: "It's not just her head that swivels," he'd been heard to say.

Sometimes he'd get a bug and fly the whole crew to New Orleans for gumbo. He rented a yacht for a Caribbean cruise—fuel alone ran $30,0000. Moonlit dinners for sixty on a terrace at a hotel in Hawaii. A $5,000 sushi dinner at Yamamotos in LA. Along with the crew were the others, a cast of luminaries that included Dizzy Gillespie, Rod Stewart, Louis Farrakhan, Princess Elizabeth von Oxenberg, Steven Stills, David Crosby, Donny Osmond, Duane Allman, George Clinton, Sly Stone, Diana Ross, Willie Nelson, OJ and Nicole Brown Simpson, Denise Brown, Stevie Wonder, and Marvin Gaye.

And, wherever James went, there were women. They threw crotchless panties on the stage when he played. They climbed the gates and knocked on his door at three a.m. They arrived in cars sent for them. Teena Marie, Catherine Oxenberg, Catherine Bach, Grace Jones, Jan Gaye, hundreds of others: groupies, twins, mother and daughter teams, one time five women at once. All he had to do was open his bedroom door and point to someone at the party going on in his living room.

Now, at the Red Parrot in 1981, the security manager came over to James's table, told him there was someone upstairs who wanted to meet him.

"Who is it?" James asked.

"Can't tell you right here," said the manager.

"Well, whisper in my ear," said James.

"I think you'll want to meet him."

James shrugged his shoulders, Why not? He made a motion in the air with his finger like a trail driver: *Head 'em up, move 'em out.* The crew began to rise.

"Just you and one other person, if you please, Mr. James."

Rick James hovered there a moment, half out of his chair, slightly taken aback. Who, he wondered, could command more juice than the King of Funk himself? Now he was *really* curious. He gestured to his friend Taylor Alonzo, the manager of Xenon. They'd met one night at the club when the bouncers had refused to let James and his crew inside. Their friendship was solidified the day James took Alonzo along with him to buy a Rolls-Royce. James settled on a vintage silver blue Cornice. Then he asked the salesman to install wire wheels. "Rick," said Alonzo, "only a pimp would put wire wheels on that car." From that point on, James had come to rely on Alonzo to help him, as he put it, "separate the flash from the trash."

Now James and Alonzo followed the manager upstairs to the private room.

"Rick James, this is Mick Jagger."

Jagger rose unsteadily from his seat, at a table strewn with bottles of Cristal and Jack Daniel's. He was totally drunk. "Rick James!" slurred the legendary front man of the Rolling Stones. "Oh man! Super Freak! I just *had* to meet you!"

Fourteen years later, on a spring day in 1995, Rick James shuffles into a small office within the Gothic walls of Folsom State Prison, near Sacramento, Calif. He is chaperoned by a prison official, who will stay at his side for the duration of the interview. James's trademark extension braids are gone, his hair is cut short, combed forward to conceal a receding hair line. He's put on 30 pounds in jail—a combination of fatty prison food and care packages from his fiancée, Tanya Hijazi: tiny marshmallows, hot chocolate, jelly life savers (when she can't find Dots, his favorite), peanut butter and jelly, after dinner mints, raman noodles, and cartons of cigarettes to trade.

Now 48, James is serving the final days of a sentence for assault, false imprisonment and furnishing drugs, the result of two separate crack-fueled incidents involving James, Hijazi and two other women. To prison authorities, the King of Funk is just another resident of a two-man cell, with bunk beds and a shiny metal commode with no seat: James Ambrose Johnson Jr., Inmate #J29237.

James has passed his days inside the prison with grace, humor and good behavior, prison officials say. He has worked in the prison library. He's nearly finished with his autobiography, *Memoirs of a Super Freak*, and he's written several screenplays, a lot of new music. From a computer in the library, he contributes to his personal web site, put up by some fans. He speaks every day by phone to Hijazi and their 4-year-old son, Tazman. Taz has long yellow ringlets, blue eyes, his daddy's sensual lips. He works occasionally as a model. He likes to bang on the piano and sing "Super Freak."

Rick James sits down and folds his hands demurely on the table. "I've been up and I've been down," he says, a mixture of pride and pain discernible in his large brown eyes. "I been to hell and back. What you want to know?"

Monday afternoon, Aug. 30, 1993, California superior court, Los Angeles County. The defense lawyer, Mark Werksman, continues his cross examination on the witness, a woman named Mary Sauger: "Did (Tanya Hijazi) then commence to beat you again?"

"There was more hitting, yes," said the woman on the stand, one of two alleged victims of James and Hijazi.

"Was she doing it in such a way that suggested she thought it was a sexual act?" asked Werksman, turning toward the jury. His client, Rick James, was facing three life sentences: there were things these 12 workaday citizens had to be made to understand—they were a jury, yes, but they weren't exactly his peers.

"No," answered the witness. "It seemed they were getting their kicks out of hitting someone, beating someone up."

"There had never been any sexual involvement between you and Mr. James?"

"Absolutely not."

"Between you and Tanya Hijazi?"

"Absolutely not."

Werksman paused a moment, scanned his notes. The trial was entering its second week; the prosecution was still presenting its case, leaning hard on the lurid details. Werksman was doing his best to rebut.

Werksman was a Yale graduate, a former assistant DA, in his third year of private practice. Yet even in his rarified world, he had never before had a client come to the office with his girlfriend and his personal lawyer in tow. James had sat on the leather couch for a few minutes, then asked his lawyer for $5,000 in cash so he and Hijazi could go shopping. Here was a man at liberty on $750,000 bail, facing fifteen felony counts, including supplying cocaine, assault with a deadly weapon, false imprisonment by violence, torture, aggravated mayhem and forced oral copulation. The district attorney had told Werksman: "I'm going to get him. He's evil and I'm going to send him away for life."

James, however, appeared unfazed. In his constellation of reality, this whole case was a bunch of shit, period. "Fill each other in on what's happening," he'd said over his shoulder to his lawyers, strutting out of Werksman's office in thigh-high boots.

Since that first meeting, Werksman had begun to like James quite a bit. Reviewing the facts, getting to know his client, he began to sympathize with the King of Funk—and to disdain the alleged victims in the case. In his mind, the two women were drug users and groupies, drawn by the magnet of his client's fame from the ooze of the Sunset Strip, a five-dollar cab ride up Laurel Canyon Drive to James's mountaintop aerie, formerly owned by Mickey Rooney. The place was palatial, complete with guest house, gazebo, swimming pool and prize rose bushes. James would tell Werksman that he had noticed the roses for the first time when police were carting him away in handcuffs. He'd spent the six months since he'd leased the house inside, mostly in his bedroom, sometimes in a walk-in closet, freebasing cocaine. For the past ten years, James had smoked up to $400,000 worth of the drug each year, most of which he cooked himself, though he had for a time employed an assistant he called Chef Boyardee.

Now, in court, Werksman cut his eyes to the witness, Mary Sauger, a brown-haired secretary at a small film company. She had told the jury that she'd visited James and Hijazi in a hotel room in Los Angeles to discuss working for his new label, Mamma Records. She said James and Hijazi beat her up. She also said she still had recurring headaches and constant throbbing in one eye. For her pain and suffering, she would later be awarded $2 million in civil suits filed against James and the hotel.

"Miss Sauger," Werksman began.

Suddenly, the quiet air in the courtroom was shattered by a series of thick, adenoidal snores.

All heads turned.

The King of Funk was sound asleep at the defense table, pencil still in hand, head lolling. His long extension braids, slicked into a pony tail with Let's Jam jell, were leaving stains on the back of the state-issue leather chair. He wore a red uniform coat—a rocked-out HMS Pinafore number with epaulets, stripes on the sleeves, and double rows of big gold buttons crowned with anchors.

The judge looked down at James, incredulous, the tips of his ears growing scarlet. A former LAPD police captain who'd attended law school at night, he'd served ten years as an assistant DA. This was the second time James had nodded out in his courtroom today.

"Mr. Werksman?" the judge intoned.

"Your Honor, may we have a sidebar conference please?"

James A. Johnson Jr. was born under the sign of Aquarius, the third eldest in a family of eight kids living in an all-black housing project in Buffalo, N.Y. His father was a handsome rogue with Native American blood who worked the assembly line at Chevrolet. "Mostly, he wasn't much of a dad," remembers James. "When I think of him, I think of the constant fights. He would beat my momma, and I'd sit at the top of the stairs with my brothers and sisters, crying, wishing I was grown up so I could kill him." He left the family when James was 7.

Momma was Mabel Gladden Johnson, known to her friends as Freddie. She had her first child at 13. Later she danced with Katherine Dunham's troupe, worked as a showgirl at the Cotton Club. She regaled James with stories of her days as the queen of the Rum Boogie during the Harlem Renaissance.

In time, Momma moved her family to a housing project across town, peopled mostly with Irish and Italians. James remembers cross burnings, rocks through windows. A gang of greasers claimed the turf near the corner store; they terrorized James and his siblings until the day his eldest brother Carmen came home from prison and whipped their butts. James remembers his father showing up to join the fight; it was the last time he ever saw him.

By day, Momma mopped floors. By night she ran numbers for the Italian mob, James says. Though she made a lot of money, she kept the cleaning job and the apartment in the projects as a cover, she would later explain to her son. There were rats and roaches in their apartment, but the refrigerator was well stocked, the kids had nice clothes, Momma always had a nice car. Though James would come, over time, to regard his mom as his best friend in the world, he remembers his childhood being rough, Momma beating him with a knotted electrical cord "to let out her frustrations," he told a court therapist.

James attended Catholic school for a time, was an altar boy. In public junior high, he played football and basketball, took drum and trombone lessons, marched with a hi-stepping drill team, hung on the corner with friends singing do-wop and drinking Thunderbird. Entering his teens, James joined a gang, began smoking pot, committing petty crimes. Then his closest brother, Roy, was knocked from his new bike and dragged down the street by a car. Roy was in the hospital in a body cast for a year. Momma visited every day. In the family, Roy was known as the smart one. He would later become a lawyer. James was known as the troublemaker. James felt his mom somehow blamed him for Roy's accident. Between her jobs and visiting Roy, James hardly ever saw her. He began skipping school. Sometimes, he'd steal money from her purse and take a bus to New York City, haunt the coffee houses in Greenwich Village. At 13, police in Rochester found him hiding in the bathroom of a bus and he was placed in a juvenile home for several weeks. "Momma finally came to get me," James recalls. "She asked me why I was running and what did I hope to find. I told her with tears in my eyes, I didn't know. I just wanted something more out of life. She would just look bewildered and cry. I hated to see my mother cry."

At about 14, following a gang rumble in which a boy was shot, James was sentenced to several months in juvenile detention.

It was in high school that he settled on his life's course. "I signed up for a talent show. I was center stage, alone. A spotlight hit me and I started off with a bongo beat. Then I began to sing out this chant. I asked the crowd to sing along and they did. As they sang, I picked up my mallets and my tom drum and played this funky beat, adding rim shots. . . . The crowd chanted louder and louder until the auditorium seemed to be moving. The rhythm seemed voodoo-like. I don't remember how long I played before I started dipping off the stage while the audience continued the chant. The feeling of the crowd singing, the people dancing in the aisles, calling out for more . . . All of it cast a magic spell on me. From that day on, music was my life."

James eventually dropped out of school. At 15, with his mother's permission, he joined the U.S. Naval Reserves. His obligation was two weekends a month. He went the first time to basic training with his stripe sewn upside down. At home, James started a group called the Duprees. They sang Motown tunes, practiced their harmonizing every day. He also had a jazz quintet; James played drums on covers of Herbie Hancock and John Coltrane, and on funky, straight-ahead bebop. The groups did well; they started to gain a local following. The big problem was that the gigs were on weekends. James failed to attend his mandatory reserve meetings.

In 1964, after numerous warnings, James was placed on active duty, ordered to report to the USS *Enterprise.* Though he made it to Rochester, where he was supposed to register, he overslept. Faced with disciplinary action, he fled to Toronto.

In the mid sixties, Toronto was home to Yorkville, a gathering spot for draft resisters, a petri dish for a nascent coffee house and rock scene similar to the one developing in New York's Greenwich Village. Many future big names were there: Richie Havens, David Clayton-Thomas, Joni Mitchell, Gordon Lightfoot, Kenny Rogers.

New in town, James was walking down the street in his Navy uniform when he was accosted by several men in sharkskin suits. A fight ensued; three hippie strangers came to James's rescue. Among the trio were Garth Hudson and Levon Helm, later of The Band. One of the guys took him to a coffee-house; James ended up performing with the group on stage, singing "Stand By Me" and "Summertime." The leader of the group, Nick St. Nicholas, asked him to join.

As James had no civilian clothes, it was decided that the band would wear the contents of James's ditty bag—denim bellbottoms, blue workshirts and dixie cups, white sailor caps. They billed themselves as the Sailor Boys. Being AWOL, James took a new name, Ricky James Matthews, after the dead cousin of a friend. He became well known in Yorkville as Little Ricky. The Sailor Boys begot the Myna Birds, financed by a wealthy Englishman who fancied himself another Brian Epstein, the manager behind the Beatles. He dressed the group in yellow and black leather outfits, had them cut their bangs into a V. He staged publicity stunts, paying women to chase the Mynas through department stores. Soon, Neil Young joined the band. There were Canadian TV appearances, sold out concerts, groupies swooning in the front row.

Motown called: The Mynas were signed. They recorded a single written by James and Young. Then Motown discovered that James was AWOL. The record was not released; James was advised to turn himself in.

Nine months later, sitting in the Brooklyn naval brig, awaiting his court-martial, James picked up a teen magazine. There was an article on the "new California sound." Mentioned were Buffalo Springfield, featuring his old Myna partner Neil Young; and Steppenwolf, with Sailor Boy Nick St. Nicholas. "I was happy, sad and pissed, all at the same time," James recalls. "I decided I'd been in the brig long enough." He busted out.

Eventually, at the urging of his momma—who said her phones were being tapped by the FBI—James turned himself in. He received a dishonorable discharge and several more months in the brig. Following his release, he went directly to California. He hooked up with his old friends, made new ones: David Crosby, Steven Stills, Jim Morrison, Donovan, Michelle Phillips. After a few months of dropping acid, smoking pot, jamming with other bands, collecting free love, James decided to fly back to Toronto and assemble a group of his own.

Within hours of arrival, James was in a club in Yorkville when the owner told him someone wanted to see him outside.

"Welcome back to Canada, Mr. Johnson," said one of the two Toronto cops who were waiting on the sidewalk. James was charged with possession of stolen property and jailed without bond, detained by the Canadian immigration department. Nine months later, he was deported.

Back stateside, Motown took James on staff, put him up in a hotel. His first project was with Tommy Chong, a guitarist who would later become a comedian and actor. The song was an interracial love story about Chong's wife and the birth of his daughter, Rae Dawn.

Eventually, James quit Motown, unsatisfied with the glut of talent in line ahead of him. For the next several years he kicked around the U.S. and Canada. He was a pimp for a while, he says. He smuggled cocaine from Colombia and hash from India, where he also took time to learn the sitar. In 1977, he finally got the financial backing to record an album at the Record Plant in New York City. After hawking it himself, enjoying local success, he was signed once again by Motown. The single "You and I" went to No. 1 on the R&B charts. It became the anthem at Studio 54. The album, *Come Get It*, was touted in trade magazines as the year's biggest album by a black artist.

About this time, James attended two performances that would shape his public style as the King of Funk: spandex jumpsuit, superhero boots, bare chest, big bulge, long extension braids. The hair concept came from a troupe of Masai Dancers. Their coiffures were elaborate configurations, braided with extensions of horse and lion hair. For $300, James had the troupe's stylist give him a new look: long, flowing braids with beads and bangs. Then, he saw a performance by Kiss. They wore tight black costumes, had big-time pyrotechnics going on, loud drums on risers 25 feet in the air. "I knew then that my concerts would be like the Fourth of July—a big party. I knew what my image would be," James says.

With *Come Get It* hitting double platinum, James received his first royalty check, $1.8 million. He leased a mansion formerly owned by William

Randolph Hearst. He set up a rehearsal studio in the great room, began assembling a permanent band.

Danny Lamelle was the arranger and director of the horn section of what came to be known as the Stone City Band. Between 1979 and 1986, he made 16 albums with James, nine of which James produced for such finds as Teena Marie, the Mary Jane Girls, and Process and the Do-rags. Making his records, James was exacting, demanding, obsessive, instructive. He had an instinct, an ear. He'd order tracks recorded again and again until every note was perfect. He brought out the best in everyone. Once, Lamelle remembers, just after a marathon recording session, James and the band were headed from L.A. to Sausalito in a Winnebago. They were drinking and smoking herb, listening to the final cut of "Give It to Me Baby," which was being sent to NY the next day for mastering. "We're layin back, listening to the song, when suddenly Rick has the driver stop the Winnebago. 'Did you hear that?' he asked us. And we're like, 'What?' He rewound the tape again and again, playing this one section. We sat on the I-5 for an hour. He cursed us out, fired us, threatened to drop us off on the side of highway." During the entire time, no one in the band had an inkling of what the problem was.

Finally, James condescended to explain: in one section of the song, for several bars, the horns, which were supposed to be stereo, played only out of one speaker. "Y'all would have mastered this, printed it, and it woulda been out there and it woulda been wrong," he told the band. "My shit gotta be perfect."

"We used to rehearse, boy," says Candi Ghant, one of the original Mary Jane Girls. "The band would rehearse from 12 to 5. Then the girls would rehearse from six till two in the morning. Whatever it took, you know, with him there were no hours. We had a choreographer we worked with five days a week. We had a vocal teacher. Rick was like a slave master. We didn't party, we didn't go wild. We weren't supposed to have boyfriends. After the shows it was interviews, pictures and we was escorted to our rooms. And they would take a bed check to make sure you were in there. He was like a boss, a husband, a mother. He was hard on us. But if he did something to hurt your feelings, in the end he always gave you a gift to say he was sorry."

In 1980, the entire entourage moved onto a seven-acre ranch near Buffalo. When they weren't working, James and the crew played equally hard. The house was equipped with a jukebox, a stereo system in almost every room, a pool table, video games. James was competitive. He'd bet hundreds of dollars on Galaxian, his favorite video game. When other groups were touring the area, basketball tournaments were held. James played power forward, was a good assist man, never a ball hog. Grandmaster Flash fielded a team against James's crew, as did Cameo and Luther Vandross's band. Eddie Murphy was also a frequent player. James's teams always won.

Though James employed a 24-hour, on-call chef (for a time it was one of his sisters; most of his family was on the payroll, including his momma), he often woke early and cooked enormous breakfasts: eggs, pancakes, bacon, grits, toast, milk. He was a consummate host. At parties, he'd go from room to room, checking to see if there was enough food, enough drink, enough toilet paper in all the bathrooms.

Frequently, James would go to New York City, driven in a van or in one of his cars at high speed by an off-duty New York State patrolman who was on his payroll. He'd pick up Taylor Alonzo, the manager of Xenon, and check into the Plaza Hotel. Then the party would begin. "He charmed everyone he met," says Alonzo. "He was always on. He loved this Indian restaurant Bombay Palace. He'd do his Indian accent the whole time he was in there. Or he'd just start singing at the table. I remember once he sang Beatles' songs the whole evening."

"Rick was kind of a connoisseur," says his brother, Carmen Johnson Sims, who headed James's security staff for several years. "He liked his Japanese food, his French food. He used to amaze me. We'd be in Mr. Chow's in New York, and he could order in French. He was down with the wines too."

Back at the Plaza, James would usually have a whole floor at his disposal. Says Sims: "We had guys stationed at the elevators to give us privacy and control. We'd have suites for all the crew, and two or three suites that were loaded down with groupies—the choice ones, the weeded out ones. We called them the 'Stockpile.'" The parties would go until dawn. Often, Alonzo remembers, James would be the last one left standing. Stepping over the sleeping bodies, James would come over and wake Alonzo. They'd leave the suite, walk for hours through Central Park.

James was a regular at Studio 54, the reigning Mecca of Disco. He partied with supermodels Iman and Janice Dickerson, with whom Alonzo says he had "this *Fatal Attraction* relationship. He'd sometimes have to duck her, if you know what I mean." Peter Max, Ted Kennedy Jr., Andy Warhol, Jim Brown, Ben Vereen, Robin Williams, Jack Nicholson—James partied with everyone. Drugs, of course, were abundant. In his own words, James "had never done a drug he didn't like." His second single, "Mary Jane," was a love song to marijuana. Cocaine, however, was his drug of choice. By now, he was snorting about an ounce a day.

"Nobody knew coke was so bad at the time," says James. "Nobody knew anything about detox. There was no Betty Ford. When you snorted it you could function just fine. We made records doing it, sitting at the console with ounce-full bags. It was just part of life. Everybody kept a big box full of pills: Quaaludes, Valium, Halcyon. Dishes of cocaine, trash bags of weed, bottles of bourbon. It was all about, hey, good drugs, leather clothes, horses, cars and fucking women. That was the criteria for the times. When we went on tour, my accountants figured out that we were spending like $250,000 on coke for everybody. They wrote it off as payment to this employee they named Jose Coca."

In the spring of 1981, James and Lamelle went to see Sly Stone in San Francisco. Sly was freebasing—sitting in a back room at a recording studio with his butane torch and his pipe, totally out of it. "When we left, Rick turns to me and says: 'Look, we smoke herb, we snort, we drink. But we will never do this. Sly is a legend. He's in the history books. Now look at him, and he did this to himself with this drug. We can never allow this to happen to us.' And right there, on the spot, we made a bond that this would never be."

A few days later, in a hotel room in Chicago, James took his first hit of freebase, supplied by one of the leaders of the fabled Blackstone Rangers.

And a few days after that, James flew back out to the coast, went to see Sly again. This time, he joined him in the back room. They stayed in there for a solid week.

For the next ten years, with brief periods of sobriety, James would smoke up to $10,000 worth of coke a week. He had a special briefcase for his paraphernalia. It was the only thing he always carried himself.

Incredibly, he continued to make hit records. In the five years that followed "Super Freak," James recorded four albums, earned two Grammy nominations. He produced "Ebony Eyes" with Smokey Robinson and "Standing on the Top" with the Temptations. He made the rounds of the television shows—from *The Merv Griffin Show* to *The A Team*. He was a presenter at the Grammy awards; *People* magazine named him to its best dressed list. He was also black music's most outspoken voice in the fight with infant MTV over equal time for black artists, a powderkeg of an issue at the time.

In the inner circle, however, things had changed markedly. "It wasn't a group effort anymore. We would be downstairs working and Rick would be partying in his bedroom. He would come down, listen, give his okay, or tell us to change something. Then he would disappear again," says Lamelle. "He was the classic Dr. Jekyll/Mr. Hyde. When he was smoking, he became downright abusive. Like, before, he may have been blunt, but he was never brutal. Now the words were like knives. You started taking it personal."

In time, things around the ranch began to erode, says Linda Hunt, who still works as caretaker of the place. "He got rid of the horses because he didn't ride anymore. He stopped paying for rental cars for people. The games, the trips with the whole crew, everything stopped. Fewer people worked here, fewer people lived here. He just didn't want them around. I guess it was paranoia from the drugs."

"I found myself isolating more and more," James writes in his autobiography. "If I wasn't in my room (where my housekeeper would leave food by my locked bedroom door), I was flying here and there in private planes getting high in the clouds. I was slowly but steadily losing control. I'd stay up six or even ten days straight. I had my staff put aluminum foil on all my windows so no sunlight could get in.

"I OD'd a couple of times, but it had been kept secret. My security or a doctor I had on the payroll would bring me back. My life on the inside was dark and lonely, while on the outside I always made it look like I was together. I felt like I was the loneliest person in the world. When I would try to explain my pain to friends, they would just laugh. 'You're Rick James,' they'd say. 'It will be all right.'

"It got to the point where I lost my desire to write music. When it was time for my eighth album, I had nothing in my head. It seemed my creativity was gone, lost in a world where smoke was all I could create and rock coke was the only music I understood."

At 4 one July morning in 1991, a young woman came up the hill to James's house on Mulholland Terrace; she was one of hundreds of people who had made the trip in the four months he'd been living there. This one was a blonde with a southern accent. She called herself Courtney.

Courtney's real name was Frances Alley. Twenty-four years old, she'd recently dropped out of a drug rehab program near her home in a small town outside Atlanta. Now she was working at a massage parlor in Hollywood, living in a transient hotel on the Sunset Strip.

Alley was visiting a run-down motel on the Strip called the Seven Star when she encountered a friend of James's named Kathy Townsend. Townsend was a former backup singer who'd descended into a life of drugs. She was leaving the motel room occupied by a friend of hers, a pimp. She'd wanted to borrow some of his girls to take to James's house. James, she'd told the pimp, had been very unhappy because his mom was dying. Some girls would cheer him up, she'd said.

The girls would also serve to get Townsend some free drugs. She visited James occasionally, would smoke coke for free for days. Everybody at James's smoked for free. There were always a couple of dealers attending the 24-hour party going on in the living room. They often charged him as much as $100 above the going rate for an eightball. As a binge went on, they'd add more baking soda to the weight.

Townsend, unlike most of the hangers-on, would try to do something for James in exchange for the drugs. She'd help around the house—cleaning or cooking, running errands. Or she'd bring him a girl. James wasn't interested in Townsend that way. He called her, lovingly, "Fat Ass."

At any rate, the pimp refused Townsend's request, fearing his girls would never return. Upset, Townsend slammed the door behind her, whereupon she encountered Alley, who was knocking at that moment on the door of a room occupied by a Mexican coke dealer. This was the first time Townsend had ever seen Alley: she looked kind of pretty in the dark. Townsend asked Alley if she wanted to go to Rick James's house and do some drugs. Oddly—or maybe not so oddly, this was the second time in her two months in L.A. that someone had offered to take Alley to James's house to party. "I guess I just felt like I was destined to meet him," she would later say.

For the past five years, James had been unable to work. At first, his problems were legal. In 1987, James filed a suit against Motown, seeking $2 million and a release from his contract. Motown, meanwhile, was suing James for not fulfilling his contract. As the lawyers exchanged paper, as the civil suits wended their way through the legal system toward a court date, James moved to L.A., on call for his lawyers. He spent his time at home, sucking on his glass pipe. He called it the devil's dick.

Then, just as the suits were being settled, mostly in James's favor, he learned that his mom was dying. Her passing, he says, "was a stunning, terrible, terrible experience for me. She was my best friend, the best woman I've ever met in the world."

James became depressed. He'd smoke straight through a week or ten days at a time, women coming and going through the binge. Then he'd take a handful of Halcyon and sleep a few days. Then he'd wake up and start again. Month after month. "One of the things about it that really attracted me was the consummation of time with basing," James says. "The ritual of preparing it, the ritual of doing it, the manipulation and almost mind control that you would have over everything and everyone while you were doing it. It was complacent. It consumed your mind. There wasn't time to think about everything that was bothering me."

Arriving at James's house, Alley was admitted to James's bedroom right away. She partied with James and his girlfriend, Tanya Hijazi, for six straight days and nights. James liked Alley, he would later say, because he'd never before met a woman who could smoke as much coke as he. Finally, when Alley got tired, James had one of his staff make her up a bed in a spare room. She was given a boom box and a night table to make things homey.

After sleeping for 24 hours, Alley woke up, walked naked down the hall to James's room. She said hello, then went to the kitchen to get a soda and a candy bar. When she came back to James's room, she recounted, they smoked a little freebase. Then, according to Alley, James discovered that an eightball of cocaine—3.5 grams, about $200 worth—was missing. He accused her of stealing it, she said.

According to Alley, James became enraged. He ordered Hijazi to bind Alley to a chair with some neck ties, one from Dior, the other from Barneys. Then, Alley alleged, he smashed her across the face with a gun and poured rubbing alcohol on her waist, stomach and legs. An interrogation ensued for the next several hours, Alley alleged, during which James continued smoking cocaine. After a hit, she alleged, he'd place the hot pipe on her legs or stomach, causing small circular burns. At one point, she alleged, he ran a hot butcher knife along her leg, causing severe burns. During the interrogation, she told police, Hijazi stroked and held her hand; later, she told police, she was forced to have oral intercourse with Hijazi, after which Hijai urinated on her, causing great irritation to her burns.

Finally, after several hours, Alley convinced James of her innocence.

"Okay, fine, then" James said. He proffered his pipe. "You wanna hit?"

"Sure," said Alley.

The party resumed.

And so it was, about two days later, after coming and going several times from James's house—where she was living as a guest, telling people she was James's new girl—that Alley went to the hospital for treatment of her burns. Doctors called the police.

James and Hijazi, who was then 21, were arrested and charged with nine felony counts, including supplying cocaine, assault with a deadly weapon, aggravated mayhem, torture, false imprisonment and forcible oral copulation. Bail for James was set at $1 million; Hijazi's was $500,000.

Both spent three weeks in jail. Their lawyers claimed that Alley had been burned and tortured by a pimp, that she and the police were targeting James with trumped-up allegations due to his status as a superstar.

By November 1992, James and Hijazi were out on reduced bail, living with her mom in the L.A. suburb of Agoura Hills, awaiting trial. A son, Tazman, had been born in May of that year. One weekend, Hijazi and James left the baby with her mom and went to the St. James Club and Hotel for a little break. The usual partying ensued; a young secretary with experience in the music business named Mary Sauger was invited over to discuss a job at a new label James was starting. It was to be called Momma Records.

Sauger arrived around 10:30. The trio smoked coke, drank, talked, ordered room service, made phone calls to friends on both coasts. Sometime in the early hours, Sauger would testify, Hijazi became angry and slapped her. James joined the fracas, grabbing Sauger by the throat, dragging her into the bathroom, beating her. When she passed out, she told police, Hijazi and James revived her with ice water.

The torture and beating continued, Sauger said, through a room change—other guests had complained of the noise. Hours after that, she was finally allowed to leave, taking a cab home with $5 Hijazi had given her. Two days later, Sauger went to the hospital. A doctor called the police. Hijazi and James were arrested again. Prosecutors combined the two cases and brought James to court.

"Will Mr. Johnson please rise?"

On January 7, 1994, James stood in his place behind the defense table, his lawyer at his side, waiting to learn his sentence. Hijazi sat behind him in the gallery with Tazman and her mom. She had already plead guilty to one count of assault with a deadly weapon. She was due to begin serving a two-year sentence. In her purse, she had a set of gold wedding bands. The judge had hinted that he'd possibly consent to marry the pair before they went off to jail.

Though he had faced 15 felony counts, James was found guilty of only three: false imprisonment, assault and furnishing cocaine—all of those charges stemming from Mary Sauger's visit to the St. James Club. The jury found him not guilty on three other charges, deadlocked on all the rest. James faced a maximum of nearly nine years in prison.

However, while James was awaiting sentencing, information surfaced that an investigator from the district attorney's office may have been having a love affair with a woman in jail who'd been called as a witness against James.

Further, it was alleged, he was supplying the woman with heroin during the trial. The woman, who was serving time on burglary charges, had testified about a night in which James supposedly smoked a kilo of cocaine and then broke her arm. James contended he'd never met her. Hijazi, however, knew her well. They'd shared a jail cell.

Now, with an investigation of the alleged police misconduct underway, the district attorney's office was forced to cut a deal. James would be sentenced to five years and four months. With good behavior, he'd end up serving about two years. Given this development, the judge had to reduce Hijazi's sentence as well, cutting it in half from the original four years. She would end up serving a little more than one year.

"Mr. Johnson," said the judge, looking down from his bench, addressing the King of Funk by his legal name, "when this is through, I want to rub your tummy, because you are the luckiest man on earth, and I want some of that luck to rub off on me. If I'd had my way, I'd have thrown away the key."

With that, the judge banged the final gavel on People of the State of California vs. James Ambrose Johnson Jr., a.k.a. Rick James. Then he turned to the other business at hand, James's and Hijazi's nuptials.

The judge asked the lovebirds to stand. He regarded them a moment, the tips of his ears growing red. "There is no way on God's green earth that I will marry you." he said. He smiled, satisfied. Then he banged the gavel. Next case.

Back at Folsom State Prison, the corrections officer chaperoning the interview looks at his watch and coughs. The rules specify that press visits may last no more than 90 minutes. Inmate #J29237 must follow the rules. He must eat, shower, sleep, work, exercise when they tell him, where they tell him. His mail is opened and read before he gets it. Some of the items in his care packages are always missing. Phone calls must be collect; time limit: fifteen minutes. His visitors are closely screened. Hijazi, a convicted felon now, is barred from visiting. James hasn't seen her or Tazman for three years, since that last day in court. A wedding is planned upon his release.

July 1996: That is when he hopes to walk out the gates a free man. Though he has declared personal bankruptcy, there is money enough left in the coffers of his record company to ensure a comfortable launching pad for Phase 2 of his career. Things look promising, he says. *Bustin Out: The Best of Rick James*—a collection released in 1994 by Motown, has done well. His collaboration with Evan Dando on a Lemonheads song was touted by critics as the "most powerful cut" on *Come On Feel the Lemon-heads*. Another collection of previously recorded songs, entitled *Wonderful* is due out from Reprise Records later this year.

Though the King of Funk remains in contact with the recording industry, his old friends seem to have abandoned him. At James's suggestion, Neil Young, David Crosby, Steven Stills, Stevie Wonder, Eddie Murphy, Smokey Robinson and Teena Marie were all contacted for this story. None chose to comment.

James looks on the bright side. The current resurgence of 70s sounds and styles, "excites me, gives me lots of hope. Good old funk is back. People got to have it in their lives; there's too much thick shit out there. It's a relief. Reality sucks, and that's what they're selling today. There's too many rappers out there talking about death and MacI0's and all that shit. What happened to the fun, man? What happened to the funk?"

James insists, vehemently, that he wouldn't be in jail if "I wasn't black, if I wasn't who I am, if I didn't say what I was saying, if I didn't fuck so many white girls. Torturing a girl for stealing an eightball? *Shit.* There was probably a half pound of crumbs stuck in the carpet! Gimme a fuckin break. And the DA gives that bitch heroin to testify!"

He realizes, however, that he was bound for fall. He couldn't stop himself. Someone had to. These last two years in prison haven't been so bad, really. He's been reading a lot, finishing his book, his screenplays, writing new music on his guitar. In a way, he says, prison is the best thing that could have happened.

"It stopped me from doing drugs. It gave me a good chance to get clear. It gave me a chance to rest, to get my thoughts together, to eat three meals a day, to get healthy again. I see now that I can love again, that I can love me again. I'm not a has-been and I'm not just a nobody. I'm not a cold-blooded maniacal killer and I'm not a black Marquis de Sade.

"What I am is James Johnson, also known as Rick James, who happened to let his life run amok because of a fucking pipe and a rock of cocaine."

(1996)

Rob Lowe's Girl Trouble

Sex, lesbians, litigation and videotape: A trip to the 1988
Democratic National Convention led to a party Rob Lowe
will never forget.

Nine in the morning was not an hour that Susan Sullivan much cared
for, but there she was at her desk in the office at Club Rio, a ruby in her
nose, circles of black mascara painted thick around her eyes, a telephone
cradled against her ear. Monday, July 18th, 1988. The partying for the
Democratic National Convention had already begun. The streets of downtown Atlanta were cordoned, the sidewalks were crowded with name tags
from out of town. Club Rio, one block from the convention hall, was
booked solid with private parties. Employees were on round-the-clock alert,
sleeping shifts in a warehouse next door. Susan's head was pounding, her
nose was running. A party of Nebraska farmers was due in at noon. Now
this cheery voice on the phone.

"Guess what Jan and I did last night!" sang Tara.

"I already heard what you did last night. You went home with Rob Lowe."

"Yeah!"

"Did you have a good time?"

"We videotaped ourselves."

"You what?" asked Susan.

"We videotaped it. And you know what else? We stole the tape."

"No!"

"Yeah! Rob passed out, and we took $200 out of his wallet, and a bottle
of pills, and the tape."

"Why didn't you take the camera? I woulda taken the camera."

"No. We just took the tape. We wanted to see it. Listen. Do you guys have
a Video Eight player?"

Susan Sullivan, 32, self-described death rocker and midtown lesbian, publicity director of Club Rio, Atlanta's hot spot of the moment, may well have

been the first to hear of the thirty-nine minutes of home-movie porn that has come to be known as the Rob Lowe Sex Tape, but she wouldn't be the last. Within a day, two VHS copies of the tape were available. Within a week, the underground axis of hairdressers, gays, lesbians, fashion punks and new-music rockers was abuzz with blue talk of the events that transpired in the early morning hours of July 18th in room 2845 of the Atlanta Hilton and Towers. The tape had been played in homes, at parties, in a gay club, at a fashion show. It was the inside joke on the scene, their little secret, a source of perverse pride and endless talk among the near hip in the New South: Rob Lowe Fucked Here.

Then, nearly ten months later, a civil suit against Lowe was filed in Fulton County, Georgia, on behalf of Tara's girlfriend Jan, who was sixteen on the night of their encounter with Lowe. Brought on May 12th, 1989, by Jan's mother, the suit alleged that while attending the Democratic National Convention, Lowe "used his celebrity status as an inducement to females to engage in sexual intercourse, sodomy, and multiple party sexual activity for his immediate sexual gratification, and for the purpose of making pornographic films of these activities." An unspecified sum for damages was sought.

One week later it was reported that the Fulton County district attorney was investigating. If charged with the sexual exploitation of a minor, Lowe could face a maximum of twenty years in prison and a $100,000 fine. Said a source from the DA's office, "I think Rob Lowe is going to have an awful lot of difficulty explaining his conduct. I think a Georgia jury isn't going to like it."

Equally difficult to explain would be the revelation, in sworn statements filed in late June of 1989, that the Fulton County DA was given a copy of the Lowe video as early as August 1988 but had taken no action. Such an investigation could have had a disastrous effect on the Dukakis campaign and on the reputation of the Southern city that was so proud to host the Democratic National Convention.

When news of the tapes first surfaced, district attorney Lewis Slaton told reporters that the Lowe matter had been under investigation by his office for "weeks." Later, Slaton amended his statement, saying that his office had had the tape in its possession since the summer of 1988 and that "the decision was made to hold it for a while," though he declined to say why.

Slaton, a Democrat, has held his elected post for twenty-four years. In a recent interview, Slaton acknowledged that he'd had the video since last August and that he'd yet to contact Rob Lowe. Asked if his decision to hold off prosecution was politically motivated, Slaton said, "What I've done through the years is try and stay out of the political side. If I try and figure out how to work with politics, I get all screwed up."

The story of the Rob Lowe Sex Tape begins thirty commuter miles north of Atlanta—I-75 to exit 114A, to Route 5, past Al's Carpet Depot, Joe's Salvage, Sam's Warehouse Wallpapers, north along the dual lane in the suburban wilds of east Cobb County—at a two-story storefront with a shocking-pink facade: SuperHair Three-13.

Twenty years ago, east Cobb was a pine forest in steep, remote hills, sliced by dirt roads, overhung with kudzu. Now 40,000 commuters daily ply the choked, congested asphalt highways in the burgeoning county, en route from subdivisions with names like Ward-Meade Farm and Chattahoochee Plantation to jobs in the aerospace and telecommunications industries nearby, or in law, sales and business offices downtown. A land of black Jeeps and baby strollers and blow-dried hair, of pillared houses on postage-stamp lots, east Cobb is a melting pot of white immigrants drawn from all over the nation by the promise of upward mobility in the gem city of the Sunbelt.

Despite its outback location, SuperHair has become a prosperous business, highly visible on the Atlanta fashion scene, regularly doing shows, videos and exhibitions. The salon has also become over the years a safe haven for the young, affluent and disaffected of idyllic east Cobb. It is run by a trio named Marian, Lester and Tony. The two men and Marian live together. Marian, for the moment, wears her hair cropped close and striped white. Lester wears several dozen bracelets; people say he reminds them of Martin Mull with an attitude. Tony's tattoo, on his left biceps, says, BORN TO PRIMP.

"We dress different, we look wild," says Lester Crowell, 33. "We let men wear makeup if they want to. Girls can shave their heads. We're a shock to some people when they first see us, but we're very devoted to hairdressing, and to fashion and everything, and to making our own look in our own way."

Marian and Lester, having started young and from the bottom themselves, recruit and train their staff from the legion of young punk hopefuls on the waiting list. They hire them as apprentices, teach them the ropes, help them qualify for hairdressers' licenses and bind them to three-year contracts. The staff of fifty is tight. "They're a unit," says Rebecca Weinberg, a stripper and performance artist and the live-in lover of Susan Sullivan. "Lester fosters complete devotion to the salon." Until recently, Rebecca was an apprentice at SuperHair.

In Atlanta's underground, the people who work at the salon are known as the SuperHair kids. "Basically," says Rebecca, "they're into sex, gossip and hairdressing." They work together, eat together, go to clubs and movies together. They couple and uncouple, dish all day, go home and call one another on the telephone at night. "Some people call us a cult," says Lester, "but it's not a cult. It's a way of life."

In the spring of 1988, Lena Jan Parsons came to work as an apprentice at SuperHair. She was sixteen, a pretty, five-foot-four blonde with a cute boyfriend and "a nice body," according to a high-school girlfriend. Once an A-B student, Jan, as she is known to her friends, let her grades plummet to Fs after she received a red 1966 Porsche from her father on her fifteenth birthday, court documents said. By tenth grade, according to friends, Jan had dropped out of school and "turned punk," dying her hair Kelly green, wearing white face powder and black clothes, frequenting downtown clubs and hanging out with lesbians.

At the same time friends noticed the changes in Jan, her parents were undergoing an ugly divorce and child-custody battle. "The problems in this marriage are many and complicated," according to court documents, which characterized the Parsons home as "unhealthy, degenerate, criminal and dangerous."

Jan's mother, Lena Arlene Wilson Parsons, according to a motion filed by her lawyers, "has her shortcomings: she is uneducated (having had only the benefit of an eighth grade education), she is conservative in her opinions regarding religion and the training of children, she can have a temper when provoked, she has no marketable skills other than home making, but she loves her children, she has devoted her life to them."

Jan's father, John C. Parsons, a retired air-force major, earns $60,000 a year as a computer consultant and an additional $15,000 in military retirement benefits. According to court papers filed by his wife, John "engages in strange rituals in a hidden space in the closet in a bedroom in the basement" of their spacious, modern home in a leafy subdivision called Tremont. John, it was alleged, "fails to discipline the children and refuses to support the wife when she attempts to discipline the children"; "uses his income in manner totally unknown to the wife"; and "attempts to convince the wife that she is mentally unstable."

Court documents alleged that Jan and her adopted brother, Ashley, also sixteen, "are engaged in the heavy use of alcohol and marijuana. The children punch holes in the wall for which the father refuses to discipline them." And, documents said, "the husband has allowed a twenty-three-year-old female by the name of Tara Seburt to move into the residence and has made it known to various people in the neighborhood that he wishes to have sex with her. The subject, Tara Seburt, is a known lesbian."

Furthermore, according to an affidavit by Amanda Hinson, a neighborhood friend of Jan's, John Parsons had "patted me and rubbed me on the rear." Jan's friend also swore that John Parsons allowed Jan and Tara to "sleep together in the same room in the same bed."

Soon after beginning work at SuperHair, says Rebecca, Jan became "a new believer, like she had THREE-13 tattooed on her head. She was a very reserved lady, very quiet. She'd just sit back and watch. SuperHair was a lot to take in at first. You're learning so much and seeing so many weird people for the first time."

About the same time Jan began at SuperHair, Tara Seburt became the receptionist at the salon. Formerly a manager of a Domino's Pizza franchise, Tara, 22, had short, spiked blond hair, a butch demeanor, a midnight-blue pickup truck and a female lover who also worked at SuperHair. When Tara broke up with that woman, she began seeing Jan. Though friends say Tara is "honestly gay," they believe that Jan was "probably just experimenting."

"From what I hear," says Lester, "Tara wanted a lot more than what Jan was giving."

"From what I saw," says a hairdresser named Paula, "Jan and Tara were very much in love."

On Sunday, July 17th, Atlanta was primed for its first Democratic National Convention. The city had been prepping for months, painting curbs and planting trees, holding seminars for cabbies, sending out packets of best-foot-forward literature.

"As Atlanta's courtship of the nation's favor reaches zero hour," said the *Atlanta Journal Constitution*, "the city is delighted. . . . Since the Civil Rights era, Atlanta has worked tirelessly for respect. It has sought to be an American city first and a Southern city second."

The night before, Rob Lowe had flown from Paris to Atlanta and checked into the Atlanta Hilton and Towers downtown. Wearing an L.A. Lakers T-shirt, Lowe was shown to room 2845, where he pulled a handful of French francs from his pocket, shrugged, then told the bellman that he had no American dollars and would have to tip him later.

Lowe was in town as part of a delegation of about three dozen Hollywood luminaries under the auspices of California assemblyman Tom Hayden. Though the group was composed primarily of producers and other off-camera insiders, the most visible were the young stars like Lowe, Judd Nelson and Ally Sheedy.

"It was an educational effort, a political education, an opportunity to meet the leadership of the party," says Hayden spokesman Bill Schultz. "It was a very serious group of people."

After spending his Sunday at the ballpark with Tom Hayden—donning an Atlanta Braves baseball uniform, taking batting practice with the pros, answering questions for a Savannah TV station and watching a game against New York—Lowe returned downtown, skirting an anti-Klan rally that was raging near his hotel. That evening, he went to a convention party hosted by Ted Turner and CNN, where he was photographed with Laura Turner, Ted's twenty-seven-year-old daughter. Lowe told *People* magazine that he might run for president someday but that he had "to learn a lot more about acting first."

Lowe, 25, has had "a peculiar acting career," one reviewer has written, "based until very recently on little more than his outrageous handsomeness." With his sculptured cheekbones and bright-blue eyes, Lowe is arrestingly pretty, the very model of a modern movie heartthrob: A *Seventeen* magazine reader poll two years ago found that forty-eight percent of teenage girls named Lowe as their favorite star.

Lowe was born in Charlottesville, Virginia, while his father was attending law school at the University of Virginia. Soon after, the family moved to Dayton, Ohio, where his parents were divorced and his mother was remarried, to a Dayton city planner.

From the beginning, Lowe has said, he wanted to be an actor: "I liked to recite dialogue and make-believe and do stuff like that." By the time he was six, he was modeling in ads. By eight, after seeing the musical *Oliver!* at a local theater, he was appearing on local TV shows, in Midwest summer stock, on radio and in several college stage productions, playing "every child role available." "There wasn't a lot of competition for roles," Lowe has said. "No boy in my neighborhood wanted to be an actor. I took a lot of flak. . . . Acting took me away from gangs and stealing cars." When Lowe was twelve, his mother was married for a third time, to a Malibu psychiatrist, and the family moved to California.

Upon arrival in the exclusive beachside community, Lowe intensified his efforts to become a Hollywood star. Every day after school he'd ride a bus two hours to Hollywood to take meetings and leave head shots.

On weekends he hung out with his friends Emilio Estevez and Charlie Sheen, making home movies and dreaming of fame.

"All Rob ever wanted to be was an actor," says Lowe's good friend Cassian Elwes, a thirty-year-old British producer who's been friends with Lowe for six years. "He'll hate me for saying this, but when he was in high school, he was a longhaired geek with glasses, and he never had any girlfriends, and people didn't take him very seriously. It was only when he cut his hair and put the contact lenses in that suddenly he became the Rob Lowe we all know."

Finally, Lowe got his start, skipping high-school graduation and appearing in two *After School Specials;* in a short-lived TV series; and then, with a cast full of pretty, young Hollywood boys, in a feature film for Francis Ford Coppola called *The Outsiders.* He went on to major roles in *Class, Oxford Blues, The Hotel New Hampshire, St. Elmo's Fire, About Last Night . . .* and *Masquerade.* His best notices (and a Golden Globe nomination for Best Supporting Actor) came with his 1987 role as a mentally retarded youth in *Square Dance.* Despite the presence of Jason Robards and Jane Alexander, *New York Times* critic Vincent Canby wrote that "the most arresting performance is Mr. Lowe's." Lately, according to industry insiders, Lowe has been receiving $1 million or more per film.

Though Lowe has been quoted as saying that he is "the most shy when it comes to girls," he has been cast opposite Nastassja Kinski, Jodie Foster, Jacqueline Bisset, Cindy Gibb, Demi Moore, Ally Sheedy, Mare Winningham, Jenny Wright and Virginia Madsen. Romantically, he's been linked with Princess Stephanie of Monaco, Melissa Gilbert, Fawn Hall, Jane Fonda, Grace Jones and many others. Of the beautiful women and leading ladies in the Hollywood firmament, Lowe has said, "If I haven't been with 'em, I know 'em or have been engaged to 'em."

Today, Lowe lives in the hills above Hollywood, in his first house, a renovated multimillion-dollar bungalow with a pool and a basketball court. Decorated in grays, blues and white, the house is furnished with repro deco, California modern and Japanese electro-tech. On the walls is a collection of paintings by obscure artists in a style described by Elwes as "Jean-Michel Basquiat meets Pee-wee Herman." Lowe drives a gray Porsche 948.

"To describe Rob would make him sound like he lived in Ohio," says Loree Rodkin, personal manager to many of the young stars in Hollywood. "He's no different from your average twenty-five-year-old, other than he's got more money and he's famous. He's prone to barbecues and going to the movies with a girl or the guys or going to the beach. He knows he's pretty, but he fights it. He's witty, he's funny, he's very self-deprecating. He's very, very humorous. He's smart. He's not a stupid boy. He's not abusive. He's really pretty wholesome. I think if you can say anything, you can say his only indulgence is women."

Lowe also likes to Jet Ski, go to ballgames, watch videos on his wide screen, hang out with the guys. He and Nelson, Estevez, Sheen, Elwes and several other Hollywood prodigies form a tightly knit boys' club. They go to the Hard Rock Cafe for beers and French fries or go "mindless bowling" at a Japanese alley called Rock and Bowl, which features automatic scoring. Lowe likes wearing jeans, T-shirts and thrift-store casual, though he also frequents the pricey men's stores on Melrose Avenue. Lowe is known for his imitations of Mr. T, Richard Gere, Marlon Brando and Cary Grant, his marshmallow-and-toast sandwiches, his loyalty to friends.

"It's mainly the weekends that we get together," says Elwes, who met Lowe on the set of *Oxford Blues,* one of the fourteen films Elwes produced in the last seven years. "People stay home during the week. The one thing about all these young actors is that everybody is very work obsessed, and they don't think about partying like James Dean and Marlon Brando did in their heydays. All they're thinking about is what the next job's going to be. They want to work, and they want to work hard.

"Rob would like to be Cary Grant," says Elwes. "He's very funny, and he's very charming, though he'd like to be Clint Eastwood, too. He has, as you get to know him, lots of little soft spots. His weaknesses are his strengths. He's sort of clumsy, he's kind of a geek sometimes, and yet he's very strong. He has a tremendous magnetism to him. There's something that draws you to him."

And, says Elwes, "Rob absolutely adores women. He loves them, he's crazy about them. He still loves every girl that he ever met. In every girl there's something that he can find that is the good part. I think that's what women respond to. He can make any girl feel like they're capable of going out with Rob Lowe."

On Sunday afternoon in Cobb County, inside SuperHair Three-13, there was little talk of conventions or politics or even Rob Lowe until a client called with a proposal. A friend of his, John Roca, a photographer for New York's *Daily News* and a stringer for the *Star* tabloid, was in town looking to freelance. Would SuperHair supply some models?

At 6:30 that evening, Roca met about fourteen employees of SuperHair at their small in-town satellite salon, Extension Three-13. After shooting several rolls of film, Roca says, he arranged to meet the SuperHair kids at Club Rio later that evening. He had in mind a piece on Atlanta night life during the convention. He thought the kids, with their blue, green and yellow hair, wild outfits and good looks, would dress up the shots nicely.

"I called Rio," Lester says, "and Rebecca Weinberg answered the phone and said she was the hostess that night. I told her we had some underage people and we were just going to come in for a photo shoot, would it be okay. She said, 'Fine, get here before it gets really busy, and we'll comp you in.' "

"Ten minutes to nine, they all showed up, thirty of them, and they all looked great and perfect," says Susan Sullivan. "The owner was thrilled to have the club so full so early. She said not to charge them admission. That didn't mean they didn't have to have an ID. Maybe Jan was using someone else's ID, but she had to have one or she wouldn't have gotten into the club."

While the SuperHair kids waited for Roca to show and take the pictures, they milled, gossiped, danced and drank in the cavernous two-story club. Three years old, Club Rio occupies a building that was once an RKO Pictures promotion center and later a warehouse used by *Hustler* magazine. The club has six different bars in three big rooms, high-intensity disco upstairs, cutting-edge live rock downstairs. Along a hallway, film vaults converted to minigalleries feature avant-garde installations. "The whole concept of Club Rio is that life is an illusion and so are nightclubs," says the club's current PR director, Eron Thomas. "We create illusions. That's why people keep coming back."

Catering to a diverse crowd, Rio has at its core a group of fashion punks whose lives are based on clothes and style. "Sometimes clothes are like armor," says Thomas. "Certain people in life will judge you based on your clothes, and if they do, you never have to deal with their bullshit. It's like a flea collar. It keeps them away."

Rio, along with two or three other clubs in the city, constitutes Atlanta's underground. The club brings in bands like Slaves to the Siren, Thelonious Monster and Urban Blight, and the action starts late, continuing at a thundering, strobe-lit frenzy until closing, at four in the morning, whereupon the scene shifts to one of several twenty-four-hour bars nearby. Low-grade cocaine and bootleg ecstasy are easily available from small-time drug dealers who make the rounds of the clubs.

"People get into the club scene," says Marion Crowell of SuperHair, "and that becomes their whole life. The idea that you're going out to have fun gets lost. Instead, the clubs are all they live for. Going out, partying, drugs. It really happens. It's sad. I've seen a lot of people who were pretty good kids just get mixed up. I don't want to say it's because of the bars, but maybe it's because of their perception of what the scene is supposed to be. They see it on TV and the movies and on cable. They think this is how they live in Hollywood, how all the glittery people and celebrities live, so this is how they're trying to live here."

On Sunday night at ten, with the SuperHair kids waiting for the photographer, Susan was in her office. "Someone from the door staff called up and said somebody from Rob Lowe's entourage had just come by and said that Rob, Judd, Ally Sheedy and some guests would be coming by," she says. "I went and found Rebecca and said, 'Listen, we got VIPs coming in,' and I told her to get champagne, buckets, ice and a private room ready. As we were doing that, I saw Tara and Jan sitting at a table. I walked over and said, 'I can't really talk, because Rob Lowe is coming in,' and the both of them said, 'What? That's great!' And I said, 'Yeah, yeah, I'm getting the VIP room ready.' And they said, 'Really? We want to meet him!' And I said, 'I'm sure he'll be in and out of the VIP room—that's fine, just introduce yourselves.' So they took their drinks and, like, ran over to the table right outside the VIP room and sat down."

Susan left Rebecca to take care of the VIP room and walked downstairs. There was Rob Lowe. She introduced herself to Lowe and to Sheedy, Judd Nelson, Holly Robinson, Justine Bateman, Alec Baldwin and the rest, then took them up to the VIP room, an alcove just off the dance floor with a velvet rope across the entrance. "Rob was okay, you know?" says Susan. "He had his little Poindexter glasses, a jacket, a polka-dot shirt. Mr. Young Democrat. He was polite."

"I was working strictly the VIP room," says Rebecca. "I was kind of socializing. Judd Nelson was following me around with two cocktails in his hands, weaving, saying, 'You're so beautiful, wanna come home with me?' " Meanwhile, Jan and Tara waited outside, just a few feet from the VIP room. Jan kept coming up to me and saying, 'When's Rob gonna come out? When's he gonna come out?' " says Rebecca.

"The place was packed with people," says Sheedy. "Atlanta was different than being in other towns. In New York and Los Angeles, because there are so many actors, people are kind of more relaxed about it. In Atlanta, everybody knew we were in town, and the word got out that we were at this one club. . . . People were coming up to the door of the room, looking in. They weren't allowed in, but they were coming in anyway. I felt like I was trapped. I left with Judd and Alec."

Lowe remained behind and continued to party. Finally, all at once, Lowe came to the door of the VIP room, Rebecca opened the velvet rope, and Jan and Tara rushed over.

"Rob, this is Jan and Tara," said Rebecca.

"Jan was real excited," says Rebecca. "Tara was less excited. She's not really into boys. But Jan, you know, this little sixteen-year-old, she was really excited. I mean, here's this girl who's never been anywhere, and she was meeting Rob Lowe. I could see it in her eyes: *Rob!* She was really hyped up about it."

Jan and Tara disappeared into the VIP room. The partying continued. At about eleven, Rebecca says, she went to the employees' lounge to take a break. There she found Lowe and two boys. "They were doing blow," she says, "and then one of the guys asked Rob if he wanted some ecstasy, and he just took it. I stayed a few minutes, hanging out, catching what was going on. I asked Rob about Ally Sheedy, like is she a lesbian. He didn't say anything. He was really drunk." By 12:20, according to one witness, Lowe "was hanging on people, really drunk. It was pretty sickening." Lowe asked Rebecca to call him a cab. With Jan and Tara in tow, he headed for the exit.

"That's when I popped them," says Roca, the photographer, who was just arriving for his shoot with the SuperHair kids. "I got off a few shots, then ran out of film." According to Roca and several other witnesses, Rob, Jan and Tara piled into the cab and sped off into the night.

Exactly ten months later, the Rob Lowe sex scandal surfaced out of the underground. On May 18th, 1989, six days after the civil suit was filed, Atlanta's WXIA-TV, acting on a tip from a courthouse insider, was the first to break the story. It wasn't until the next day that Jim Shuler, a reporter with the local CBS affiliate, WAGA-TV, became the first member of the media to actually see the tape.

Shuler jumped on the story Friday morning. "That afternoon I got a call from an insider in the club scene," he says. "He laid out this entire scenario for me: Lowe, the girls, the videotape, all that, and it just sounded so bizarre and so unbelievable that we decided the responsible thing to do was not to air it." On the five and six o'clock broadcasts, Shuler summed up the charges in the lawsuit against Lowe and interviewed district attorney Slaton about possible criminal investigations. The phone lines lit up with tips, outrage and offers of access to the tape.

By eleven that evening, after a clandestine meeting in the suburbs, Shuler had a dub of the tape in hand. The station ran with highly edited, electronically censored clips. "Once we realized what the liabilities were, we knew we'd best be very careful about the way we handled it," says Shuler. In Atlanta, possession of such a tape for distribution carries a one-year jail sentence and a $5,000 fine. Making even one copy could constitute intent to distribute, according to the Fulton County solicitor general.

The thirty-nine-minute tape was divided into three segments. The first twenty-five minutes were made in Paris just before Lowe came to Atlanta for the convention. They show Lowe and a twenty-one-year-old male friend having sex with an American model named Jennifer. According to a source, the friend, a production assistant from New York, had met Lowe sometime earlier on a movie set, and the two had become "great friends." In Paris, Lowe and the other man were "in the middle of a bout of partying for, like, three weeks in a row," says the source, who has spoken to Lowe of the events and has asked not to be identified. The night the tape was made, says the source, Lowe and the friend were out partying until the early hours with Grace Jones. On the tape, Rob and Jennifer are called by first names; the friend is called by his first and last.

The segment opens with the friend laboring atop Jennifer, who is visible to the camera only by her kneecaps. The room is dark, the quality of the video poor. After some time, Lowe enters the scene, carrying a bottle of beer. He sits on the bed, then says, "Go on. I'm watching. I'm watching." While the friend continues, Lowe places the beer on the night table and manually arouses himself until Jennifer complains about the friend. "You're torturing me!" she moans, a comment on the friend's prodigious endowment.

Then Lowe takes over, and for the next six and one-half minutes, his rear end to the camera, Lowe continues to pump, uttering a guttural "uh-huh . . . uh-huh." At the same time, Jennifer fellates the friend as he stands at the head of the bed. The friend coaxes Lowe as he goes, suggesting at one point that Jennifer would like to be treated more roughly. The sounds of slaps are heard. On it goes, the two men taking turns. "Do you like all this attention?" Lowe asks the girl.

Finally, Jennifer says, "Jenn needs a ten-minute break." Lowe responds, "Is it hot in here, or is it just me?" and a discussion ensues, wherein Rob and Jennifer talk about holiday plans, St.-Tropez and Grace Jones.

The second segment of the film lasts about seven minutes and documents Lowe's Sunday afternoon in Atlanta. There's a shot of Lowe in a glass elevator in a downtown hotel, of Lowe's gym bag with his baseball glove inside, of Lowe's taking batting practice with the Braves, of Lowe and Tom Hayden (Hayden says many people have mistaken him for Lowe's father), of Lowe's being interviewed by a reporter from Channel 22 in Savannah, of the Goodyear blimp, of the California Raisins and of an anti–Ku Klux Klan demonstration downtown.

The final seven minutes begin with Jan coming naked out of the bathroom, carrying a newspaper. Tara is seen drinking a beer. Then Jan and Tara begin having sex. The camera is at the foot of the bed. Lowe says, "I want to see what girls do . . . I want a serious lesson," and the girls proceed to kiss and engage in oral and manual sex. A hand, presumably Lowe's, darts now and again into the frame, stroking one or the other of the girls. Then Lowe is heard to say, "I want to show you this after, show you how you look. Jan, you're so sexy." The girls giggle and smile, appear to be having a good time. At one point, the camera zooms in for a gynecological shot. Tara, in a mock instructional tone, starts labeling body parts. "This is Jan's clit," she says. At another juncture, Jan can be heard to say, "This is fun. Give me a pucker," whereupon she picks up the camera and focuses on Lowe, who mugs, smiles and kisses for the camera.

Coming as it did in the midst of television-ratings sweeps, the airing of the tape on WAGA brought a stampede of broadcast and print media to Atlanta. Stories were carried in publications as far ranging as the *New York Post*, the *Washington Post*, the supermarket tabloids and the London scandal sheets. Arsenio Hall quipped that "finally, Rob Lowe has made a movie that everybody wants to see." David Letterman, in his list of reasons the Ayatollah had to live, posted as number 5 "Hasn't yet seen the Rob Lowe sex tape." In Atlanta, crews and reporters camped outside Club Rio and outside Jan's home and school. Several different video journalists brought hidden cameras into SuperHair. They paid for hair cuts but got no information. Craig Rivera, Geraldo's brother, on assignment for *Inside Edition*, chased Tara, camera klieg blazing, through a club and into the ladies' bathroom. He was booed roundly by patrons and shown the door.

The day after broadcasting the video, WAGA was offered $10,000 for the tape by a nationally syndicated television show. Later a representative from the same show offered Shuler $3,000 in cash on the spot. When other staffers at the station received offers of bribes, an internal memo was posted in the employees' break room advising them to report any offers for their own protection.

Soon, other stations and programs came up with copies of the tape, though most included only the first segment of action, the part with Lowe, his friend and Jennifer. Because of this, viewers were given the impression that the first segment of the tape had been made in Atlanta and that the girl seen with Lowe and his friend was Jan. In reality, few people have seen the portion of the tape that landed Lowe in trouble.

According to several sources, when Tara first called Susan on the morning after, she asked if Rio had the facilities to copy the original Video Eight cassette onto VHS format. When Susan couldn't help, Tara and Jan took the tape to Lester at SuperHair. As a favor to Lester, a local video freelancer made two VHS copies, putting sound and color effects onto one. The freelancer, to his later disappointment, did not view the tape before copying it and did not keep a copy. Lester, as a favor to the girls, kept one of the tapes at home. Lester erased the part with Jan and Tara and on several occasions, he says, lent it out to friends. For a while, Lester says, he lost track of the tape. He stresses that neither he nor anyone else at SuperHair made copies. It is believed that Lester's edited tape, dubbed and redubbed, is the one that circulated around Atlanta for ten months prior to the filing of the suit.

According to Susan and other sources, Tara has said that there were "several eight balls" of coke in Lowe's room on the night of their encounter. She has also said that at one point, while Lowe was having sex with Jan, she picked up the camera and tried to shoot some footage of the two but that she couldn't make the camera work. Court documents filed in the case also said that drugs were used and that Lowe had sexual intercourse with Jan. In addition, Tara has told friends that at one point, while she sat in a chair, drinking a beer and watching Lowe and Jan have sex, Lowe looked at her, stopped, crawled over to Tara and ripped her shirt off. Tara also said that Lowe was having a hard time achieving orgasm due to the cocaine and ecstasy ingested that evening. In the end, Tara brought the actor to climax orally, whereupon he passed out and the girls left, taking with them the tape, $200 for a cab home to east Cobb and a bottle of prescription pills.

In the days following, the underground glowed with the neon gossip of Jan, Tara and Rob. "I think Jan was a little more embarrassed of it and Tara was a little more proud of it," says Lester of SuperHair. "Tara came up with the idea of having a party and showing the video to everybody, and Jan sort of agreed to it, but knowing in her mind that there was no way it was going to happen. That's another reason they took the tape. They didn't want Rob Lowe to have it. And they didn't want Jan's parents to find out she had been with another woman. They realized what had gone on, but they were mesmerized by it. It was like 'Hey! We were with Rob Lowe! We're gonna be stars around the Atlanta area!' "

Soon after, according to an affidavit given by Amanda Hinson, Jan "came over to my house and told me that she had had sex with Rob Lowe and to come over and see the video tape of the sex scene. Jan Parsons told me that if I told her mother, Lena Parsons, that she would kill me. Subsequent to that, Jan Parsons told me that she was going to have a party over at Super-Hair . . . and have a showing of the film." In addition, Hinson swore, "Jan Parsons is now being treated for a vaginal infection."

Then Jan's brother, Ashley, found the tape in a closet in her room and watched it. He promptly told their mother.

Papers filed on June 14th, 1989, by J. Hue Henry, attorney for Lena Parsons, continue the saga: "This film was discovered by Plaintiff in early August of 1988 and immediately was conveyed to the appropriate law enforcement officials in the jurisdiction where the pornographic film was made." That jurisdiction was downtown Atlanta, in Fulton County.

The filing of Henry's affidavit has called into question the actions of Fulton County DA Lewis Slaton. When first questioned about the incident in mid-May, Slaton told reporters that the case had come to his attention just weeks ago, and that he was just then "looking to see if any prosecution is merited." In a recent interview, however, Slaton confirmed that he had had the tape in his possession since August 1988.

"There's been some holdups, some places where we purposely held up," said Slaton. "There's a whole lot of things we needed to know. Where they met, how old the girl looked, if any force was used, a whole lot of factual stuff we had to find out." Asked if Lowe had been questioned, Slaton said he had "not yet attempted to contact Mr. Lowe."

Could Slaton have held off prosecution to avoid harm to the Dukakis campaign? Was Lowe spared for political reasons?

"I haven't covered it up too much," said Slaton. "The media's been following it. I do run as a Democrat, but I have prosecuted an awful lot of Democrats in my time, about 10,000 a year. There aren't many Republicans down here. A lot of cases around here are older than this one. By law, I have to act within four years. Different cases take longer than others."

At the time Lena Parsons found the video, she and her husband were in the midst of a bitter divorce. The tape added fuel to the fire. Affidavits from Amanda Hinson stated that Jan told her that "she was going to use the film to blackmail Lowe for $2 million."

Whether such boasts were the product of a teenager's imagination or the truth is a subject of contention between Lowe and Lena Parsons.

Documents filed by Lowe's attorneys claim that the Parsons family attempted to "extort" half a million dollars from the actor in order "to avoid adverse publicity." A motion also claims that an attorney for John Parsons told Lowe's attorneys that his client was "interested in attempting to have any criminal investigation of Mr. Lowe dropped," but only in return for the $500,000. John Parson's attorney, Pamela G. Guest, refuted this charge, saying, "I never stated to anyone I could or would get the criminal investigation dismissed or dropped. I have no such power."

Lowe's attorneys asked the court to dismiss the suit and impose sanctions against Mrs. Parsons. Lowe's attorneys deny that Lowe seduced Jan Parsons. They said that Lena Parsons has no claim to seek damages for emotional stress she says she suffers as a result of Lowe's alleged seduction of her daughter. Her claims, said Lowe's attorneys, lack any "substantial justification" and are being pursued "for an improper purpose" through "extortionist tactics."

Lena Parsons's attorney countered with sworn affidavits stating that Lowe's Century City attorney, Dale Kinsella, told them that he "conferred with Mr. Lowe, who had admitted that he met my client's daughter in Atlanta and that he had appeared in the pornographic video tape." (Kinsella has not returned phone calls.) In regard to the charges of extortion, Parsons's attorneys claim that they "have conducted themselves in an exemplary manner throughout negotiations," in contrast to Lowe's attorneys, "who have engaged in a pattern of threats, profanity, temper tantrums, defamation and mendacity. . . . His attorneys have used the process of this Court as a public relations gimmick."

In early July, a federal-district-court judge granted Lowe's motion to dismiss that part of the Parsons suit that asked for damages to be paid to Mrs. Parsons for the pain and suffering she endured as a result of her daughter's alleged liaison with Lowe. They let stand, however, Mrs. Parsons's right to sue for damages for Lowe's alleged seduction of her daughter. Both sides were refused their request for sanctions.

• • •

In the aftermath of Jan and Tara's night with Rob Lowe, much has changed in all the players' lives. When the news of the civil suit broke, on the heels of Lowe's embarrassing musical performance with Snow White at the Academy Awards, the actor was in France for the Cannes Film Festival. Though he told a reporter from *People* magazine that he was "not worried about the allegations," a friend who was with him in Cannes says he had been preoccupied for some time with "being sued or blackmailed." The friend also says that Lowe, fearing prosecution or other reprisals, had several months earlier destroyed a library of videotapes showing similar encounters with other women. "I don't think he had any inkling this was going to come out," says the friend. "Rob's being very evasive about this. I think he's embarrassed."

Though Lowe refused to be interviewed for this story, he did ask several of his friends to agree to interviews. Through his publicist, Lisa Kasteler of PMK, a picture of a kinder, gentler Rob Lowe was portrayed. Stressed were his longtime interests in the political affairs of Malibu and in charity foundations, most of which benefit children.

Lowe, says Cassian Elwes, "was devastated by the Atlanta thing. We all went up to the house. And he was, like, 'Listen, I'm going to somehow make it through this, and someway I'm gonna find my way out of it, and I feel bad for all my friends to have to put you all through this, and I'm apologizing to you for that.' "

"Rob has a very strong sense of humor," says Ally Sheedy. "Basically, that's what he's using to deal with this whole thing. He's, like, 'Okay, this happened. I really want to get it all cleared up and get over with it.' Working as an actor is very important to him. He's worried about everything that's happened and how it will affect him."

Shortly after the revelation of the sex tape, Lowe was pulled from the cover of *Teen* magazine's back-to-school issue. A spokesman for the magazine said it was "inappropriate to publicize a public figure of Lowe's nature when serious charges are challenging his reputation." In early June, a women's clothing line bestowed upon Lowe their No Excuses Award. Lowe was pictured in a full-page ad in *Women's Wear Daily*. HOW LOWE CAN YOU GO? read the copy. In July, following the airing of the Rob Lowe Sex Tape on Al Goldstein's cable program, *Midnight Blue*, copies of the tape—featuring only the first segment—have been selling in L.A. for $29.95 and are the talk of the town.

Though the incident has proved a public-relations nightmare, it has not necessarily dashed Lowe's career. While some in Hollywood are obviously outraged at his behavior, others believe the scandal rounds out his appeal, adding an edge to his pretty-boy image. Lowe began a previously scheduled nine-week shoot in Los Angeles on June 20th. The movie, ironically, is titled *Bad Influence*. In it, Lowe plays a drifter who surreptitiously videotapes a businessman having sex with a woman. Lowe's character, says producer Steve Tisch, is "a guy who we have all had in our lives, a bad influence."

Tisch, who produced such hits as *Risky Business* and *Soul Man*, says he is standing by his choice of Lowe for *Bad Influence*. He and Lowe have become close through the ordeal. "I think that Rob has experienced his own mortality," says Tisch. "In the business he's in, he will be destroyed by the same people that created him: his audience, his fans, the people who believed him. There is an element of Rob Lowe who knows he has got to become a better actor and less of a personality. And I got to admit, selfishly, that the timing cannot be better. I think what he faces is the ultimate challenge. Can you turn a liability into an asset? He's acknowledged to me that this has changed his life. He's said to me that some of his little-boy rudeness, some of his little-boy attitude, has got to now become part of Rob Lowe's history and not his present.

"This incident has focused him. Between setups he's not looking out the window and saying, 'Look at the tits on that seventeen-year-old.' Instead he's, like, 'I've got to get serious about my work.' I've seen the guy go from an attitude of 'Where's the party tonight, dude?' to 'I'm gonna really get focused on my work, because what I've got to do is come out with a movie, a character, a performance, not an item in *People* magazine about who I'm taking to the Academy Awards.' "

Lowe's friend who appears in the first segment of the tape was, according to a source, scared at first. His parents know Rob, and they watched the footage on *A Current Affair* while eating dinner. "He hadn't had a chance to warn them that he was in it too," says the source, who also said that Lowe's friend was offered $5,000 for an interview with a syndicated television show. He refused, remaining loyal to Lowe.

John and Lena Parsons, Jan's parents, have since divorced. Lena Parsons has gone to work part time as a $4.50-an-hour clerk in a Kroger supermarket. John Parsons, who received custody of Jan and her brother, said in a television interview that Jan never intended to blackmail Lowe and that "she's a very modest girl. It may not appear that way on the tape, but she's a very modest girl yet today."

As for Jan, she was ordered by the court to stop work at SuperHair and to attend an alternative high school in Cobb County. In the fall of 1988, soon after the tape was discovered, Jan spent ninety days in a psychiatric facility undergoing treatment for depression. She is furious with Lester for "fucking her over" on the matter of the tapes, Lester says, adding that "she is real mixed up" and that her Porsche is out of commission. In a recent telephone interview, Jan referred a reporter to her attorney, saying, "Please, please, I don't want to talk."

Tara, meanwhile, was fired from her job at SuperHair for what Lester says was nonperformance based on alcohol abuse. Since the ambush by Craig Rivera, she is lying low. She refuses to be interviewed, saying that she has already turned down a $25,000 offer to talk about that night.

"You know," says Susan Sullivan, "people have two opinions about this whole thing. Either that Rob Lowe's a scumbag, a cradle-robbing pornographer, or that he got taken. You have to see both sides. Everybody was in the club. Jan was acting like an adult, she put herself in an adult situation. She enjoyed being with Rob Lowe. If it was some guy named Beauregard from Clayton County, you would never have heard that he videotaped it.

"It's stupid, because America makes such gods out of its matinee idols. Years ago it was Rudolf Valentino, now it's Rob Lowe. Hollywood puts him up in a sexual position. That's the whole focus. That's the publicity. They market him so that little girls will go to the movies, buy his posters, fantasize about fucking Rob Lowe. So why wouldn't Jan want to fuck him if she got the chance? Why shouldn't she?"

(1989)

Murder, My Sweet

When his romance with an informant proved to be more than he'd bargained for, the model FBI man committed the perfect crime . . . almost.

The last time Shelby Jean saw Susan, the heavens were thundering over Appalachia, a late-spring downpour that had lasted for days. The creeks were roiling and the river was up, the fog hung thick across the hollows and the hogback ridges, obscuring the mountains and the trees. Shelby Jean Ward and Susan Smith sat at the kitchen table, each clicking her manicured nails against the Formica, the shared habit of sisters, a counter-beat to the drumming rain. It was getting dark now. Through the open door, they could hear the rumble and swish of dump trucks along the dual lane, gearing down toward the railhead, laden with thick chunks of black Kentucky coal. Susan cut her eyes to the clock. Shelby frowned. They were waiting for Mark to call.

Mark Putnam had left a month earlier, on a Friday. His wife had gone ahead to Florida to look for a new house, and Susan had driven the forty snaking miles to Pikeville, as she had so often before, this time to say good-bye. They met as usual in the Wendy's parking lot and then took Mark's car to his house, on Honeysuckle Lane. He made spaghetti. They made love several times.

The next morning, Mark hitched a U-Haul to the car, then drove Susan to hers. She had a Dodge Diplomat just like his, a car so obviously federal, only hers without the little screw-tail antenna on the trunk. He bought Susan a tank of gas, told her he'd be back in a few weeks, that they'd talk about child support then. "Remember, I love you," he said. Then he drove away.

After Mark left, Susan moved in with Shelby. She would sit day after day at the round kitchen table, always the same seat, and stare out the door. "I'm going right out of my mind," she'd say.

Mark did call while he was gone, though Shelby didn't always convey the message. Shelby Jean was 35, the eldest of nine kids. Susan was 28, number five; Shelby had always treated Susan like a daughter, and she didn't like Mark at all. He was 30 and handsome, real handsome, had gone to some uppity school in New England. He had Susan working as an informant, singing to the Feds about bank robbers, drug dealers, even her neighbors in Freeburn. Susan was putting her life in jeopardy, and Mark was making a name for himself as a rookie agent in the FBI. Plus, he was getting sex. He was drinking the milk but had no intention of buying the cow.

Susan, of course, didn't see things that way. The FBI had paid her almost $9,000, tax-free. She had two new cars. And she had Mark. How many East Kentucky girls with two kids and an eighth-grade education found themselves an FBI man?

Now the phone rang. Susan jumped.

"Heeeey!" said Ron Poole, agent in charge in Pikeville, Mark's former boss. Ron, who was from North Carolina, always opened that way: "Heeeey!"—like Andy Griffith. Ron called once in a while and had become pretty close to the sisters since Mark had left. Too close, some would say. At any rate, they thought he was sympathetic. When Susan had come by the office with a copy of her pregnancy test, Ron had Xeroxed it, promised to leave it on Mark's desk.

Now Ron giggled over the phone line. "Guess who just walked in?"

"Put him on!" cried Susan.

She had a lot to say. She told Mark she'd been beaten up by a bank robber's girlfriend. She reminded him that he'd promised witness protection. She also mentioned the baby. She was four months along now, planning to name it Mark junior, or Markella if it was a girl. It must not have occurred to her that there was already a Mark Steven Putnam Jr., the 2-year-old son of Mark and his wife, Kathy.

Mark said he was back in Pikeville only briefly, to get ready for a trial, one of his big cases, against some outlaws from the hills who'd been stealing earthmovers and heavy machines and breaking them down for parts. He didn't know about seeing Susan. He was pretty busy, he said.

Susan hung up, then took a shower. She asked Shelby to lend her an outfit. Shelby had a hair salon; her husband, Troy Ward, had a pension, drove trucks. Theirs was about the largest house in Freeburn, two stories, painted green. Susan borrowed a brand-new shorts set and a little cross necklace, then called Ron Poole at home.

"Come pick me up," she told the FBI supervisor. "Mark's a-wantin' me over to the Landmark Inn."

• • •

Like many little girls in Pike County, in eastern Kentucky, near the Virginia and West Virginia borders, Susan Daniels Smith was raised by a miner and his wife, in a house at the head of a hollow near Barrenshea Creek. Tracy Daniels was "a model wife, a good woman," says Shelby Ward. Daddy Sid "was a hell-raiser."

Susan was a little more outgoing than Tennis Ray or Billy Joe or some of the other Daniels kids. She was friendly, a sixth-grade cheerleader with long hair, skinny legs, a high-pitched voice. When she was 15, Susan moved out of her parents' house and into Shelby's. Soon after, she quit Freeburn High School and fled the county with Kenneth Smith, her boyfriend from Vulcan, West Virginia, across the Tug River. Susan, like many raised in Freeburn, had a lust for the outside world, a need to make sure it really existed. She and Kenneth were married in Columbus, Indiana, in 1981, then moved around to Chicago, New Orleans, West Virginia, sometimes getting jobs, other times dealing in drugs and scams, according to Shelby. Along the way, they had a daughter, Meranda.

When Susan returned to the Tug Valley, everyone commented on how much she'd changed. Not that people wouldn't have had something to say in any case. Nothing escapes comment in Freeburn. The town's 400 souls live close together at the base of a hill, below the state road, on a level spot covering an area about the size of a city block. Two rows of houses in various states of repair face one another across a street just wide enough for one car. Coal bosses live alongside welfare mothers, church ladies down the way from felons.

For years, the Tug Valley had been known as a kind of forbidden zone, an Appalachian Hole in the Wall, a haven for bank robbers making forays into neighboring states and for drug dealers growing some of the highest-grade marijuana in America. With a force of only twenty-five men, there is little the Pike County Sheriffs' Department can do about Freeburn and the Tug. It took Daniel Boone three tries to find the area now known as Pike County; the territory has always been known as a lawless wild. Its settlers were the original hillbillies, crack marksmen who would later come down from the mountains to fight—on both sides—in the Civil War. The late 1800s saw the bloody feud between the Hatfields and the McCoys; Prohibition brought the moonshiners. About ten years ago, a new era was born when some boys from the valley crossed over to Virginia and robbed a bank. Though two were tried and imprisoned, an accomplice went free.

Since then, according to law-enforcement officials, bank robbery has become a ruthless legacy of these hills, like crack dealing in city ghettos, a way out for the criminally ambitious.

Life outside Freeburn had made Susan more sophisticated. She wore makeup and fashionable clothes now and had Northernized her down-home accent. She and Kenneth settled in a little yellow house in Vulcan. Though they had divorced three years earlier, they continued living together. Susan collected welfare. Kenneth sold drugs. "They were happy," Shelby says.

Then, in 1987, Kenneth and Susan became involved with a big-time bank robber named Carl "Cat Eyes" Lockhart. Cat Eyes had done time for three bank robberies, one of them the largest ever in Virginia. On September 10, police say, a man stole $12,807 from a Pikeville bank. As he fled in a stolen van, a pack of dye, placed by a teller in the robber's pillowcase along with the money, exploded all over the bills. Cat Eyes was arrested after he'd tried to exchange the red dollars at a bank.

For some time, the FBI had been working the Tug Valley, on a task force with state and local officials from surrounding jurisdictions. Now, with Cat Eyes and the red money, the FBI had its break. They brought in a rookie to tie up the case. His name was Mark Steven Putnam.

Mark was the eldest of three children raised by a truck-driver and his wife in Coventry, Connecticut, a mostly rural town about thirty miles east of Hartford. He started out in a public high school, then switched to the Pomfret School, an exclusive all-boys academy. He went on to the University of Tampa, where he majored in criminology, made the dean's list and became captain of Tampa's NCAA-champion soccer team. He was known as a silent leader, an overachiever who motivated his teammates through example.

After graduating, in 1982, Mark came home to Connecticut and took a job as a lowly clerk in the FBI bureau in New Haven. In three years, he'd qualify to take the entrance exam for the FBI Academy.

One night in July, Mark was hanging around the house when his mother called. She was listening to some music at a local bar. "I just met this girl, Mark," she said. "I think you better get down here."

The girl was named Kathy. She was two years younger than Mark, dark-eyed, thin, lovely. She and Mark's mom had gotten to talking. Kathy was the residential manager of a luxury-apartment complex; she was also studying for her paralegal degree. The daughter of a construction worker and his wife, who had shared hard times and come through strong, Kathy believed in love, long and lasting, forever. She told Mark's mom she was tired of all the heartaches and the breakups, of all the men who acted like dogs. She was a hard worker who enjoyed her job, but at the same time, she says now, "I always wanted to be a mother. I wanted to bake cookies and play with the kids."

Mark was the guy Kathy had been wishing for. "He was charismatic," she says, "the kind of guy who just melted you." He'd always wanted just two things out of life, he told Kathy. He wanted a family, and he wanted his kids to be able to say, "My father's an FBI agent."

"We fit perfectly," Kathy remembers. They went home together that night.

For the next two years, Mark and Kathy lived together in her free apartment. They didn't have many friends; they had each other. On weekends they went to New York City for dinner and a show; in the summer they hit the beach in Rhode Island. They talked a lot, planned their dream: two kids, a house in Florida, Mark an FBI agent.

They were married before a justice of the peace in New York City on Easter weekend, 1984, and Kathy became pregnant almost immediately. She quit the resident-manager job, went to work for an insurance company. Mark, meanwhile, got a promotion at the office. He worked nights there and days in a liquor store to build a nest egg.

Mark applied to the FBI, the IRS, several police academies. Finally, after a stint with Burns International Security, Mark was appointed to the FBI Academy, in Quantico, Virginia. In February of 1987, Mark got his first FBI assignment, to the two-man office in Pikeville. Usually, says Kathy, new agents are assigned to a big office. There, under supervision, they learn how to work in the field, handle informants, live with danger. But Pikeville was another thing altogether. The agent in charge was nearing retirement; some say he was more interested in his boat than in crime. Mark wasn't sure he was ready to jump headfirst into an office where he'd have so much responsibility. He told Kathy he was scared. But he also knew he couldn't complain. Being in the Bureau is like being in the military. During your first years, you do what they tell you.

So Mark and Kathy and their baby daughter, Danielle, went to Pikeville. They bought a nearly new seven-room house for $89,000, a wood-sided rambler in Pikeville's only subdivision, just outside downtown. The city is the seat of Pike County, the largest in the commonwealth of Kentucky, 785 square miles, beneath which is one of the largest underground veins of bituminous coal in the United States. Nestled beside the Levisa Fork of the Big Sandy River, at the bottom of a bowl made of sheer rock cliffs and thickly forested mountains, the town of 6,000 is sleepy, friendly, provincial—a college town with one movie house, where tickets are $2.

At first, Mark and Kathy were happy. "Mark had the job he wanted, I loved our house," says Kathy. "We were talking about how good this could be, because in a small office in a place like Pikeville, with everything that was going on, he could really make a name for himself." Every Friday night, Mark would take little Danielle on a date. Kathy would dress her up, curl her hair, and then Daddy would drive her to McDonald's, the pet store, the Dairy Queen. Kathy got her special nights too. In 1987, little Mark was born. The day he took his first steps, Kathy called the state police, had them patch her through to Mark's radio. He came home immediately, Code 2, with the siren. If Pikeville wasn't exactly idyllic, well, the Putnams were resigned to the fact that they had to do their time. In a year or two, they'd get to submit their top twelve choices. After that came the OP: office of preference. Florida, here we come.

Soon, however, Pikeville started getting to Kathy. The mountains blotted out the light, and "there was nothing there for me. There was the grocery store and the Kmart. That was it. I was used to civilization. You couldn't even get in your car to drive. It was only a matter of time before you were caught in the mountains, and I was scared to death to drive in them."

Pikeville, she says, was like a fishbowl. On her third day in town, she went to the bank and the teller looked at her and said, "Oh, you must be the FBI's wife. How you like your house up there on Honeysuckle?" People in Pikeville stood at their windows, sat on their porches, watched. They told stories about one another, then smiled and said hello. Once, after Mark had been gone all night, meeting with his supervisor across the state, a neighbor knocked on the door and told Kathy, "I couldn't help noticing that Mark's car wasn't in the driveway last night."

When he wasn't working, Mark coached a YMCA soccer team, attended Friday-night high-school football games. Mark Sohn, a neighbor and a psychology professor at Pikeville College, remembers Putnam in three mental snapshots. In the first, he is kneeling in the town's tiny Catholic church. He always sat in the same pew, in the same seat. He worshiped but never stayed for the social hour. The second picture is of a muscular Mark in shorts and a tight shirt. He'd take off full tilt up a mile-long hill, do a set of very fast chin-ups, then run 440's around the track.

The third is of Mark on the street after work. He's pushing a stroller, talking to neighbors. "You know the game Clue?" asks Sohn. "That's Mark

Putnam, his life, you know? He was a detective. His primary focus in all his conversations was on this Clue stuff."

Not long after Cat Eyes was arrested with the red money, Kenneth Smith, Susan's ex-husband, was also arrested. Cat Eyes, it turned out, had used Susan and Kenneth's house to plan a robbery. Rather than take a fall on drug or accessory charges, Susan decided to talk. She met Mark for the first time, at the Federal Building in Pikeville, in late September 1987.

Remembers Shelby: "She came home and said she was going to seduce this guy."

And so Susan and Mark and Kathy began their odd and ultimately disastrous relationship. With Susan's testimony, Cat Eyes was sentenced to fifty-five years in prison. Susan went to work on other cases. The FBI refuses to discuss the particulars of Susan's work, but Kathy says that Susan, for a while at least, was an effective informant. Like the other habitués of the Tug, the criminals knew one another's business, and all the crimes were interrelated; some of them even seemed to follow a trail to the doors of state and local officials. Susan and Kenneth had always been drugstore cowboys. Susan knew a lot of names, a lot of what was going on. Her problem as an informant was her mouth. She *told* everyone she was an informant.

An agent assigned to the Pikeville office spent most of his time in the field. If an informant wanted to contact his agent, he called headquarters in Louisville and was switched to the agent's home. Mark learned quickly that this wouldn't work. People in the Tug were too paranoid. The only answer was to give out his home number.

Stuck in the house, Kathy became Mark's clerk, and more. She knew all the cases, all the informants. And none called more than Susan. "She'd phone two or three times a day, and we'd talk for two hours—her PMS, the kids, Kenneth, this and that. She asked me all about Mark. All about myself. She'd say, 'I love Mark, there isn't anything I wouldn't do for him.' She always made insinuations that she and Mark were sleeping together."

And so it went for months and months. Any time, day or night, straight or drugged, Susan would call: Kenneth was horrible. Her life was rotten. The kids needed clothes. Someone was trying to kill her. Several times, Susan called threatening suicide; once, she kept Kathy on the phone from ten at night till four in the morning. "You felt for her. You had to. She had such a rotten life," says Kathy.

Somewhere along the way, probably in the fall of 1988, Susan and Mark became involved. According to Shelby Jean and her brother Billy Joe, Mark and Susan met frequently in the evenings at the Wendy's in Pikeville. Billy Joe's girlfriend has a record of thirty-two trips in her diary—times she went along for the ride to drop Susan off. Mostly, though, Susan drove herself. Sometimes, Shelby says, Susan and Mark went to the Landmark Inn. Often they had sex in the car.

"She would come home and tell me everything they'd done, go into details about their lovemaking," Shelby says. "He treated her real nice. But he never bought her nothin'. I would give her money to take him and her to Wendy's, 'cause he said his wife wouldn't give him no money."

Meanwhile, the FBI announced budget cuts. Rookie agents would have to stay at their first posting for five years instead of three. Already, Kathy was miserable. Mark would come home and she'd break down sobbing. She couldn't last any longer. No way. The couple huddled and decided to take desperate measures. Kathy began working undercover, on a big political case, and she did it for one reason—to put herself at risk. If she was personally in danger, she and Mark both knew, the FBI would get her and the kids out, and Mark would soon follow.

As it happened, the Putnams got what they wanted, and then some. When the indictments for the heavy-machinery case came down, the threats began. Again and again, the phone rang. Kathy called the Putnams' insurance company and asked around obliquely about their coverage in case of arson or bombings. One night when Mark was away, A man called and announced politely that he was on his way over to kill her. Kathy stayed awake all night in the living room, aiming a .357 magnum at the front door.

In late February of 1989, both of the women in Mark Putnam's life got what they wanted. Kathy and the kids were removed from Pikeville—in the middle of the night—by the FBI. Susan began waking up nauseous.

It was her second pregnancy since she'd taken up with Mark. The first had ended in a miscarriage. Susan told Mark she was determined to have his baby.

In April, Mark and Kathy got their dream assignment, to the Miami bureau of the FBI. In June, Mark came back to Pikeville. Susan was determined to see him.

On the evening of Monday, June 5, Ron Poole, Mark's former supervisor, picked up Susan at the Freeburn post office, across the road from Shelby's house. He drove her through the dark and the rain to Pikeville, to the

Landmark Inn, and rented her a room at the FBI's expense. Over the next three days and nights, Mark worked on the loose ends of the heavy-machinery case. In his spare time, according to Shelby, he and Susan talked, went out for meals, made love. Susan called Shelby every day. On Thursday morning, Shelby asked her if she'd discussed the baby. Susan said they had, that Mark wasn't going to pay child support. "You're makin' a fool of yourself," Shelby said. "You're better off on welfare."

At around 10 P.M., according to a confession by Mark, written in consultation with his lawyer, Susan came to his room, began pressing him about the baby. "Susan started being more vocal and argumentative. I began to worry about other guests of the motel overhearing us, so I asked her to go for a ride with me."

They took his rental car, a blue Ford Tempo, rode out into the hills of Pike County, toward Freeburn. "All during the drive we discussed the pregnancy. I kept asking her what she wanted me to do. She kept telling me the baby was mine and that she was going to 'hang me' over this. She said she would tell the FBI, my family and the newspapers. I was getting extremely uptight."

At midnight, halfway to Freeburn, at the top of Peter Creek Mountain, Mark pulled off the road. He turned to Susan. He told her he and Kathy would adopt the baby, that they could give it a much better home than she could. Susan became enraged, "started striking me with her hands in a slapping-type motion. In an act of extreme rage, I reached across the car and grabbed her by the throat with both hands and straddled her by actually sitting on top of her in the seat. I started choking her and telling her to shut up.

"I estimate that I must have choked her for two minutes, during which time she continued to struggle and strike me about the face. After she ceased struggling, I released my grip. I believed she was unconscious. I checked for a pulse and found none. I began to administer mouth-to-mouth-resuscitation techniques. I also took my fist and hit her chest in an attempt to get her breathing again. She still had not moved."

Mark got out, walked around the car, grabbed Susan under the armpits. "She felt extremely heavy. I was exhausted and feeling faint. I sat her on the ground and she was leaning back against my legs. I released my grip and she fell to the side, with her head striking the ground with a 'thud.' At this point I realized she was dead."

Mark looked down at the body, tried to think. He noticed that Susan was wearing his gray shorts and his T-shirt. He removed the clothes, placed Susan's nude body in the trunk of the car and drove back to the Landmark. He stayed awake the rest of the night, sitting on the edge of his bed. In the morning, he took a shower and drove to Lexington for a meeting. The car sat all day in a parking space outside the federal courthouse with Susan's body in the trunk.

Mark returned to Pikeville, went to McDonald's, then set out looking for someplace to hide Susan's body. Nine miles north of town, he turned off on Harmond Branch Road, then turned again onto an old mining road. He backed up the Tempo, hoisted Susan, carried her down seventy-five feet into a ravine and laid her on her back. "She was nude and after I laid her down, I sat there for a minute, then kissed her on the cheek." Then he climbed back up to his car.

Mark drove back to the Landmark. He called Kathy. "Tell me about the kids," he said. "What did they do today?"

Kathy began talking about the ducks. Mark and Kathy had bought a condo near a canal in Fort Lauderdale. There were ducks everywhere. That afternoon, a family of ducks—a mother with all her babies in line—had come to the back porch. Kathy gave Mark junior some bread, and he went out there like a little bull moose. He picked up one of the ducklings by its neck and began pushing bread into its beak. "No, no, little Mark!" called Kathy, and he threw the duck down. It was so cute. He'd thought it was a toy.

The next morning, June 10, 1989, Mark went to the car wash and vacuumed the Tempo. He threw away the gray shorts and the T-shirt, an earring and the floor mat from the trunk. Then he went back to work.

Meanwhile, in Freeburn, Shelby was getting nervous. Friday and Saturday passed with no word from Susan. By Sunday evening, distraught, she had taken to bed. As the shadows leaned deeper through her window, the tiny digital clock on the nightstand clicked 5:00. The phone rang.

"Heeeeey!" It was Ron Poole. "Has that sister of yours made it home yet?"

"I ain't seen or heard from her since Thursday."

"Gosh. She shoulda been home," said Ron.

Shelby filed a missing-persons report the next day. Eight days later, on June 20, the state police interviewed Mark. He said Poole had brought Susan to the Landmark for undercover work. He said he'd talked to Susan about her pregnancy, offered to pay for an abortion, but that she'd never indicated who the father was. He also said he and Susan had discussed her plans to hook up with some out-of-state drug dealers, and that he'd offered to follow as backup, but she'd declined. He didn't know where she was.

Ron Poole told police a different story. He said he'd brought Susan to the hotel to discuss her pregnancy with Mark. He also said he'd found Susan's purse, makeup and shorts outfit in her abandoned room at the Landmark.

Mark went back home to Florida on June 25. State-police investigators, with no body as evidence, had no crime, just a missing person. But Shelby knew Susan was dead: She would never have gone anywhere without her purse and makeup. Shelby called the FBI regional office in Covington, Kentucky. She spoke to the supervisor, Terry Hulce.

"I'm reportin' that my sister's missin' and that she was last with Mark Putnam," Shelby blurted, speaking faster and faster. "She was his informant. . . . They were having a love affair. . . . Two years. . . . She's pregnant. . . . He killed her. He—"

"Whoa!" Hulce told her. "From what I heard, your sister slept around with everything in Pikeville."

"He just talked to me like dirt under his feet," Shelby recalls. "He acted like Susan was just some ol' rat informant, and that Mark was Mr. Perfect."

The summer dragged on. State police, at the FBI's suggestion, made a desultory effort to find Susan's out-of-state drug connections. In August, they began to focus their investigation on Susan's ex, Kenneth Smith. They searched five months for him. But not too hard, apparently, because during that time he was living in Freeburn with Susan's brother Billy Joe, serving a home-incarceration sentence for traffic violations, an electronic band around his leg. Had Smith moved more than 150 feet from his telephone, a buzzer would have sounded at a monitoring station.

Finally, on January 12, 1990, police located Kenneth Smith. A lie-detector test revealed that he knew nothing about Susan's disappearance. In March 1990, nine months after the murder, Shelby went to Pike County Commonwealth Attorney John Paul Runyon. Runyon's father had also been the commonwealth attorney; Runyon himself, an imposing white-haired man often taken for a judge, had served for twenty-one years.

Runyon listened to the story. He gathered that Susan wasn't exactly the most upstanding young woman in the county. (Many said that Susan had a lot of flings—with another FBI man, with a Chicago cop, with a prominent Pikeville citizen who, she claimed, was the father of her son, Brady.) He also suspected that she may have brought this whole thing on herself by attempting to dig her hooks into Mark. Still, it didn't make any sense that the FBI would ignore the disappearance of an informant. But if the informant was having an affair with a federal agent, it was easier to understand their inaction. Runyon could envision a row of falling dominoes, cases overturned because of Mark's involvement with Susan.

"I mean, the FBI flat ignored the case," says Runyon. "I sat down with [an agent from the Department of Justice] in Washington, and I said, 'Look, this is your case, you people are involved up to your eyeballs.' " If the FBI didn't start moving soon, he told the Fed, "You're likely to find someone like Geraldo Rivera coming through your office door."

By the following Monday, says Runyon, there were ten agents assigned to the case.

Meanwhile, Shelby had closed her beauty shop, started drinking and downing Valium. She'd begun poring over newspapers for baby announcements and obituaries. She called the Welfare Department, Legal Aid and post offices in three states to see if Susan was getting any mail.

In Florida, Mark continued working, but all was not well. In the midst of interviewing a suspect, he'd think, After what I've done, how can I hop on this guy for stealing his own computers? At night, driving home from the office, he would look down at his speedometer, find himself going 100 mph. On his nocturnal runs, he'd pick out a star, imagine it was Susan and tell her he was sorry. Kathy remembers his having diarrhea for a year. And the dreams: "I would wake up in the middle of the night and he'd be scratching his chest, just digging at it. I'd shake him and he was like, 'What did I say?' "

Finally, on May 16, 1990, the FBI interrogated Mark for six and a half hours. He denied the affair, denied knowing anything about Susan's disappearance. Apparently, the agents believed him. They asked if he would take a polygraph, just to clear his name.

The next day, Mark flew to Washington, D.C. He failed the polygraph, returned home. Kathy picked him up at midnight at the airport in Fort Lauderdale, and they drove in silence to David's Plum, a bar in a Holiday Inn. Kathy ordered a double Black Russian.

"It's really bad," Mark said. His hands were shaking.

Kathy regarded her husband. She knew what he was going to say. He'd had an affair with Susan. She hated the thought, but mistakes happen. She would forgive him; she'd already thought it out. Now, at the table, she readied herself for the telling. But first, just to eliminate the possibility, she said, "Okay. Did you kill her?"

"Yeah, I did," answered Mark.

Kathy couldn't move. She felt paralyzed. Numb. "You slept with her?" she asked.

"Yeah."

"This could have been your baby?"

"Yeah."

And Kathy backhanded him across the face, knocking him out of his chair. Then she tossed back her drink.

Three days later, Commonwealth Attorney Runyon received a call from a lawyer in Fort Lauderdale. He said Mark wanted to make a deal and confess to the killing of Susan Smith in exchange for a manslaughter charge, which carried a max of twenty years in jail.

Runyon was dumbfounded. Lie-detector tests were not admissible in court, and other than that, the state had nothing with which to make a case against Mark. By the time he had become a suspect, the rental car and all other physical evidence were long gone. And with no body, there was no crime. Pike County alone covered 785 square miles. Runyon knew he could bring in 5,000 members of the army reserve and comb the hills and hollows for a week and never find the body of Susan Smith. "We had absolutely no evidence," says Runyon. "Not one scintilla or shred. It was the first time in my career that I had a man on the phone wanting to confess to murder and I could not charge him for it.

"He could have walked away. I believe his conscience got to him. He just felt guilty. He couldn't go on."

On June 12, a few days after the anniversary of Susan's death, Mark Putnam stood before a Pikeville judge. He had resigned from the FBI, and he had led the cops to Susan's decomposed body. Now he was pleading guilty to first-degree manslaughter, the first agent in the FBI's eighty-two-year history to be charged in a killing. He was sentenced to sixteen years. Special arrangements provided that he would serve his time under federal protection. He had many enemies where he was going.

Mark's sentencing was not uneventful. When Shelby entered the courtroom, she set off the metal detector. Police found a loaded .38 pistol wrapped in a sock inside her purse. Shelby told the officers, "Lord! I wasn't gonna do nothin'," and everybody in town pretty much agreed, including Runyon, who recommended probation.

Still, it was interesting to many how, after the offense, Shelby toned down her rhetoric. When Mark's confession and plea bargaining had been announced, Shelby had been livid. "Because he was a big FBI, famous and everything, they don't want him to get justice," Shelby told the media. Four days later, after the incident with the gun, she changed her tune. She understood, she said, that the state had had no case without a body, that the police had done the best they could. "I highly credit John Paul Runyon. I am sorry. I was wrong and he was right," she told the press.

Next came the matter of the autopsy. There wasn't one. And no death certificate either. Though the remains were positively identified by forensic specialists (Susan was still wearing the little gold cross Shelby had given her), a full autopsy was not performed. Faced with a bureaucratic delay of two or three weeks by the coroner's office, Shelby opted to take the body back.

"She had laid out for a year over the hill over there," Shelby says, "and here I go up Mama and Daddy's house every day, and they say 'When are we gonna get to bury her?' But the medical examiner just left her down there like a science project, taking a look at her every once in a while. So I just said, 'Give me the body back.' "

Susan was buried on a little hill overlooking the hollow where she had been born, in a plot next to her grandma's, surrounded by a waist-high Cyclone fence. The ceremony in Freeburn was small, quiet and solemn. But down the mountain, newspapers, politicians and lawyers were locked in fierce debate. An editorial in the *Lexington Herald-Leader* asked: "Why did it take nearly eight months for the Kentucky State Police and FBI to focus on FBI agent Mark Putnam as the prime suspect?" Articles suggested classism and bias: The FBI and the judicial system, the lofty government, had trampled a daughter of the underclass. Similar editorials in other papers made it a state, and then a national, case. At issue also was the lack of an autopsy. Irregularities were surfacing.

In his nine-page confession, Mark said he and Susan had made love only four or five times. He described in detail the way he had murdered Susan, in language carefully crafted by his lawyer to meet the standards for the manslaughter charge. According to Larry Webster, the lawyer representing Susan's family in a civil wrongful-death suit against Mark and the FBI, new information has revealed that her body was missing several teeth, perhaps even several bones. The medical examiner has ordered an autopsy. Mark's lawyer has moved for dismissal of the case.

It is getting dark now in Kathy Putnam's kitchen, three steps up in a mint-green semidetached in Rochester, Minnesota, a blanket of snow shimmering in the clean orange light of a subzero sunset. She sits at the kitchen table, pushes her glass distractedly across the woodgrain Formica, ice tinkling. Mark is in prison nearby. She and the kids visit every Saturday. His release date is January 12, 2002.

"The way I see it," says Kathy, "Mark's mistake was sleeping with her. And it hurts. A lot. But when you get past that feeling, you realize there's a lot more to what you are to each other than sex or even friendship. It's being a part of each other. That's what love is all about. You don't just throw it away, even though something terrible has happened. The biggest hurt would be to be without the person."

One time zone east, Shelby Jean Ward is in her kitchen. She sits in Susan's seat at the round table, drums her manicured nails on the Formica. Through the open door, she can hear the rumble of dump trucks along the dual lane, gearing down toward the railhead, laden with thick chunks of black Kentucky coal. She's trying to get her life back on track, is thinking about reopening her hair salon. But first, she wants justice.

"All through this, I think the FBI has covered up," Shelby says. "They did it in the beginning, and they're still doing it now. We're gonna get that autopsy; we're gonna see if he really did kill her the way he said. I don't care if he was some big FBI man. If he killed somebody in cold blood, he should fry."

(1991)

The High Life and Strange Times
of the Pope of Pot

He had an 800 number and a corps of bicycle messengers, each covered by the company dental plan. Meet the marijuana pope and his faithful followers at the Church of Realized Fantasies.

There's a knock at the door and Mickey the Pope, the Pope of Pot, stubs out a joint and stashes it in a drawer. "Gotta go now, toots," he rasps, smoke leaking from his chipmunk grin, and then he laughs, *"Ah-ha-ha-HA!"* and then he coughs, a deep black hack that shudders his shoulders. He swallows hard, wipes a tear, shrugs and smiles. A trickle of blood reddens the groove between his two front teeth.

Mickey hangs up the phone, writes a number in his little book with a green pen. His entries aren't alphabetical—more experiential, like life, taken in the order that comes, always in alternating colors. He likes things around him to be beautiful, the way God intended. He closes the book, puts a finger to his lips, concentrates. Something to do . . . What was it? . . . Hmmm . . .

Mickey pans the room, in search of a clue: a refrigerator, a stack of chairs, a poster of the Italian rock & roller he has taken off the street, a hot plate with one coil glowing, his desk, a pile of bills, a birthday card. *Birthday!* Today is Mickey the Pope's birthday. He is forty-nine years old. Today is also the day before the winter solstice, the last shortening day on the calendar of seasons. This is significant somehow to Mickey the Pope, who's facing fifteen years in the slammer.

Since the bust, sales are down by more than half. Expenses, however, remain the same. It looks like Mickey will have to get a loan. He'll have to ask his little brother to cosign. His brother, of course, will insist that Mickey write something besides *pope* on the section marked EMPLOYMENT. He thinks Mickey is *meshugge*. He may be right. But the fact is, Mickey can't stop being pope just because he has no money. When you start your own church, take the top spot, register it with the City of New York, you make a lifetime commitment. You have responsibilities, toots: You have to tend the flock, buy and dispense sacrament, hire couriers—people you can trust. And then there is operations: two apartments, two offices, the church, the handouts to unfortunates, the food and the dental plan for employees, the telephone lines, 800-WANT-POT. Give the pope a call if you live in Manhattan. Leave your address, your first name, a description of yourself. Your pot will arrive by bicycle in forty minutes or less.

Mickey spies his papal miter—a high, white, John Paul crown, with underwires shaped to a peak, a nine-inch marijuana leaf pasted on the front, lace trailing from the sides. He dons it, tying the polka-dot ribbon beneath his chin. He wears the miter for all public appearances. The May Day Smoke-In at Washington Square, the Halloween parade in Greenwich Village, ACT-UP demonstrations at City Hall, Wigstock, in Tompkins Square—any occasion that requires his high-camp popely presence, any opportunity to stroll the streets, preach the gospel of marijuana and hand out free joints, the sacrament of his Church of Realized Fantasies.

Mickey the Pope swivels around in his chair, grinning, mouth agape, glasses glinting in the fluorescent light. *"Ah-ha-ha-HA!"*

The door again. Knock, knock.

Oh, yeah. The door. It is made of metal. It is very heavy. Mickey shambles over and yanks. His arm boings like a rubber band. The door doesn't budge.

Mickey giggles and shrugs. What, me worry? Used to be Mickey weighed 300 pounds. He's down a bit lately. A lot. He's a little weak. This diabetes shit. The bleeding gums, the fading eyesight. And all the time drink-and-piss, drink-and-piss, the other day he wet his pants. It was an accident. People have accidents. It'll be all right. The winter solstice is upon us, and the days will be longer, the world will be brighter. This is nature. We know this for a fact. Just as we know that when his church hits 1 million members, he'll have the best medical care available. Just as we know that when his case comes up, the jury will acquit. Some juror, the pope is sure, will know what he knows: that to follow an insane law is to be insane yourself.

Things may look bleak, but Mickey the Pope will find his way clear. He always has. He speaks with the voice and the authority of God. He'll tell you that himself. He also has experience on his side. Twenty years in the pot business, a dozen arrests, seven gunshot wounds, three years in jails, one deportation and all those men, toots, so many wonderful, beautiful men. The counselors at camp. The kids in his bunk. Ten percent of the crew of the U.S. Navy carrier *Intrepid* in the spring and summer of 1959. Two at once on public-access television, a salt-and-pepper team, the black one so big he could do it to himself if he wanted.

And then there was the guy in Amsterdam. He was hired to kill Mickey. As it was, Mickey was just wounded. Mickey was really fat then. The shot passed through the fleshy part of his right arm, down into his belly and out again. What Mickey remembers is that oil oozed from the wounds. It looked like chicken fat, nice and bright and yellow. "I felt like an oil sheik," he says. "*Ah-ha-ha-HA!*"

In the end, the guy who tried to kill him in Amsterdam became another of the many and varied lovers of Mickey the Pope. Amsterdam: that was the place, those were the days. During the Seventies, Mickey the Pope was known in Amsterdam as Da Paus Maus. He was the No. 1 pot dealer in a city of heads, unloading nickels, dimes, lids, to the tune of seven kilos a day, selling out of a room in his five-story houseboat on the Amstel River, the front hatch of which was painted to resemble a giant pair of red lips. You had to come through the lips to meet the pope.

The knock again. Mickey the Pope pulls hard on the door.

Late December in the meatpacking district in New York, the sunlight leaning into the West Side afternoon. In a few hours the crack boys will stir and the curbs will be deep in transvestites, and effeminate men wearing leathers and lots of keys will come jangling down the block holding hands, headed for a basement club called the Hellfire. Now, though, things are almost serene on this corner of Thirteenth and Hudson, just in sight of the river. Mothers push strollers, delivery trucks come and go, old Irish ladies promenade—constitutionals taken daily since the boom days on the waterfront, when corners like Mickey's were given over to pubs.

The pope's place, his Church of Realized Fantasies, is painted yellow in its present incarnation, a bright beacon against dark, slick streets and dirty brick. It's an old comic-book store—Dick Tracy painted on one side—with eight big windows, so good for his plants. Mickey the Pope loves plants.

Two men stand flat-footed outside the church. One wears a pompadour and a trench coat. He looks like a mobster. The other carries a pad. He looks like a balding Irish guy in a leather jacket trying to look like something other than a cop. The door swings open. "Michael Cezar?" asks the guy in the leather jacket.

"Howdy, honey, howdy!" rasps Mickey the Pope, beak nosed, red faced, wearing his marijuana bonnet. He giggles, raises his hands—palms out—and rubs tiny circles in the air before him, the papal greeting.

"Internal Affairs," says the guy in the pompadour.

Back now to August, earlier in the year. Across the Americas, from Bogotá to Harlem, the drug war is raging. Though the government has proclaimed drug use on the slide, curb-side dealers are trading briskly in cocaine, prices are down, supply stable, the rat-a-tat-tat of automatic-weapons fire rings across the ghettos like cash-register bells. Sales are also strong in heroin, an old drug making a resurgence as an antidote to crack. At first the police notice a sudden infusion of high-grade, low-price H into the cities. Later it is revealed, but not widely reported, that most of the stuff is China White from Asia's Golden Triangle, moved into America by Triads, many of whose members have recently emigrated from Hong Kong. What fools the police is ingenuity: Chemists are processing different batches with different recipes out of the international heroin cookbook, making some of it look like Mexican, some like Lebanese.

Meanwhile, potheads across the mainland are mourning. It is the time of the drought, the great marijuana drought of 1990, the summer of scrounging, of smoking roaches and cleaning seeds and finally just giving up. Film at eleven shows bonfires of prime buds and old tires sending thick black smoke into the ecosystem. County sheriffs in camouflage fatigues stand around smiling, pitchforks or shotguns in hand. In the cities, the police and legislators launch a massive assault on head shops. Mail-order companies are also targeted. The police seize records, mailing lists, stock. It becomes impossible to buy a bong.

One fine summer day in the midst of all this, a New York radio personality named Howard Stern—the drive-time attitude idol of the bridge-and-tunnel crowd—is sitting at his desk at the station. He's paging through a New Jersey newspaper, looking for material for his talk show, when he spies an ad. He blinks in disbelief.

"Call 1-800-WANT POT."

The next morning, live before 2 million listeners in three Eastern cities, Howard calls Mickey the Pope.

"Hey, dude!" Howard says. "You're on the air!"

"Howdy, honey, howdy!" rasps Mickey. "I'm the pope. The Church of Realized Fantasies."

"So what do you do, sell pot?"

"Oh . . . see . . ." says Mickey. "We give out sacrament for those who need it."

"You don't think it causes any—"

"No," interrupts the pope. "It cures everything. Even AIDS."

"It gives you breasts," blurts Howard. "How's your breasts?"

"My breath may stink a little. I didn't brush my teeth."

"No! Your breasts!"

"They're fine," says the pope. "They get erect, I suppose."

"So," says Howard, changing the subject. "You make a lot of money doing this?"

"I'm living on the Upper East Side. I'm comfy. And I have a palace in New Jersey."

"Really? All from just dealing pot?"

"Well, from being the pope. A lot of people admire the pope."

They talk a while longer, then Howard says goodbye.

"You know," Howard says to his sidekick, Robin Quivers, "I had seen the number in the newspaper, and I thought, 'This is kinda cool.' I mean, I don't think it's cool that he's a drug dealer, but it's kinda cool that he's getting away with it."

"It seems it would be pretty easy to catch him, wouldn't it?" says Robin. "You just call him up, make an order, he shows up, you book him."

"He ought to change his number to 1-800-ARREST-ME," says Howard.

Mickey the Pope was born Michael Ellis Cezar, in New York City's Greenwich Village, the eldest child of a Jewish engineer and his wife, the daughter of a former postmaster general of Jamaica who was the scion of an English colonial family that had made a fortune mining bauxite. Mickey's father owned an electronics factory in Paterson, New Jersey, which built transformers for radar, the space program, nuclear-power plants. Mickey's little brother runs the factory today. One sister is a real-estate agent; the other, a ceramics teacher who lives in the family "palace," a large house in Morris Plains, New Jersey, which has been stripped of all its furnishings to pay the family bills.

Mickey dropped out of high school after his father went bankrupt. Starting over in a new plant, Mickey built tables for machines, hooked up the electric and the plumbing, did everything from filing and drilling to sweeping the floor. Later, after a stint in the navy, he feuded with his father, who in turn disinherited his son and committed him to a mental institution. Upon his release, Mickey fled to Europe.

One day in the early Seventies, Mickey took the fabled Magic Bus Tour of Amsterdam. When it stopped at the Lowlands Weed Company, says Mickey, "I knew I'd found a home."

Lowlands Weed, it turned out, was owned by a bunch of Dutch Provos, anarchists who renounced the concept of work. They were known for their be-ins, demonstrations during which they sat around and did nothing but be themselves. The Provos also advocated the legalization of marijuana. They were the original potheads of Europe, the Continent's largest dealers. They would eventually place several of their number on Amsterdam's city council. Oddly, after achieving their political foothold, the Provos disbanded. It was probably the shock. Having won, these devout anarchists found themselves in charge of legislating societal order.

"They were a bunch of crazy people," says Mickey the Pope. "This one guy threw smoke bombs at the marriage of some Dutch aristocrat. He used to have sex with women and their kids. I'm telling the truth. I had people take shits on my floor. I had other people come in and eat it.

"In the beginning, they sold pot by the plant and seeds," the pope continues. "I convinced them to sell the smokable product. Buses would pull up and three-quarters of the passengers would flow into the shop to buy pot."

Soon, Da Paus Maus moved out of Lowlands and founded his own retail operation, selling out of a series of ever-larger houseboats. A port city, Amsterdam had an almost inexhaustible supply of drugs. Da Paus would get the list of ships from the harbor master, then go down to the docks at three in the morning. He'd fall into step with some sailors, say, "Howdy, toots!" and offer to share a joint.

"And then you'd go on board and there were tons of smoke pouring out of the ship," Mickey says. "Everybody had the stuff. So I'd give them a good price and they'd throw it down on the dock, and then I'd drive out, waving to the customs guy. He knew everything. The whole government was in on it. I was once visited on my houseboat by some secretary of state. He said, 'Keep up the good work. It's great for the tourists!' "

Amsterdam had always been known for its coffee bars and hashish, but the pope saw an opening and set about creating a market for marijuana. He kept long hours, stayed open seven days a week and sold at a tiny profit—even advertised in the yellow pages as "Hennep Producten." Pretty soon, says the pope, the Cosmos, the Milkyway, Paradiso, all the big clubs were selling Mickey's finest. "I was making, like, $20,000 a day," remembers Mickey.

Mickey lived the good life for a while, spending the guilders as fast as they came in. He bought a new boat, an old school to house his forty workers. He even paid for medical and dental plans. Then Da Paus Maus was busted. After seven years in business, Mickey was kicked out of Holland.

Penniless, still estranged from his family, Mickey landed on New York's Lower East Side in 1979. He met up with some anarchists, moved into a little apartment at First Street and First Avenue and began selling loose joints. Soon he started his first telephone delivery service, 777-CASH.

And thus began the pope's delivery empire. He serviced UN diplomats, rock stars, whorehouses, nightclubs, night watchmen, magazine editors, yippies, yuppies and punks. For a time the pope had a diner. For a time he operated a storefront on First Street, selling bags brazenly to all comers. When that store was busted in 1981, the pope did eight months in Rikers Island Prison, whereupon he returned to the Lower East Side and started all over again, this time at Eleventh Street and Avenue B.

"People lined up outside to buy pot all day long," says a longtime associate. "They were taking the money out in garbage bags, but the cops were so busy with all the heroin in the neighborhood they didn't really have time to fool with Mickey."

The mid-Eighties saw the pope battling the underworld. First came a Puerto Rican gang called the Hitmen Club. When Mickey refused to pay protection money, the gang members forced their way into his telephone center, holding the workers at bay with a .357 and a straight razor, taking $500. The next day they came back, demanding $1,000 a week from the pope. When Mickey refused, they ambushed him later on the street, shooting him six times with a .22. "He was so fat they didn't hit any vital organs," says the associate. "The ambulance guy didn't even believe Mickey had been shot until he opened up his coat and showed him the bullet holes."

Later the young sons of some Italian mobsters would try to muscle in on Mickey's operations. They cut the phone lines, waited outside to break Mickey's legs. Meanwhile, inside, Mickey the Pope was alone, in pain from a bowel obstruction, a complication from the Puerto Rican ambush. Weak, sick, determined, he held the fort for five days. In the end he was rescued by his father. "Well, I guess if you're dying, I can take you to the hospital," the old man said.

Over the years, Mickey estimates, he has presided over phone operations in more than forty different locations, always with modest success. Then came the summer of 1990, the drought. Nobody could find any pot except for Mickey. Business boomed.

Each morning, the bicycle couriers would meet at a secret location and check out stock for the day, four-gram bags of brown-green commercial Mexican, packaged in sealable glassine inside white paper envelopes. The couriers would hit the streets by 10:00 a.m. As calls came in, telephone operators would take down locations in logbooks and then beep the couriers, who would deliver the goods within forty minutes. Each bag cost the consumer $50. Delivery was $10 extra. At twenty-eight grams to the ounce, the pope's medium-grade pot was expensive, selling at about $350 a lid. But it was the only pot available. One hundred or 200 calls a day were not unusual.

By eight each evening, the couriers would check back in and pay up. No business was done after dark. That's when the real criminals were out, and couriers were often taken down by street thugs or fake cops with Chinatown shields. Mickey worried for his people. Usually, at night, the pope would gather around him a number of his flock and somebody would cook a big dinner. It was a happy family, mostly. And why not? The pope provided food, a dental plan, money to fix a broken bike. He gave out free pot, sometimes paid the medical bills of people he knew with AIDS. He'd even let you live in the telephone center or his extra apartment if you needed a place to squat. The police say Mickey was doing $40,000 a day. Mickey says he was probably making about half that much.

In any case, as quick as it came, it went. As Mickey says, "Money is like manure, toots, it's meant to be spread around."

Then, just as the church was hitting its stride, the New York police did exactly what Robin and Howard had suggested on their radio show. On September 22nd, 1990, the cops called the pope's 800 number. As guaranteed, a courier delivered. The police did the same again on October 12th and 26th. A few days later, during the massive Halloween parade held each year in the West Village, the pope gave a joint to an undercover cop. Handing it over—as he had to so many others that evening—Mickey giggled and declared: "I'm the Pope of Pot! If you want pot, call my number!"

That was it. The NYPD labeled Mickey the Pope a high priority. "There comes a time when you have to let people know that you are serious," said Special Narcotics Prosecutor Sterling Johnson. "He defied the authorities. He threw down the gauntlet."

On November 14th, with the press in tow, the cops raided the Pope of Pot. It was, said the *Village Voice*, "a police operation worthy of *America's Most Wanted."* The bust made all the news shows the next day and all the papers, even the *New York Times.* The *New York Post* played it on the front page with the headline COPS NAB PHONE 'POPE OF DOPE.' Police officials were quoted as saying that Mickey was taking 360 calls an hour on six telephones.

Mickey was brought out of his yellow church to a fusillade of flash-bulbs and questions. Handcuffed, red faced, blood pressure roaring, the pope had time to rasp only a quick, "Howdy, honey, howdy," before he was piled into a police car. Over in the shadows across the street, crack dealers and transvestites watched in amazement. They knew Mickey. On cold nights, he sometimes let them into the church to get warm. He gave out hot chocolate.

Then a cop in a suit, Assistant Chief John J. Hill, stepped forward into the klieg lights. His public statement: "We seized here a total of five mes-sengers, two people operating the phones and the pope himself. Also seized were seven pounds of marijuana."

Nighttime now at the Church of Realized Fantasies. In an hour or two the doors will open at a club called Mars, and a benefit will commence, a bailout throw-down for Mickey the Pope. Meantime, some of the inner circle have gathered to wait. They smoke joints, watch a video of the pope, eat sponge-cake, drink hot chocolate.

Soon after his arrest and release, Mickey was arrested again, this time for participating in an ACT-UP protest. Radical gays, demonstrating for a city-sponsored needle exchange for addicts, collected dirty syringes in a bucket. The pope was snatched when he attempted to turn the needles over to the police. Later he was arrested again for selling a half an ounce of pot to an undercover cop who came calling at the "palace" in New Jersey.

So it has gone. At the moment, the Pope of Pot is, to put it simply, des-titute. All the change from the Mason jar in his apartment has been spent. He doesn't even have a subway token in his pocket. He has plenty of church currency—poker chips in various colors stamped in gold with his sickle and marijuana leaf insignia—but nobody wants it. MCI has cut off the 800 number; New York Tel is threatening his other accounts. Landlords are clam-oring too. And, of course, there are the lawyers.

Hence the benefit, this gathering at Mickey's church. They are an odd bunch sitting on stackable plastic chairs, about two dozen of the 5,000 that Mickey claims as followers, having crawled this night from the belly of an F train from the Lower East Side, descendants of Burroughs and Ginsberg and Huncke the Junkie, of Madonna, Andy Warhol and Kenny

Scharf, the ever-changing members of the cult of near-fatal hipness that has thrived for so long in the East Village.

Quite a collection tonight. A guy in a Burberry raincoat, a silk tie, one eye stitched shut. A Russian Jew. A singer who is famous for looking like John Lennon. A man who looks like Charles Manson. A man named Mighty Man. One guy wears a black turban and little, square red plastic sunglasses. Another wears striped pants, a plaid coat, a Siberian fur hat. No one says a thing. Not a word. They sit, dumb, passing a joint.

Over in a corner, near the hot plate that heats the storefront, Mickey the Pope is being videoed as he watches the video of himself on a TV. An artist named Clayton has the minicam. He takes the thing everywhere, its red eye glowing, recording for a documentary what's been known for years in its many and varied forms as "the scene." Clayton made headlines in 1988 when he refused to surrender some footage to city authorities. His film showed cops, badges removed, beating homeless men and local residents with nightsticks during a riot in Tompkins Square Park. Clayton also has a storefront on the Lower East Side, on Essex below Houston, next to a kosher Chinese restaurant, in a Puerto Rican neighborhood known to Caucasian druggies from New Jersey as a good copping spot for Percodan. Clayton's mustache looks like two caterpillars inching along his lip line toward his nose. His goatee is long and thin like one of the Three Musketeers'. The hair along his two frontal lobes has been shaved. The rest hangs long in the back.

To Clayton's left is Mickey the Pope, who is being pumped by a woman for information about a friend of hers named Danny Rakowitz. Rakowitz is a Lower East Side artist and short-order cook who was arrested for cutting up his girlfriend, cooking her into soup, serving the soup to the homeless, leaving her skull and bones in a five-gallon bucket filled with Kitty Litter in the baggage claim at the bus station.

Rakowitz's friend is a tiny black woman with ashen skin and a shock of nappy hair. Her leather jacket is decorated with skull buttons. She looks like a skull, all cheekbones and sunken eyes and this thick top lip that flies up and to the left with every third word, a dancing sneer, a sort of visual "Fuck you." She is sure her friend didn't kill Monica. She's been interviewing people for months, gathering evidence. There's a plot. She knows this. Everyone is involved.

"But Danny had no reason to kill Monica," declares the skull lady.

"What's the difference?" asks the pope. "The girl saw the body in the bathtub."

"Doesn't that seem strange to you?"

"Of course it does."

"Why wasn't there any blood?" asks skull lady. "Where was the blood?"

"An awful lot of cleaning, dear," says the pope, lecturing. "Put her in the tub. Cut her up. Run the water, toots. *Ah-ha-ha-HA!*" He raises his palms, rubs tiny circles in the air before him. "The guy is crazy. He even had a sign on the door: SOUP KITCHEN. Everybody knew it."

"Well, why didn't anybody call the cops?"

"Why didn't anyone call the cops?" repeats the pope, begging the question. He snorts and giggles. "What do you expect? It's the Lower East Side."

Only in New York, only on the Lower East Side, could somebody like the pope be the pope.

Three centuries ago, the Lower East Side was farmland and aboriginal hardwood forest, and the Bowery—now the western edge of the district, changing to Third Avenue just north of Houston Street—was a trail, used by Native Americans in their sorties against the occupying Dutch colony of New Amsterdam. Today, this jumble of factories, tenements and storefronts, strewn from Astor Place to Alphabet City and from Fourteenth Street to Chinatown, remains the wilds of Manhattan—a campground from which the natives, with their alternative lifestyles, still launch assaults on the tastes of the mainstream uptown.

The late 1800s on the Lower East Side saw the first flowering of the immigrants. Millions of Turks, Greeks, Italians, Poles, Germans, Ukrainians and Jews came through Ellis Island to the world's newest urban frontier. It was a dense ethnic soup, the original American pepper pot—a world, according to a WPA guidebook, "of politicians, artists, gangsters, composers, prizefighters and labor leaders."

World War II, the Fifties, the early Sixties, saw new waves of immigration. Jews gave way to Puerto Ricans, winos to junkies. The Beat era was upon the East Village, a dark time of morphine, heroin and speed, of caffeine and marijuana, of bongos, berets, turtlenecks and homosexuality. Starting with writers William Burroughs and Herbert Huncke, poet Allen Ginsberg—continuing with Jack Kerouac, Neal Cassady, the Merry Pranksters, hallucinogens, communal living, free love—a new kind of culture, expressed in the widest range of perverse and irreverent and star-crossed possibilities, grew in the shabby far reaches of the Lower East Side.

The Seventies saw the rise of the club and art scene. There were punk rockers, hip-hoppers, new wavers, performance artists, fashion designers and drag queens. The club of the moment was CBGB; the musicians were Lou Reed, Patti Smith, Debbie Harry, the Ramones. Andy Warhol and his Factory were the spiritual center of the art world. Around him would revolve the likes of Keith Haring and Jean-Michel Basquiat.

"Although they sprang from varied backgrounds, the artists [who came to the area] shared a collective media-drenched consciousness, the heritage of the suburban teenager," writes Steven Hager in his book about the East Village. "In the Sixties, this pampered upbringing was frequently a source of guilt, but in the Seventies, it was dissected and rearranged, and eventually regurgitated into new forms."

In the last few years, with the fall of the economy and the rise of a new era of American Prohibition, the Lower East Side has hit hard and seamy times. "Every year it's been a different thing," says Clayton, the video artist. "Some years it's been drag queens. Other years it's been skinheads, the police, squatters, homeless. This year seems to be, you know, there's a depression happening in the country, a lot of uncertainty. They're trying to close our fire department, that's big for us. There's Mickey's bust, the Rakowitz murder, AIDS, crack. It changes down here, but it never changes. A lot of these fuckin' people are geniuses. A lot of them are nuts."

"So what's up with the telephone center," asks the hippie. "Is it cool or not?"

"I don't know," says Mickey the Pope.

"Well, we're only doing twenty deliveries a day, and that ain't shit!"

"Put me on PR!" chimes in Bartman. "Give me a minimum budget! Give me no budget!"

The pope eyes Bartman, shakes his head in sorrow. Bartman, Freddie Redpants, Larry the Libertarian . . . Why can't he find some help? Why must he do everything himself? Here in the church, a few days before his birthday, Mickey the Pope is in ruins. The other night at the fund-raiser at Mars, 700 people crowded all four floors. It was a raging success. There was so much support for the pope that you couldn't move across the room. Unfortunately, nobody at the benefit thought about collecting any money.

In the end, Mickey the Pope lost forty dollars.

So now he has gotten himself a new partner. Call him the hippie. He is bald on top with a fringe of shoulder-length hair, a gray beard cascading down his chest. He is hyper, creepy. He keeps looking all around him. Toward the windows. The back room. Under the papers on Mickey's desk.

"So what about the phone center?" he asks again, picking up the trash can, checking the bottom, putting it back down. "Is it cool?"

"Well, there wasn't a big investigation," interrupts Bartman. "They didn't freeze his bank accounts. It was just—"

"Baaaaaaart!" chides the pope.

"Listen, you little turd!" says the hippie, eyes suddenly wild, finger in Bartman's nose. "What you gotta do is one thing. Meet Red each morning, pick up, work. No talking. Got it?"

"I've cut it back about twenty percent," says Bartman. "I'm definitely talking less. I'm gonna—"

"You're gonna do what you got to do!" hollers the hippie, puffing up, ballistic, a vein popping in his right temple. He zeros in on the hapless Bartman: "Look. I got a lot going for me right now. I can't have some little pussy to fuck it up. If I'm gonna go to jail for conspiracy, I'll kill a fucker and go to jail for the same amount of time!"

"I'm with that!" says Bartman.

"You know what I'm sayin'?" asks the hippie.

"Fuck! I swear!"

"Now, now, boys, boys," says the pope, batting his eyelashes, an aging coquette with a curly gray beard. "This is the sacrament we're talking about Please. . . . Respect. *Ah-ha-ha-HA!*"

The pope is at home now, his upper East Side studio, a second-floor walk-up. He's not feeling too well, lying shirtless on his unmade bed amid a clutter of plants and clothes and videos with titles like *Hot Rocks II*, his scars and bullet wounds looking pink and ropy amid the forest of fine graying hairs covering his torso.

Over in the kitchen, a friend of the pope's is scouring the oven. The sink is filled with dishes. A flesh-colored marital aid pokes up out of the soapsuds. The friend has just been released after twenty years in prison. He doesn't want his name mentioned, but he intimates that he had something to do with an art heist and a murder at a big museum in New York City. He met the pope in prison. All the Jewish guys in there knew each other. He looked out for the pope. They also took ceramics together. The pope is letting him crash in a basement apartment while he looks for a job in his old field, public relations.

It is time now for a papal audience. Why? the pope is asked. Why is he setting up business anew? Why is he letting a reporter see all this? Does he have to have an 800 number? Couldn't he just chill like the other eleven delivery services in Manhattan, do a thriving underground business? Perhaps Howard Stern is right. Is he begging to go to jail?

"I'm the bringer of wisdom and truth," explains Mickey the Pope. "I'm doing what's right. I'm the kind of person, you're not gonna intimidate me. Marijuana is the saving plant. It should be legal. People want it that way. The voice of the people is the voice of God in a democracy. If you get enough people into it, the politicians have to listen. I think what we should do is, sort of set up our own society and do our own thing. Let all the others go do what they will. We're doing what's right and proper and screw 'em, our little group should live better than they do. We should win by example."

With that the tape recorder clicks off. The pope takes a long slow drink from a gallon jug of water, then grins, bats his lashes. "So how'd I do, toots?" he asks. "This is serious. I don't want to go to jail. I really don't want to go to jail."

Now it is Mickey the Pope's birthday, the day before the winter solstice, the last shortening day on the calendar of the seasons. There's a knock at the church door, and Mickey opens up and finds two undercover cops. One wears a pompadour and a trench coat The other carries a pad.

"Oh! Internal Affairs!" giggles Mickey the Pope, remembering the appointment he'd scheduled. "I called you, didn't I?"

"Yes, sir," says the cop with the pad. He regards Mickey for a moment, beak nosed, red faced, wearing his marijuana bonnet. The cop rolls his eyes to the heavens. "Mind if we come in?"

"Of course, toots," rasps the pope, bowing, gesturing, showing the guests to some chairs.

"So what happened?" asks the cop with the pad.

"Well, when I was busted, there was this big media thing, you know, and John J. Hill said there were seven pounds confiscated in the raid."

"John J. Hill?" asks the pad.

"Yeah, he's an assistant chief."

"Oh! Chief Hill!" exclaims the pompadour, leaning forward.

"He said there were seven pounds?" asks the pad.

"Right there on the news," says Mickey.

"Oh," says the pompadour.

"So how many pounds were there?" asks the pad.

"Close to five."

"So, close to five pounds were taken into evidence by the police?"

"Right," says the pope.

"So, what's the problem?" asks the pompadour.

"Well, I was only indicted for two and one half pounds."

"So what's the problem?" asks the pad.

"See," says the pope, grinning. "Two and one half pounds are missing! Cops shouldn't be stealing the evidence. I mean, I don't steal. I don't jump turnstiles, none of that shit. I really don't. I live the pure life. I don't take from nobody, and that's the truth."

"I see," says the pompadour.

"The thing is, if the cops want pot, they should have to buy it like everyone else," says the pope. "If you're not gonna charge me for it, I want it back. After all, it's the sacrament. This is the church. The marijuana church. The Church of Realized Fantasies."

(1991)

The Corruption of Ed O'Brien

He was the highest-ranking DEA agent ever arrested for dealing drugs. Was it simple greed or was it inevitable? A look at the early days of the drug war.

A man code-named Jack eases a white Cadillac Seville into the driveway of the airport Hilton. He brakes, shifts to park, reaches beneath his shirt, switches on a tape recorder. "Two a.m., 28 July, Boston," he says into the humid darkness. "Meeting with Ed O'Brien."

Jack sees Ed coming through the glass doors, taps the horn lightly three times. Ed acknowledges the signal, smooths his tie, sets a course for the car. He carries a man's leather purse with a .22 derringer inside. Strapped to his ankle is his service revolver, a .38. He is muscular, round-faced, not unhandsome, a black-Irish fireplug wearing a Rolex and an expensive suit.

"Holy shit! I'm back in this gaw-damn automobile," says Ed, sliding across the seat, his voice a nervous, high-pitched Boston brogue.

They have a good laugh and Jack reaches into his breast pocket, pulls out an envelope. "Here," he says, handing it over. "There's the other twelve-five. Use it in good health. Everything went fine, beautiful, smooth. Oh—and lemme tell you. Before Bill went to sleep, we had a couple of minutes to talk. I liked the idea that you gave him. You know, about swapping the car?"

"Yeah. I didn't want to drive this thing up the New Jersey Turnpike," says Ed. "That's the gauntlet. You had three of the five reasons to pull somebody over with this machine."

"Really?" asks Jack. He thinks a moment. "You know, that's why I look to your input. Bill said to me, 'We got the right guy in Ed.'"

"This car here was a drawback," says Ed. "For one thing, it was a rental, and you pulled the Dollar Rent-a-Car sticker off. And you left the residue from the old sticker on there. And it's a Y plate; Z and Y are both rental plates. So, if I were a cop on the New Jersey Turnpike, and I saw this car— there's enough probable cause to pull this vehicle over for a search."

"Well," says Jack. "I appreciate the fact that you were driving."

"I didn't mind. Say Bill was driving and we were stopped. If I had to get out of the car from the passenger side and come around and talk to the cop, it looks even worse. Whereas if I'm on the driver's side—"

"You just flash the badge and that's it," says Jack.

"Yeah, ha-ha," says Ed O'Brien, laughing nervously.

They called him Ed the Fed, an eighteen-year veteran of the Drug Enforcement Administration (DEA). Fluent in Russian and French, he had served in New York, Paris, Nice; he'd even gotten a small piece of the infamous French Connection case, pinching a water glass with a suspect's fingerprints from a table in a restaurant. Then, in the early years of the current Drug War, Ed was transferred to Springfield, Massachusetts, to set up a new bureau. He came in with both barrels blazing, the high-profile agent in charge. He was respected and reviled in Springfield, often by the same people, but he was good at his job. He had a mind like a steel trap. He was dogged and relentless. And when he came up behind you at the bar at Tilly's or Lucky Pierre's and patted you on the back and said hello, your spine straightened and the hairs on your neck tingled. He made you feel guilty, even if you weren't. In 1984, he was commended by Governor Michael Dukakis for breaking up one of the largest coke rings in the Northeast.

Now, on a summer night in 1989, he is in a Cadillac in a hotel parking lot with one of the bad guys, a person he thinks is a bad guy anyway, and in his lap is an inch-thick envelope of hundred-dollar bills, his cut of a drug deal.

Maybe it began with Camille, his secretary. Ed's divorce from Claire had been tough. They'd been together since Assumption College, and had four daughters. Child support alone was running him almost two grand a month. Then there was Jamie Short, a fast talker and bunco artist with rotten teeth and a taste for cocaine. Why had Ed gone in on a car business with him? And there was the $147,000 in cash that Ed had taken from the bureau, the personal loans, the defaults on the personal loans, the foreclosure on his second home. And the family business, down on Cape Cod. It was hurting too.

In the spring of 1989, Ed had been looking for another loan, this one to help finance the purchase of a building on the Cape. There were facilities for a restaurant, and enough rental space to carry the load on the note. Jamie, learning of Ed's need, told him about Jack. Jack was rich, Jamie said. He was looking to invest in property, Jamie said. How could Ed have known the truth?

On June 20, Ed and Jamie flew to Miami for the introduction. Jack picked them up in a white Rolls-Royce; they went to Bennigan's, near the airport, for drinks. Ed said he needed money for a real-estate deal. Jack said he wasn't interested, and the subject died. Then Jack broached a now topic. As well as being a businessman, he said, he also dealt in cocaine. If Ed wanted to join the team, he could. Ed was surprised that Jack was so bold about his business. Jack had to have known that Ed was a DEA man. Jamie told everyone. He had a Fed in his pocket. It was great leverage. The three men talked some more, then went back to the airport. Ed told Jack to call his brother John if he was interested in financing a business.

And so it happened that Jack called John and told him that "the wedding was on." The morning of July 25, Ed got on a plane. He was supposed to go to West Palm Beach, but there was someone he knew from work on the flight, so he went to Fort Lauderdale instead. Once there, he called Jack's beeper. Jack was angry. Now plans were delayed. Schedules were blown. I'll be there, Jack told Ed. Wait.

Outside the Embassy Suites Hotel, near the Fort Lauderdale airport, things didn't seem right. Ed thought he was being shadowed. He noted suspicious-looking characters parked nearby in a Jaguar. He thought, Maybe Jamie and this fuck are setting me up.

Finally, after Ed watched two other drug deals go down outside the hotel, Jack showed up in the Rolls. With him was Bill, who'd be riding shotgun on the trip north. The three men first drove south to Hollywood, where the white Seville was waiting in a parking lot. Inside the trunk were twenty-five one-kilogram bricks, six of which were cocaine, nineteen of which were a harmless white powder that looked like cocaine. For his role as courier, Ed was to collect $1,000 a key, half up front, half after delivery. Twenty-five thousand for a few hours work. His annual salary was $59,541.

Now, thirty-six hours later, the coke has been transported, the money has changed hands. Jack and Ed sit together in the Seville, discussing times and dates. Next trip, they decide, Ed will fly and avoid the Jersey Turnpike altogether. They talk baggage.

"Canvas or nylon?" asks Jack.

"No, no, no. I'm talking about the kind of suitcase that photographers use."

"Those heavy metal ones?"

"Yeah, aluminum. I've taken twenty-five kilos of evidence in one of those."

"And you can put them under the seat? I don't want no fuckin' checked luggage," says Jack.

"I can put them overhead."

"Overhead? Okay. Are you gonna put some kind of label on it?"

"I don't have to put the label on it. I can just fuckin' finagle it. The last time I came up, in fact the first time I met you, I had to finagle putting two machine guns into boxes. I put them into a cardboard box and I walked on the plane. I could have had 400 pounds of coke in those fuckin' boxes. And I just put them up front with the captain. It's amazing that the obvious is never questioned."

"No shit," says Jack.

"Yeah," says Ed. "I could do a dry run for you, just to let you see how I go through—"

"No, Ed. Again, whatever you feel comfortable with. Let's face it. I'm buying your expertise."

"Right," says Ed.

Three weeks later, Edward Kevin O'Brien, 44, supervisory special agent for the Drug Enforcement Administration, would be arrested at Logan Airport with two aluminum suitcases. Inside were twenty-eight kilos of white powder, all of it real cocaine. O'Brien, the highest-ranking federal agent ever to be arrested for dealing in drugs, faces up to forty years in prison and $4 million in fines.

The sting, according to Boston bureau chief John J. Coleman, was "a closed loop." The dealer, Jack, and his helper, Bill, were recruited and paid by the DEA, as was Jamie Short. The coke in the deal was DEA coke. The money was DEA money. The plan was the agency's, too. "No expense was spared," said a federal source.

The DEA refuses to comment on Ed O'Brien's arrest, his character or on any of the cases he worked on during his eighteen-year career. Ed O'Brien has also refused comment. He is awaiting trial, confined to his home in Herndon, Virginia. An electronic monitoring device is strapped around his ankle. Should he wander more than 150 feet from a central telephone in his house, an alarm will sound in an office in Alexandria and U.S. marshals will be dispatched.

At a time when the Drug War has become a lead item on the nation's political agenda, the case of Ed O'Brien is particularly disturbing. Also awaiting trial on drug charges, in courts in Los Angeles and Miami, are six other DEA agents, all members of an elite corps that numbers only 2,800 worldwide. In 1988, the DEA reported a 176 percent increase in misconduct cases investigated by the agency's office of internal affairs.

Though corruption within the criminal-justice system is an old theme, the DEA has long been considered special and beyond reproach, sort of the Green Berets of law enforcement. Today, however, faced with low salaries, limited resources, increased public scrutiny and the frustration of having to play by the rules when their opponents do not, the pressures on DEA agents are greater than ever before. The temptations are many, as are the questions about Ed O'Brien. Did he step across the line, or was he pushed?

Here was Ed O'Brien, a Boston Irish Catholic of humble means, with a good education and high moral principles, engaged in the situational ethics of the Drug War. In the simplest, most fundamental sense, Ed fought a battle daily between good and evil, between duty and temptation. DEA agents are among the most freewheeling of federal operatives. They have latitude. They make judgments in the field. They cover their own tails. Ed was juggling cases and informants, dealing with criminals and sociopaths and liars, talking their talk, walking their walk, trading some of his soul for some of theirs. He planned stings, which are really just elaborate crimes perpetrated by the government, and his foot soldiers were convicted criminals as often as they were cops. Ed, a man who had always seen things as black or white, was dealing in very gray areas. The men he busted lived in mansions on mountaintops. They drove, wore and ate the best. Hundreds of thousands of dollars' worth of cash and drugs passed through Ed's hands on a weekly basis, as did his paycheck for $1,146, signed by Uncle Sam. After eighteen years of dealing with criminals, maybe you become one too.

Growing up in Somerville, Massachusetts, outside of Cambridge, O'Brien went by his middle name, Kevin. He was the eldest of six boys, the sons of a painting-and-drywalling contractor and his religious wife.

It was a close-knit, working-class, bedrock Irish family. All the boys were dark, compact and muscular, with thick hair, wide jaws and innocent, twinkling eyes. Among them were the constant intrigues, combats and shiftings of allegiance; the subtle, changing mixture of love and hate, loyalty and betrayal that makes a large brood so complex. They were altar boys. They did fairly well in Catholic school. They played hockey, basketball and musical instruments. They never welcomed a fight, but they never ran away from one either. As a group, they liked fast cars, pretty girls, nice things. As individuals, each had his own style.

Ed was the eldest by six years. The rest of the boys—John, Eugene, Thomas, Paul and Michael—followed one another at two-year intervals. Ed was the brother on a pedestal, an enigma. When Ed left for college, the rest of the family moved to the Cape. Ed was 17, John was 11 and Michael, the youngest, was 3.

The brothers saw Ed as being "straighter than hell," says one of them, and later, in the Seventies, when they were old enough to question, the younger O'Briens wondered why anyone would want to bust people for a living. Yet, their feelings about Ed were a bundle of contradictions. They loved him, but they didn't like what he did. They respected him, but they didn't trust him. Still, they'd do anything he asked. For the O'Briens, it seemed, blood was thicker than common sense.

Ed was successful, smart, talented. "He could have been a concert pianist. He could have been an architect. He could have been a lot of things," says one brother. At the same time, Ed was aloof, a bit frightening. He never discussed his own life with his brothers, but he was "quick to bad-mouth you if he thought you did something wrong," says a brother, who spoke at length on the condition that he not be identified. A friend of the family's remembers Ed, the young DEA man, telling the boys stories of French gangsters, beautiful women, automatic weapons, loads of hashish trucked across the Middle East. Once, Ed came downstairs, where the boys were hanging out with some friends, and whipped out his .38 from his shoulder holster. He pointed the gun around, then laughed.

"I was pretty much in awe of him," remembers the friend.

Another old friend of the O'Briens' remembers Ed's brother John as the "caveman" of the family. Quick to holler, quick to fight, he was the strongest. Once, says another friend, when he was a kid, John arranged to have his grandmother's purse stolen. His accomplices found $15. John split the money with them and took the purse. Hidden inside was another $225. He kept that for himself.

Brother Eugene was the funny one. Thomas was the quiet one. Paul was the eclectic: a bartender, a singer in a rock band, a graduate of the University of Hawaii. Michael, the baby, was a basketball star.

Says the friend: "There are people you think are your friends, but when it comes right down to it, they aren't. When the O'Briens are your friends, they'll do whatever's necessary. They'll always stand up for you. They're good people."

Ed graduated from Matignon, a Catholic high school in Cambridge, in 1962, and went on to Assumption College, seventy miles away, outside of Worcester. After a year of classes and ROTC, he joined the navy, serving six years in naval intelligence during the Vietnam War.

Ed returned to Assumption after he was mustered out of the service, to pursue degrees in political and natural science. While there, he won honors for his study of Russian, and married Claire Teresa Smith, a pretty, dark-haired social worker.

In the Sixties, Assumption was a small Catholic college with no national reputation, but among its students and faculty there was a certain spirit, a love of ideas and learning. The students were motivated, bright locals from parochial-school backgrounds who wanted to become professionals but didn't want to leave home for such bigger-name Catholic schools as Notre Dame or Georgetown.

The school was run by a French order, and the education was distinctly European in flavor. At 24, Ed was a serious student. He gravitated toward the professors rather than his classmates.

Patrick Powers, a professor of political philosophy at Assumption, was his teacher, adviser and friend. He remembers that Ed "wasn't the best of students in an academic sense. Not that he wasn't bright, thoughtful, sharp, disciplined. But the important thing was to go out and do it. He was a man of action.

"Ed believed in morality," Powers says, "and I don't mean in any narrow Catholic sense. I mean upright and moral. He had a certain notion of nobility, right and wrong, justice. Something of the hero on the white steed. He didn't articulate all that, but it was in his demeanor. There was a quiet-ness to his speech, but he wasn't shy. He was serious, high-minded. He always took the high road in an argument. He cared about ideas."

Though he went to college and served in the military during the Sixties, Ed was not a child of those times. He was of the mold of the post–World War II American man, the generation that wore ties to high school and had their hair trimmed once a week. Like many of his contemporaries, says Powers, "Ed wasn't a narrow-minded conservative. He wasn't angry at the times. He just wasn't really a part of them."

Powers was struck by Ed's appreciation of the good things in life. "He was a man of taste. I can picture vividly the last time I saw him. He had just mar-ried Claire and I was seeing them off at Kennedy Airport. They were leaving for France. He was wearing a long camel's-hair coat. He was impeccably groomed and tailored. It was a taste. He was not a show-off. It was what was proper. I would look for its roots in his background. The oldest boy in a family that's making its way up, Ed could see what his next step was. There was a combination within him: There was a certain boyish innocence, a sense of do-goodism. But he was also calculating how to survive in life."

• • •

After college, Ed joined the Bureau of Narcotics and Dangerous Drugs, the precursor to the DEA. His first posting was to New York City in 1972; by the late Seventies, he was put in charge of the DEA office in Nice, France, making him a member of a small, elite group of overseas agents. In Nice, Ed helped mop up the infamous *French Connection* heroin case. He also saw duty all over Europe and in the Middle East. He is remembered by one who knew him there as "intelligent, jovial and modest."

Ed's posting to Springfield, Massachusetts, population 152,000, in 1980, as a lone operative attached to the Hartford office, coincided with the early rumblings of the Drug War. Nancy Reagan was soon to take up her "Just Say No" campaign and Springfield was a perfect base camp for the years of combat to come. In the early Eighties, the city—birthplace of basketball, the Springfield rifle and the monkey wrench—was a decaying industrial center with an Irish government, an Italian Mob and a large, multiracial underclass. Its proximity to New York City, Albany, Boston, Hartford and Montreal made it a perfect hub for domestic and international drug traffic.

A federal-district-court seat had recently been established in Springfield, and part of the reason Ed was sent there was to fill the court docket. "It was dead out here," says an attorney who clerked for Springfield's first federal judge. "You'd get these welfare-check frauds, or some kid from U. Mass. who got caught with a bag of dope. It was just crap stuff. They weren't making big cases out here."

Ed started from the bottom, working with state and local police, building a network of informants by arresting small-time users carrying $10 or $20 bags of drugs. He stairstepped to mid-level dealers and from there to the big boys. The locals saw Ed as a treasure trove. While the state police and Springfield narcotics detectives had only hundreds of dollars with which to make drug buys and pay informants, Ed had access to federal intelligence, federal money, federal expertise. And he was sharing it.

"Here was this big boy on the block coming in, giving us thousands of dollars," says a police official who worked with Ed. "They had computers, automobiles. The federal seizure statutes gave us a lot more latitude than the state, plus we got a share of the seizures. Eddie was kind of like a conductor. He could direct all of us into the places we wanted to be to form successful cases."

Ed had dozens of informants, and always had four or five cases going at once. "A lot of times our investigations paralleled," says a local narcotics officer. "I'd say a name and he'd come up with names, dates, places. It was like talking to a computer."

"He had perseverance," says a former U.S. attorney. "He put together some of the best cases I have ever seen. These were some of the most involved conspiracies in Western Massachusetts. He knew the details that had to be accumulated to take the case from the street and ram it home in the courtroom. Things were documented, corroborated, double corroborated. He was right on the fuckin' money all the time."

In court, Ed was fast on his feet. "He thought it was good if you pointed out to the jurors that he had worked on the *French Connection* case and had been stationed on the French Riviera," says another former U.S. attorney. "He fancied himself as someone who, on an intellectual level, could joust with any attorney, and he would very much enjoy putting in the occasional zinger if a lawyer gave him too much of an opening. He really enjoyed sticking in the knife."

By 1982, the DEA had officially set up the bureau in Springfield with Ed in charge. "All of a sudden there was Eddie O'Brien," says the former court clerk, "and all of a sudden there was a whirlwind of activity. Cases were being made left and right. They seemed to be getting more and more significant. He was good for me and a lot of other lawyers. Business was better. Bigger. Bigger cases, bigger fees."

Springfield was a small town, and Ed was everywhere. He worked the bars and restaurants in Springfield's downtown, often bringing his striking, married secretary, Camille, with him. He wore impeccable clothes, carried a leather purse with the .22 inside, drank white wine sparingly. He patted shoulders, shook hands, told stories. He dropped names and thinly veiled threats.

Ed even gave interviews to the press, something the DEA rarely does. Late in 1982, in an article in a local newspaper, he trumpeted that "the pillars of the community" of Springfield were under investigation for using drugs. Doctors, lawyers, politicians—no one was above suspicion.

"They all know I am coming," he told Springfield's *Valley Advocate*. "I have interviewed quite a few of them anyway. They know I know about them. It is now a *fait accompli*."

Needless to say, the pillars of the community were not pleased. "It became apparent after a while that much of this whirlwind around him was coming from his own mouth," says an attorney. "It became clear that this was part of his MO, just to shake the place up, let them know he was here. He came in, made a big bang. The new sheriff in town. Ed O'Brien, the federal posse. He was really driving some people wacky. He had people really upset, really paranoid."

"In his mind, everybody was evil," says another Springfield lawyer. "People who used drugs, people who sold drugs, lawyers who represented them. Even people who were sort of left-wing, politically. People in the peace movement. People in politics. People who had nothing to do with drugs. He was very tense, very puffed up, very pumped up. I have a memory of a glazed look, a guy whose attention levels were so high that he was kind of out of it."

"The DEA guys, O'Brien, they were always out of control," says one Springfield attorney. "Clients were hurled around the rooms. Their heads were banged on radiators. The DEA would bust a house and they would write on the walls, on the furniture. I had this one case where they wrote 'COCAINE SUCKS' on the walls. They tore this place apart. They had it all down to a science. For example, a picture on a wall could contain cocaine, so you had to slice it. I compare them to the Tontons Macoutes in Haiti.

"I never had a drug case, except minor local ones, in which a client didn't complain about something missing. Whether it be a camera, an antique knife, money or drugs. You know, ten kilos are busted, but only eight show up in evidence," says the attorney.

Soon, informants began complaining that Ed wasn't paying the DEA stipends they had been promised. A federal judge chided Ed for sending one informant to a meeting between several attorneys and their clients. A federal appeals court reprimanded him for failing to follow proper procedure in a case in which he seized the entire contents of a man's home, including his toothbrush, on the grounds that the man was a drug dealer.

Ed began having problems with state and local law-enforcement officials, as well. They complained that he was stealing their informants, breaking promises of deals. He also failed to pay the overtime due to local police who worked on federal cases. One former district attorney remembered Ed as a disruptive influence. "We wouldn't deal with him," he has said.

"There's always a little rivalry between the Feds and the locals, and Eddie, unfortunately, was not gifted with a real personable, cop-buddy-buddy-type personality," says a former prosecutor who was close to him. "Eddie didn't fit in. Those guys have a tight brotherhood. You'd give your life for the next guy. You have a tragic sense that no one understands what you're doing, that no one understands the pressures. With them, when you're not with the guys, you're really not with the guys. Eddie just didn't fit in."

"With narcotics, you go out and you dig up; you are what you do," says a narcotics detective who worked with Ed. "If you're a successful investigator, you make your own name, you make your own bones in the business. Ed was always looking for the next target. A case better than the last one, more newsworthy than the last one. He was a very aggressive, competitive guy."

"He became Machiavellian," says a former colleague. "He burned a lot of people."

Meanwhile, Ed had begun what a neighbor called "a very curious relationship with his secretary." Camille McGail—a police officer's wife—was dark, attractive, well-dressed, sophisticated beyond her station. "They were always together. Every day for lunch. After work, having a drink," says the neighbor. "It was open and obvious, to the point where people began to look and say 'What the hell is going on?' It was almost like he didn't care what people thought. It struck me as bizarre. If you're going to carry on an affair with your secretary, you try to be discreet, especially in a small town. This is not midtown Manhattan."

While Ed was out all hours of the day and night—chasing gangsters, meeting informants, trysting with Camille—his wife, Claire, was home with their four daughters in leafy Forest Park, a few miles from downtown Springfield. In a brief interview, Claire says that during that time she was mainly trying "to keep up appearances, to live with the sacrifices that had to be made for 'the company.' He was a company man. Everything was for the DEA. I had to keep this idea alive that Daddy was always gone because he was a very important man working for the government."

Says a neighbor who lives on the next block: "His youngest girls didn't even know who their daddy was."

In September 1985, Claire and Ed separated. In their divorce agreement, Ed was ordered to pay $450 per week in child support, a monthly car payment of $170, plus all his daughters' medical and dental bills. He was also ordered to pay off a $9,000 home-equity loan on the Forest Park house, and to sign ownership over to Claire. All this on his annual pretax income of $59,541.

To the people in Springfield who knew Ed O'Brien, 1985 was the year things appeared to fall apart. Not that he told them anything. A U.S. attorney with whom Ed worked every day had no idea that he'd gotten separated. Ed's brothers heard about the split from their mother. Ed shared his secrets with no one, but people knew something was up. For five years, he'd been living not one double life, but several. Husband and lover. DEA bureau chief and undercover cop. Crusader for justice and denizen of the underbelly.

"I really think he started burning out," says a detective Ed used to work with. "I noticed things like involuntary twitches in his face."

As time went by, Ed was less and less visible in Springfield.. He began spending more time in Sandwich, Massachusetts, on the upper end of the Cape, where his brothers now lived. "My brother Ed figured he wasn't going to make too many friends in Springfield," says one of the O'Briens. "I think he eventually wanted to retire on the Cape."

Besides Ed, the only O'Brien boy to finish college was Paul, the eclectic, and neither Paul nor the rest of the brothers displayed any desire to become professionals. John and Eugene, like their father, did painting and dry-walling, and spent winters working in Florida. Paul bartended. The other brothers worked, as they had on and off for fourteen years, for the Ice Man, an ice-making-and-delivery company in Hyannis.

In 1986, soon after his separation from Claire, Ed, along with Paul, Thomas and Michael, opened Cape Cod Ice. The brothers controlled 60 percent of the company. A lawyer and a businessman owned the other 40 percent.

Now the intense focus that Ed had trained on his job seemed to turn toward enterprise. Between March 1987 and August 1988, Ed would borrow more than $140,000, most of it in short-term loans from acquaintances in and around Sandwich. Also within that period, according to the confession Ed made upon his arrest, he stole at least $147,000 from the DEA bureau in Springfield, most of which he says he replaced. But according to court tes-timony, the DEA, despite the internal audit they conducted, has no idea how much money was stolen or returned. Ed would tell DEA agents that he put the stolen money into the ice business to help cover the more than $230,000 that he claims his brother John had skimmed. Brother Paul would tell agents that Ed had put some money into the business, but nowhere near $147,000. John has said he worked eighteen hours a day for three years at the ice plant, that he never stole anything.

Of all Ed's financial dealings, one—a loan for $50,000 from a restaurant chef named Robert Wayne Oulette—would prove the most damaging. It was arranged by Jamie Short.

John O'Brien was the first in the family to meet Jamie Short. It was the winter of 1987, at the Saltwater Cafe, a bar in Clearwater, Florida. Jamie was originally from Quincy, between Boston and Cape Cod, and he had a thick

Beantown brogue. It was the accent that brought them together, two Boston boys far from home.

John O'Brien, like many seasonal workers from the Cape, was in Clearwater trying to get things going. He was doing a little painting and drywalling. For a time, the balding, husky 37-year-old escorted rich older women on Caribbean cruises. One woman bought him $35,000 worth of clothes, John has claimed. Later that year, however, John would be arrested and jailed for twenty-one days on a bad-check charge in Pinellas County, Florida. According to court testimony, John had bad-check charges and default warrants in Florida and Boston going back to 1982. He had, according to a court magistrate, "the lousiest record I have ever seen in showing up for court." When Ed was arrested, he would tell the DEA that his brother John was a "gigolo," "a bail jumper" and "a con man."

Late in 1987, Jamie and John met again, this time in Fort Lauderdale, at a bar called Shooters. John was there on vacation with his brothers, including Ed.

According to court testimony, James Carlton Short, 36, used three different names and lived in seven different cities between 1986 and 1989. He'd worked the used-car market up and down the East Coast since his youth; he started out doing bodywork and mechanics and moved on to sales. The buying and selling of used autos has traditionally provided a fine, shady oasis for all sorts of scams, and Jamie Short, by all accounts, was perfect for the business. With his longish, silky black hair, he was a good-looking man, until he smiled. Then you could see his rotten teeth.

Jamie, according to court testimony, had a penchant for "crimes committed by design and trickery." Court records show arrests dating back to 1973, in Massachusetts and Florida, for larceny, obtaining a motor vehicle with a worthless check, larceny by fraudulent check, attempted larceny of a motorboat, possessing stolen property and falsifying a title. Court records also show that, in Boston, Short romanced a waitress long enough to steal $5,000 from her checking account, and a tax-refund check. In Syracuse, New York, he ran up $40,000 on charge cards belonging to a woman named Regina Durose, leaving her bankrupt—and with child. In Pinellas County, Florida, working under the aegis of James Short Enterprises, he sold cars with phony titles, and sold titles to cars that no longer existed.

"My brother Ed wasn't a good judge of character," says one of the O'Briens. "You could impress him if you were a good salesman. After he met Jamie, I told him, I said, 'Ed, don't have anything to do with this dirt ball.'

But the next thing I hear, Jamie's coming to Cape Cod. He talked Ed into financing a car dealership with him."

Apparently, Jamie's first order of business with Ed involved his vendetta with a Florida drug dealer named Patrick Perkins. Jamie was currently enmeshed in a dispute with Perkins over a speedboat they had built. According to court testimony, Ed referred Jamie to special investigator Robert Allen, of the Boston DEA office. Working for a DEA stipend that would amount to $23,000, Jamie Short arranged to buy cocaine from Perkins. Upon making the buy, according to court testimony, Jamie "took it upon himself . . . to open the package of cocaine and spill some out" for himself, before delivering the package to the DEA.

Jamie relocated to Sandwich in early 1988, with Ed picking up the tab for his move. They incorporated a company called O'B II (O'B I was the parent company for Cape Cod Ice); James Short was the president, Ed and Paul O'Brien were the vice-presidents and the treasurer was Judith Sorenti, John O'Brien's girlfriend. It's unclear why Ed went into business with Jamie. As a DEA man, he had access to Jamie's arrest record. He had to have known it was against DEA regulations for an agent to do outside business with an informant.

Nevertheless, Jamie and Ed set about procuring high-end used cars: Jaguars, Mercedeses, Porsches. Witnesses estimate that the pair had on hand as much as $200,000 worth of cars at any given time, most of them financed by Ed's loans.

Once in Massachusetts, Jamie began making contacts of his own. As the winter of 1988 progressed, the bay-side car lot became a hangout. Business didn't begin until around eleven each morning, and there was, according to witnesses, constant drinking and drug use. Along the way, Jamie made friends with a convicted drug dealer named Cliff Crowley. Crowley and his wife owned a bar in sleepy Sandwich called Pilots Landing. The party shifted back and forth between the dealership, Pilots and Jamie's apartment as the days and nights wore on. There were always girls and drugs on the scene.

The testimony conflicts as to whether Ed was ever around when the drugs were. One of Ed's brothers says Jamie would never do any drugs in Ed's presence. While some say that Ed and Jamie spent a lot of time together, and that they frequently drove to Boston for dinner, no one interviewed has alleged that Ed did drugs himself.

One man who was on the fringe of this party group remembers car-buying trips with Jamie. Four or five men would pile into a car, bound for a wholesale lot in Boston or Springfield, drinking and smoking joints and doing lines along the way. "We'd get to the car lot and Jamie would just say 'I'll take this one and this one and this one.' He wouldn't even start the cars," says the friend. "One time, my nephew gets in this car. It had no brakes. None. We left that one there. Another time, I drove a truck back and the thing was blowing oil. He was *paying* for these."

Gradually, Jamie Short became entangled with the O'Brien family. He told people he was a shareholder in Cape Cod Ice. The checks for the car business said "O'B II." Consequently, when customers had problems with Jamie, they came to the O'Briens.

As a car salesman, says one of the O'Briens, "Jamie was brutal." According to court testimony, Jamie sold the same car to different people more than once. One time, after one of the lot's cars had been accidentally smashed beyond use, Jamie went to Falmouth National Bank and obtained a $5,000 loan, using the car as collateral. According to a witness, the dealership was once picketed by angry customers.

In the late spring of 1988, Jamie was having a few drinks with a friend of his, Robert Wayne Oulette, who also split his time between the Cape and Florida. Oulette happened to mention that he had recently received an insurance settlement for a back injury.

Remembers Oulette, "Jamie says, 'You know, Ed needs a loan. You could make five grand!' So me and Jamie went across the street and met Ed. He seemed all right. Very straight-faced, very serious. He tells me he's having this financial difficulty, a divorce, and blah-blah-blah, and he said, 'You think you can lend me that?' And I said, 'Yeah, I think I can arrange it.' "

Later, Oulette says, it came out that Ed wanted the money to buy a building in Bourne, a nearby town. There was a restaurant, some office space and room in the back for a company John wanted to start, called Cape Cod Chowder. Oulette, a chef, was interested in the idea. He had contacts with some men with a fishing boat, and recipes for a whole line of frozen foods.

The $50,000 loan was made by cashier's check. It was secured with shares of the ice-plant business and was to be repaid, with $5,000 interest, in ninety days.

Meanwhile, in May of 1988, the DEA transferred Ed to Washington, D.C., where he was made staff coordinator of the office that oversees operations in Europe and the Middle East. Though it is possible that Ed's activities in Springfield and his erratic behavior had something to do with his reassignment, it is unlikely. As an administrator in Washington, Ed had access to information about major investigations inside the United States and around the world. If the DEA was suspicious, they probably wouldn't have put him there.

Ed and Camille, along with her two children from a previous marriage, moved to the Virginia suburbs of Washington. They purchased a house, putting the deed in her name, and then they were married.

Back on the Cape, with Ed far away, things were beginning to spiral out of control. Jamie was seen riding around Sandwich one night with two girls and a stash of cocaine in a Lincoln Town Car that Ed had bought in order to start a limousine service. And, as if the pickets and complaints weren't troublesome enough, people began suing the officers of O'B II for restitution for Jamie's bogus sales and broken leases (according to the O'Briens, Jamie let rents and telephone and utility bills, to the tune of $40,000, go unpaid). And according to court records, Jamie charged about $4,500 on Ed's credit cards, and he bought a fur coat for his girlfriend with a card belonging to Michael O'Brien.

Another matter involving Jamie remains murky. According to one of the O'Brien brothers, Jamie may also have been involved in a car business with another DEA agent, Robert Allen, the one he had worked with on the Perkins case. In a recording of a phone conversation between Jamie and John, submitted into evidence by Ed's attorneys, there is mention of the sale of a car, and a payment, by check, of $6,500 to Allen. When asked about Allen's dealings with Short, a spokesman for the DEA's internal-affairs division, the Office of Professional Responsibility, said, "The whole matter of O'Brien and anybody else that was involved in the situation is still open. We're looking at everything that has come up in that investigation." Jamie Short refuses to comment on Allen.

Short claims that the O'Briens cheated him. "Ed's a thief," says Jamie. "He can talk you out of anything you have. I was paying him $300 a week as an officer of the corporation, and I was putting my salary back in the business. I was sending cars down to him in Virginia and he was selling them there, but I never got a penny from any car he ever sold down there. I had 51 percent of the place, and they sold it out from underneath me. They have a license to steal."

In the early fall of 1988, Jamie Short skipped town.

On November 26, Ed's IOU to Oulette came due. When the check didn't arrive in the mail, Oulette called Ed at home in Virginia. "A man answers the phone," says Oulette, "and it's Camille's ex-husband. He's watching the kids. Ed and Camille had gone to Europe for three weeks. I knew that was it."

Oulette waited for three weeks, then began calling Ed repeatedly at his office. Ed would stammer and tell him he'd call right back, but he never did. Oulette saw only one course of action.

"I called his boss. I told him all about Ed and Jamie. I told him all about the loan. I wanted to see the motherfucker hang!"

And so it was that the DEA learned about Ed's financial problems, and about his business with Jamie Short. The agency contacted Jamie and put him on the payroll of the Office of Professional Responsibility. Ed was transferred again. This time, he was assigned to research a history of the organization and to set up a DEA museum near Washington. By all accounts, Ed was not suspicious about the transfer.

By this time, however, there was no doubt in anyone's mind that Ed O'Brien had gone off the deep end. The cases, the informants, the netherworld. The lawyers, the police, the pillars of the community. The divorce, his four little girls, the remarriage. The stolen money, the loans, the foreclosures. He told one woman at the time that he was ready "to bite the bullet," according to court testimony.

"He had what I call a standing meltdown. He had an emotional breakdown on the job," says Henry Rigali, a friend of Ed's and a former U.S. attorney. "It's never a simple thing. It's like the layers of an onion. And with every deeper layer, there's a deeper reason, and who knows what you find at the core. If it happened to you or me, we'd be in straitjackets. But Eddie is a fucking bull of a guy. He could go through it and keep walking around."

The investigation continued for two or three months. Then, according to court testimony, Jamie suddenly remembered something. A while before, he couldn't specify exactly when, Jamie had been at the home of a used-car dealer in Springfield when Ed arrived, driving a Rolls-Royce. In the trunk of the Rolls, Jamie recalled, was a suitcase with three kilos of cocaine inside. Or maybe it was thirty kilos. Jamie wasn't sure which.

Nevertheless, with Jamie's information, the DEA felt it had what it needed to engineer a sting—proof that Ed was predisposed to dealing in drugs. The plan was formed.

Jamie introduced Ed to Jack, a rich man looking to invest in real estate, and Jack declined the business offer, but gave Ed a job as a courier. On July 27, Ed, along with the informant code-named Bill, drove the first load from Florida to Boston—six kilos of cocaine and nineteen kilos of powder—for a fee of $25,000. On August 14, after changing flights and arriving late in Miami, Ed and Bill took the second load, twenty-eight kilos of real cocaine in two aluminum suitcases, on a Northwest Airlines flight to Boston. Though John O'Brien had agreed to rent a car and pick up Ed and Bill himself, he instead sent Ed's unwitting brother Paul to get them at Logan Airport.

At 5:45 p.m., after loading the coke into the rental car and watching Bill drive away, Paul and Ed walked back inside the terminal. There, they were arrested by John J. Coleman, head of the Boston bureau of the DEA and one of Ed's oldest and closest friends. Friendship, however, was not mitigating. "When you accept work on the public payroll, you agree to be held to a higher standard," Coleman would later say. John O'Brien, who allegedly knew about Ed's plan, was picked up the next morning at his home. Charges against Paul were later dropped.

Currently, John and Ed await trial on four counts of conspiring to distribute cocaine. At a bail hearing in Boston, lawyers for the O'Briens argued that Ed had been entrapped, and that Jamie Short's information was insufficient evidence of Ed's predisposition.

"What we're really talking about here," argued one of the lawyers, "is all of the frustrations with the national drug problem we have.

"Yesterday, the court asked a very good question: 'What does the DEA do with a broken agent?'

"The answer is very clear. They consume him themselves."

(1990)

The Death of a High School Narc

The citizens of Midlothian, Texas, cared deeply about the future of their town, but their war on drugs claimed an unexpected casualty.

It was cool that Friday, the sun just gone, the night settling in upon the prairie. Midway between the towns of Venus and Midlothian, a brown-on-tan pickup juddered down a two-lane, a blond-haired boy at the wheel. He drove past fences and cattle, past fields of stubble and hay, up a rise and then down. It was eight miles from Midlothian to Venus. So far, he had covered the distance three times. Now, outside Venus, he slowed, signaled, turned around again.

This is stupid, Jonathan Jobe was thinking. *Why the hell are you down here? Driving around in the dark, in the cold and the drizzle. You know that nothing's going to happen. There's no way they're gonna be down here. . . .*

North now on Highway 67, back toward Midlothian, the place Jonathan had lived all his life, where his parents had lived all their lives, a jumbled little town of 7,000 at a crossing of two railroads and two highways. It was also a town that was about to lose its innocence, though at the moment, at 7:30 P.M. on Friday, October 23rd, 1987, no one hereabouts suspected. As always, Jonathan could see in the distance the ghost skyline of the cement plant. It rose from the flat black of the north-Texas plain, obscuring the stars, looking to him like a post card of a big city, but really just a tease, a shimmering mirage above the town that the chamber of commerce called the Cement Capital of Texas, that the kids called Middle of the Ocean.

Jonathan checked his rear-view mirror, then his watch. The wipers squeegeed across the windshield. He dialed the radio across the frequencies—static, commercial, strings, twang—and then he gave up, slotted a tape by a heavy-metal band called Slayer.

He'd installed the tape deck first thing after buying the 1979 Chevy Scottsdale, or rather Greg Knighten had installed it for him. Jonathan and

Greg were neighbors. Back in the summer, when they were both fifteen, they had hung out together all the time. Then Jonathan turned sixteen. He got his license and his truck. Greg installed the stereo, tuned the engine, lubed the chassis. For a while, Jonathan drove him everywhere. Then school started and Jonathan met Richard Goeglein.

Jonathan and Richard took homemaking class together. They sat in the back of the room, on the right. Richard was funny. Richard was weird. One time he wrote, "What are you looking at, Dick-nose?" on the cover of his notebook and held it up in class. Everyone laughed so hard the teacher had to stop the lesson on color coordination and sentence the students to thirty minutes of "quiet time." Richard wore a pentagram around his neck; he told people he worshiped the devil. Sometimes he'd prick his finger and draw pictures with his blood. Richard could make his face rubber and do all kinds of accents, and he could draw anything, and almost from the day he and Jonathan met, it was Richard riding everywhere, Greg left behind at home.

Richard, 17, turned Jonathan on to Slayer and other heavy-metal bands, and the two were always together, talking mostly about bands like Anthrax and Metallica and Iron Maiden. Sometimes they played with a small, black, heart-shaped Ouija that Richard called Terry's Heart. Richard carried Terry with him everywhere he went. It was homemade, of black plastic, sort of like the kind Milton Bradley sells. Sometimes when he was getting high, Richard would blow smoke on Terry and tell it, "I'm gonna get you stoned."

Some of the kids at school heard Richard explain that Terry was a dead girl and that the Ouija carried her "essence." The story was hazy, but apparently Richard had to find a girlfriend, and if he was with her for a year, she would change into Terry. Not change physically. She would take on Terry's "attitude."

The police in Williams, Arizona—a town of 3,000 near the Grand Canyon where Richard had lived before moving to Midlothian—would later speculate that Terry could have been Angelina Estrada, a girl about Richard's age who died in 1983. One rowdy night, the police say, Angelina was at a party. When someone threw a rock through the window, Angelina dropped dead. The cause was said to be heart failure.

Sometimes when Jonathan and Richard were together, Richard would set Terry on a table, press his fingertips to the edge, then close his eyes. In a few moments, Terry's Heart would move, all by itself, in figure eights. Jonathan saw this. Some other kids saw this. All by itself, it moved in figure eights.

Anyway, Jonathan began dating Richard's sister Becky. Richard, in turn, fell in like with Jonathan's best girl friend, Gina. The night before, Thursday, Richard had kissed Gina for the first time. It had taken him a long while, six weeks if you start counting from their first encounter, which was also in homemaking. One day, Gina had stretched and accidentally hit Richard in the head, and he had exclaimed, "Hey, what's up, bitch?" She turned around, angry. That's when she noticed his "meltin' blue eyes."

Even before the kiss, Richard and Gina and Jonathan and Becky had formed their own little clique. They didn't consider themselves dopers, ropers or preppies, the recognized categories of kids at Midlothian High. Instead, they called themselves thrashers. The thrashers' music was hardcore, but their habits were not. Once in a while they smoked dope, but considering how little else there was to do in Midlothian, the thrashers were, as a group, pretty straight-arrow, especially compared with the dopers, who got high at least every weekend. Mostly they spent their time cruising and laughing in Jonathan's truck.

As it was, four kids across the front bench of the pickup was tight, and there was no room left for Greg. Kids being the way they are, it didn't occur to Jonathan that this was a big deal. They still saw Greg more than enough anyway, at school and around town. Besides, Jonathan and Richard were much closer than Jonathan and Greg had ever been. They were together day and night. They had plans to get an apartment the next summer and to party together for the rest of their lives. In early October, Richard and Jonathan made themselves brothers. Each boy cut a two-inch slit in the meat of the other's thumb, and then the two of them pressed their hands together, mingling their blood.

An hour earlier, Jonathan, Richard and Greg had met in Greg's bedroom. There was Marlboro smoke in the room, and the air was thick with alarm and raw nerves and indecision. As usual, Greg was begging.

It seemed that the rail-thin lad was always begging for something, most often for a ride. He had to go to Dallas to score dope. He had to go see his girlfriend, Jamie. He had to come along, just to come. This time, he was begging for something else.

"No way, man," said Richard. "I ain't going with you to do that shit."

"Man, he probably won't do nothing anyway," said Jonathan. "You know how he is."

"Yeah?" said Greg, rising up to his full sixty-eight inches. "That's what *you* think. I'm gonna do it. You can be sure of that."

"Damn, man," said Richard. "I ain't going *nowhere* with you."

"Come on, dude, *please!*" said Greg. "I got to have you down there. If you'll do this, I'll never ask you to do anything else again. I promise."

Richard looked at Jonathan. He looked at Greg. Then he said, "Okay, dude, if it means that much to you just for me to go down there, I'll go down there."

And so it was that a horn honked outside the house, and Richard and Greg went out the front door and got into a red GMC truck driven by a senior they knew as George Moore. Jonathan went out the back door and then toward Venus, with instructions to drive back and forth until about eight, when he would pick up his two friends along Farm Road 875.

This being a Friday in the fall, Jonathan knew that a lot of the kids would be over in nearby Red Oak, watching the Midlothian Panthers play the Red Oak Hawks. Neither the dopers nor the thrashers ever attended the games or any school activities that weren't required. There were too many rules.

The truth is, they had rules for just about everything at Midlothian High. The student handbook was eighty-three pages long. Printed blue on white, the school colors, the book enumerated, in extremely fine detail, dictums concerning hair length, metal shoe taps, suspenders, discipline classes, bus etiquette, delivery of balloons, facial hair, dress, earrings, parking, driving. On page 11, the Pregnant Homebound program was explained. According to one teacher, twelve Midlothian High girls qualified for that program during the 1986-87 school year.

There was also the Just Say No program and the Student Assistance Program. S.A.P. was a committee of teachers and administrators who sat in judgment of students. If a student was showing behavioral changes of any sort, a teacher could fill out a checklist and submit it to the committee. The committee would then hand out more checklists to teachers who knew the student. After evaluating the secondary reports, the committee would call the student's parents.

So the dopers and the thrashers steered clear of school events, and that was pretty much okay with everyone, because the preppies and the ropers didn't like the dopers, and the dopers thought the preppies and the ropers were symbolic of everything that was wrong with their school and their town. "They call us the problem kids," said one doper, "but I see the kids who are clean, and I see they're the ones with the problem. They're too hung up on society. I'm sixteen, you know?"

As Jonathan drove, he thought about school and the dopers and the thrashers for a while, trying to keep his mind off the plan, but his thoughts kept drifting back to George Moore, the kid who'd picked up Richard and Greg almost an hour before. Things, he had to admit, were adding up.

George was new to school, and he seemed all right at first, shy like a new kid, eager but not too eager to make friends. But as time went on and he started hanging out with Greg all the time, it began to be apparent that something wasn't right.

George's truck, a cherry-red, step-side 1986 GMC pickup was too nice for a high-school kid. The truck had a great stereo, but George never had it on. You had to ask. He always had money, but he didn't have a job. He said he lived with his uncle in Midlothian, but nobody ever went to his house, and you rarely saw him on weekends. He bought cigarettes, but he didn't inhale; the ashtray in his truck was spotless. George's wallet was weird too. All he had in it was his license and his money. There were no pictures of friends, no phone numbers, no scraps of paper. And George wore the kind of clothes a father wears. He always wore a polo shirt, blue jeans, a blue windbreaker—it seemed he was wearing a uniform. He always had a five o'clock shadow by three.

He did buy dope, though, lots of it. Come Friday night, the average doper would have maybe ten dollars in his pocket; it always took a few partners to buy a quarter-ounce bag of marijuana. George, however, always bought at least two, or two quarter-gram bags of powdered amphetamine—fifty dollars' worth. Plus, George was always driving Greg to Polk Street, the curbside drug market in Dallas, but he would never ask for gas money. One night he round-tripped with Greg, then round-tripped with another doper. Both times he bought dope.

When it came to smoking the pot he bought, well, George acted strange. He made these raucous sucking noises, but he didn't blow out any smoke. And then there were the allegations.

Once, George went to a doper's house, and when he left, the doper's father—a former doper himself—said George looked like a narc. Jamie's mother, who worked at the post office, said she'd heard that there was a narc in school and that his name was George. Cynthia Fedrick, a twenty-three-year-old cashier who let the dopers party at her apartment, said she didn't like the look of George. Another doper, who'd ripped George off for fifty dollars, reported that he had swung on George—smacked him right in the face—and that George had not fought back. Word also began to filter back from Polk Street: dealers were getting busted after selling to George's red truck.

Then, on Wednesday night, two nights before, Greg and George had stopped at Cynthia's to smoke some dope. On a table was an expensive stereo. Cynthia had two kids, few clothes and an ugly blue '69 Plymouth Valiant that she had bought for fifty dollars. She had just lost her job at the Road Runner convenience store; she never had much money. Everyone knew the stereo was hot.

The next afternoon, Thursday, the police came to Cynthia's apartment. They confiscated the stereo.

That was it: Greg and Cynthia and the others were now sure. George Moore was a student goody-goody who was telling the police what was going on in town.

They were almost right.

Now, traveling north on Highway 67, Jonathan took a hard right turn, and the tires spewed gravel. He headed east onto Farm Road 875, toward Mountain Peak.

You're gonna get there, and the road's gonna be empty, Jonathan was thinking. *You'll go back to town, and you'll find George and Greg and Richard sitting in town, you know, drinking a Coke out there at P&S Foods. Greg is a fuckup, he'll never do it. He'll never go through with it. You'll see. . . .*

Then, up ahead, walking by side of the road . . .

Shit! Jonathan thought. He jammed the brakes, slid to a stop. Richard jumped in, then Greg.

"Did you all just do what I think you all did?" asked Jonathan.

"Yeah, man, come on, let's go!" said Greg. "Let's get out of here."

Jonathan floored it. Richard looked really scared, just scared, no emotion to it at all. His eyes were huge. He hung his head. Greg, by the door, was hyper. Paranoid and real hyper.

"Man, did you really kill this dude?" asked Jonathan. "I mean, is he dead? Is he layin' out there in the fucking field dying, you know, dead?"

"Yeah, man," rasped Greg, "Shut up! Just keep on driving!"

"Shot him three times, man," said Richard. "He's dead."

"Fuuu-uuck," said Jonathan, low and long, in two syllables. "Fuuu-uuuck."

Charles "Chuck" Pinto first saw Midlothian in the spring of 1986. It was a Saturday, and he and his wife had packed a bag and driven 250 miles north from Live Oak, bound for the town that was courting him for a job as city manager.

Though Pinto craved the challenge of a new town, he was first of all a family man, and he knew well the heart pull of uprooting. As a city manager, he'd be working late, attending countless meetings. The entire community and its entire portfolio of problems and pissing matches would be his responsibility. In short, taking a job in Midlothian meant that he, his wife and his two kids would have to live there.

Pinto, who was thirty-six at the time, probably realized that he had the advantage on this job transaction. Midlothian was badly in need of a city manager, and he was known as a dynamo. A former Houston Police Department traffic-accident investigator and small-town police chief, Pinto had turned around the city of Live Oak, his first assignment, in just six and a half years. An air-force veteran with a bachelor's degree in criminal justice and a master's in public administration, the lean, clean, hard-working Pinto typified a trend in city managers in recent years, a move away from engineers or native sons toward law-and-order, can-do professionals.

The citizens of Midlothian knew that they too could have prosperity if they planned for it. They had watched over the years as one by one their neighbors to the north had been transformed magically from sleepy farm towns into bustling suburbs. In the last ten years, Midlothian had already become a bit of a bedroom community, and the numbers were ripe for exploitation. Between 1970 and 1986, the city population had more than doubled, as workers from Dallas sought housing within a commutable distance. By the late Eighties, only ten percent of Midlothian's residents were working at the steel and concrete plants that for years had employed most of the residents in the area. Median family income had risen from about $23,000 in 1980 to $34,000 in 1985. And although Midlothian, in 1986, encompassed only thirteen square miles, surrounding it were twenty-two square miles of land that could be legally annexed.

As always, Pinto had done his homework. Midlothian, he could see, had excellent prospects. The city had recently begun turning a profit with its electrical franchise, selling electricity to its neighbors. It had begun work on a new reservoir, a water-processing plant and a million-gallon storage tank. The U.S. government had just awarded Midlothian and neighboring Waxahachie a grant to plan a commercial airport. It had also declared the town and some surrounding areas an international free-trade zone, creating the opportunity for the high-profit deferred-duty sale of imported products.

And so it was that Chuck Pinto and his wife pulled their Olds Cutlass into Midlothian after a five-hour drive on that rainy Saturday afternoon, intending to look around, check the shopping, eat dinner and stay overnight.

Pinto was shocked. Was this the place he had researched? No curbs, gutters or street signs. No hotel, no shopping center, nowhere to stay overnight. No drainage. Helter-skelter development. "In a town facing high growth and development," Pinto said, "there's always a lot of controversy. Here, I knew I'd be in for it."

The Pintos drove around town for two hours. Then they drove all the way back home.

But Midlothian kept after Chuck Pinto, and he returned for interviews. He met the people, toured the schools. He changed his mind.

"I guess when you compare values," Pinto said, "you always compare yourself. I'm from a modern but yet very conservative attitude. That's what I saw. A lot of people with good values. There were good church values, first. Now that doesn't mean a hill of beans to me, because a lot of people can go to church and it doesn't mean a thing. But what I saw was people who had religious values about them whether they were in church or not. I saw it in practice. I saw the stability in the community."

So Pinto took the job and moved his family, and beginning in July 1986, he began the task of modernizing Midlothian.

He computerized and organized, helped put the city in the black for the first time in years. He urged the city to annex four square miles of land. He brought in paid firefighters, folded the ambulance service into the fire department, initiated a policy of cross-training whereby a firefighter was also a paramedic and a building inspector. Road signs were erected, community services were put in place, the police force was overhauled and retrained, and a new police chief, a twenty-year man from Dallas, was hired.

In addition, a "comprehensive plan" was commissioned—at a cost of $160,000, more than five times the average amount spent on similar small-city plans. The plan specified that future development should take into account "that the character of Midlothian is primarily that of a small town, and that community facilities should provide a sense of community identity."

And perhaps most important, Pinto was a key player in Ellis County's bid to land the U.S. Department of Energy's Superconducting Super Collider, a $4.5 billion energy project. Pinto knew that if the county was chosen as the site, it would instantly become the energy capital of the world. The project, Pinto knew, would bring higher standards of education, sophistication, permanent stability and economic boom. The proposed location for the facility was next door to Midlothian.

So times and hopes were high in the city. Then one morning in early 1987, Pinto pulled into a gas station and convenience mart near city hall.

"I watched some kids trading drugs and money," said Pinto. "You could see it was routine. We had received some information from various sources that we were a distribution point for drugs, in that a lot of the trucks come through here. I was sitting here thinking, 'Are we furnishing the world with drugs?' "

As Pinto saw it, before anything could be done, officials had to learn the extent of the drug traffic in town. He went to the city council, asked for funds for a "covert" drug operation. As Pinto said, "You come into a town like this and you tell them, 'I'd like to have some money to buy some drugs. . . . ' Well, you've got to break people into that slowly."

In the end, however, there was little fuss over the proposal. Though Pinto said the council members weren't told "exactly what we were doing," they were given the general idea. There was a drug problem in town, and Pinto knew something they could do about it.

In a community like Midlothian, *drug problem* means any drugs at all. Two years into Nancy Reagan's Just Say No program, Midlothian was highly aware of drugs and their toll on the nation. With nearly every home wired for cable TV, even a rural town like Midlothian was linked by satellite to every fashion and fad, every event, attitude and phobia experienced by the collective national mind. The citizens and leaders of Midlothian knew well about the war on drugs, and they knew that *everyone* had to fight. They appropriated $20,000.

Surely another reason the council went along was the recent installment of Roy Vaughn as chief of police. Vaughn, 53, a big man with a full head of white hair, had spent twenty-two years on the Dallas police force and had been the assistant coordinator of Dallas's Organized Crime Unit. Equally important to the townspeople was the fact that Vaughn was one of the family, a twenty-year resident of Midlothian. He was a member of the chamber of commerce and had put five kids through the school system. When he retired from the Dallas force in 1980, he had opened Midlothian Glass and Mirror.

In January 1987, Vaughn beat out forty-one other applicants to become chief. "I think I missed the police work," he said.

To help with the narcotics investigation, Vaughn brought in Billy Fowler.

Short and dark, with a deeply creased face, Fowler was given the rank of lieutenant in the twelve-man, nine-car Midlothian force. Like Vaughn, Fowler had spent more than twenty years with the Dallas police force. For a time, he'd worked exclusively in narcotics, usually as a "control agent," the in-house contact of the man undercover.

For their operation, Vaughn and Fowler borrowed police officers from nearby Cedar Hill. Between May and August of 1987, the "undercover agents" bought marijuana, cocaine and amphetamines in small but felonious quantities from sources around town. By August, when the operation ended, seventeen adults had been arrested on twenty-eight felony counts.

"Through this investigation," said Vaughn, "we determined we had a problem in the high school. We had good information. I can truthfully say that in May we arrested two 17-year-olds for sale of methamphetamine. Neither of them were students, but during the investigations we readily found places where high-school kids were buying and using marijuana on the premises. We determined we had a problem in the high school."

"We weren't just picking on Midlothian," said Pinto. "We had a lot of kids coming over here from other areas. Some of the other towns around here had been doing some pretty good drug enforcement, and there was a void in Midlothian. If I put a dead-bolt lock on my door, and you leave yours open, and somebody wants to do a burglary, they're going into your place. Well, other towns were throwing some drug dead bolts up, and we had our door open.

"So we just closed the door. We said, 'We need to get to that younger group.' And the way to get into that younger group was to get somebody that fit into the high-school age."

George William Raffield never knew his father, who left the family before George was born. When he was seven months old, his mother, Shirley, who worked in a nursing home, married Don Moore, a machinist. It was Moore's second marriage as well, and among the seven children in the newly combined household was another George, so the baby was called Tiger.

Tiger was one of those boys who declare one day early in life that they want to be policemen, and he never wavered from that goal. By his sophomore year at Mesquite High, southwest of Dallas, George had joined the Police Explorers, and by his senior year, he'd risen to captain.

A straight kid who never smoked or drank, Tiger had one vice: cinnamon rolls. The habit produced a small spare tire around the midsection of his five-foot-five-inch frame—and not a little teasing from his sisters, Sheryl and Sherrie. He was extremely close to the girls, his natural sisters, especially Sheryl. There were only thirteen months between Tiger and Sheryl; they were best friends. Tiger introduced Sheryl to David, the boy she would marry. Sheryl, in turn, coached Tiger before his first kiss. It was Tiger's freshman year, the Valentine's dance.

Sheryl and David and George and Dolly had doubled, Sheryl remembered. "Dolly was sitting next to me, and she said, 'Is your brother gonna kiss me?' and I said, 'I don't know.' So I asked him. I said, 'Tiger, are you gonna kiss Dolly?' He says, "Well, I don't know. . . . How should I do it?' and I said, 'Just go up to her and lay one on her!' And that's just what he did."

George's accounting teacher at Mesquite remembered that the 1985 graduate "was not the typical nerd. George was a well-rounded kid. He could horse around, but he could read people. If I said, 'Okay, now, y'all get busy,' he would go around and tell everyone to get busy. . . . He wanted to clean up the world."

After graduation, George continued on at Minyard's Food Stores, where he had worked since he was fifteen, giving all but thirty-five dollars of his weekly paycheck to his mother. He also enrolled at Tarrant County Junior College and took an eleven-week course to earn his basic police certificate. Though busy with work and studies, George also found time to join the reserve police force in Red Oak, the town where his family had recently moved, five miles northeast of Midlothian. As a reserve officer, he wore a uniform and carried handcuffs, and almost every Friday night he'd patrol Red Oak High School activities. Often, George would ride in patrol cars with Red Oak officers, putting in three or four times the required sixteen hours a month of service, working Christmas and Thanksgiving so the regulars could stay home.

When George graduated, he received his police certificate and his first handgun, a nickel-plated, wood-handled Smith & Wesson .357 Magnum, purchased for about $300 at the police-supply store in Grand Prairie. "He was nineteen," said Shirley Moore. "He wasn't old enough to buy the gun or the bullets to go in it. We had to buy it for him. He always carried that gun. I used to get so frustrated because he put it in his back waistband when we'd go into a big shopping center. And I'd say, 'Tiger, do you always have to carry that?' and he'd say, 'Yes, Mother, we always have to carry it.' "

In September of 1986, George got his first real job, with the Wilmer police force. Not long after he started, George wrecked two patrol cars while chasing speeders. "He didn't do anything wrong," said Wilmer police chief Preston Parks. "He just had some bad luck." Nevertheless, George was let go after three months. Sergeant Michael Pigg, the officer who had trained George, said he was fired for "failure to meet minimum standards for probation . . . for violating policy involving the operation of patrol cars."

"George was a damn good man," said Pigg. "He would have made a fine officer. He just couldn't handle the cars."

Returning to Red Oak, George began working part-time as a police dispatcher. Then, in June of 1987, Roy Vaughn called. Vaughn had heard about the enthusiastic young cop who was looking for a job. He told George he had an assignment that was perfect for him. He couldn't discuss the details on the phone.

"I looked at several candidates," said Vaughn, "and George kind of fit the role for what I was looking for. He was an impressive type kid. He was an average type Joe. Good, clean-cut disposal. Followed instruction well. I was looking for someone I could put out there and know he could do the job. Some guys go out there, they get too close to the people they're working against. They can go bad. We knew that wouldn't happen to George."

In August, George was sent for about a month of training with the Dallas Police Department's narcotics unit. They "took him under their wing, showed him the dos and the don'ts," Vaughn said.

According to his mother, George participated in several drug raids in Dallas. "One night he came home and said he'd just been out on this bust, and he said he was so tired of counting money. He said that's all he'd done, was count money. He said, 'Mother, you wouldn't believe the drugs and the money.'"

Following the training, George worked closely with Billy Fowler. First, they "laid down his cover." For the purpose of the investigation, George William Raffield would be known to all as William George Moore, though he'd still go by George, so he'd remember to answer to the name.

George Moore's story was that he had come from Temple, Texas, was living with an uncle in Midlothian and was buying the drugs to resell in Temple, where he had a girlfriend he visited on weekends.

One day in late July, George and Fowler drove to Temple. "We wanted him to be well acquainted with the town," said Fowler, "in case he ran into somebody at the school who might ask him where the Dairy Queen is."

George and Fowler also went over to Temple High School. With the help of the principal and a guidance counselor, William George Moore was entered into the computer system, given a Temple address, vaccine records and a transcript of courses from grades one through eleven. George Moore's grades were made a little lower than average. "We didn't want to have him working eight hours on the street and then going home and busting his ass doing a bunch of homework," said Fowler.

With his cover established and his mustache shaved, George was enrolled in Midlothian High as a twelfth grader. None of the school's officials was told of the existence of an undercover officer in the school.

Still, George had much to learn. "All this stuff was really new to him," said Fowler. "He'd never been around drugs at all. He didn't smoke cigarettes. He didn't even drink. We asked him, if he was forced to, could he drink a can of beer. He said he probably could if he tried, but he never had.

"We told him, 'If you're buying weed, you're probably going to run into a situation where you're gonna at least have to simulate smoking it.' We showed him how to pinch it off and actually not get any of the smoke but to still act like you do. We told him, 'Number one, go over there and don't rush into it.' We really didn't care if he didn't make any buys for the first four or five or six weeks. We told him to try and sort the kids out in his mind, you know, who were the dopers, who were the ropers, who were the preppies. We told him not to ever buy any drugs in school, never to be in possession of any drugs in school. Not to get in trouble in school. To maintain a rapport with the teachers. Not to be a problem student. To call us every night. To call us before and after a buy. To be in school every day or, if he wasn't gonna be in school, to let us know. We'd check the school parking lot two or three times a day to see if his truck was there. We knew that playing hooky would be part of the game, but we told him, 'Just let us know first, 'cause if you're not there in school, we don't know where you are.' "

George Moore registered for English, typing, math, computer science and health at Midlothian High. When the first fall-semester grades came out, the undercover agent was on the honor roll.

In English, he wrote an essay about horse racing and chose to write a book report about *The Sword in the Stone*. His handwriting, according to his teacher, Harriette Fowler, was a lovely cursive, and he was "just a little more advanced than most of the kids as far as vocabulary and writing skills."

In health class, George's handwriting was sloppy, and he often left the bottom half of test papers unfinished. "The only thing he'd say was, you know, 'It's Friday! We're gonna party!' " said his teacher, Cathy Britton. "He was no more vague than your normal type of kid."

In typing, George sat himself near the lower-level students. Asked to type a history of himself, he wrote, "My name is George and I am a seventeen-year-old senior. I like to go cruising and partying. . . . I think school is boring." In the opinion of George's typing teacher, Barbara Whitham, his was "the work of a very low-level student." On one occasion, however, he made the teacher wonder. While taking a timed test, George typed for a period, then stopped. The clock was still ticking. When the papers were handed in, Whitham saw that George had typed exactly twenty-seven lines, just enough for a D. Every line was perfect.

Students remember George tossing balled-up pieces of paper around the room, helping a classmate cheat on a test, hanging around and watching people. One girl thought George was "laid-back and nice and real quiet . . . real intellectual." A boy remembered Friday nights with George. "We'd park our trucks and sit on our tailgates in town and holler at people."

By all accounts, George's first three weeks went smoothly. "He met some guys up there during the first three or four weeks that probably used dope but didn't sell dope," said Fowler. "He liked the guys, they liked him. They'd go out and play flag football, take their four-wheel-drive vehicles and carry him out to the country and ride some mudholes. He was getting paid a good salary, getting all the spending money he needed. He really enjoyed it."

Because there were no movie theaters or teen centers in town, the kids of Middle of the Ocean took their fun where they found it. The video arcade, the bowling alley and the McDonald's were eleven miles away, in Waxahachie; the mall was even farther away, in Duncanville; the liquor store was farther still, in South Dallas. Most of the Midlothian kids didn't have much money anyway. Their parents worked blue-collar jobs; their allowances were pretty slim, five or ten dollars a week. The major form of entertainment in Midlothian was cruising. An offshoot of cruising was "rafting." The kids would park their cars and pickups close together, side by side, and put the windows down, and they'd all tune their radios simultaneously to Z-ROCK, and they'd yell back and forth between cars.

That was about it in Midlothian, besides sex and drugs.

By the dopers' own rough estimate, about ten percent of the 750 students at the high school smoked dope on occasion. Half of those considered themselves "true dopers," kids who got high, according to one of them, "at least once a day, several times a day if we can."

To tell the truth, the dopers of Midlothian couldn't afford to take drugs in massive quantities, but they did well in the area of variety. Marijuana and hashish. Cocaine, both powder and crack. LSD of varying kinds and strengths. PCP and crank, a powdered amphetamine.

Since Midlothian's summer offensive against drugs, the only place to score, according to the dopers, was out of town, either on Polk Street, in Dallas, or in neighboring towns and cities. Because of this, the dopers operated in a spirit of cooperation and trust that mirrored the small-town ways of their parents. If someone was going to Dallas to make a buy, he would buy for a few others as well. It made sense: less money was wasted on gas; not everyone had a car; and some kids weren't yet old enough to drive. Though their parents would never have understood this, drugs were a matter of friendship to the dopers of Midlothian High, a common denominator that crossed differences in age and class and status. Drugs were something to share, something to gather over, something to do in the Middle of the Ocean.

After three weeks at school, George began spending less time with the "fun" kids and more time with the dopers. One of his new friends was Greg Knighten.

Since Greg couldn't drive and had pretty much lost his regular ride now that Jonathan and Richard were hanging around together all the time, George came in handy. He began picking Greg up for school and taking him home afterward. And as it would develop, George would buy many bags of dope with Greg's help.

According to Fowler, George's first opportunity to make a buy came on Thursday, September 18th. When school was over, George met a doper friend in the parking lot, at the red truck.

The doper asked if George had seen a friend of theirs.

"No, but his truck's still over there," said George.

The doper walked to the other truck, waited for the kid, spoke to him and returned. "He's gonna bring me some weed tomorrow," he told George.

"And here, George seized the opportunity," said Fowler. "He told the doper to get him a twenty-five-dollar bag."

The next day in school, Fowler said, the doper asked George for the money. Later that day, during a pep rally in the cafeteria, George watched money change hands. "He said this kid had a pad and a pencil out and two or three kids were standing in line. He was taking their orders, taking their money. Right in the cafeteria."

George called Fowler and told him that the deal would go down before the football game. Fowler said he'd meet George at the game. "We had a prearranged signal that he was to give me in the crowd. I told him that when we made eye contact, if he had scored, just to run his hand through his hair, which he did.

"I went into the restroom, and he came into the restroom, and he told me he had the dope in his truck, locked in his glove compartment. I told him I was gonna leave at half time and for him to leave as soon after that as he could, because he was supposed to be going to Temple to see his girlfriend."

After an interval, George left the game and drove out in the country to Fowler's house, looping around, making sure he wasn't being followed. As would become standard procedure, Fowler left his electric garage door open, and George pulled in silently and shut the door. George surrendered the drugs, then sat and drank a Coke and related the details of the buy.

As weeks passed, this late-night scene at Fowler's place would become more regular. "George would give Knighten money and say, 'Well, when you score, will you get me two quarters?'—or three, or whatever he was buying," Fowler said. "So they'd go to Dallas, and George would remain in his truck. That's the way the cases would be made on Knighten. We in turn were keeping Dallas narcotics informed of where they were scoring.

"George was real proud of what he did. I know one time he brought me either four or six bags that he scored at one time. He'd made two round trips to Dallas the same evening. Boy, he thought he'd really done something."

George was still living with his parents in Red Oak during this time. After coming home from school, he'd eat dinner and go back out. "He'd say, 'Mother, I'm going to make the buy,'" said Shirley Moore.

"He'd never tell me who, but we would discuss what he was going to buy. Sometimes it was marijuana. Then he got on something called crank. I'd heard of crack, but I'd never heard of crank. So he goes in and takes a little sandwich bag out of his drawer, and he says, 'Mom, here's twenty-five dollars' worth.'

"Of course, all that would make me worry, but Tiger used to tell me, he'd say, 'Mother, don't worry; this is high-school kids.'"

If you asked people about Greg Knighten, said a former close friend, "they woulda said, 'He's weird, he's nuts, he's a heavy druggie, he's always in trouble, always.' He hated school. He wanted to get the hell out of his parents' house, but he couldn't, 'cause he couldn't get enough money. He thought that life sucked. He said it very often, you know: 'Life sucks.' And he was just waiting until he could get money. That's all he wanted, enough money to get out on his own. That and some friends, some friends to talk to."

Greg Knighten was the adopted son of a Dallas police corporal and his wife, a phys. ed. instructor at a fundamentalist Bible academy. The Knightens, along with Greg and their younger son, had moved to Midlothian two years earlier from Duncanville, a suburban city fifteen miles to the north that had once been a quiet rural town like Midlothian.

Before being assigned to a patrol car in southwest Dallas, Tom Knighten, 44, had worked for many years at the police shooting range, where he met Vaughn. "He was a very good individual, a very helpful individual," Vaughn said. "If you went out to the pistol range, Tom Knighten was the type that if you had problems, he'd go out of his way to help you."

Knighten said that his son, when he was younger, was a quick boy, eager to help his father work on cars, eager to hear police stories, which reminded the young boy of "something just like he'd seen on TV."

"We were a good family, tried to give our sons the right things," said Knighten, who bought the boys, at different times, a swimming pool, a dune buggy, a three-wheel ATV, an off-road motorcycle and a racing go-cart. "There were good times—lots of them."

According to his father, Greg's problems began in Duncanville. All of a sudden, it seemed, Greg became tired of church. He'd gone to his mother's Bible school since first grade, and now he was insisting on going to a "normal school." He began hanging out with the unsavory kids in town. It seemed to the Knightens that Duncanville was going to the dogs and that Greg was being dragged down with it. It was time to move.

The Knightens found Midlothian. "It was a little town that seemed like the place where I grew up," said Tom Knighten. "We felt like in a nice little town he wouldn't get into much trouble because it just wasn't there."

In Midlothian, Greg became even more distant, and Tom Knighten did not like the look of his son's new friends. Once, Knighten patted down a neighborhood boy for drugs. Later, he questioned teachers about his son's friends, searched his son's room for drug paraphernalia, sent Greg four times for drug tests.

After Greg put a red streak in his hair, the Knightens took him to a psychologist in Dallas.

"We just decided it must be low self-esteem, especially since he was adopted versus our other son being our biological child," Tom Knighten said. "We tried to tell him that being adopted meant he was the chosen one, but to what extent that he heard or believed anything we said, who knows?"

Meanwhile, Greg was having a hard time making friends. Most of the dopers wouldn't go near his house, fearing his father. Many said Greg was a thief. A boy said he stole a camera; a girl said he stole a tape, a hat and a cross earring; another boy beat him up for stealing a Mötley Crüe cassette.

"He was always screwing somebody around," said one doper. "Like even on a little half-ass deal. He'd go, 'Yeah, I'll get you a dime on Polk Street,' and then he'd come back and give you a nickel and shit, like two joints, and you'd beat his ass for it.

"He wasn't popular. He was kind of a down person, a low person, kind of like a nerd or something. When he hung around us, you know, he was in the way and stuff. He always tried to get us to take him places."

Greg's girl, Jamie Cadenhead, saw him differently. "I know that a lot of people say that he was bad, and he wasn't," she said.

Jamie and Greg planned to get married when they turned seventeen. Then they were going to get an apartment and finish high school. Greg, a talented mechanic, believed he'd have little trouble finding a job. "A lot of people are saying that he didn't care about life," said Jamie. "He did. He made people laugh. When somebody was upset, he'd just get them to feeling better."

Cynthia Fedrick was also fond of Greg. The two had met through her brother, Randy Marcott, another student at Midlothian. Cynthia had married at fifteen and divorced at seventeen. She had two daughters, aged six and four. One lived with the child's father, the other with Cynthia's parents. Cynthia had a bad knee and many worries. "Greg was caring," said Cynthia. "Every time I had a problem, he's been there to talk to."

Though he seemed to have good friends in Jamie and Cynthia, Greg couldn't go see them because he couldn't drive. That's where the new kid, George Moore, came in. Unlike Jonathan Jobe and the others, George seemed willing to take Greg anywhere he wanted to go.

The two boys became fast friends, or so it seemed. Even Greg's parents liked George. When the Knightens had a family dinner for Greg's sixteenth birthday, George was invited to come.

"He just seemed real nice, clean-cut," says Tom Knighten, "and he'd look at you when you talked. . . . That night, we all held hands to say the blessing, and we just felt like he was one of our family. We just felt so pleased that he was there for our son."

On Friday, October 23rd, the Midlothian Panthers were scheduled to play the Red Oak Hawks. A pep rally was set for that morning, and the late bell would be ringing any minute. The weekend was coming, and lockers were banging, and couples were snatching French kisses, and kids were bombing through the hallways, laughing and high-fiving, walking fast but not running, caught in the spirit of a free period at Middle of the Ocean High.

Richard and Jonathan were at Richard's locker, which was decorated inside with drawings of skulls and pentagrams and things. Down the hall, coming fast, was Greg Knighten.

"Richard! Jonathan! Hey, dudes!"

"Wonder where he wants us to take him now," mumbled Jonathan.

Richard made one of his faces, a real roper face. He spoke in a roper accent, a thick prairie twang. "*Wayyyyy-elllllllll, Ah jus' don' know, duuuuuuuuuude.*"

Greg was out of breath, hyper, oblivious to the joke. "We pieced together a puzzle, man," he said. "That guy George is a narc. There's got to be something done about it!"

Jonathan stared at Greg a few seconds. Then he said, "What are you talking about?"

"Well, we just pieced it together, believe me. We know this dude is a narc."

Greg ticked off the evidence. The expensive truck. What Jamie's mother had said about a narc at school. The dealers on Polk Street who had been arrested. The police confiscating the stolen stereo from Cynthia.

Jonathan leaned close. He knew that Greg was real smart about putting things together. Usually, if there was anything Greg wanted to do, or wanted to know, he would figure it out. Jonathan also knew Cynthia, and that worried him even more.

Once a doper had ripped off Cynthia for fifty dollars. Greg was friends with this guy, and he wanted Cynthia to know that he wasn't responsible. Greg begged Jonathan to drive him to Cynthia's apartment.

Cynthia was "big, fat, mean, crazy, nuts," said Jonathan. When Greg tried to explain, Cynthia flipped. She pulled down a whole set of shelves; tapes and a radio fell all over the place. She busted the table and busted the chair. She screamed, stomped, kicked stuff around, kicked the wall. Then she grabbed a bottle of bourbon and downed three shots. That's when the boys left.

Now she was pissed again. Some kids would tell the police that Cynthia had grabbed Greg, pushed him against a wall. She had told him to kill George and that if he didn't do it, she'd do it or find someone else to do it.

" . . . and Cynthia said we need to do something about it because George is using us to bust everybody," Greg was telling the other two boys.

"She said that when George was done, he's gonna bust me too. Man, that guy has been using us! He's gonna bust me. He's gonna bust Jamie! She's been to Polk Street with me and George! Man. . . . Shit. . . . That guy came to my birthday party!"

Jonathan looked at Greg. Granted, this was serious, but granted also was the fact that Greg was always getting ready to kick someone's ass, though he rarely ever went through with it.

"So what are you gonna do, kick his ass?" asked Jonathan.

"Yeah, right," said Richard.

"No, man," said Greg. "I'm gonna get a gun."

On Fridays, George's last class was typing. When the bell rang, everyone bolted. George stood a few moments by his desk, waiting for the room to clear. Then he walked toward the teacher's desk. He mumbled something.

"Pardon me?" asked Barbara Whitham. She was a bit shocked. George had rarely spoken in her class.

Now George turned, gestured toward the bulletin board that Whitham had decorated for Halloween. On a black background were orange letters that spelled, DO THESE GHOSTS HAUNT YOU? Surrounding the letters were white construction-paper ghosts. Each ghost was labeled with a different hindrance to good typing: POOR POSTURE, POOR RHYTHM and so on. "These ghosts haunt me," George said.

"Which one?" asked Whitham.

"All of them," said George.

George stood, silent. It seemed to Whitham that he wanted to talk, that he had something to say, but he wasn't saying it.

Whitham walked toward him, smiled. "Well, let's not worry about it," she said. "We can start working on those things Monday."

At 6:30 that night, Richard was holding a séance in Greg's bedroom. He had his eyes closed, and his ouija, Terry's Heart, was on the dresser. Greg and Jonathan stood to either side of him. All three boys pressed their fingertips to the dresser top.

Terry's Heart began to shudder.

Holy shit, thought Jonathan.

Jonathan and Richard had arrived twenty minutes earlier, as Greg had requested. Much to their surprise, Greg actually had a gun. He also had a plan.

It would be a cinch, Greg had said. Who would ever suspect them? George would be dead; the cops wouldn't know anything. And best of all, nobody would go to jail for drugs.

The gun Greg planned to use was one of his father's .38-caliber pistols. Greg had fired it before at the police range. He said that when he took the gun, it had been loaded with fancy bullets. He had removed the fancy ones and replaced them with homemade reloads he had found in the workshop. When they were finished, Greg said, he would put the fancy bullets back, and no one would ever know they'd used it.

Then Greg begged Richard to go with him. For ten minutes he begged, and in the course of that time, Richard's attitude slowly changed from "No way" to "I don't know" to "What could it hurt?" to "Okay, if it means that much to you, dude."

Now, a few minutes later, Terry's Heart was on the dresser. The question lingered in the air: "Is George Moore a narc?"

Terry's Heart shuddered. It moved to the left.

Left meant yes.

Other questions were put. Terry answered.

"Take care of it," it told the boys.

It also had a message for Richard: "Don't do it. Don't go."

A light mist was falling as George's red truck pulled off Farm Road 875 and bounced a quarter mile along a dirt lane through a pasture. George parked facing south. The cement plant glowed in the distance. He engaged the emergency brake, killed the engine, turned the key to auxiliary and tuned the radio to Z-ROCK. Then all three boys got out of the truck, leaving the doors open so they could hear the music.

They sat on the tailgate, talked about nothing. Everything seemed normal. No allegations were mentioned. Nothing was said about narcs. After a while, one of the boys said, "George, would ya go and turn that music up some?"

George hopped down, turned and started toward the driver's door, with one of his hands in the pocket of his navy-blue jacket.

The first shot hit George square in the back of the head. As he fell, the second shot grazed the side of his head. The third shot missed. George was dead by the time he hit the ground.

"Fuuu-uuck," said Jonathan, low and long. "Fuuu-uuuck."

At about 7:45 P.M., Jonathan saw what he had hoped he wouldn't see,

Richard and Greg walking along Farm Road 875. He stopped his truck, and the boys tumbled in.

"Get the hell over to Cynthia's," said Greg. "We got his wallet, man."

"Fuck, man," said Jonathan. "I want my fucking gas money and then you get the hell out of here."

"Man, you got to take me to Jamie's," said Greg. "Please, man."

On the way to Cynthia's apartment, Greg opened George's wallet, divided up the $18 he found inside. Had the boys checked the front pocket of George's blue jeans, they would have found $50.52. They would not, however, have found his gun. George's nickel-plated .357 Magnum was not on him. Unlike the undercover cops on *21 Jump Street*, his favorite TV show, George was not allowed to carry a weapon on assignment. George's gun, along with his real wallet, was back in his apartment. Twenty-two days earlier, two weeks after his twenty-first birthday, George had moved out of his mother's house for the first time. He shared his new place with his fiancée. They were to be married in April.

When the boys arrived at Cynthia's apartment, the usual crowd was partying, some of them students, some not. According to Cynthia, "Greg started to tell me about having his daddy's gun, and how he'd switched from the fancy bullets to regular bullets. That's when I told him to shut up."

Nevertheless, Cynthia took the wallet from the boys, and she went into the bedroom, where she burned George Moore's driver's license over an ashtray. Why she did this is not clear. Later, the police would find the wallet intact in her trash.

Next, at Greg's insistence, the boys drove to Jamie's. They said little en route. When they pulled up, Greg stepped out of the truck, and Jamie came running out of the house. They hugged. Greg cried.

"It's all okay now," he told her.

In his bedroom, Jonathan had his collections of G.I. Joe dolls and samurai swords, and like many of the kids in Midlothian, he also had his own phone, complete with call waiting and conference call. When he and Richard returned from Jamie's, Richard phoned Gina, his girlfriend, and told her what had happened.

Gina said she and others had heard Greg talking about his plan at school, had heard him saying, "He's a narc, man. I'm gonna kill his ass." Other kids had heard about the events from the partyers at Cynthia's. Tales of the séance and the shooting were buzzing in bedrooms all over town.

Richard and Jonathan couldn't sleep. Jonathan was pretty freaked out, but he knew he hadn't done anything, and he knew his parents would believe him. Unlike his two friends, he'd never been in any trouble. The very worst thing he'd ever done in his life was start a fire in a field.

Richard, on the other hand, was scared out of his mind. He was there. He'd seen George dead. It wasn't the first time he'd been present during a felony. Four months earlier, in June, Richard had witnessed the bludgeoning of a sixteen-year-old boy. Frank Ross, a nineteen-year-old, was charged with the attack, which took place in a trailer on a farm owned by Richard's grandparents. Richard's father, a hairdresser and heavy-equipment operator, and his mother, a waitress, lived in the main house of the farm. Richard, who lived alone in the trailer, was the only eyewitness. The victim survived, though he suffered six skull fractures and was comatose for nine days.

Richard and Jonathan talked most of the night in Jonathan's room. They didn't know what to do. They discussed hiding out in Arizona. Richard knew someone there who might help, the son of a highway patrolman who lived in Williams. They decided to call him in the morning.

Meanwhile, Billy Fowler was getting worried. George always checked in at ten or eleven in the evening. Fowler called Vaughn.

"It was the middle of the night," Vaughn said. "We came down here to the office and started making calls and checking places. Sometimes, for an undercover officer to disappear for a short period of time, you know that's normal. Billy had talked to him some, ten minutes to seven. George said he was going out to meet some people and just piddle around. There wasn't any planned drug buy, so we weren't overly concerned, but we were concerned. Our city limits is cut up. We got much rural area. I felt, and there was no doubt in my mind, well—I called the Texas Rangers prior to ever finding the body."

At 6:00 A.M., Vaughn called George's mother and told her George was missing. George's stepdad and brother-in-law went hunting for him in their truck. Meanwhile, hundreds of police officers, state and local, on duty and off, joined the search for their missing colleague. Horses, pickups and four-wheel drives swarmed through the tiny town and the surrounding prairies. Once the cloud cover lifted, helicopters flew concentric circles around Midlothian.

At home, Shirley Moore and her daughters monitored the search with a police scanner her eldest stepson had purchased that morning as soon as the stores had opened.

"I was going crazy," she said. "I knew Tiger was dead. I just wanted them to find his body. I knew as soon as the call came, 'cause he was not the type not to check in. He was too dependable.

"I knew his cover had been blown. Right before he moved into his apartment, he told me he had gotten ripped off on a deal, and the chief had told him to go back and stand up, either get his money or his stuff, and what happened was he ended up having an altercation with one kid in a parking lot of a drugstore. That day he told me, he says, 'Mother, the kid hit me, but I couldn't hit him back. Mother, I couldn't hit him. He's only seventeen, and I'm a police officer. I couldn't hit him 'cause he's a minor.' He said the kid accused him of being a narc, and the kid said, 'My dad thinks you're a narc too.'

"And that was the last time I saw him, standing right here. And I said to him, 'Get out. Your cover is blown. Get out of it, or you're gonna be dead.' And he said, 'Oh, Mother, I'm gonna be all right.' And I said, 'No. You tell them. You get out of it.' "

At about 4:00 p.m. on October 24th, Shirley Moore heard the message on the scanner. "Victim and vehicle found," a voice said. "Search discontinued. Notify family." A few minutes later, on television, she saw Tiger, lying face down in the field. A few minutes after that, she got word from the police.

An hour later, at about 5:00 p.m., Jonathan, Richard and Gina pulled up to Richard's house. They'd spent the day at a flea market in Waxahachie. They'd walked around awhile, and then Richard decided he wanted to buy Gina a silver necklace. It was only two nights before that he'd kissed her for the first time; they'd decided to go steady. Richard didn't have enough money to buy the necklace, so he and Jonathan pooled what was left of George's. Gina kicked in what she had, fifty cents.

Now, as Jonathan set the emergency brake and reached to open the door of his truck, a van pulled up across the street. A man stuck his head out of the window and yelled.

"Hey, come here, man, we want to talk to you."

Jonathan, Richard and Gina exchanged looks. They stepped slowly out of the truck.

Suddenly, there were police cars everywhere. Thirty, maybe more. They came from the left, the right, straight ahead. Cops jumped out, their hands on their guns.

Fuck, man, thought Jonathan. *We're dead. We're gone. Right now, man, this is the end of everything.*

Then he thought, *This is like* Miami Vice!

• • •

In late January, after the murder, Chief Vaughn leaned back in a chair in his smoky office. Across the desk was Lieutenant Fowler. Chuck Pinto was in the doorway; he'd come by to talk about the porn busts at two video stores in town.

"The stereo was taken in a burglary," said the chief. "It was an expensive stereo. It was a rented stereo. In a sense, it was a kind of a judgment call. We didn't think any way in the world that it would be connected with George. In all honesty, we searched our souls and everything else. Realistically, hell, if we had to go back and do it again, no, we wouldn't have done it. But that's what happened."

"The whole thing was so unbelievable," said Fowler, and Pinto and Vaughn shook their heads in agreement "If you were dealing with a bunch of Jamaicans or Puerto Ricans or some hard dudes like that, you might have thought . . . But here, to think that some kid from Midlothian would shoot someone, well, how can you even think that?"

"Yeah," said Pinto. "I mean, you might think that if they thought George was a narc—and there was never any indication that he was compromised, believe me—you'd think they woulda whupped his ass, something like that."

Vaughn creaked forward in his big wooden chair and leaned his forearms across the desk. He looked at Pinto and Fowler, and he sighed, and then he searched for the right words. "Quite honestly . . . Had we . . . You don't think . . . Realistically . . . Oh, hell." He shook his head. "You can sit back and try and reason all day long, and you never come up with a solution. What I can't figure out is why. You know, why?"

At this writing, Richard Goeglein, 17, is being held in lieu of bond at the Ellis County jail, indicted on a charge of capital murder, which carries a possible sentence of death by injection. Greg Knighten and Jonathan Jobe, now both sixteen, have been declared adults for trial and have also been indicted on charges of capital murder. As minors, Knighten and Jobe are exempt from the death penalty. Conviction, however, carries a mandatory life sentence. Knighten, whose lawyer has told reporters that his client did not fire the fatal shots, is in the county jail. Jobe is free on a $50,000 bond and is making good grades at Midlothian High.

Cynthia Fedrick, 23, has been indicted on charges of criminal solicitation for capital murder and conspiracy to commit capital murder; both crimes are first-degree felonies. She too is in the county jail, facing penalties of five years to life.

George Moore was buried in his Midlothian P.D. uniform with full police honors and a twenty-one-gun salute. More than 570 officers attended his funeral, and hundreds of townsfolk lined the streets of Waxahachie to see his half-mile-long procession. Five days after his death, he was inducted into the American Police Hall of Fame, in Northport, Florida. A memorial scholarship has been funded in George's name, to be awarded each year to a student participating in Midlothian High's Just Say No program.

Ellis County, Texas, with participation from the city of Midlothian, is one of six finalists in the bidding on the U.S. Department of Energy's Superconducting Super Collider. The winner will be announced soon.

(1988)

The Temple of Doom

Police were baffled when nine Thai Buddhists were killed execution-style in a temple outside Phoenix—the worst mass murder in Arizona history.

It was to be a special day at the temple, so Chawee Borders arrived early, a bouquet of flowers in her hands. August in Arizona, the flat valley west of Phoenix. By ten a.m. the temperature was already pushing triple digits. Chawee squinted into the blazing sun, shook her head, made a noise behind her teeth, *tsktsk.* Heat eddied through the rubber soles of her shoes: It felt like walking through a skillet. No matter how long she lived here, Chawee couldn't quite get over the idea that they called *this* the monsoon season. Baked earth and cotton fields, battered Chevys, migrant pickers, mountains rising in the distance, barren and craggy against a wan blue sky. Half a world away, in her native Thailand, it was also the season of monsoons, all lush and wet and green, the time of rains and contemplations, of Buddhist retreat.

In Thailand, it is said, there is a temple on every corner, and every summer, one percent of all males become monks. In Phoenix, there is only one temple, Wat Promkunaram, an L-shaped stucco building with a red ceramic roof on five acres of lonely scrub in the western part of Maricopa county. This year, two boys had entered the temple. Matthew Miller, 17, had just arrived. David Doody, 14, had just left. The celebration tonight was for them.

Along with Matthew, there were six monks, a nun, and a young acolyte living in the Wat. Matthew was the son of an American Air Force vet and his Thai wife. Born in Myrtle Beach, SC, Matthew spoke Thai but had never been to Thailand. He was a friendly kid who played electric guitar, called his buddies "dude," cooked part-time in a Chinese restaurant. His nickname was "GQ," earned for the thrift-shop three-piece suits he painstakingly ironed and accessorized. None of the other kids wore suits to school. It was Matthew's own style, part of his need to be his own person. Half Thai, half

American, he'd found something special in his difference, was in the teenage process of puzzling himself together with pieces from many worlds.

Lately, Matthew had become more curious about his roots, something his mother traced to his Grandma Foy. Foy Sripanpiaserf was a youthful 71, one of the few mothers who had followed their daughters to America. Though she had learned to love hot Ovaltine and pro wrestling, she still spoke no English. After years of farming rice paddies, raising water buffalo and chickens along with children, picking her roots and vegetables from the ground free of charge, America seemed a very strange place to live. She worried that when she died, her spirit would inhabit an English-speaking place, too.

The Temple was thus a great comfort to Grandma Foy; she spent most of her time there—cooking, cleaning, gossiping, giving advice. Often Matthew came along. It surprised no one this summer, when Grandma Foy declared her intention to become a nun, that Matthew decided to follow.

Matthew planned to stay in the temple about a month. He didn't want to spend his whole vacation sitting around acting holy, and this was fine with the abbot. When a man becomes a Buddhist monk, he can stay for a few weeks or a lifetime. He can leave and return. It is honorable to be a monk for any length of service; they are living icons of the highest spiritual pursuit.

The first monk was Guatama Buddha, a Hindu prince born in the 6th century B.C. Buddha understood life as a complex universe of endless rebirth, with many heavens above, many hells below, one lifetime affecting the next. Buddha taught that a person could build merit for his fortunes in each successive life by practicing right thoughts and good deeds, by keeping a pure heart. Beyond this, there is the ultimate reward, Nirvana. Reaching Nirvana, he said, entails study, meditation, simple labors, a removal from material concerns. The key is coming to understand the Truth: "The way things really are." When the Truth becomes clear, suffering ends. The soul leaves the cycle of rebirth and rejoins the universe, much as a drop of water rejoins the ocean.

Being a practical religion, Buddhism recognizes that everyone can't be monk. For one thing, monks are celibate. For another, they're not supposed to cook or work for money. Most people, therefore, take for granted that other lifetimes are in store. Meanwhile, they seek karmic merit by serving the monks.

Since Chawee Borders lived right down the dirt road that led to the temple, she cooked lunch every day for the monks. Like Matthew's mother, like many of the women in a community of 2,000 Thais who settled in this unlikely outpost near Luke Air Force Base, Chawee was a Vietnam-era war bride.

Beginning in the late sixties, the Thai population of Phoenix had burgeoned. GI brides, working class families, professional men, they set up housekeeping and surgical practices, went to work in factories, opened restaurants and businesses. By 1983, the only thing missing was a Temple. A committee of wives was formed. Letters were written to Thailand, requesting monks for a spiritual center. To raise money, the women sold eggrolls, hosted a beauty pageant, recycled cans. Finally, five years ago, Wat Promkunaram was built.

Now, on the morning of Saturday, August 10th, 1991, Chawee shut her car door, walked with her friend Premchit Hash across the parking lot toward the temple kitchen. Just shy of the grass, the women stopped. The grounds were flooded. The monks hadn't turned off the irrigation. "Why would they forget?" Chawee wondered out loud. Premchit shrugged. Her arms were laden with trays of food. The two women circumnavigated, seeking a drier entrance.

At the east side, as was custom, they removed their shoes, stepped into the ceremonial hall. As Chawee padded toward the altar, she was struck by the silence. So quiet. The monks should have been up now for hours. But then again, she'd known the monks to sleep late. She put a finger to her lips, "Shhhhh," she urged Premchit, speaking in Thai, a language with no plurals. "The monk sleeping."

The monks were pampered and beloved figures, led by their abbot, Phra Maha Pairat Kanthong. Phra means something like Father or Reverend. Maha is a title denoting rank. Pairat, as he was called, was 36 years old. He'd been in Phoenix since the beginning of the Wat. To an American mind, he conjured the image of Spencer Tracy in *Boys Town*, known for his enthusiasm, his strength, his devotion to boxing, gardening and TV news.

Though he liked to tease and laugh, some say Pairat was troubled. The congregation was thin, the coffers were low. The children, almost all of them half-American, didn't attend very often. Sometimes, on Sundays, the congregation sparse, he almost despaired. He knew his concerns were earthly, unworthy for a monk. Yet still he worried—a human with responsibilities, a holy man, still a man.

As there were others under his charge, Pairat did his best to show a good face. Suthichai Annutaro, 32, was the eldest of a large family with a history of producing monks. Boonchuay Cahiyathammo, 37, was from Chang Mai, the poppy growing area in the north known as part of the Golden Triangle, the heroin center or Asia. Somsak Sopha, 47, had lectured on Buddhism, worked among the hill tribesmen of Thailand, traveled to Taiwan, the

Philippines and Sri Lanka. Siang Mahapanyo, 28, was an artist, sculptor, inventor and toy maker. Chalern Kittipattaro was 29. Little else about him was known. A monk can be collegial or choose to keep to himself. Like the rest, Chalern's main duty was to seek personal enlightenment, help others along the path.

Also under Pairat's care this summer was Chirasak Chirapong. Known affectionately as Boy, he was the abbot's nephew, 21, the long-haired son of a wealthy branch of his family. Chirasak had not entered the monkhood; he was just vacationing. He'd made friends with David Doody, and with his older brother, Jonathan. The American Thai boys had turned him on to malls, Slurpees, Arnold the Terminator, *Boyz N the Hood.* Boy bragged of having more than $2,000 in a small safe in his room. He spent it freely, financing all the outings.

Now, on the morning of the celebration for the novices, Chawee placed her flowers on the altar, bowed to the six-foot brass and gold leaf Buddha. She and Premchit passed behind the altar, into the kitchen. They busied themselves unwrapping platters. Maybe the monks were outside somewhere. No doubt they'd be back soon.

Then the telephone rang. There was a pay phone right next to the kitchen. Chawee picked it up, heard a click, then silence. Thinking she might have answered the wrong phone, she walked out of the kitchen a few steps, over to the private line. The chord was cut.

Puzzled, Chawee turned, surveyed the living room. Over in the middle, beyond the sofa, she could see all the monks sleeping on the floor. She'd known the monks to sleep on the floor. It wasn't too unusual. But then she noticed someone wearing white. Nuns dressed in white. Grandma Foy was sleeping with the monks! This was *not* allowed.

"Wake up!" she called gently, "Wake up, my monk." She took a cautious step forward.

"My monk!"

Matthew, Boy, Grandma Foy, Pairat, the monks . . .

All of them were dead.

It took three tries for the first officer on the scene to count the nine victims. "I guess it was mind boggling." he would later say.

Within hours, Wat Promkunaram was cordoned roundabout with yellow crime scene tape. Inside more than two dozen police combed for clues, some wearing rubber boots against the copious bloodflow. Other policemen—rubberneckers, top brass—trampled about, unwittingly contaminating evidence, what little there was: seventeen expended .22 caliber long-rifle shells, four expended yellow shotgun shells. Medical examiners would conclude that each of the nine had been shot execution style with the .22—at close range, above the base of the neck, while lying on his or her stomach. All except Boy had been shot twice. Several had superficial wounds from the birdshot. There had been no struggle. All nine had lain motionless, waiting to die, one at a time.

Though the ceremonial room was untouched, the living quarters had been ransacked. There were no usable fingerprints; the assailants had worn gloves. Police removed a section of wall on which the word "Bloods" had been carved in two-foot letters. This information was kept mum, as was the curious evidence that someone had set off a fire extinguisher, sliced open a bag of rice, poured soda into Pairat's computer. Guarding such details is standard in police work. When a suspect mentions secret details, detectives know they have the right man.

In the coming weeks, a sixty-six person task force would be assembled under the command of Maricopa County Sheriff Tom Agnos. The media were calling this the worst mass murder in state history, and Agnos—a gruff, chainsmoking, good old boy, serving his first elected term—was in charge. He coordinated personnel from local and state police agencies, the FBI, the Immigration and Naturalization Service, the DEA, even the Bangkok police. People around the world were watching in horror.

At first, police speculated that robbery was the motive, citing jewelry and ancient treasures kept in the temple. Then, upon learning that monks live in virtual poverty, they blamed Asian gangs. As each day passed, new theories were bandied about: It had been the work of a "lone psychopath," an "isolated bunch of kooks," a "Laotian mafia figure from Fresno," the KKK, a heroin trafficker.

Over the next two years, things would only get more complicated. What began as a gruesome, incomprehensible massacre of innocents would degenerate further over time into a complex, confusing, disturbing case that highlighted America's myriad ills: clashing cultures, fractured morals, family dysfunction, the tragically easily availability of firearms, the frightening latitude taken by law enforcement groups during increasingly martial times. In the end, the case of the murders at the Wat would become more than just another senseless tragedy. Some would say it was a sign.

• • •

For the first several weeks after the murders, police ran in circles. After 15,000 man-hours of investigation, they were clueless. Then, lead No. 511 lit up the switchboard. The tipster said he had the scoop on the murders at the "Budapest" temple.

Three hours later, detectives pulled up to the Tucson Psychiatric Institute. There they met the tipster: a short, heavy-set Mexican American, 25 years old, "alert and eating a graham cracker," according to a police report. The tipster asked the detectives if they had found blood on the walls at the temple.

Bingo. The cops had found the word "Bloods" carved in two-foot letters. Michael Lawrence McGraw was brought in for questioning, advised of his rights. Waving his right to a counsel, he confessed, implicating himself and four others.

Acting swiftly, police made arrests. Sheriff Agnos held a press conference. Five arrests, five confessions, he told reporters. Case closed.

One week later, McGraw and the others recanted their confessions. "I had nothing to do with this," McGraw told the *Arizona Republic* in a jail house interview.

In the southside barrio of Tucson, a dusty patchwork of poverty, neighbors and relatives rallied in defense of their own. McGraw, they said, was known as "Crazy Mike." According to a 30-page probation file, McGraw had been arrested twice for false reporting of crimes. One counselor questioned McGraw's "discrimination of reality to fantasy." Said a longtime neighbor: "If the police had stopped to ask anyone about Michael, we would have told him."

Unfortunately, the police had not asked. They had obtained search warrants without consulting the county attorney. SWAT teams in black hoods broke down doors with battering rams, threw stun grenades into empty apartments. Not one shred of physical evidence was recovered from the suspects' homes.

Then it was announced that one of the confessed killers was to be released. The man worked at a Greyhound track. Video tapes of races placed him atop the starting gate at the time of the crime.

Soon, defense attorneys began crying coercion. The ACLU concurred. The Tucson men, it was alleged, had been questioned for ten to twenty hours without a break. They had been denied food, sleep, lawyers and phone calls. Some interrogations were taped, some were not. The men were shown a roomful of evidence from the temple—including pictures and crime-scene drawings—before they were questioned. All five men said that the police had threatened them with the gas chamber, with having their fingernails pulled out, with a lake and an anchor. A lawyer characterized the cops' technique as "World Wrestling Federation tag-team interrogation . . . tantamount to a rubber hose."

Four of the men were bound over for trial.

"Okay, Jonathan, we're gonna go though this thing again," said Det. Rick Sinsabaugh, tired and exasperated in the ninth hour of interrogation. Sinsabaugh was a ten-year veteran of the Maricopa County Sheriff's Department, a long drink of water in cowboy boots. It was early in the morning of October 26, more than two months after the murders.

The kid across the table sobbed, then sniffled. His name was Jonathan Doody, the older brother of the novice monk David. He was dressed in a baby-blue ROTC uniform. He sat up a little, stared at the cop. Tears began to flow. "When you caught those people in Tucson, they were laughing at you! They had nothing to do with it!" he said.

"Who was laughing at us?" asked Sinsabaugh, outraged.

"They beat the system."

"Who?"

Jonathan cut his eyes to the floor. "Them," he mumbled.

Sinsabaugh sighed. "Listen, Jonathan," he said, his voice warming. "We're not going to be going out and telling people what you told us, okay? Come on, pal, join the team. Be a soldier, Jonathan. Come clean, my man. Hey! Jonathan! Look at me!"

Jonathan was 17. His mother, Laiad, was a regular at the temple, and Jonathan knew Pairat and Boy and all the rest. Though he was born in Thailand to a Thai father, and spoke English with an accent, Jonathan knew no Thai, had no interest in Buddhism. He'd been baptized in Valdosta, Georgia, by a Pentecostal minister. His nickname was LT, for "lieutenant," his rank in the ROTC. He considered himself American.

Jonathan's step-father was career Air Force; Jonathan wanted to become a pilot. In school, he was a gung-ho commander in the Air Force ROTC. On weekends, he maneuvered with the Civil Air Patrol. He was quiet and serious, had a military bearing. He knew ROTC was his only chance for college. He studied hard, drilled hard, practiced good manners. In sum, he was seen by all who knew him as the model boy, the model immigrant, a throwback to the old ideal: That people could come to the Land of the Free, shed their old ways, assimilate, live out the American Dream.

It was now the morning of October 25, more than two months after the murders. Last night, the Agua Fria High School Owls had a home football game, and Jonathan, as always, commanded the honor guard. After the anthem was played, Jonathan marched the squad off the field, and Sinsabaugh walked over and tapped him on the shoulder. Jonathan went quietly. He had no reason to do otherwise. He liked Sinsabaugh. Up till now, Sinsabaugh had been treating him like a fellow soldier—an inside agent who could help police solve this mess.

The file on Jonathan Andrew Doody had been opened inadvertently ten days after the murders. Police at Luke had stopped two cars, a silver Mustang and an orange Nova, for "suspicious activity." Jonathan had just bought the used 5.0. The Nova belonged to his friend Rolando Caratachea, known as Rollie. On the back seat of the Nova was Rollie's .22 caliber rifle. The police told him to stow the rifle in the trunk, then let him go.

Two weeks later, as cops on horseback and in helicopters combed the desert between Tucson and Phoenix, looking for the murder weapon, the Air Force called about Rollie's .22 rifle. Sinsabaugh later drove out to the base to see Rollie. He asked if he could borrow his .22 for routine testing, telling him it was part of a sweep for stolen arms. Since Rollie's mom had bought the gun on sale at Kmart for Christmas, he gave it up willingly. Sinsabaugh took the rifle to the lab, put it in line behind eighty other .22s to be tested.

That night, Lead No. 511 came in over the phone. The cops focused on Tucson. Rollie's rifle was forgotten.

Six weeks later, there was still no shred of physical evidence. The task force had become a nightmare of infighting, all of it followed closely by the press. Detectives were beginning to believe that the Tucson suspects were innocent. The top brass was clinging to their confessions. Detectives were being ordered to rewrite reports, according to news reports.

Then the lab got around to testing Rollie's Marlin .22. There it was. The murder weapon.

It didn't take much footwork to pinpoint Jonathan as a new suspect. Rollie had lent the gun, on the weekend in question, to Jonathan and another ROTC cadet, Alessandro Garcia, known as Alex. The exchange occurred outside a party; there were many witnesses. Likewise, on the night before the killings, Jonathan told his girlfriend that he was going to "play in a game" involving "intrusion alert" near the temple. Another friend says that after the murders, Jonathan had bragged about killing the nine Buddhists on behalf of the Office of Special Investigations of the Air Force (OSI) because they were "invading national security and had to be eliminated." Jonathan had claimed he was a paid OSI sniper who'd killed the Thais "mercenary style." Once a person commits a mercenary killing, he said, "you will always see and hear the blood rushing from their heads."

Now, in what his attorney would later characterize as a "brutal, nonstop, 14-hour interrogation," teams of deputies implored, begged, beseeched, yelled at and comforted Jonathan. They called on his patriotism, his sense of team spirit, his need to get things behind him. At one point, his attorney suggests, Sinsabaugh may have even "de-Mirandized" Jonathan when he said that the police "won't be going out and telling everybody what you told us."

Throughout the taped proceedings, Jonathan said as little as possible. Listening to the seventeen forty-five-minute tapes—acquired though a source by *GQ*—the story that emerges sounds improvised, as if he was trying to please the cops, weaving together details that were fed to him.

Jonathan claimed that he and Alex had been approached by a friend of Rollie's, who was a member of a gang. The friend wanted help to breach the temple's security system, which consisted of two motion-detector lights in the parking lot.

Jonathan said he didn't know who shot whom, or who had which gun. He didn't know the names or races of his accomplices. He could, however, describe the shots. He imitated them for police, making the sounds like a kid playing war. *Pow, pow . . . Pow, pow . . .*

Afterwards, Jonathan said, they all reconvened at a dry riverbottom. The gang members warned Jonathan and Alex: If they talked they'd be "eliminated."

"While you were being fingerprinted, I asked you how you were doing. Do you recall that?"

"Yes, I do," said Alex Garcia, Jonathan's closest friend.

"And do you remember what you asked me?"

"I said, 'What's going to happen to me?' "

"Correct," said Det. Russ Kimball, reviewing their previous conversation, speaking not so much to the blanket-wrapped tenth-grader sitting across the table as he was to the hidden microphone. It was 8 a.m. on October 26, in an interrogation room next to the one in which Jonathan was being questioned. Kimball was recollecting a conversation he'd had with Alex a short while ago, attempting to get it onto the record.

"My recollection, Alex," said Kimball, pointing with his Mountblanc pen, "is that I said there was a possibility that you wouldn't go to jail. And you could . . . what? Do you remember what I said?"

"Walk out."

"Walk out. Okay. At that point in time you asked me what?"

"I asked what if I told the complete story without any lies."

"Good, Alex, good!" said Kimball.

Five hours earlier, after questioning Jonathan for a while, police had obtained a search warrant and raided the Garcia house. Jonathan had been bunking with Alex since school began. Police were searching for several cameras, a flash, a boom box, a bullhorn, a pair of binoculars, a portable CD player, some gold leaf paper—items that had been taken from the temple. They found those things, along with a pair of air force snow boots and a Stevens Model 67 20-gauge shotgun, the other weapon used in the temple murders.

Two hours into his interrogation, at 5:33 a.m., Alex asked for a lawyer. The police called his father. Then they took Alex for mugs and fingerprints.

Presently, Juan Garcia arrived in a squad car. Before he saw his son, he talked to the detectives, their captain, even Sheriff Agnos. They offered him donuts, told him Alex was a good boy. They said Alex could tie the Tucson four to the murders. They mentioned a sentence of seven to nine years, a deal. If only Alex would talk.

Juan Garcia was shocked. As far as he knew, his son had never been in trouble. He baby-sat neighbors' kids, fixed bikes in his driveway. He was a smart boy who'd skipped seventh grade. Six-four and beefy, Alex was a lineman on the football team. "He was a Gentle Ben type," Juan would later say. "He would apologize when he hit someone too hard in practice."

Alex talked to his father several times. There was a lot of hugging and crying. Juan—himself six-six and nearly four hundred pounds—urged his son to tell the truth. "I love you, *mijo*," he said.

"I love you too, Daddy," Alex said.

Just after 8 a.m., the questioning began anew. Through the wall, Alex could hear Sinsabaugh screaming at Jonathan. The tape rolled. Alex began.

"It was just an idea that me and Jonathan . . . Should I mention names?"

"Absolutely," said Kimball.

". . . that Jonathan Doody had come up with. Basically for money. Because

Jonathan was attempting to purchase a car, a used Mustang 5.0. He needed $2,000, and Boy had said he had $2,000 in a little safe.

"To start out, we collected information from his brother. David, his younger brother, attended the temple. We asked, like, were there security cameras, there weren't any. Alarms, there weren't any. How many people were there, if they had weapons underneath the beds. And we just collected information and it came to the point of, well, that it was a go. . . ."

The boys drew a diagram, made a plan. Next, they decided, they needed guns. There were four rifles in Alex's house. He would take the shotgun kept in his father's closet. It was hidden. Juan wouldn't notice it missing. For Jonathan, they decided to ask Rollie to borrow his .22.

On Thursday, August 8, they got the rifle, a Marlin .22. That night, they went out into the desert to test it. They tried to fashion a silencer from a length of pipe and some bottle caps, following instructions from a book. Though the silencer worked, it was only good for two or three shots. They nixed the idea. For clothes, they decided on BDUs—battle dress uniforms or camouflage fatigues—along with web belts, knives, right angle flashlights, caps, bandannas, tank goggles: everything military issue, from either ROTC or Luke. And air-force surplus snow boots. The boots were very large; they would leave oversized footprints, confuse the cops.

At 10 p.m. on Friday the boys turned onto Maryland Avenue, doused the headlights of the Mustang Jonathan had just picked up on credit from a friend. They turned right into the temple lot, synchronized their watches.

Doubletime in a half squat, they ran to the nearest wall, worked their way around to the kitchen door, the west side.

Jonathan hit the door first. "Police!" he yelled.

The monks and the others were watching television. They were startled by the masked soldiers. "We told them to get on the floor, and we told them that, you know, we were here," Alex said.

Jonathan cut the phone line and went to the bedrooms. Alex could hear things breaking, shelves tossed, a lot of noise. After some time, Jonathan returned to the living room, and Alex went back through, making sure Jonathan didn't forget anything. Along the way, Alex came across a fire extinguisher. He'd always wanted to shoot one off so he did, spraying foam around the hallway. He cut the bag of rice. Poured Coke into Pairat's computer. Then he carved the word "Bloods" on the wall in two-foot-high letters. *That'll throw a wrench in the works,* he thought. He packed the loot into two duffel bags.

When Alex returned, Jonathan was standing on a sofa, holding the gun on the prostrate monks.

"Then Jonathan said it was time to go," Alex told Kimball. "He said: 'No witnesses.'"

Kimball raised an eyebrow.

"Listen," Alex pleaded, "I'm being completely honest. I will sign anything. I will take a lie detector. This is true: I'm in the doorway, and he's on the couch, pointing the gun down at the monks, and he looks at me, you know, like, 'Go ahead, start.' And I just stood there, like, 'What do you mean?' And then I told him to come over here, I motioned him over. I told Jonathan that I didn't want to kill them. I seriously did not want to kill them. But he just said 'No witnesses!' That was his exact words, 'No witnesses.'

"And he walked back to the monks and just started shooting, okay? And at that point of time I was like, something came over me, you know? I just stood in the doorway and kept pulling the trigger, pumping, pulling the trigger, until, you know, nothing was left. I don't know where I aimed. I just shot my four shots. Jonathan went around shooting the people in the back of the head with the .22 caliber, a couple of times to make sure that they were completely dead. He went from one to the next, kind of like *bang, bang . . . bang, bang,* you know, like enough time between each to like aim at the head, just like a steady beat, not like *powpowpow.*

"It was just me and Jonathan. The four people in Tucson, they had nothing to do with it. *Nothing.* I don't know how they come about to the story. Rollie, nothing. We just used his gun. It was just me and Jonathan. No one else had anything to do with it."

The next night, October 26, Master Sgt. Brian Doody and the other members of his family—his wife Laiad, his step-son David, his bio-kids Crystal and Michael—pulled into their driveway in a cherry red truck. It was a military-issue house at Maxwell Air Force Base in Colorado Springs, same as every other on the street, enlisted country. The Doodys had been living there—without Jonathan—since September 1.

Brian, 38, was a seventeen-year air-force veteran, a munitions specialist who had recently cross-trained into satellites. He'd been raised in Connecticut, son of a construction truck driver. Always a loner, a bit of a nerd, Brian was scrawny and four-eyed growing up, the object of pranks and beatings. A few years after high school, his prospects dim, he joined the air force.

They sent him to Germany, where he serviced missiles. He began lifting weights, studying Tae Kwon Do. Two months in-country he was set up with Laiad on a blind date. She was the widow of a Thai. Her sister—a GI wife— had paid her way to Germany. The pair had been dating five months when her visa expired. There was only one thing to do. "She had it in mind to marry me. I guess I was the last to realize it," he says now.

Laiad had two sons, ages 8 and 5. They were living with their grand- mother in a one-room house of corrugated tin in a village north of Bangkok. "The most excitement for the kids was waiting for it to rain so the dirt streets would fill up full of water and they'd take off all their clothes and go play in a puddle," recalls Brian.

Within two weeks of his wedding, Brian adopted the boys. Veerapol and Veeraphan Khan Kew became Jonathan and David Doody.

Once in Germany, Jonathan fixed on the fighter jets. There were F4s and FI6s at the base. They'd take off trailing brilliant flames, bank low over the Doody house. Jonathan would squat for hours, Thai style on his haunches, watching the takeoffs, feeling the ground shake beneath him.

Within a year Crystal was born and the family was transferred to Valdosta, Georgia. The boys were put into public elementary school. Neither spoke English. They failed everything the first two years but were promoted anyway. Laiad spoke no English, didn't seem to want to learn. There they were, trying to make things work in a place were Asians were generally referred to as nips or gooks—and no one in the family could communicate. Laiad could speak to the boys but not to her husband. Brian had only a rudimentary knowledge of Thai. He carried his dictionary wherever they went. There was a language gap, a culture gap, a chasm. Brian despaired. He began drinking.

When Jonathan was 13, Brian was transferred to Guam. By this time Jonathan could read and write English. He refused to speak Thai at all. "Jon's and my relationship was really funny," says Brian, "maybe because he knew I wasn't his real father, even though he did call me Dad. . . . A lot of things he did, I took personally. Like he'd spend all his time in his room. I felt it was against me, like, 'I'm gonna close the door so I won't have to look at Dad anymore.' "

Before long "Jonathan's hormones kicked in," Brian says. The distant boy became even more oblique. He found a first girlfriend, started staying out late at the base canteen with the other military brats.

"I'd tell him, 'Jonathan, be home by nine.' And he'd come home at ten- thirty. I would work myself up into a frenzy, just like a shark, you know? They'll tap at the meat and the more they tap the more they get excited. And that's the way I was. He'd get home late and I'd ask him why, and he'd just stand there, no expression on his face at all. It would aggravate me more. And more and more. And finally I'd start grabbing and roughing him up. I used to hit him a lot. I used to slap him. I used the belt on him. Jonathan, he was total defiance. He wouldn't say one word. He'd just stare at me."

The wars continued until the Doodys arrived at Luke in the summer of 1989. The Civil Air Patrol had a unit on base; Jonathan immediately joined. In the fall he entered ROTC. Brian sought help for his abusive behavior, received counseling and quit drinking.

"Jonathan changed overnight," Brian says. "He talked to me about things. I gave him books of mine, manuals and stuff. He was more mature, responsible, he did what I told him the first time I asked.

"It's like he'd found a place for himself. For all those years, especially in Georgia, he was so concerned about being accepted because his eyes were different, his skin was different, he had an accent. When he found ROTC he just found his niche. He was going to make a perfect military person because he loved America. He said, 'This is my land of opportunity.' He meant it."

Jonathan worked two jobs, rising before dawn to peddle five miles to McDonald's, then going to the base commissary after school to bag groceries. He gave all his earnings to his mom, who kept meticulous records on little slips of paper, stashed safely in a drawer with her underthings.

Soon after he got his driver's license, Jonathan went halves with his parents on a used Ford Escort. The head needed rebuilding. Brian envisioned it as a father-son project. Jonathan did not. He didn't want to learn how to work on his car. "Dad," he said, "someday I'll be able to afford people for that."

Goddammit, thought Brian, Jonathan was getting uppity. He aspired to be an officer, a pilot—a class above his enlisted step-father in the rigid caste system of the military. "Jonathan said, 'I'm gonna be better than you.'" Brian says, "It cut into my heart like a knife."

Then, in early 1991, Brian announced his pending transfer to Colorado. Come September, he told his family, they would be gone from Phoenix.

As far as Jonathan was concerned, however, come September, he'd be a junior at Agua Fria High School, the commander of the ROTC honor guard. Up in Colorado Springs, the schools didn't have ROTC. He wasn't going. Period. There were fights. Big ones.

Brian left Phoenix for a month of training, returned just in time for the funerals of the temple victims. The family went together; Jonathan placed flowers and incense on each casket. To those around him, he seemed genuinely moved by the killings. He went back to the temple every day for a week afterwards to help out.

At home, Jonathan wasn't quite so respectful. He was set on staying. Laiad was against the idea, but she helped him find an apartment, put down a deposit. Then she reminded him over and over that he was breaking her heart. Jonathan told Brian: "My friend says I could take you to court if you don't let me stay."

"I surprised him," says Brian. "I told him: 'Go ahead and get out now.' "

From mid-August until this October weekend, Jonathan had been living with Alex Garcia, sharing his bedroom. When Brian and the rest of the Doodys came inside, he noticed the telephone answering machine blinking. He hit play.

"Mr. Doody, this is the Durango Juvenile Detention Center. We have your son. He's been arrested on nine counts of murder."

One month later, November 20, 1991, *The Arizona Republic*:

> Maricopa County Attorney Rick Romley will ask Superior Court judges Friday to dismiss charges against four Tucson men held since September in the slaying of nine Buddhists monks.
>
> "The sheriff just wouldn't accept the fact that the Tucson men and the Phoenix boys did not know each other," Romley said.

Following Alex's confession, he and Jonathan were booked on nine counts of robbery and murder. Rollie, after questioning and a lie detector test, was charged in two unrelated burglaries.

Weeks of controversy and political infighting ensued, culminating in the release of the Tucson 4. The men had been in custody for 70 days. They filed multimillion-dollar lawsuits. All except "Crazy Mike" McGraw. He went back to the Institute.

Time passed. The boys were adjudicated adults for the trial, transferred from juvenile to county court. There were preliminary hearings, motions, legal maneuvers. Attorneys tried desperately to have the confessions thrown out, to uncover evidence and exhibits from the helter skelter investigation, to overcome what felt to them like malicious prosecutorial zeal.

Eight months later, in July of 1992, Sheriff Agnos was still pushing his Tucson scenario. He even went so far as to visit Crazy Mike again. Mike told the Sheriff that after the murders, he and the others had posed for a picture in front of the temple, with Mike holding up a newspaper to show the date. The photo, he said, was buried along with some ammunition, a watch and a bag of rice on a butte outside Phoenix.

Agnos sent deputies up the mountain with picks and shovels. Nothing was recovered.

In November, Agnos was defeated by a landslide.

Alex Garcia shifted his weight in the hard metal chair, trying to get comfortable. He crooked his knees, slanted his legs to one side like a debutante from Miss Porter's, ankles kissing, foot shackles jangling against the concrete floor of the interview room. He held a pen awkwardly in his big fist, wrists cuffed, following each word of every sentence across the pages before him, lips moving ever so slightly as he read.

Thick iron bars framed his face. From a three-quarter view he seemed handsome, with high cheekbones and almond-shaped eyes. The jaw, thick and square, his father's, lent a sort of haughty, rakish air to the face of a teenage boy. From dead on, though, the impression was altered. You saw the stick-out ears, the chipped front teeth, the meaty expanse of forehead; he appeared vaguely feral.

The document before him was a plea agreement. Though the police believed Alex's scenario, when it came right down to it, Alex was in bigger trouble than Jonathan. Courtroom justice is a game, with each side trying to win points inside carefully drawn boundaries, the rules of law and procedure. In the hands of the court, the narrative and nuance—the story of a complex happening—tends to get lost. Featured instead are tiny pieces of truth: singular details, items of evidence, shards. Those incriminated Alex.

The cops, in fact, had no hard evidence on Jonathan. He had confessed only to witnessing the murders. On Alex, they had his thumbprint on the shotgun, his air-force boots. And they had the cameras and the other stolen property found in his bedroom. Though Jonathan was living with Alex, in legal terms, it was Alex's room. The goods were on Alex, even if he wasn't the shooter.

Alex was in trouble. He was the easier target in a big case with a freakish history and heavy ramifications, local and worldwide. And he was living in a Republican stronghold with a reputation out of the wild, wild west. A state with Mormon roots, cowboy sensibilities, an ever-growing population of Mexicans and foreigners of color, a reigning philosophy that seemed to mix

Libertarianism and Prohibitionism. You could walk around Phoenix with a gun on your hip, go to a head shop and buy a crack pipe. Get caught using either, however, and you'd find Arizona's sentencing guidelines to be among the toughest in the nation.

Under Arizona law, complicity in an armed robbery is equal to pulling the trigger. Facing death by lethal injection, Alex made a deal—his testimony for his life.

So now he checked the pages carefully, asking questions of his lawyer, Luis Calvo, wondering if he was doing the right thing.

In the eleven or so months of their friendship, Alex and Jonathan had talked a lot about The Code. It is honored in the military, among thieves. It's about keeping your mouth shut. No one likes a snitch, especially not in jail.

But then again, in Alex's mind, he didn't pull the trigger. Fuck Jonathan. He was a comrade of interests for a time, sure. But mostly he was this funny, stupid, arrogant kid who couldn't pronounce the letter "r" and never put the "s's" on plurals—"*Come on, you guy, we go for a lide.*" He carried the instructional diagram from a package of condoms in his wallet. He seemed not to grasp exactly what was going on a lot of the time; he was always watching you to see what to do next. In sum, Jonathan was a dweeb, but he was also Alex's only friend with a licence and a car. He would pick up Alex whenever he called. When you're 16, that's more than enough for friendship. But not enough to die for.

Reading through the agreement, Alex came to a clause that said he must state any knowledge of crimes committed prior to his arrest on October 25th, 1991. Failure to disclose would void this deal, make him eligible for the death penalty without a trial.

Alex read the clause again, then again. Finally he looked up. "Mr. Calvo?" he asked his attorney. "What if I know about another crime?"

As it turns out, Alex Garcia wasn't quite the Gentle Ben his parents knew.

As Alex tells it, in an exclusive jailhouse interview with *GQ*, he grew up hard, son of a repo man and a factory supervisor, "below average middle class." He'd lived his whole life in Maricopa County, in the West Valley. Suburban, exurban, rural in spots, the area has an equally eclectic population. There are snowbirds—named for their hair color and seasonal migrations—in retirement villages like Sun City; military housing around Luke; professionals in Litchfield Park; bluecollars and farmers in Litchfield. Trailer camps for migrant workers; modest, ad-hoc developments of second and third generation Chicanos; apartments filled at dinnertime with a symphony of exotic smells from Asia and the Middle East.

From the time he started elementary school—bussed each day to Litchfield Park, an affluent suburb nearby—Alex says he felt "like a poor boy, someone who wore the same clothes three days in a row and heard about it." Alex was a loner. "It was always like, 'What the fuck do I want to deal with them for, anyway?' " he says. He didn't need people or have the same interests as them. Then, as now, "I lived in my own mind," he says.

He did play with other kids sometimes, a group from the neighborhood. "We did a lot of shit," Alex says. "Like, there was this one house across the street, it was empty, and we just tore the shit out of it. I mean, I wanted to blow the damn thing up. Or we'd, you know, get sticks and our bikes and, what do you call that? Joust? We'd fly at each other down the street, try and knock each other off. I broke my arm from that.

"If you wanted to go somewhere where we lived, you walked or rode your bike. It wasn't 'Mom, take me here.' You walked. You didn't have malls, you didn't have three wheelers or ATVs, so we made our own fun. We had the desert: Let's make a clubhouse. It was fun, but at the same time, it was hard because of the family situation. A bullshit lazy faggot for a father, a mother that works all the time, and a dick for a brother. I was the younger one. You know? The younger one gets beat? Well I got beat a lot of times. To me, it was like, fuck you, life's too short. I didn't want to be told what to do. I'd go where I wanted, I'd wear what I wanted, I'd say what I wanted. It was like, fuck it, you know?"

If Alex had his druthers, he would have been born earlier. "I'm a Vietnam freak," he says. His favorite movie is *Apocalypse Now*. He would have fucking fought. Jimi Hendrix on the tape player, humping an M-60 through the slop, twin bandoliers of ammo across his chest. Vietnam: he would have fucking loved it. "It's the paranoia of not knowing," he says. "One second you can be sitting, the next you're dead. It's like, 'Hey, this shit's for real!' "

ROTC was thus a natural choice, though Alex would have preferred army or marine if they'd offered it. He met Jonathan the first day of freshman year. It was a perfect match: Alex the poor boy, the loner, the thinker; Jonathan the immigrant trying to blend in. Both of them had families from hell. Both were crazy for all things martial. They bonded instantly, an alliance of outsiders.

One night, at the beginning of summer vacation in 1991, the boys found themselves at a house party. There, they met a new group of friends. One of them was Rollie Caratachea. He lived way out there in the boonies, had the distinction of being kicked out of his house and living in his car. He was said to have ties to the Avondale Barrio Locos, a Mexican drug gang. Altogether, there were like 10 or 15 of them hanging out in a knot at the party, drinking beer, goofing, everybody starting to get to know each other. As the night wore on, someone decided it was time to go to Sonic Burger.

"If you can imagine a Nova, a Mustang, a Camaro and a little Ford Escort, racing off down the road in a cloud of smoke, that's what it was," says Alex.

And so the summer took shape. "We did a lot of shit," says Alex.

The first thing they did was name themselves: AM Posse, for After Midnight: That was when the mischief always started. You could call the AM Posse a gang, though in times past you might have called it a frat or a club or an affinity group, a garage band, a softball team. All over Phoenix, all across America, nineties kids are forming posses or gangs or crews. Modeled upon the glorified media vision of the L.A. Crips and Bloods, they call themselves "posses" after the infamous Jamaican hoods, or maybe after Arsenio's band, or Ice Cube's homeys, or maybe just after the sheriff's vigilantes in the cowboy movies. Hybrid groupings, composed of kids of both genders, from different neighborhoods, all races and social strata, they organize not over traditional missions like turf or respect or drugs, but rather over the newer scourges of boredom and alienation.

Proliferating in cities and suburbs and rurals alike, what the members of these new-age gangs have in common is dysfunctional families. In this era of working parents, shifting values, societal chaos, the kids have no other choice but to go to each other. Today's kids find their structure, protection, opportunity, acceptance, love in the comfortable surrounds of their posse.

The AM Posse was also bonded by something else: a love of mischief and mayhem, violence and guns—the drugs of choice for the Just Say No Generation. "If you think about it," says Alex, "there's always something to get in trouble with. It's fun. It's free. It's living on the edge."

The AM Posse started out racing cars, laying rubber, doing donuts. When that got boring, they moved on to yanking stereos and siphoning gas, and then on to stealing cars. Jonathan and Alex liked to add military wrinkles. They'd patrol the perimeter, monitoring a police scanner. Counterintelligence, they called it.

Inevitibly, guns came into the picture. Rollie had his .22 in the back seat. Others had guns of their own. They shot out street lamps, pumped shotgun pellets into cars—drive-by assaults on inanimate objects. They kept doing car stereos, packing heat now for "protection." And then they moved on to "capers." Rollie and some others hit a mini-storage place twice. Another time, Alex, Jonathan and Rollie went to rob a friend who had several large bottles of coins. They dressed in BDUs, each carrying a gun. The kid wasn't home. The mission was aborted. "It was like living in a movie," says Alex.

Guns have become a major problem in America, but in Arizona, where owning firearms has always been a way of life, they are "epidemic," experts say. In Phoenix, a kid can get a .22 pistol or a sawed-off shotgun for $25. For a little more he can buy a .38, for a little more a Mac 10 or a .9mm or an Uzi. Even in states with more restrictive gun laws, the black market thrives, with weapons being dealt out of car trunks and duffel bags. "Guns are magnetic," says Alex. "It's all about power. It's all about I've got control. You're gonna hit something if you aim at it. You're gonna blow it away. I like guns, I really do. I like knives too. I generally like weapons. Hell, if I could have got a .50 caliber machine gun in the back of a pickup truck, that would be cool."

There is something magical about guns and violence, Alex says. The American public seems to agree. Studies of television and movies have shown that by the time a child reaches 18, he has seen over 18,000 simulated murders, 100,000 acts of violence, according to studies of programming. Seventy percent of prime time TV programs include violence. The average home viewer witnesses 16 violent acts a night. Children's programs have three times the amount of violence as adults'.

Witnessing so much feigned violence, a kid today has a sort of virtual reality experience with killing. Even if he's never held a gun, he's seen one used enough times that it seems second nature. Not suprisingly, the homicide rate among juveniles in America has more than doubled in the past decade.

"To me, what we were doing didn't seem wrong," says Alex. "I don't know, I'm weird with it. A lot of people would consider us, okay, a bunch of criminals. But what makes us criminals? If you get caught? 'Cause everybody does things wrong, everybody. To tell you the truth, we could have done a lot. We could have been the beginning of another kind of organized crime. We lived in a small community. We had several gun stores where we could have easily broken in. We had the houses out in the desert. Isolated settlements. We could have really made something of it."

By midsummer, however, the AM Posse had dissipated, and Jonathan and

Alex were back on their own. For money, for something to do, they planned the temple caper. On August 9th, 1991, they moved.

"You gotta imagine," says Alex, recalling the scene. "You got nine people, all laying face down with their hands clasped behind their heads. Every time a bullet hit, you know, every time the sound went off, you could just see them jerk. Like their body jerking. And then I remember the gurgling, the gurgling of blood in their throats. I wish I was a good enough artist to draw it. It's hard to put into words.

"The weird thing was the money, counting up the money and splitting it. We had a big grudge about it. We got I think $2,650. Jonathan owed $2,000 on the Mustang, and it was like he wanted to take that much and give me $650. Shit. I wasn't gonna play that. You're getting a fucking car and I'm getting a couple shirts and a pair of shoes? Fuck that. We split even. Then we went over to Circle K and bought Thirst Busters. . . .

"To this day—You know, it's funny. You can pull a caper, and when you're there, you can say: 'Yeah, this looks right,' and then afterwards you're like: 'Why in the fuck did we do *this*?' That was the only thing: If we could have gotten rid of the .22, we could have, hell, we could have had robes, we could have had jars of blood in our closet, we could have had anything from the temple. As long as they didn't have the murder weapon. That's what caught us. We could have dumped it in the river, filed off the serial numbers, just thrown it on the street. We were stupid.

"There was a lot of mistakes. I shouldn't say I'm sad, but it's kind of fucked up. I mean, right now, after my case and everything, I could write a guidebook about how not to get caught. You could follow my handwriting and do all the crimes you wanted.

"To tell you the truth, if me and Jonathan couldn't have been caught, I think there would have been more crime. I know for a fact there would have been. A lot more crime. A lot more murders."

"All right now, Alex. Are you ready?"

Deputy County Attorney Kenneth C. Scull was a distinguished veteran with a sculpted grey beard. He removed his glasses, rubbed his tired blue eyes. It was the first week of February 1993. He'd been working the temple case since the beginning, seventeen months before. Now Alex had asked for this meeting. There was something on his conscience that he wanted to say.

Shifting in his chair, Alex began his story. It began inside of a pickup truck in the sand dunes near the White Tank Mountains. Alex was at the wheel. Michelle Hoover was in the passenger seat. It was October 14, 1991, ten days before Alex and Jonathan had been arrested.

"So what do we do, Alex?" Michelle asked. She was 14, a freshman, less than five feet tall, the biggest love Alex had ever had. The pickup belonged to her mother. They were stuck in the sand, it was a school night, after three in the morning.

Alex slumped in the seat, stared out the windshield. The sky was black, freckled with a million stars. Michelle had a million freckles across her nose, beautiful blue eyes, fine long reddish hair with a new perm, the front moused and standing up off her forehead. In the glow of the dashboard, she looked scared.

"Can you call your father?" asked Alex. "He can tow us out."

"Oh no! He's asleep." said Michelle. "He'd kill me!"

In fact, Ted Hoover had never even raised his voice to his daughter. She was an only child, a tomboy, an honor student, daddy's pet. When she was born, six years into their marriage, Ted quit his job as a cop to spend more time with his family.

The Hoovers lived in affluent Litchfield. They had four Doberman dogs, a good piece of land. Ted was a boss in a big construction firm in the West Valley. Mom Kathy worked there too. Their daughter was known by all to be responsible, artistic, sweet, "one of those few people who's a saint." She took ballet and tumbling, was fair skinned, tended to be heavy. She liked Troll dolls, the New Kids on the Block, going to the mall, eating. Summers she taught Bible school.

Michelle had just entered ninth grade at Agua Fria. The first week of school, one day after class, her friend Liz invited her to watch ROTC practice. Liz had a crush on this guy Alex.

Liz's plans went slightly awry. When Alex met Michelle, "there was an instant flame," says Alex. "She was outgoing, she was funny, she was bursting with energy." He gave her his number and she called that night. "He was scared because he thought his girlfriend was pregnant," says Michelle. "We talked and I just said it would be okay. And then he found out she wasn't pregnant and he started talking to me more. And then he picked me over her."

The kids became close, very close. Closer then they'd ever been to anyone. For Michelle, it was her first boyfriend. And Alex—he'd never had someone like her. She came to ROTC practice every day. When they got home, they talked on the phone before and after dinner, late into the night, also the first thing each morning.

Michelle began to change. She wore makeup, fussed with her clothes, went on a starvation diet. Kathy would tell her to get off the phone and find her on again five minutes later. She no longer did her chores, had no interest in clubs or events. Kathy never met the Garcias, nor did they ever offer to carpool.

As the Hoovers saw it, Alex was the love interest from the other side of the tracks. In his days as a cop, he said, Ted had seen how Mexican men treated their wives; he wasn't happy with this at all. But the Hoovers didn't say much. What could they say? Michelle was head over heels. "I was drawn to him," says Michelle. "On a scale of one to ten, it was a ten, you know. I cared so much about him."

At midnight on October 14th, while Ted and Kathy slept, Michelle and Alex were cooing to each other from the the phones in their respective bedrooms. They'd been dating for three weeks now; this was their custom, watching TV together, giggling, declaring their love. Sometime during the conversation, Alex suggested that Michelle commandeer her mom's truck and pick him up. Though the 14-year-old had no license, she'd been driving with her parents in the car for years. She was due to take drag racing lessons next summer. Michelle was hesitant.

"If you love me you'll do it," Alex told her.

"I do love you," said Michelle, "but it's a school night."

Eventually, Michelle assented. They made a plan: Michelle would take her dad's .9mm semi-auto and his .22 magnum, steal outside to the truck. Underway, she'd call Alex from the car phone and let it ring once, his signal to jump out his bedroom window with his brother's .22 rifle. They'd go shooting out at White Tanks Mountain.

Michelle picked up Alex, drove out to the dunes, parked and left the headlights on so they could see what they were shooting. For targets Alex had brought along a plywood board and a stolen motorcycle helmet. When they got tired of shooting, Michelle let Alex drive around the dunes. Now they were buried up to the hubs. Michelle was scared, worried that her parents would be worried. On the other hand, this was a grand adventure with the boy she loved. She knew she shouldn't be there, but it felt right.

"It's funny," Alex says. "In my mind I'm saying: 'Come on, you're 16, you've got this girl that likes you, let's try and do something. Let's have sex.' But on the other hand I'm saying, 'Fuck no! I'm not doing that to her.' With some girls, it's only sexual. But I liked who she was. I mean, here you've got a guy who does what he wants when he wants, and he's got to live for himself. But then you get a girl that you really need, that you really like—It's weird how that shit works."

At daybreak the kids dug out, drove to Alex's house. He stole money from his mother, gathered up his BDUs and some camping supplies. They hit the road, on the run, north toward Horseshoe Dam.

After stopping at a mini-mart to buy provisions, Alex pulled into the Mesquite Campground in Northern Arizona. They found a spot, built a fire, slept in the bed of the truck. For the next two days they hung out, walked, talked. They discussed sex but Michelle said she wasn't ready. Alex didn't press. They were having fun. The campground was empty except for a nice hippie lady and a crazy guy, like a homeless vet, all shaggy and dirty with a beard.

On the third night, Alex asked Michelle if she wanted to go home. She said she did but didn't. She was confused. "I tried, you know, to act happy around him and I was happy," says Michelle. "But I knew I should be home. I was hoping the police would find us."

Even if Michelle had wanted to go home, they had a problem: They were out of gas, money and food.

"We're gonna have to rob somebody," Alex said.

The hippie woman was the obvious target. She was camping right near the Verde River, a secluded spot. Before it got dark, Michelle went over to her site to ask for matches, to case her out. "She's a nice lady," Michelle reported.

In fact, many people thought Alice Cameron was a very nice lady. Fifty years old, Alice was a little kooky, a kind of hippie holdover. She'd married a divorced man with children and raised them like her own, then split. A gifted paralegal, she'd freelanced for many Phoenix attorneys over the years, turning down dozens of offers of full-time work. She'd had no contact with her birth family or her married family for 15 years. She was a free spirit dressed in flowing clothes, working just enough to finance her next walkabout.

"We're gonna have to kill her," Alex told Michelle. "No witnesses, you know what I mean?"

"I guess," said Michelle.

"Do you want to do it?" asked Alex.

Michelle looked up at Alex. It's not like she was surprised or anything. He had told her about the temple. He talked all the time about doing crimes. She wondered if he'd kill her too. She didn't say anything.

"If you love me you'll do it," urged Alex.

At around 1 a.m. on October 17, Alex and Michelle walked to the woman's campsite, Alex sticking to the tree line with his brother's .22 rifle, Michelle walking out in the open on the path. They found Alice reading in a chair on the bed of her pickup. Her back was to Michelle.

Michelle hesitated, looked over at Alex. He had the .22 shouldered and aimed, his finger on the trigger. He nodded.

She fired her dad's .9mm. She shot twice—*pow pow.*

Alice was toppled by the blasts. She screamed and kicked.

Michelle dropped the gun. She got very cold, began shaking uncontrollably. She turned her back and crumpled to the ground.

Alex ran to the truck, jumped up into the bed. He jammed a scarf into Alice's mouth, told her to shut up. "Hold her down!" he told Michelle.

Michelle climbed into the truck, held Alice's legs. She told Alice to calm down, that everything would be all right. Then she got Alex to help her wrap the woman in a sheepskin blanket. Alice quieted and Michelle took her hand.

Alice was bleeding heavily. Michelle was a pretty good shot: two bullets, two hits. Alice asked Michelle to get help. Michelle said she was sorry, she couldn't.

Almost two hours later, still in the truck, still bleeding, Alice looked up at Michelle. She seemed calm, serene. "I forgive you," she said. Then she died.

Now Alex and Michelle wiped down Alice's truck for fingerprints, ran back to their own truck with the loot: a bank card, four good-luck stones, a one dollar bill, 59 cents. As they drove away, Alex threw the stones out the window. A clerk in a gas station confiscated the card.

Police found them a few days later at a cabin not far away, owned by Michelle's cousins. Their parents were called. They never saw each other again. . . .

"And how do you feel about Michelle now?" asked the county attorney, KC Scull. He was visibly shaken.

Alex was pale and drained. "I'd rather not say."

"Why are you doing this?"

Alex looked at him. Why was he doing it? He didn't know. *Fuck! Stupid!* He was already sorry. Why did he rat out Michelle? He still loved her. A lot. He still had a picture of her; he still had one of her pony tail bands. "To protect my ass," he finally said.

"Okay, that will be all," said KC. He closed his files, gathered his papers. He was in a hurry. There was a major mess to clear up.

Just after Alice's murder, police had arrested the shaggy Vietnam vet who'd been living at the campground. George Peterson, 46, was an ex-marine. He'd been hospitalized 13 times for mental illness.

Peterson had endured only three hours of police interrogation before he confessed to killing Alice Cameron.

He had spent the last 14 months in jail.

It is to be a special day at the temple, so Chawee Borders arrives early, a bouquet of flowers in her hands. It is August in Arizona, monsoon season, the time of Buddhist retreat.

Two years ago, nine Thai Buddhists had left their earthly lives in a senseless, bloody massacre: Pairat, five monks, Boy, Matthew Miller, Grandma Foy. This afternoon, the anniversary, the congregation will gather for a special ceremony; eight sets of ashes will be sealed into a monument on the grounds of Wat Promkunarum. The ninth set, belonging to Boy, was sprinkled by his parents over a river in Thailand.

Just about the time Alex was telling the county attorneys what he knew about Michelle, six new monks had boarded a flight in Bangkok, bound for the Phoenix. One congregant, a western convert named Peter Angel, arrived at the temple just in time.

"They were obviously very tired, very disoriented, they'd flown all the way non stop. They got out of the van, filed directly into the temple, started chanting. They kept that up for like a half hour, then stopped. Then they all turned around in their places and looked at the people. It was beautiful, so wonderful. The people had been waiting so long for them to come. We didn't know their names or anything. But they were here."

There is a wall now around the grounds of the temple, an alarm system, bars on the windows and doors, a German shepherd. There are two portable cellular phones, one always recharging. And walkie talkies. When a monk goes outside to work in the garden, he remains in constant touch.

To this day there are some in the temple who say the monks "died bad," that hanky panky was going on. Sometimes—when a stiff breeze blows, when the lights blink, when Pairat's cat spontaneously arches its back and purrs like it's being stroked—some members of the temple say that the dead monks are trying to speak. Likewise Von Miller: Matthew's mother, Grandma Foy's daughter. One morning, she woke up to Grandma Foy, sitting on the bed, patting her leg, asking for a hot cup of Ovaltine. Mrs. Miller has stopped going to temple. It is said she is not well.

Mostly, the people in the congregation are trying to live the Buddhist way, in the present. They have gotten to know their new monks, special men themselves. Wenai, who learned English entirely from watching soap operas and cartoons, is now taking courses at the local college. Boontechr, the youngest, can fix anything. And Supab? An older man who speaks no English at all, he saw the other monks getting driver's licences and wanted one himself. He got the manual, turned to the sample questions, memorized each one by sight. He scored 100 percent on the test.

The attendance has grown at services, births and weddings, and special occassions go on. The people will always remember their first monks, but they are trying to forget the events of two years ago. They are trying not to feel anger or hatred. They are trying not to wish for revenge. In the end, said the Buddha, one gets what one deserves, good or bad. And indeed, the waters have been leveled. Misfortune has visited; the perpetrators of the ghastly happenings at the Wat have become victims.

In July 1993, after a three-month trial as strange and convoluted as could be expected, Jonathan Doody was found guilty of nine counts of murder. His attorney, Peter Balkan, argued that Jonathan was an unwitting accessory to the murders, that he had been duped by others into participating in what he believed was a military exercise, not a robbery. Over and over at trial, Balkan sought to convince the jury that Rollie Caratachea was the gunman. It was, after all, his gun. He was said to never lend it out. He had gang connections, a record. Balkan's artful work was aided inadvertantly by the zeal of the judge and prosecutor: Indeed, it seemed at intervals to observers that the case had been rigged against the boy. Time and again, defense evidence and testimony was ruled inadmissable. Balkan called for a mistrial on more than twenty occasions. A great deal of sentiment was created in the courtroom for Jonathan, more mature now, beefy and thick-necked with bad skin, a close-cropped haircut. For his part, Jonathan sat impassively throughout the trial, showing emotion only when Alex testified. Then the change was remarkable. He narrowed his eyes, glowered at his former best friend, diddling a ball-point pen so fast between the first two fingers of his right hand that it blurred.

Despite the procedural handicaps, Balkan managed to create enough doubt that the jury found Jonathan guilty of felony murder instead of premeditated murder, a lesser charge, but still one that carries the possiblity of the death penalty. Jonathan's sentencing is scheduled for early January. Life without parole; death by lethal injection: His fate up to the judge.

Like the jury, psychologists who have interviewed Jonathan have questions about his involvement, and some also believe that Alex and Rollie may have played larger roles. They have found Jonathan to be deferential, respectful, "stereotypically Asian in his total lack of ability to emote or be demonstrative." Though news reports characterized Jonathan as being without remorse, these experts say that, in fact, Jonathan lacks the cultural vocabulary to show remorse, or even to explain himself, though he may indeed feel remorseful. They found his English and his knowlege of American society and convention to be almost nil. "A lot of the time," says one, "He just doesn't get it. He doesn't have a clue what's going on."

Still, along with these doubts and sentiments are certain irrefutable facts. If Jonathan was a hapless accomplice, would he have come away with half of the loot? Why would Alex protect Rollie? And why didn't Jonathan's attorney put him on the stand to tell the jury, simply, "I didn't do it."

If indeed Jonathan was the killer, say the psychologists, then what occured that night at the Wat was a terrible splintering of his personality, a break from reality, from his normal function. Certainly the foundational fractures were there. The trauma of his real father's sudden death; his mother's dissapearance to Germany; his change of name; his transplantation to a new culture; the constant moves to strange places like Valdosta and Guam; the lack of understanding of American language and culture; his militaristic, abusive stepfather; his guilty, isolated, passive-agressive mother.

"If he did do it, it was because he totally freaked," said a psychologist who has interviewed all of the Doodys. "Something went awry in the boys' plan, and Jonathan just lost it, went into some other mode. He withdrew into a corner of his being that no one will ever get to. We'll never know for sure."

Asked by the psychologist what he thought would be his fate, Jonathan said, so quietly he could barely be heard, "Death penalty."

And what of all the rest?

Brian and Laiad Doody maintain their son's innocence. They have instituted a letter-writing campaign, have won the affections of the head monk in Los Angeles. Laiad has been back to the temple, has made her peace with the monks and her old friends. She was not forgiven; there was no need, for there was no blame. It was not her fault—deep in her heart, she can't entirely believe that to be true.

Brian Doody is thinking of mustering out of the air force early, even if it means a much smaller pension. In the military, a man is the commander of his dependents. If his family screws up, he is responsible. Master Sgt. B. Doody is the stepfather of a mass murderer, the worst in Arizona state history. No one will let him forget. He too is plagued with guilt.

Alex Garcia will be sentenced shortly after Jonathan. He faces 25 to 271 years. Alex regrets his decision to rat out Michelle. Of greater regret, perhaps, is his standing among inmates as a snitch. He's in segregation, must move about the prison under the protection of three guards. Jonathan, in the twisted world of cons, has come off cool: A mass murderer commands respect. As he would have made a fine soldier, so he makes a model prisoner.

Michelle Hoover, after a horrible year of silence and inner turmoil, copped a plea, full of remorse. She is currently serving 15 years. Her dad, meanwhile, has undergone by-pass surgery. Her mom has been diagnosed with multiple sclerosis. It is likely both will die before Michelle's release.

Sheriff Agnos remains in retirement. The new sheriff has ordered a review of all confessions, as well as an independent investigation of the entire temple investigation. Capt. Jerry White, the commander in charge, has been reassigned to transportation. Det. Rick Sinsabaugh has left the force to become a probation officer. Det. Russ Kimball, the sergeant in charge, has been banished to uniform patrol, midnight shift.

Now, at the temple, the chanting and the prayers for the dead are about to begin. Pete Angel, a member of the Wat, says it doesn't matter who is guilty of the murders. "Things like this are expected," he says.

"As long as there are people on this earth, the world will be full of suffering and greed," says Pete. "Maybe in America it is a little worse. A nation of children and their evil toys. A complex society, full of complex rationalizations.

"You see, the Buddha looked at the world in very simple terms. He saw the answers in simple terms. Right thoughts, good deeds, a pure heart. To care instead of kill. To tell the truth. To love. To give people a break. To eschew violence and revenge and greed. To live and let live, to give all people their due. This is the Buddist way. It is the only way. It is something that people must learn."

(1994)

Inhuman Bondage

The Animal Liberation Front believes that meat is murder, that science is torture, that animals have the same rights as humans. A report from inside a 1987 guerrilla raid on a USDA laboratory near Washington, D.C.

Saturday afternoon in the suburbs, a split-level in a leafy cul-de-sac. Holly and Alice are side by side at the kitchen counter, making sandwiches, sipping club soda with lime. Holly is thin and pretty and wears a miniskirt. She's twenty-two, a hairdresser at the mall. Alice is short and funny and wears hiking boots. She's thirty-four, a social worker with the county. Both women are a little nervous. Tonight's their big night.

"Yuuuuuuuck!" groans Holly.

"What's the matter *now*?" asks Alice

Holly makes a face, points her knife at the glob of vegetable pâté that Alice is troweling across a slice of seven-grain bread. "You're probably one of those people who put two inches of jelly on a peanut-butter-and-jelly sandwich."

"Yeah? Well, look at yours," says Alice. "What are you doing, painting it on? You barely touch the knife to the bread. It looks like . . ."

"Children! Children!"

The voice comes from the living room. It's Ramona. She lives here with her husband, two kids, four dogs. The dogs were all rescued from roadsides. One of them, Fred, is asleep in the corner of the kitchen. Above him is a cork board pinned with snapshots, crayon drawings, a poster with a photo of two baby raccoons. Above the photo it says, THESE BABIES MISS THEIR MOTHER. IS SHE ON YOUR BACK?

Ramona enters, hands on hips. She regards Holly, then Alice, then shakes her head. *All this bickering!* she thinks, but she says nothing. She understands. She feels it too.

Ramona has long, thick, wavy hair, parted in the middle. She's wearing stiff new jeans and a white gauze blouse with embroidery at the neck, and there are soft, concerned lines around her eyes. Ramona looks like someone who marched against the war many years ago, and she did, though she never got arrested or anything. Making her body limp was not her idea of how to bring about change. For a long time she didn't know what her idea was. Nothing ever seemed to work. Today she's a librarian at a county annex. Her hobby is backyard gardening. No one would ever believe what she's getting ready to do.

Until last night, when she was called, she wouldn't have believed it, either.

In thirty minutes or so, Holly, Alice and Ramona will pile the sandwiches, the sodas, two coolers and a change of black clothes into Ramona's Honda wagon. They'll pick up vegetarian Chinese carryout for fifteen, drive to a hotel, listen to a briefing, wait.

At 1:25 a.m. they'll commit their first felony.

Wearing face masks and cotton gloves, Holly, Alice, Ramona and twelve other members of the Animal Liberation Front (ALF), an underground terrorist organization that advocates radical animal rights, will penetrate security at the U.S. Department of Agriculture's Animal Parasitology Institute, in Beltsville, Maryland. It will be the twenty-sixth strike on an American research facility by the ALF since 1982.

Working in teams, the raiders will enter two different research labs, remove twenty-eight cats and seven miniature African piglets. The animals will be put in boxes and knapsacks, hiked across a pasture, loaded in vans and spirited along an "underground railroad" to foster homes.

The raiders will leave behind recipes and quotations Xeroxed from *The Cookbook for People Who Love Animals.* The recipes will include matzo-tofu bake, curried cauliflower, Chinese bean threads and garlic. The quotations will include one from Leonardo da Vinci: "From an early age, I have abjured the use of meat, and the time will come when men will look upon the murder of animals as they look upon the murder of men."

When the raid is over, thirty-five animals will be saved from science, and fifteen people will feel pretty good about themselves, having risked their own safety for something they believe in. And even more important, tonight's action will be tomorrow's news: front page of *The Washington Post*, big play on CNN, Sunday feature in *The New York Times.* The flame beneath the animal-rights issue will be upped a notch, and millions of Americans will hear the message one more time. A few more will begin to believe.

The raiders will also destroy two years of scientific research, the work of

Dr. Jitender Prakash Dubey, a renowned parasitologist. Dubey's cat project is funded by federal taxes, $250,000 a year. The disease being studied is called toxoplasmosis. Cats show no symptoms of the disease; the parasite, *Toxoplasma gondii*, doesn't hurt them at all. It lodges in their intestines, and leaves the body when they defecate. Cats, however, are the only known transporters of the disease. They are to toxoplasmosis what mosquitoes are to malaria. Dubey, from Delhi, India, discovered this fact in 1970.

Toxoplasmosis causes abortions in commercially raised sheep, goats and pigs and kills millions of young lambs each year. In humans the disease causes birth defects, dementia and death. One in a thousand babies is born infected with the parasite, which can cause hydrocephalus and blindness, sometimes twenty years later. The hospital bills for these children run to half a billion dollars a year. Toxoplasmosis is also the cause of death for one-fourth of the people with AIDS.

In the opinion of the ALF, however, Dubey is another egghead engaged in redundant, costly, worthless research: another sadist torturing animals in the name of science.

"He's been doing the same experiment for fifteen years," the ALF members will be told at their briefing. "He's been feeding infected mice brains by stomach tubes into the cats, and then he kills them or lets them die of vomiting, diarrhea, convulsions, and then he either uses their tissue for injection into other animals or disposes of them."

This is not exactly true.

To the ALF, however, the details don't matter. Human animals have no right to exploit nonhuman animals for *any* purpose whatsoever. Not for food, not for clothes, not for research, not for sport. This is what the ALF believes. This is what 10 million Americans in animal-interest groups believe.

Meat is murder, they say, and so are leather and fur. Wool, eggs, cheese and honey are theft and exploitation. To the ALF, the world is an animal Auschwitz: the death toll is in the billions.

Nine in the evening, a hotel somewhere in the suburbs. By now planes have landed, cars have parked. The team has assembled, seven women and seven men, ages twenty-five to sixty. They sprawl on beds, in chairs, on the shag carpet in one of two adjoining rooms, watching Julie Andrews lead the Von Trapp children through their do-re-mis. The raid is set for midnight.

Holly, Alice and Ramona sit together in the back corner. There is equipment everywhere—a half dozen walkie-talkies, a video camera, several still cameras, two cellular phones, a portable computer with a telephone modem, a tap-proof voice scrambler. Cans of spray paint and bug repellent and a few tiny flashlights sit on the dresser alongside the Chinese food and some paper plates and plastic utensils.

Ramona keeps checking her wrist, forgetting she's left her watch home. They arrived on time, three hours ago. Since then all they've done is sit. Looking around, Ramona recognizes a couple of people. One she's always suspected. The other she can't believe. She kind of nods to them; they kind of nod back. No one speaks. It's weird. Ramona doesn't know exactly what she expected, but it wasn't this. *This is a raid?* she thinks.

Time passes. Finally there is a knock at the door and a shuffle of movement in the next room. The adjoining door opens, a man steps inside. He moves to the front, turns off Julie Andrews. He is M., mission commander.

"Try to listen well the first time around," M. says. "What doesn't make sense, I'll explain a second time. If it still doesn't make sense by then, you're in trouble."

M. pauses at this, his little joke. The commandos titter.

Ramona and Alice trade glances. Alice shrugs.

M. looks around, shifting his gaze from person to person, making eye contact, holding it a moment, moving on to the next. Some of them he knows; some he's heard about.

Of the new ones, Ramona shows much promise. Like most of the others in the room, Ramona's early involvement with animal rights was mostly personal. She became a vegetarian and then a vegan, abstaining from eggs and other stolen products, eating nothing that wasn't grown in the earth or artificially produced. She read newsletters from animal-rights groups, saw vivid pictures of animal abuse on farms and in labs: Baby chicks with their beaks amputated. Veal calves imprisoned in tiny crates. Baby beagles burned with torches. Sheep mortally wounded with Soviet AK-47 assault rifles. Chimps turned into heroin and cocaine addicts. Baboons strapped to a special table equipped with a piston designed to smash their skulls.

For years she gave money, volunteered, demonstrated. She joined several above-ground animal-rights groups, and when someone needed a favor, Ramona was always there. Then, about a year ago, Ramona confided to someone that she was fed up with volunteering, fed up with politicians, fed up, frankly, with all the bullshit you have to go through to bring about change. For all these years since Vietnam, she'd been trying to find a way to really *do* something. Now, she said, she'd decided. She wanted to join the ALF.

For twelve months after that, Ramona heard nothing. She continued as before, volunteering, doing whatever she was asked, totally unaware that she was being watched, discussed, considered by the ALF. Then, on Friday, yesterday afternoon, someone called and asked if she was free this weekend. That was the question: "Are you free this weekend?"

Ramona knew what was being asked. She talked it over with her husband, a systems analyst. Contingencies for child care and prison terms were discussed in their living room after they'd put the kids to bed. Ramona wanted to go for it. She wasn't asking for permission; she was asking for support.

Alice was a draft pick. She'd been watched and invited. You wouldn't believe it to see her, this tiny suburban single with too much gold and a nasal voice, but Alice is one fierce woman. Once she tried to stop a father from beating his son in public. The father turned on her and beat her up. On vacation in a foreign country, Alice heard the cries of a female dog who'd been tied to a pole in a back yard with a male. She returned the next day and heard the dog's cries again. She went to the local authorities, but they were no help. She stole the female from the yard.

A man called the Twin is a veteran member of the ALF. Fortyish, he wears a Rolex watch that says 6:30. It is 9:30 p.m. in the hotel room. The Twin is a great technical person, good with communications, strong. For a raid you need a few people who are physically strong. There are locks, fences, doors to penetrate. And one of these times the ALF is going to be surprised by a guard who won't take the $1,000 in cash the raiders always carry. He'll have to be subdued, without injury. The Twin is trained in martial arts.

R., H. and L. are also veterans. R. has been around since the first ALF action, at the University of Maryland in April 1982, when forty-two rabbits were taken from a class called Rabbit Production and Slaughter.

H. participated in the largest single action in ALF history, the April 1983 raid on the University of California at Riverside. Almost 500 animals—cats, rabbits, pigeons, mice, gerbils, opossums and a five-week-old stump-tailed macaque named Britches—were rescued from labs. Computers were smashed; monitoring equipment was destroyed; hundreds of thousands of dollars' worth of research, lab animals and hardware was lost.

L. is known for her part in the Memorial Day 1984 raid on the Head Injury Laboratory at the University of Pennsylvania. It was L.'s idea to wreck the computer system by pouring chemicals into the mainframe. It was her idea to destroy all the files. The mother of three did these things spontaneously, freelancing the plan, outraged with what she saw in the lab, a dark room that seemed to her a torture chamber of exotic devices and bloody rags.

No animals were taken in the University of Pennsylvania raid. Stolen instead were seventy hours of videotape, some of it containing graphic footage of scientists inflicting brain damage on baboons. At one point in the tapes a researcher is seen making an incision in the head of a baboon. The animal writhes and struggles. A colleague complains: "It hurts him, for chrissakes!"

As a result of the University of Pennsylvania raid, of the viewing of the tapes and of the four-day takeover of an office at the National Institutes of Health by a coalition of above-ground organizations, Margaret Heckler, then secretary of health and human services, suspended funding for the brain study. It was the ALFs greatest triumph to date.

Among the others in the hotel room are a security-systems expert, a veterinarian, a computer expert, a man with extraordinarily good night vision, several good drivers, a woman with a great sense of humor. You need a few jokes at a time like this. M.'s glad to have her along.

Behind M., above the television, a map of the parasitology institute is taped to the wall. It is crudely drawn on poster board with Magic Marker. Alice bought the board and markers this afternoon in the back-to-school department at a Zayres discount department store. Green on the map means tree line and cover, brown means roads and paths. Buildings are blue; staging areas are red.

"Now, A., listen up," says M.

A. is Alice. They do this, use initials instead of names, whenever and wherever they meet, in case of bugs. They also do this so names won't be known. An important tenet in the ALF code is "need to know." If you don't need to know, you won't. What you don't know, you can't tell the police.

"A., you'll have the keys to the sedan, a nice shoulder bag, insect repellents, a portable telephone and a special item you'll get later on."

"What item?"

"I'll let you know privately."

"Okay."

M. continues his outline, switching his focus from Alice to each of the raiders in turn, explaining in detail the steps they'll take, answering their questions, throwing in tips.

When you get out of the van, he advises them, make sure you stay away from headlights and taillights. There are gopher holes in this area, be careful, point them out to the person behind you. Watch for a security guard coming over this hill. Patrol cars sometimes drive with their lights off, so listen for the crunch of gravel. If you have to break a window, wrap a towel around the hammer. If you have to use a flashlight, put your fingers over the bulb. If one of the cats gets wild, shine the light in its eyes. Three people should work one cage. Take the cat by the scruff of its neck, hold it out and away from your body, don't let go until it's inside the cat carrier. If there's a mother with kittens, keep them in the same box. If you've got a flashlight, you're the most dangerous person in the room. People get in trouble not thinking. Spray-paint the slogans on the back of the building, not the front; security could discover them while we're still inside. If the pigs make too much noise, abort and join the others. There's a big herd of cows in one field—be careful not to start a stampede. . . .

Standing in front of the room, gesturing in the air with an expandable pocket pointer, M. looks like a salesman outlining projections for the coming year. He's in his forties, balding but still boyish, chubby, wearing corduroys and a striped sport shirt. He doesn't look like a guerrilla commander, and he doesn't feel like one, either. Once he was just like Ramona. Someone who believed strongly but didn't know what to do about it. Someone who got a call from the ALF on a Friday night.

M. was never a joiner. He always felt stupid walking around in a circle, chanting a slogan, carrying a sign on a stick. He always hated the cliques and internal squabbles and petty political intrigue that make doing good such a pain in the ass.

M. was convinced a great wrong was being committed, but he didn't know what to do about it. Like Ramona, he contributed money to the animal groups, wrote letters to his congressman. Sometimes he went to protests but only if they really needed another body in the line.

Then M. was contacted by the ALF. The members of the organization had seen him around, knew who he was, liked what they saw. They had a mission, and they needed his special skills.

The call was a total surprise, but M. made his decision very quickly: it was as if he had already done the thinking in advance.

Now, in the hotel room, M. finishes outlining the plan, moves on to contingencies and escape routes. If the police come, he says, scatter. Go through this creek bed, these woods, to this subdivision. Find a pay phone. Someone will take calls.

Ramona, in the back corner of the room, chews her lip. *Where are we going, anyway?* she wonders.

Ramona has no idea what research institute they're raiding, no idea where the institute is located. Apparently these are not details she needs to know. She accepts this. It's part of the decision to join. But anyway, she can't help imagining. She sees a picture in her mind: Ramona in black clothes and a mask wandering through a maze of subdivisions. Ramona being stopped by the cops.

She considers this for a moment and then raises her hand, remembers she's not a schoolgirl, pulls it back down. Then she blurts out a question: "If the police stop us, do we have to show any kind of identification?"

"I think you should," M. says calmly. "If I was a police officer and I stopped you and didn't quite believe you and you showed me your driver's license, I'd feel safe."

"So we should offer the ID?"

"I wouldn't offer anything. But if they ask, you have it. I would be open and normal with them. You could say, 'I had a fight with my husband and we were driving along and I just got out of the car. . . .' "

"I can see it now," says the woman with the sense of humor. "Ten people walking along the road and they all had fights with their husbands and wives."

"Yeah," says M., laughing. "Tell the cop it's a trend."

M. pauses at this, his little joke.

No one titters.

"Look, folks," he says. "If we get arrested in the process of this, it's some-body's bad luck or six people's bad luck or whatever. We all have to stand firm. However many draw a short straw, the same rule applies: Nobody says anything, no matter what. And everyone will always be looked after, what-ever needs to be done. Lawyers, court, whatever, it will be done."

M. smiles, rubs his hands together.

"Now, who wants some Chinese food?"

"Okay, folks. This is it. This is it! Coming up on first drop. Get ready, Number One."

Lights out, the van slows, breaks asphalt, crunches gravel. M., in front, whispers commands.

"Number One . . . Number One? . . . Who's Number One?"

"That's you, Alice, oops I mean A.," whispers Ramona.

Alice rises, duck-walks over a tangle of legs. Fifteen people and all that equipment are crammed in a small Dodge van. Alice reaches the side door. It slides quietly open.

"Ready . . . go!"

"But we're moving!" Alice croaks.

"Jump!"

Alice jumps.

"Okay. Okay. One away. Pig group next. Then the cat group. Get ready, people."

On a cloudy, damp, moonless summer night, August 23rd, 1987, the landing has begun. Alice moves to her post at lookout. M. leads the pig group across a pasture and through a fence. L. takes the cat group, single file, Ramona at the rear, up a narrow track between the tree line and a chain-link fence. . . .

Though the case for animal welfare has been debated since the latter part of the nineteenth century, animal rights—in Western society at least—is a relatively new political issue, having emerged only in the last decade. In the past, groups like the American Society for the Prevention of Cruelty to Animals (ASPCA) and the Humane Society of the United States (HSUS) concerned themselves mainly with promoting kindness toward animals. Use the animal, but don't abuse it. That was the thrust for 150 years.

Then, in 1975, an Australian named Peter Singer published *Animal Liberation*. In what has become a landmark book, Singer evokes the Eastern religious notions of species equality, challenging the Judeo-Christian belief that man alone is made in God's image, that man alone has dominion over all other animals. "We have always assumed that we are justified in overriding [animals'] interests, but this bald assumption is simply species-selfishness," wrote Singer in a collection of essays called *In Defense of Animals.*

Though most people had never stopped to think in these terms, once they did, Singer's philosophy seemed to make sense. People had always said they "loved animals." Now, thanks to Singer, they knew why, and there was text to prove it. Meat *is* murder. It makes sense if you're inclined to think that way.

Apparently, many were so inclined. In the wake of Singer's book, interest groups were formed to collect money and spread the message. A new issue was born.

Unfortunately, few people cared.

Founded in England in 1972 as the Band of Mercy, the organization

became known as the Animal Liberation Front in 1976. In 1982, 700
protesters, armed with flares, sticks and wire cutters, stormed the Hunt-
ington Research Center, in England. The rebellion was quashed, but it
made headlines all over the world.

The American ALF was founded later that year. How, where and by whom
remains a secret. After its first raid, on the University of Maryland during the
1982 Easter weekend, the ALF would strike again and again, sometimes
calling itself the Band of Mercy, the Urban Gorillas, the Wild Geese or True
Friends to throw police off the trail. Raiders stole valuable lab animals,
wrecked labs, ruined research. Animal activists have also taken responsibility
for planting a bomb outside the house of a well-known researcher in Chicago
and for setting fire to a farm-animal diagnostic lab at the University of California at Davis. Damages were estimated at $3.5 million.

Now people care.

Using the spectacle of crime, the dramatics of laboratory abuse, the
hunger of public and media for action and splash, the American ALF has
managed, over the last six years, to make a public issue out of something that
was never an issue before. In this age of ambivalence, the militant altruism
of the ALF has appeal. People risking their lifestyles for something they
believe. Little people up against odds. Ultimate underdogs. Since 1984 the
number of Americans belonging to animal-rights groups has increased five-
fold, to 10 million.

Since 1982, inspired by the example of the ALF, more than 100 new,
above-ground animal-rights groups have been formed in the United States,
most of which are radical in their stance on the issue, calling for an end to
use of animals in laboratories. The effects can even be seen on old-line
organizations like the Humane Society. "HSUS is definitely shifting in the
direction of animal rights faster than anyone would realize from our literature," said a former executive of the society in 1986.

Washington is responding as well. "These days most of the congressional offices have aides assigned to animal affairs," says Jeff Diner, president of Bioscan International, a research-consulting firm that monitors
laboratory-animal issues. "There's a lot of constituent interest, and I think
that is because the ALF has been able to put the animal-rights issue in a
context that people can understand. The ALF is emotional; they deal with
action and images. They make news. They have moved the whole debate
to the left of center. It's amazing what a few people can do; the ripple
through society that they have caused is astounding." Indeed, in the last

several years, state lawmakers across the country have considered more than eighty bills that would restrict animal research, and three major labs have been shut down.

On a federal level the Animal Welfare Act has been amended with restrictions, and a bill for stricter oversight of federally funded research has been passed. In addition, the National Institutes of Health have made in-house efforts to improve the standards of animal research, as has the Department of Agriculture, which is charged with overseeing all lab animals used in federal research.

Meanwhile, science is on the retreat. Though animal research is credited with important discoveries about cancer, heart disease, AIDS, transplant operations, virtually the entire spectrum of medical research, scientists are finding themselves hamstrung by new laws, buried in new regulations. The price of animals is soaring as restrictions make them more expensive to produce and harder to obtain. And millions of dollars that could have been used for research are going instead to security.

"Every single major medical breakthrough in this century has involved animal experimentation," says Dr. Ronald Fayer, director of the Animal Parasitology Institute. "Measles, mumps, chicken-pox vaccines. Open-heart surgery. Virtually every single item that you can think of has been possible because we've been able to use animals.

"People like the ALF appeal to the public," he says. "They say, 'Oh, these poor animals.' The fact is, we have pets. We're not unsympathetic. But the animal people think we want to hurt animals. We're concerned about animal health. Sick animals are no good to us. Healthy animals equal good science."

Dr. Fayer points to an eight-inch-thick folder of regulations for animal use in experimentation, all of them issued over the last fifteen months. Size of cage, amount of feed, the humidity and temperature of the air, hundreds of details involving the care of lab animals are specified. "We have all these guidelines to follow before we can even get an animal in here, never mind the experimentation," he says.

It's difficult to say how many animals are used in research labs each year, but according to a report issued by the Congressional Office of Technology Assessment, the number may be as high as 100 million. While some animal research has been replaced with mathematical models or studies using cell cultures, much of it, scientists say, cannot be done without animals. To science, the question is life or death, us or them.

"People are uncomfortable with the image of an animal in a cage being used for research," says Carol Sheman of the Association of American Universities. "But we are also uncomfortable about seeing a sick child in bed hooked up to tubes. We are uncomfortable about pain and suffering, and we should be. We're human beings, and that part of our humanity is important. But what's also important is using our heads to understand the whys and effects of doing certain things."

On a hilltop overlooking the institute, a thunderclap of static breaks the quiet.

"Number Two?"

"Two," responds M.

"Clear?"

"In service."

M. rubs his ear, takes a deep breath, gropes for the volume knob on the walkie-talkie. The first communication. If things are going as planned, the cat group has settled into the thick underbrush near the institute, and the scouts have slid under the chain-link fence for a final look-around. Phase 2 of the mission has begun.

Although it is cloudy, the sky is awash with ambient light from the city, a thick amber dome above the trees and rolling hills and cinder-block out-buildings that make up the institute. The effect is eerie; the whole complex seems to glow.

The idea of raiding this place surfaced eight months ago. The ALF receives tips constantly, channeled to it from laboratory insiders, some of them disgruntled, some disgusted. Though the ALF is loosely organized into several cells, based in different regions of the country, targets, ideas and cell members are shared among them; raids are ultimately a unified action. As the tips come in, the ALF sorts, considers, researches. It narrows the possibilities, sets up surveillance, chooses.

The first time he took a look at the institute, M. knew it was perfect. It was a federal facility; it was near the nation's capital; security was weak. The horrors, he thought, made the risk worthwhile.

"One of the buildings had two baby calves chained in metal restraining devices," he says. "They were only about four weeks old, much too young to be away from their mothers. They were chained at the neck, in metal crates. The sheep reminded me of slaves in slave ships, when they would pack them into the hold and chain them.

"The calves had continual liquid diarrhea," he continues, "and all the fur on their back legs had been burned off by the diarrhea, and their knees were completely raw from kneeling on the metal mesh at the bottom of the crate. They were just terrified of me. We went in quietly with one little flashlight, and they just went berserk."

On other nights, ALF scouts found sheep, cats, pigs. They decided to take only the piglets and cats because they were small and could be carried on foot. Usually the ALF is able to load the animals directly into trucks, but the layout of the institute called for a different plan. They knew it would be impossible.

Besides, the many are more important than the few. Taking the cats and piglets would be practical, symbolic. The political statement would be made.

In a tangle of leaves and vines and shrubbery, Ramona, with the cat group, waits for word from the scouts. Though she is trying to concentrate on the raid, all she can think about are bugs.

The mosquitoes are driving her wild. Buzzing her ears, flying up her pant legs. Already she has a welt on her forehead. Worse, she is sitting in thorns. Every time she shifts, her face and arms get scratched. *Of all the places to sit, she thinks, I choose thorns. I should get up and find another place. No, that would make too much noise. I wish they'd hurry up.*

The last time Ramona was in the woods was 1974, the summer she camped her way across the country. In Chicago she visited a friend who worked in a packinghouse, "They gave us the grand tour," Ramona says. "I couldn't believe what I saw. I'd watched pigs and cattle and chickens slaughtered before, but never like this. It was so . . . just such severe pain. There were animals crying everywhere. It was a huge place. They had a whole plant just for slaughtering pigs, another one for chickens, another for cows. And it was just so intense. They beat the animals, right there in front of me, with canes, they beat them about the face and head, severe beatings. There was so much brutality I couldn't believe it.

"The chickens, they'd pull them out of the crates and hang them upside down on this conveyor belt. Some of the hangers were already filled with just the legs of the chickens. They'd slapped them down so hard that they'd broken their knees backwards and snapped off their legs from the knees down. And the guy who was slitting their throats would slice with his knife and then stop and pull it out and show it to me and smile."

In the stand of trees on the hill overlooking the institute, M. keys his walkie-talkie. A little red light flashes on and off.

Good, he thinks, *still on the air.* He was beginning to wonder if his batteries were dead.

He checks his watch. Forty-five minutes since the first communication. *What's taking the scouts so long?*

M. runs through the possibilities in his head. Security is pretty irregular here, he found on surveillance. No rhyme or reason. It just seemed like, every now and then, the guards would decide to take a run around the place with their lights off. Maybe the scouts have been caught. Maybe security surprised them and they didn't have time to warn the others. Maybe the cat group was discovered in the underbrush. Could Alice have panicked? Did the cops find the vans?

Christ! M. thinks. *I could be home watching television.*

"It's weird," M. says later. "Before I was involved with this, life was really pretty comfortable. I mean, I'm taking risks now that don't need to be taken. I have a wife, some kids, some cars. I've worked hard to get where I am. I'm a businessman, for chrissakes. What do I have to gain from this? It's not like I'm robbing a bank and spending the money.

"Up to this point, I've had a pretty enjoyable life, and compared to those animals, it's been a pretty damn nice life. I may be caught; I may have to spend some time in jail. A lot of time in jail. But it would balance out in the end. It would be okay. Looking at the costs and the benefits, it's worth it."

"Number two?"

"Two in service," responds M., with the pig group.

"Number Three?"

"Three in service" responds L., with Ramona and the cat group.

"Proceed! Proceed! Proceed!"

L. rises from her seat in the bushes, motions to Ramona and the rest of the cat group. "Let's go!" she whispers.

Someone cuts the fence with the bolt cutters, a four-foot vertical gash in the metal links. The raiders go through single file, stooping, moving fast. *This is like playing spy as a kid,* Ramona thinks as she goes.

Two, three hundred yards. They pass some pigpens, see the scouts. Ramona feels like waving, but she doesn't. A little to the right they find the cat lab. The door is unlocked.

L. takes position out front. She is the lookout. The scouts evaporate. Ramona and seven others enter the lab.

Inside, it is pitch black. The building is a rectangle. A row of windows, a corridor, a row of doors. It's not what Ramona expected. She expected a sterile kind of bigger building. This is so little and grimy. It looks to her like a shed in someone's back yard.

A great scuffling ensues as the raiders try in the dark to assemble the cat boxes. The cardboard has to be creased and folded a certain way. A bottom has to be inserted. The edges have to be taped together. It's hard to do. It's not getting done.

This should have been practiced! Ramona thinks. *Everybody's moving around and nothing's getting done fast enough! We have to do this fast. We have to get out of here. We need to be efficient. Nobody's in charge.*

Meanwhile, outside, L. hears the racket. She was afraid of this. Earlier, waiting in the bushes, she thought maybe she should go ahead and assemble the boxes so they'd be ready. She decided against it, but now she knows she was right the first time. The noise! It sounds to her like they're tearing the lab to pieces. *What if security comes down the road? Should I tell them to stay inside and lie low? Should I tell them to run? Maybe the pig people have been seen. I don't want to lose the cats, but I don't want to lose the people, either. I don't want to make a wrong decision. . . .*

Inside, scuffling, movement, noise. The raiders mill about. Time is passing.

Why isn't anybody taking charge? Ramona wonders. She's scared now, unsure, lost. She doesn't know what to do. Her stomach hurts. Nothing's happening. They'll all be caught. They'll all go to jail. *Somebody has to do something!*

Ramona thinks about the slaughterhouse, the crying cows, the newsletters, the checks, the errands, the protests at fur stores. She thinks about the night the ALF finally called. She thinks about taking action.

Suddenly she feels calm.

"Listen. Everyone. Stop!" she says, rasping in the darkness.

Everyone stops.

For a moment, Ramona stops too. She looks around, surveys the dark shapes in the room, as if she too is trying to name the voice that has spoken out.

Then, all at once, she starts whispering orders. She points at people. "You. Go get a flashlight from L. . . . You. Take the tape. . . . You and you, make the boxes. . . . Everybody else, get the cats. Let's move! Hurry!"

Mission accomplished, the members of the ALF ride back toward the hotel in the Dodge van. Their voices are low, controlled, tired.

"Yeah! The pigs were real easy to catch."

"Did they make a lot of noise?"

"Well, if you put a hand under their mouth and kind of petted them a little bit, they hardly said a word. They went right to sleep as soon as you put them in the box."

"Did you have to wait long for the cat people?"

"Fifteen, twenty minutes."

"Wow, that was good timing!"

"Yeah. When we saw you guys coming, we weren't sure whether you were cattle or people at first. It was great. You should have seen you guys coming over the hill, this herd of black shapes. It looked like fifty of you. . . ."

Meanwhile, another van travels in a different direction, spiriting twenty-eight cats and seven miniature African piglets toward new lives in a different part of the country. M. doesn't know where the animals are being taken; he doesn't need to know, though he knows the drill. After the UC-Riverside raid, M. drove Britches to freedom.

Britches was five weeks old when they rescued him. A stump-tailed macaque monkey, he'd been taken from his mother at birth for use in blindness experiments. His eyelids were sutured shut; a sonar device was attached to his head. He'd lived his whole short life isolated in a soundproof cage.

"When we got him," says M, "even after the vet removed the stitches and the sonar, Britches clutched himself constantly. He would have these very abnormal, almost seizurelike movements. Like spastic, you know? If you touched him, he would just, he'd go into this seizure thing and clutch at his own body. The way he kept clutching, it was like he was desperate to touch someone or something. The cage he'd been in was just metal, nothing soft on the bottom, and he was all raw and bleeding on his haunches from being in the cage. He was in such bad shape. He was really off the walls.

"It was really sad, really gross, but on the other hand it was great. Britches was free. I was taking him to get better. It's hard to describe how good that made me feel. The camaraderie. Just being with this guy who was free for the first time. Knowing he'd never be locked up again. Knowing he wasn't going to be experimented on anymore, it really makes all this worth it, worth it for a while, anyway. . . .

"Then, when you come down off the high of a mission, you feel this disappointment. They use 20 million animals in the lab every year. You saved twenty. What you've done makes such a small dent. You start thinking, 'Christ, I'm going to be seventy years old and still breaking into labs.' "

• • •

Slumped next to M. in the van, Ramona is deep in thought.

I think I was born to do this. I really do. Something came over me in the cat building. A whole new sense of calm. A whole new purpose. A whole new way of looking at social change. I can't imagine a more satisfying extracurricular activity.

It's funny. Me on a raid. People are going to think the raid was the work of radical extremists. I don't feel like a radical extremist. I feel normal. I feel like I'm having the normal reaction and everyone else is having unreasonable ones. We don't need meat. We don't need to experiment. We don't need to use animals for our own purposes. It's not fair to the animals, but they can't speak for themselves. Somebody has to speak for them. That's what we did. Hah! We spoke out in a big way!

The van rocks and bumps along the highway. Ramona breaks her reverie, whispers to M.

"That was great, wasn't it?"

"Um-hum," says M., smiling.

"We really did something good."

"Um-hum."

Ramona smiles. She's quiet for a while. Then her face darkens. A shade slides down, and the light goes out. She leans toward M., whispers, "Did you see those sheep in the pen?"

"What about them?"

"I wish we could have saved them, too."

(1988)

Raised in Captivity

Gary Fannon lost the best years of his young life to a trumped-up drug arrest and a draconian law. The decade he spent in prison taught him lessons no man should have to learn.

He rode out to quarantine on a bus full of stinking guys, all of them under 21, convicted as adults of felony crimes. He was going to Riverside to be processed, three hours away, in Ionia, Michigan. The town had four prisons. They pronounced it *I-own-ya.*

Gary Wayne Fannon Jr. pressed his nose to the vent by the window, seeking fresher air. He wanted to scream, to cry, to smash his head through the glass. The state of Michigan owned him now. He'd drawn the mandatory penalty for his crime: life in prison without parole. It was a death sentence, really—a long, slow death by natural causes.

He stepped off the bus, his wrists shackled to a belt around his waist, his legs chained together at the ankles. He shuffled forward in a single-file line, through a door marked Intake. They removed his shackles, locked the heavy gate behind him. They gave him his number, 189196. He bent over, spread his cheeks and coughed. He got his blues. The shirts were too big; the pants were too small. The underwear was made by convicts in a factory for 28 cents a day. Since it was summer—August 20, 1987, to be exact, his nineteenth birthday—they were giving out rubber flip-flops. He reached down into a huge laundry cart, held his breath against the smell. The rubber was worn, impressed with the toe prints of previous owners. *Fuck it,* thought Gary. *Happy birthday to me.*

One week, one month, two months, three. An eight-by-ten-foot cell, twenty-three hours a day. No TV, no radio, no roommate. If you needed to piss, you used a plastic bottle. If you needed to do more, you had to bang on the door and wait for the guard. Sometimes the guard wouldn't come, and you'd have to use your trash can. Then you'd tie up the plastic liner bag and throw it out the window, into the courtyard.

345

The guards at the Riverside Correctional Facility liked Gary. He was polite and well mannered. He was white, as were most of the guards. He seemed like a regular kid. How he had gotten here, how he had ended up with a life sentence—Gary wondered about that himself. Before all this happened, he had lived with his mom and little brother in an apartment complex in Westland, a blue-collar suburb northwest of Detroit. He played guitar, smoked pot, paid $120 a month on his black Mercury LN7, was a regular at the midnight screening of *The Rocky Horror Picture Show.* He graduated from high school by the skin of his teeth. He'd been in trouble with the law once: nabbed at age 13 for shoplifting a pack of batteries. The cops never found the other item he'd taken, secreted in his coat pocket, a small ceramic statue of a blond guy in a striped prison suit, a ball and chain affixed to his ankle. Now it seemed like an episode of *Tales From the Crypt,* some eerie prophecy fulfilled.

Why me, oh Lord? Gary asked this many times. He made a list of everything he'd done wrong in his life, looking for a reason he was being punished like this now. When he was 7, he had broken a pinball machine in a bar his father had taken him to. When he was 13, he had smashed a window in the front door of an apartment complex. The manager had denied his mother an application; he had a policy against renting to divorcees with kids. When he was 12, Gary fell in with a bad crowd. They jimmied apartment doors, stole spare change and radios, rearranged furniture. Later they stole car stereos and radar detectors. And there were the little things. Like the time he broke that girl's virginity and then called her a blood witch. The time he hit his kid brother for squealing. The time he raised his fist to his mom, a selfless woman who slept on the sofa in the living room.

Because the guards liked Gary, they gave him the job of cleaning the courtyard. He didn't get paid, but he did get to go outside by himself for an hour. He'd rake the shit bags into a pile and carry them to the Dumpster. Then he'd mow the grass. At least it was something to do.

One day he was in his cell and there was nothing to do, he was going insane. He'd written all the letters he could, his hand was numb and there was nothing to do, he was going insane. He'd read as many books as he could, his eyes were killing him. There was nothing to do and the window was open and the sun was shining. He wanted to be outside. He was going insane.

A fly buzzed into his cell. It landed on the windowsill, on the bed, on the desk. Gary watched it.

The fly rubbed its legs together. It flitted around nervously. Gary inched toward it. Closer. Closer. He tried to quiet his body and his brain, to make himself still like deep water, like Caine on *Kung Fu*.

He snapped out his arm and caught the fly in his hand. He put it in a large Doritos bag, purchased in the prison store, contents devoured, bag kept folded on the shelf. He watched the fly buzz around inside the Doritos bag. Time passed.

A bee flew into the cell. Gary watched it. He concentrated, trying to send the bee a telepathic message. *Come to me. Come to me.* The bee settled on the back of his hand. He cupped it in his palm, put it in the Doritos bag; the bee on one end, sectioned off with a pencil, and then the fly, and then a book to seal the opening, all of it on top of the desk.

Gary watched the bee. He watched the fly. Every once in a while, he'd remove the pencil, open up the sections, make them meet so they would fight. But they wouldn't. They just buzzed and walked around.

Time passed. A wasp flew into the cell. The shit bags in the courtyard were like magnets for all these bugs. It was a regular insect zoo. Gary stalked the wasp across the room, caught it in a Styrofoam cup. He put it in the Doritos bag.

He watched some more. He set up fights between the wasp and the fly, the wasp and the bee. The bee and the fly wouldn't fight, but the wasp, he would fight anybody. Gary took turns pitting the wasp against the fly and the wasp against the bee. That was the best match, the wasp against the bee. Lots of buzzing and stinging. Just hours of amusement, you know.

In the end, the fly got crushed. The bee suffocated. The wasp drowned in the Styrofoam cup.

By then it was time for chow.

December 10, 1986. One year earlier. . . .

Gary sat at the wheel of his Mercury LN7, listening to Pink Floyd's *Dark Side of the Moon*, using the rearview mirror to study a new zit budding on his chin. He was parked behind another place called Riverside, this one a roller rink, waiting to meet a guy named Kurt Johnston, a friend of his buddy Lance's.

Gary and Lance had been hanging out for about a year. Lance had a beer belly and wore a lightning-bolt earring. Most people thought he was a dip-shit, but Gary thought he was funny. He chauffeured Lance around, found him a job and a girlfriend. Lance, in turn, kept Gary's car running. Lance's dad had taught him auto mechanics. He was a cop. He didn't like Lance's friends, his hours, his behavior, his attitude, his foul mouth, his pot smoking. Lance lived in the basement, kept a footlocker full of weapons. He had baseball bats with screws stuck in them, brass knuckles, several guns. Lance and his dad fought so much that his dad had recently kicked him out. Gary's mom was letting him stay at their place.

The beginning of Lance and Gary's friendship corresponded roughly with Gary's entry into the pot business. Gary started out selling loose joints during his junior year, later moved into grams and quarter ounces. Occasionally, he sold mescaline or acid. His buyers were students on school grounds at lunchtime. Much of the stuff was consumed on the spot.

Looking back, Gary thinks the reason he started dealing was his new girlfriend. Kathy was a year older, more experienced, a twelfth grader. Kathy liked smoking pot before sex, which was fine with Gary, but it started getting a little expensive. Gary had worked since he was 13—busing tables at Chuck E. Cheese, washing dishes at the upscale surf-and-turf roadhouse where his mom waitressed. Wouldn't it be cheaper, Gary proposed, if they bought a quarter ounce of pot and sold joints for a dollar apiece? With the profit, they could smoke for free.

Making Kathy happy was Gary's number one priority. She'd had a shitty life. She didn't know her dad. Her mom worked in a box factory, spent her off-hours sniffing glue. Gary had this thing about taking care of people— running errands, driving them places, lending support. You might say that Gary was searching constantly for love and assurance, trying to be the kind of father figure he had never had.

Gary Sr. was a Tennessee native, an early-'60s greaser who combed his hair into a waterfall. Gary's mom, Linda, the fourth of fourteen children in a loving Catholic family, had gotten pregnant by Gary Sr. when she was 17. Gary Sr. and Linda were separated when Gary was 6 and his brother, Robert, was 3. For a long time, Gary hated his name. He vowed that someday he would find his father and beat him up, like he remembered him doing to his mom.

When Lance needed a place to stay, Gary, of course, came through. One day, in the fall after graduation, Lance was hanging out with a friend named Bob. They were smoking pot, playing with Lance's .45. Bob picked up the gun, pointed it at his own temple. "Heh-heh, heh-heh, heh-heh," he giggled, and pulled the trigger.

Luckily, the bullet just took out a chunk of Bob's skull, and he eventually recovered. Lance was arrested on a weapons charge. The cops told him that they'd drop the charge in exchange for the names of any drug dealers he knew. Lance gave up Gary. Then Lance moved back home with his father, started acting like he was mad at Gary. Gary didn't understand; he'd done so much for him.

Even so, when Lance called a month later and asked for a favor, Gary was ready and willing. One of his buddies needed some pot. Could Gary help out?

So it was, on the afternoon of December 10, 1986, that a car pulled up behind the Riverside Roller Rink and parked. Gary got out of his car and walked over, slid into the passenger seat. Kurt Johnston was in his thirties, with slicked-back hair and sunglasses on a bleak winter day. He reminded Gary of a character on *Miami Vice.*

This was the second time Gary had met with Johnston. He said he worked at the Ford plant and sold dope to fellow employees. The day before, at their first meeting, Gary had sold Johnston four small bags of pot—five grams in all, less than one-quarter of an ounce—for $60. Johnston smelled one bag, seemed pleased. Then he asked if Gary could get him some cocaine. Gary said he'd never even done cocaine. Johnston pressed. "A friend of Lance is a friend of mine," Gary declared, giving Johnston a soul handshake and vowing to try.

Now Gary handed Johnston the coke he'd scored, one-eighth of an ounce, $200 worth. Johnston opened the bag, took out a mirror and a bill. He dumped some of the white powder on the mirror, laid out some lines. He snorted, sniff, sniff. Then he handed the mirror to Gary.

Gary took the mirror, the bill. *I don't know,* he thought, a spooky, singsong voice in his head. *I don't kno-ooow.* He'd never done coke before. The way they talked about it on the news, it made you kill your kids, rape your granny, run around naked in the streets. Johnston watched and waited. *I guess this is what happens in a coke deal,* Gary thought. He snorted, sniff, sniff. It hurt his nose at first, but he didn't really feel anything. *What the fuck is this?* he thought. *Why do people do this?*

Then it hit him. BANG! He felt this power surge, like he could pick up the car and throw it over the roller rink. Just that much power. Superpower. He wanted to dance. He wanted to sing. He tried to maintain. "I think I'm gonna go now," he told Johnston.

Gary walked back to his car. When he opened the door, it felt like he was ripping it off the hinges. He cranked Pink Floyd, pulled out of the parking lot, onto the street, squealing his wheels. *Whoa!* he thought. *This is fucking great!* Weed made him sleepy. Alcohol made him sick. Mescaline and acid were

OK, though he hated coming down. But coke, whoa! *This is my drug of choice!* he thought. *This makes me fucking whole.*

In a few minutes, the coke began to wear off. Gary wanted more. He made a U-turn, drove back to Detroit. He bought a gram of coke, took it to Kathy's.

They each did some, and then they started fooling around. They did more and more. Gary had never heard a woman scream like that. He had never lasted so long. They stayed up until dawn.

"Everything is set for tomorrow," Gary said into the pay phone one month later, standing on a nasty corner in Detroit. He had lost fifteen pounds, had bags under his eyes. "I just wanted to say, you know, see ya."

"What are you talking about?" asked Kurt Johnston.

"I'm gone, man," said Gary. "I'm taking my girl to Florida."

"Why don't you just wait a couple days?" asked Johnston. "Let's get this thing done."

Since that afternoon in early December, Gary had supplied Johnston with coke on two more occasions, a half ounce and then an ounce. Then Johnston said he wanted to buy a kilo—thirty-six ounces, 2.2 pounds. The deal was set for January 7. Johnston met Gary and Michael Thompson, the Detroit man who now supplied Gary with pot and coke, in a crummy apartment in Dearborn. Johnston produced $32,000 cash. Gary counted it, all hundreds and twenties and tens. "This is $32,000, all right," Gary announced. He handed it back to Johnston.

"Where's the dope?" asked Johnston.

"We don't have it yet," said Gary.

"Were you planning on getting it?" asked Johnston.

Gary and Thompson left the apartment. They spent all day making phone calls and waiting, trying to get the dope. No luck. The next day, they tried again. Still no luck.

By late afternoon on January 8, Johnston was ballistic. Gary was getting scared. *Maybe this is fucked up, you know?* At first he'd gotten Johnston the drugs as a favor to Lance. Then he'd gotten them as a favor to Johnston. Then he'd gotten them to get free coke. With each deal, he'd skim some coke off the top. Johnston did it; why not he? *I guess this is what happens in a coke deal.* But now, well, things were getting really out of hand. "You guys are a bunch of shit," Johnston bellowed. "Get the hell out!"

Gary drove Thompson back to his house in central Detroit. On the way, they decided to call the supplier one more time. He finally had the stuff. Or most of it, twenty-six ounces. Gary rang Johnston from the pay phone. Johnston agreed to buy the twenty-six ounces for the same price he'd agreed to pay for the thirty-six ounces. The deal was set for the next day. Gary felt his obligations had now been fulfilled. He wasn't getting a cut; he wanted no more part. "Look," he told Johnston from the pay phone, "I'll catch you guys later." He hung up.

Gary took Thompson to the supplier's house, bought an eighth of an ounce for himself and drove to Kathy's. Then the couple went over to see some friends of Kathy's.

The two couples played a snorting game involving dominoes and pencil-thick lines of coke. Around dawn they fell asleep.

At eleven the next morning, Kathy woke Gary. His beeper was going crazy, she said. Gary raised his head off the pillow, tried to focus on the digital readout. Mike Thompson's number. Kurt Johnston's number. Each of them several times. "Fuck them!" he said. He went back to sleep.

He finally rose at 6 p.m. A few hours later, he and Kathy left for Florida, setting out in his LN7 through a snowstorm.

The next afternoon, January 10, one hundred miles from the Florida border, Gary was pulled over for speeding.

After a license check, the cop walked back to the driver's side. "You'd better get out of the car, sir—there's a warrant out for your arrest."

"For what?" asked Gary.

"For delivery of over 650 grams of cocaine," the cop said.

"You sure it's me?"

Gary stood before the judge with his head bowed, trying not to cry. It was August 19, 1987, the day before his nineteenth birthday. Gary was wearing an olive-drab prison jumpsuit. Counting today, he'd been in jail 193 days. A month ago, a jury had found him guilty. Now he was back in court for sentencing.

Gary's handsome face was twisted into a hideous mask of pain and remorse and anticipation. He already knew what was going to happen. It was mandated by state law. But he also knew that some judges in Michigan had refused to follow the law, calling it cruel and unusual. Part of him was praying that his judge, an auburn-haired older woman named Marianne Battani, would somehow see the light too. Gary's vision clouded; his knees buckled. His lawyer caught him with an arm around his waist.

"Have a seat for a minute," said the judge.

Behind Gary, in the front row of the gallery, Linda Fannon was surrounded by family. Her mom sat at her side. "They will not do this to an 18-year-old boy," she told Linda.

Neither Linda nor her mom knew about Michigan's "650 drug lifer law." It was passed as a one-paragraph rider to a health-code bill. Very few people knew anything about it, including most of the legislators who had voted for it. The law provided that conviction for delivery of more than 650 grams of cocaine, about 1.4 pounds, carried a mandatory sentence of life in prison without possibility of parole. To be found guilty, you didn't have to deliver any drugs. You didn't have to see any drugs or any money. All you had to do was conspire to possess.

Johnston, of course, was an undercover cop. He lived down the street from Lance's dad. Though Gary was recruited and turned on to coke by the police, and though he was on the road to Florida on January 10 when the twenty-six ounces (723 grams) of coke was delivered, Gary was tried on the same charge at the same trial as Michael Thompson. The jury found the two equally guilty.

Now, at his sentencing, Gary was helped to his feet.

"All right," said the judge. "I have here a stack of letters attesting to how good a person you are and what a nice family you have. And you know what? The court believes all of these things.

"But this court has no discretion whatsoever. It is the sentence of this court that you be committed to the state Department of Corrections for a period of your natural life."

Gary swallowed hard. *They will carry me out in a pine box*, he thought.

Gary walked into the gym, right on time for band practice.

Basketballs stopped bouncing. The speed bag came to rest. A doo-wop quartet harmonizing in an alcove fell silent. There must have been forty or fifty black guys in there, every eyeball on him. "Here come the snitch!" somebody hollered. A chorus erupted. "Cheese eater!" "Rat!" "Bitch!"

Gary froze in the doorway, set his feet in a martial-arts T stance. He took a deep breath. He roared: "COME AND GET ME, MOTHERFUCKERS!!!"

Nobody said anything for a second, so Gary moved swiftly, heading for a door at the rear of the gym, a utility room where Gary's band, the No-Names, was allowed to practice once a week.

It was early September 1993. Gary was 25; he'd been down for six years.

After stints at Riverside and at Scotts Correctional Facility, he'd been transferred here, to Ryan Regional Correctional Facility, a new maximum-
security prison in the middle of bombed-out Detroit. Gary had long hair,
a stubbly chin, veiny arms; his trapezius muscles bulged into a hard collar
of fleshy mass that jutted up through the deep V neck of his shirt. Every
day, rain or sun or snow, he hit the weight pit in the yard, then spent an hour
throwing karate kicks against a cement wall. He had gained fifty pounds; the
other cons called him Bulldog.

Gary had adapted to prison the best he could, tried to master those parts
of his life that were still under his control. He passed the time drawing
ornate renderings of women and wolves, wrote letters, prayed. He played
cards, read Stephen King. He stopped beating off, because wet dreams were
better, more real, like you were there. He brushed his teeth six times a day.
He hooked up his radio to his guitar amp, a makeshift stereo. He learned
how to dance. How to sew. How to make a knife using a toothbrush, a pack
of matches and a disposable razor. How to get himself into a routine, to
move slowly and deliberately, to make use of every second. To count the days
that passed but never the days that remained.

Over time Gary discovered that prison was, well, put it like this: There was
no way you would choose to be here. But once you resigned yourself to being
here, and once you resigned yourself to having no control or freedom, prison
wasn't all that bad. You could wear your own clothes, work out as much as
you wanted, buy bags of fresh-popped popcorn in the yard, touch your
people when they came to visit, even have sex in the visiting-room toilet. You
could have a TV and a radio, a typewriter or a sewing machine. For a few
years, before they cut the funding, you could go to school and earn college
credits. You could work: making soap, making cigarettes, operating a forklift, doing laundry, tutoring other prisoners for their GEDs.

The real problem with prison was the prisoners. The dregs of society were
in here. They had nothing left to lose. You had to watch out constantly for
robbers, confidence men, dangerous psychos. People would split your melon
for $25. They'd fuck with you just to have something to do. You had to hold
your face a certain way, tough and noncommittal, and your eyes a certain
way, askance but all-seeing. You had to watch who you talked to and what
you said. You had to learn to sleep lightly, how to rig a nighttime barrier
around your bunk. You had to be careful of people who were too friendly.
You had to be careful of people who wanted to make you their bitch. You
had to be careful of the guards; they ran all sorts of scams. And you had to

watch out for gangs—there was constant fighting and racial tension. Overall, you learned to stick with your own, to mind your own business, to keep the faith. And to never, ever be a snitch.

Gary reached the utility room, rushed in, slammed the door.

"Dude, we didn't know if you were going to show," said JK, the lead guitarist in the band. He was sitting in a circle with the others—Big George, Snake Eyes and Tom; a murderer, an armed robber and a rapist; on bass, drum machine and keyboard. Gary was the singer. They covered songs by Metallica, Black Sabbath, Anthrax.

"Look, man, if they rush me in here, you guys just stay out of it," said Gary, picking up a tennis racket, testing its weight.

"No, man," said Tom, the drummer, rising out of his chair, picking up another tennis racket. "If they bust in here, I'm with you, man."

"Dude, you ain't gonna do nothing with me, man," said Gary. He took a practice swing, chopping the air with the racket. "I stand alone. This is my problem."

Gary's problem was tricky. It had started four years ago, with his mom.

For a long time after Gary's conviction, Linda Fannon lived in a fog. She couldn't talk to anyone about her problems; people believed that Gary was a drug kingpin who'd gotten what he deserved. When his appeal was turned down, she considered suicide, but only briefly. Her boy was in prison for life. She had to get him out. The question was how.

Then one day in 1989 Linda heard that Kurt Johnston had been dismissed from the Canton Township police force for using drugs. A quantity of prescription drugs had gone missing from the evidence room. The detectives were all screened for drugs. Johnston tested positive for coke and Valium. Though he denied stealing the drugs, he was fired.

All along Linda had believed the cops were crooked. Now she had the evidence. She called Gary's attorney, who wanted more money. She had already spent more than $30,000 on legal fees. She had to try something else.

Linda went to the library and discovered she was not alone; there were groups all across the country fighting state and federal mandatory-minimum drug laws. Michigan's, it turned out, was the toughest in the nation. A study by the *Detroit Free Press* had found that while the statute was intended to snare "drug kingpins," big dealers had largely avoided the Michigan penalties. You had to be caught with more than 3,000 pounds of coke to get life in the federal system. Like Gary, the majority of

Michigan's 650 lifers were first-time offenders. More than 50 percent were low-level functionaries—lookouts, drivers, couriers.

Linda called the newspapers and the television stations, contacted William Bryant, a state representative. After many calls and visits from Linda, Bryant was persuaded to hold legislative hearings in Lansing, the state capital. Linda testified. A reporter who worked for the *Detroit Free Press* was moved by her story. MOTHER TAKES FIGHT AGAINST LIFE SENTENCES TO LEGISLATURE, read the headline on March 18, 1991. "I will fight until the day I die," Linda was quoted as saying. Encouraged, she stepped up her efforts, crisscrossing the state, speaking out.

In the summer of 1992, while researching a story about mandatory minimums for *Rolling Stone*, I read about Linda and Gary in *USA Today*. I flew to Michigan to meet them and was so struck by their story that I featured only them in my piece.

Following the *Rolling Stone* story, there was a flood of publicity. Linda appeared on a dozen national television talk and newsmagazine shows. Gary appeared too, a disembodied head on a TV monitor. The response was overwhelming—Gary began receiving more than thirty letters a day from all over the world.

A year later, in the summer of 1993, I went to see Gary again. Though he had received a lot of media attention, his situation was unchanged. The drug war was still in full swing. Two bills in the Michigan legislature that Linda had helped bring to fruition were stalled in committee; both the Michigan and the U.S. Supreme Courts had ruled sentences like Gary's constitutional. Gary was still in prison for life. Wanting to help, I wrote a follow-up.

Rolling Stone was well circulated at Ryan, and when that second article appeared, in September 1993, everyone knew about it, though few had read it. The first article had focused on the issue of mandatory minimums; none of the cons had much comment. The second, however, focused on Gary's life inside Ryan. Though I had made an effort to protect him, I had unwittingly committed several errors of judgment. I mentioned in the article that there were gangs and drugs in the prison and that couples fondled in the visiting rooms—the kind of stuff found in every prison movie. I didn't think that I was revealing secrets.

The cons at Ryan thought otherwise.

They believed Gary had written the article himself. And they believed that Gary had broken the ultimate prison code: He was a snitch. A price was put on his life.

The guards came to the utility-room rehearsal hall and cuffed his hands behind his back, led him against his will toward protective custody, the lowest rung of prison hell, the haven of snitches and sissies and child molesters. To reach p.c., the guards had to walk Gary through the main area of the prison, an atrium affair with the cell blocks stacked one on top of the other.

As they entered the room, a guard on either side, the sergeant behind, wrenching up Gary's arms, the other prisoners began yelling and spitting and throwing things down from their cells. "There go the snitch!" "Ruff, ruff, ruff, bull bitch." "Cheese eater!"

"FUCK YOU, BITCHES!" screamed Gary. He struggled, staggered, fell to the floor, hit his head. The cons heckled and taunted.

The guards looked at one another and smirked. Gary felt like Jesus walking the last mile. The sergeant hauled him up by his wrists. "Come on, Bulldog, you're making me look bad."

"Hey, Gary, you got any of those nutty bars?"

On a crisp afternoon in November 1995, Gary pulled off his reading glasses and looked up from his typewriter. Some days he spent eight hours at his desk, answering letters, dispensing advice and updates on mandatory minimums to cons in other prisons, helping to organize Friends of Gary Fannon, writing steamy letters to several girls, including his main true love, Alita.

Alita had contacted Gary five years ago, after reading about him. She was doing five to fifteen on charges of vehicular manslaughter. At first Gary and Alita were pen pals. Then, during the two months Gary was locked down in p.c. at Ryan, the tone of the letters began to change. By the time he'd gotten to this new prison, the Lakeland Correctional Facility in Coldwater, they'd declared their mutual love.

Alita was housed at a women's facility a mile from Coldwater. He'd never seen her, never heard her voice. If he went out to the corner of the yard, past the garden, behind the greenhouse, and peered across the fields, he could see tiny people in the yard of the women's prison. Once a week, at a special time, he'd go behind the greenhouse with a shard of mirror and reflect the sun. Alita would signal back.

Coldwater was known as a soft place. Many of the prisoners were in for rape or child molestation or had been in p.c. at another facility. Coldwater was in the country, next to an Amish settlement. The buildings had once housed a children's mental hospital.

The relaxed atmosphere at Coldwater, Gary discovered, had an odd by-product—everyone had a business. One guy sold hot dogs and chili dogs; another sold sandwiches stolen from the kitchen. Israel the Rastafarian was a wizard with electronics. There were tattoo artists. Loan sharks. Leather workers. Bookies. Greeting-card makers. Portrait artists. Drug dealers. Spud-juice bootleggers. Hit men. Letter writers. Rip was the store man; he sold cookies, Kool-Aid, razors, same as the prison store. In fact, he bought his merchandise from the prison store. Rip charged $1 for a 75 cent bag of chips. But he was always open. And Rip gave credit, with interest, of course.

A few weeks into his stay, someone asked Gary if he could buy a candy bar from him, and Gary's entrepreneurial instincts stirred. He started with a box of peanut-butter cups, branched out into nutty bars, then Kool-Aid, then chips. He'd spend $100 a week and make $30 or $40 profit.

Soon Gary had jars and socks and pockets full of tokens, the coins that were used inside as tender. He cashed them in, sent money home to his mom. He started a loan business and then got an idea for a sort of prison ATM. Someone outside would send Gary's mom a check for $50, and Gary would dispense $35 in tokens to the designated prisoner. His basketball pool, 25 cents a ticket, was an immediate success. Then came haircuts, $1 a head. Typing was 25 cents a page.

By November 1995, Gary was living about as well as you could behind bars. He had cons minding his store, collecting his debts, selling basketball tickets. He paid two cons to set the point spread for basketball. Another was paid to run errands. Gary had a big radio, all the sweatpants and T-shirts he could wear. Though he never missed a prison meal—he figured the state owed it to him—he augmented his diet with special food from the kitchen, sandwiches and meats, orange juice, fruit. Even with the scams people were always pulling—like the time his consultants rigged the basketball pool and cleaned him out—he'd sent home in excess of $3,000 during the past year.

Most important, for the first time in years, there was movement on Gary's case. A dedicated young Detroit attorney, Patrick McQueeney, had managed to persuade Judge Battani to hear new evidence. He'd subpoenaed Kurt Johnston. The date was set.

Now, at his desk in Coldwater on this afternoon in November, eight months before his scheduled hearing, Gary finished a letter to his mom and turned off his electric typewriter. He cocked his head, cut his eyes upward, toward his customer. "I don't know about any more nutty bars, Lindsey. What about your girlish figure?"

"Oh Gary, don't you know it's not polite to talk about a lady's weight?"

Lindsey laughed, her voice coy and smoky. She had long, straight blond hair and big breasts. Her shirt was tied up in a little knot to expose her doughy midriff. She went about five feet seven, 160 pounds, said her name was Lindsey Starr, headlining female impersonator at all the great rooms in Vegas and L.A., best known for her Julie Andrews and her Ann-Margret.

After nine years in prison, Gary knew well that sissies could mean big trouble. But Coldwater was sissy heaven. There were guys sucking dicks everywhere in the shadows. There were super-sissies all over the yard with big-time makeup and poufed hair. Some of them had implants in their cheeks and chins and hips, and the shit had melted or something, and they looked like monsters. It was a freak show, you know. Gary was fascinated.

When Lindsey first started coming around, however, Gary refused to even look at her. In all these years, he'd never thought of doing any gay stuff. To tell the truth, the thing he missed most was spooning: He dreamed of lying in bed with Alita, her arms wrapped around him.

Lindsey chased after Gary. She frequented his store, quizzed him about the basketball pool. She watched him lift weights, made comments about his body. One day Gary got fed up. He pinned her neck against the wall. "CUT IT THE FUCK OUT OR I'LL RIP YOUR HEAD OFF!" he roared.

Lindsey got the message, sort of. Though she kept coming around, she softened her approach. Slowly, the two began to talk. Gary asked her why she was the way she was, and she told him the whole story about being a little girl stuck in a little boy's body. She was about 40 years old, and she was real attractive when her makeup was on, this tan eye makeup with the light brown eyes—it was nice.

Over time Lindsey became a fixture in Gary's routine. He'd be out in the yard with his friend Eric, or they'd be playing cards or pool, and Lindsey would be hanging around, sitting off to one side with her legs crossed just so. It was like being on the outside again, having a woman around. As Lindsey used to say, she was one slice away from being a real girl.

Lindsey was funny. She acted out little dramas, snapped her fingers in the air, did different voices. She told stories about her days onstage. She told stories about Zebra, her current lover. They called him Zebra because he had these weird patches of gray hair. Zebra was in love with Lindsey. He cleaned up her room, cleaned the mud off her shoes, followed her around, kept trying to get her alone in the shower. He had offered to transfer $1,500 into Lindsey's prison account if she'd tell everyone he was her husband.

One day in the yard, Gary and Eric were playing cards and Lindsey was hanging around. Zebra was across the way, bellowing. It was his birthday. He wanted Lindsey. "Get away from those motherfuckers!" he hollered.

Lindsey rolled her eyes. Gary and Eric laughed.

"Fuck you!" screamed Zebra. He stormed across the yard.

Gary set himself in a T stance. "You don't have to go nowhere you don't want to, Lindsey," said Gary.

"Not while we're still standing," said Eric.

"Fuck you, motherfuckers," said Zebra.

"Boys, boys, boys!" sang Lindsey, stepping between her knights, looking very pleased. She took Zebra by the elbow, aimed him across the yard. "See you guys later!" she sang over her shoulder.

Life went on, the whole incident pretty much forgotten. Then, about a week later, Linda Fannon received an anonymous letter from Coldwater. It said Gary and Lindsey were lovers. "This is gonna mess up your chances to get out, Gary," Linda sobbed over the telephone.

Gary was furious. He told his mom to get real. "Mail me that letter," he said.

The evidence arrived a few days later. Gary gave it to Lindsey, who checked it against her trove of greeting cards and love letters, kept in a shoe box tied with a lace ribbon. Now, as Gary handed her a nutty bar, she told him she'd come up with a match. "It was Shorty," Lindsey concluded.

Shorty was a little black guy, five feet four, a closet sissy who hung around with all the gang members who had recently started flowing into Coldwater. Shorty was friends with Zebra. He was also in love with Lindsey.

Gary found Shorty in a hallway near the gym, talking to one of his boys. Gary leaned against the opposite wall, a few feet away, and commenced staring at Shorty, giving him what they call a marquette—a hard, menacing glare.

He stared at Shorty, marquetting him, marquetting the little fucker. Finally, Shorty turned to Gary: "You got a problem?"

"Yeah, I got a fuckin' problem."

They went into the weight room. "Sit down," he commanded Shorty.

"I don't want to sit down."

"SIT DOWN, BITCH, BEFORE I KNOCK YOU DOWN!"

Shorty sat down.

"Now, listen here, you motherfucker," Gary said calmly. "If my mother ever gets another letter—"

"I didn't write no letters!" whined Shorty.

"Shut up, BITCH!" said Gary. He jabbed Shorty in the chest with his first two fingers—a hard, tight poke. Shorty tumbled backward off the bench, onto the floor.

"You gonna put your hands on me now, huh, is that it?" whined Shorty.

"Bitch, you're lucky I don't strangle your ass. If my mother gets another letter, I'm gonna kill you. I'm gonna fucking butcher you. I'm gonna drag your motherfuckin' dead carcass up to the control center, and I'm gonna spit on you as I walk. NOW GET THE FUCK OUT OF MY FACE!"

A half hour later, Shorty was back. He had his boys behind him, five of them, and a tile-cutting knife, sharp and curved, in his hand. He found Gary in the yard with Eric.

Shorty advanced toward Gary, slashing the air with the knife, making kung fu noises. Gary wrapped his sweatshirt around his arm, assumed a T stance.

Shorty lunged. Gary blocked with his sweatshirt. Shorty lunged. Gary blocked with a side kick. A crowd gathered. "Kill that white motherfucker!" "Butcher that nigger!" Shorty slashed, a wild swing. Gary backed up, backed up. He felt like a punk. He outweighed Shorty by a hundred pounds. He could take the knife, break his wrist. He could kill the little fucker with a snap kick or a roundhouse to the temple or the jaw. But he didn't know what to do. *I could blow my chances for a new trial!*

Shorty lunged.

Fuck it, thought Gary. He did a fancy spin, planted his front foot. He ran away.

Gary sat on his bunk with his head bowed, trying not to think. It was a muggy afternoon, a month before his twenty-eighth birthday.

Gary had been down now for just under ten years. Six weeks ago, he'd finally had his trial, a four-day hearing on his "motion for relief from judgment" before the same judge who had sent him away. At this very moment—2:05 p.m., July 25, 1996—in Wayne County Circuit Court, 150 highway miles west of Coldwater, Judge Marianne Battani was ready to deliver her oral decision. . . .

In the front row of the gallery, Linda Fannon was surrounded by family, coworkers, supporters, journalists, a carload of nuns in habit. Linda had dreamed of this day for years. No matter what happened now, at least she could finally say that the truth had come out.

Gary's original trial attorney had testified that he was a general practitioner who dabbled in criminal law. He said he had never discussed an entrapment defense with Gary because he didn't believe there were grounds.

Gary's appeals attorney had testified that, based on his review of Gary's trial record, he had believed that entrapment was not a viable option for Gary's appeal, even after Kurt Johnston had been dismissed for using drugs.

Several of Gary's old friends had testified that Gary had never done or sold coke before meeting Johnston.

Patrick McQueeney had grilled Johnston for three hours. Johnston, who had become a drug counselor after leaving the police force, denied snorting coke with Gary. He denied skimming coke off the top of drug deals. He admitted to testing positive for coke use, explaining that he'd sometimes rubbed a little on his gums to relieve certain aches and pains and that he had snorted it while working cases. Johnston also testified that he had no knowledge of Gary ever dealing coke before he himself started Gary off.

Now, in the Wayne County Circuit courtroom, the judge began delivering her oral opinion. "This court has certainly been involved with this case for a long time. It has a long and tortured history. . . ."

Linda sat on the hard bench, trying to concentrate. She sat there, listening but not listening, watching the burnished red lips of this portly woman as she spoke from her seat high over the courtroom.

Finally, Linda could hear summation in the judge's voice. She tuned back in.

"Given all these factors," the judge was saying, "the court finds that the defendant was entrapped into committing these crimes. The court further finds that trial counsel for defendant was ineffective, and of course there is ineffective assistance of appellate counsel. The court hereby sets aside the conviction of Mr. Fannon."

Pandemonium. Linda laid her head on the rail and began to cry. Everyone else stood at their seats, clapping and cheering. Even the judge broke a smile.

"Gary?" called Linda. "What are you doing?"

It was well after midnight, his first day back in the world. The light was bright and harsh. Gary's hands were buried in his pants pockets. His eyes were glazed.

"What is it, Gary?"

"Look," he said, sweeping a palm along the vista before him, two nine-foot-high rows of shelves—the cereal aisle at the supermarket.

They'd come here because they weren't tired yet and needed a few things for the morning, and because, well, just because they *could*. Entering the store, they went first to the cereal aisle. Linda left him there, told him to pick out something he liked. Gary scanned the shelves. There was Raisin Bran, Bran Chex, Shredded Wheat, Frosted Wheat-Bites, Frosted Mini-Wheats. Quaker, Post, Kellogg's, Nature Valley. Low fat, no fat, no sodium, high fiber, high vitamin. In prison they plopped oatmeal on your plate. You ate it.

Linda came back twenty minutes later, her cart brimming. Gary was standing exactly where she'd left him.

She smiled indulgently and tousled his forelock, the way she used to do when he stood waist high. "Here," she said, reaching for a box. "You used to like Frosted Flakes."

Since he walked out of Coldwater late Friday afternoon, July 26, 1996, to the cheers of friends and family and even the press, things have been a little bumpy for Gary. As Linda said, "He's like a child, discovering the whole big, wide world." The minute he arrived at Linda's apartment, the phone began ringing, and he literally ran to answer it. He hadn't answered a phone in almost ten years.

Gary had been sent away at 18—a damaged, troubled, good-natured boy just out of high school. He came of age inside prison, learned the ropes, built a life, got along the best he could. Rather than let prison corrupt him, he worked on himself, tried hard to be honest, loyal, thrifty and brave, a Boy Scout among the infidels. He had always believed God gave you what you deserved, good or bad. Gary figured he deserved to go to prison for all the things he'd done wrong in his life. He saw his stretch as his penance, an opportunity to earn a second chance, to travel a different path than he might have. He discovered over time that if you try hard enough to be something, you grow into it.

The Gary Fannon who emerged from a decade behind bars is today a fine and simple man, naive about the ways of business and social intercourse and grown-up women, an odd combination of coarsened ex-con and earnest young man, Jacobo Timerman meets Forrest Gump. Within days of his release, he was working for his lawyer as a gofer. He is now attending School-craft College in Livonia in the hope of becoming a physical therapist. After the first semester, he posted a 3.6 average. He also works the midnight shift as an order selector in a food distributor's warehouse; he became full-time after only nine weeks, a record at the company.

After a brief fling with Alita when he first got home—she'd been out a year, was six months pregnant and separated from her new husband—Gary got together with a young single mom. He's not sure of their future yet, but in the meantime he's settled into the complex, befuddling institution that is modern domesticity.

Gary has been to several lawyers about suing the state of Michigan, the police, Kurt Johnston, someone. Three different lawyers have passed, saying he has no case. Meanwhile he works all night long, goes to school in the morning, sleeps in the early evening, reports to work at midnight. He is tired. He is stressed out. He is stressed out about being stressed out. He feels as though he should be happy all the time now that he's free. He's learning that freedom brings complications.

"I'm pretty happy, I guess," says Gary. "But it seems like I'm still waiting. For ten years, I waited to be free. Now I'm waiting to get what's mine, what I deserve in life. At first I didn't feel like I was robbed. I was just glad to be out. But now I'm starting to look around at these other 28-year-old guys, and they have the wife, the kids, the house, all the good stuff. It's like I'm struggling to get to a place where I should already be. I think a lot about those ten years I lost. I'm trying to appreciate what I have. Let me tell you, bud. It ain't easy."

(1997)

An Imperfect Weekend

Lee Risler was driving to work in his Ford Econoline Van. Fifty-six hours later, he would emerge from an unthinkable nightmare—at least most of him would.

At dawn on the third day, Lee Risler awoke in bed, his face buried in the rumpled nest of his feather pillow. The sheets were warm and soft and familiar, redolent of Ivory detergent and dry Mojave air. Chickadees sang in the locust trees outside his window, the fountain gurgled in the grove. He turned his head slowly, luxuriantly, toward the night table, opened his eyes. His clock was in its usual place, as was his book, his glasses, his framed picture of Bryn and the kids. He felt his lips form a smile.

He lay there a few minutes, nuzzling into the pillow, swimming languidly upward from the depths of sleep. *Ahhh, this feels soooo good,* he told himself. *I'm so happy I made it out.* He drew a long cleansing breath through his nose, let the air fill his diaphragm, his lungs. He exhaled through his mouth—a light, controlled, sibilant stream. At last, he moved to get out of bed. He'd been gone for a while. There was much to do.

But he couldn't get up. He was stuck.

What in the world?

The odor of dirt and rot and petroleum began filtering into his senses. The Dopplered rush of early-morning traffic, the scratch and skitter of small animals. The softness, the sheets, the bedroom faded away, dissolved like a scene in a movie.

And he was inside the van again. It was dark and humid. He was trapped.

The van, a white Ford Econoline, was upside down, planted hood first on a steep slope in a dense thicket of bushes and trees, near the bottom of a ravine, just off the shoulder of the highway. Lee was lying nose to roof. The sharp corner of the dome light was beneath the point of his left hip, digging in, stabbing at the same raw spot. His body, outstretched, was tilted at an angle, feet elevated higher than his head. He was buried in an avalanche of shoe boxes and leather sandals, about eight hundred pairs in eight different styles, each crafted painstakingly by his own hands. The steering wheel was behind his head, which was crowded against the herniated ruins of the fire wall and dashboard. Thick, overgrown branches—silk oak, Chinese elm, eucalyptus, pepper trees—intruded through the crumpled frame of the windshield and driver's-side window, impaling the vehicle against the slope, twisted under its weight. Tangled within the branches were Lee's left arm and shoulder. Exactly how they were tangled he couldn't tell. His left eye, the hazel one, had been blind since birth. His right eye, cornflower blue, was extremely myopic. Given the condition of the van, his position, and his partial blindness, his field of vision was nil—maybe fifteen inches, 45 degrees. He felt as if he'd been crucified horizontally, nailed by one arm.

Slowly he became aware of the pain, a catalog of pain, varying types and degrees and dimensions. He called out hoarsely to his wife, "Bryn! Bryn!" his voice echoing inside the van, thinking that maybe he was dreaming, that maybe he was still in bed and Bryn was in the other room, but there was no response. *Fuck!* he screamed inside his mind, *FUCK! This isn't fair!* He jerked frantically at his left arm, trying to pull it free, throwing all of his weight against his shoulder and his arm, trying to jar it loose, but the limb wouldn't come, it just wouldn't come, it was stuck, still stuck, and it was throbbing now. He bucked again, knocked his head against something sharp. Stars appeared, shimmering motes of silvery light floating in the air before him. He paused, winded, wiped his forehead with his hand, came away with a sticky palmful of blood and ants. He'd seen kittens and other baby animals killed by ants, ants crawling out of their mouths and eyes and noses. Soon, when daylight came, the flies would return. They would lay eggs. Maggots would hatch. He imagined his body in the van in a week or so. *I have entered the food chain,* he told himself. *I have left the top of the food chain and become part of the lower order.*

He closed his eyes and tried to collect himself. *Suck it up,* he thought. *Breathe through your nose to conserve moisture.* His thirst was unbearable, worse than the pain. His tongue was shriveled at the back of his mouth. Dry and leathery and hard, it didn't feel like a tongue at all, more like the meaty flesh of a walnut.

And then it hit him: *Maybe I'm dead.*

Lee searched his memory, trying to put things straight. He was sure he'd gotten out. He was sure he'd awoken in bed. In his mind, he could see himself shattering the back window of the van with his feet. He could see himself climbing out of the ravine, strolling into 7-Eleven, telling the Armenian guy behind the counter to pour him a supersize Slice and to please call 911, there'd been an accident. He remembered asking for a baggie full of ice, carrying his thumb and fingers with him into the ambulance.

His brow knitted with concentration. *That's what I was going to do,* he told himself at last. *That's what I was planning to do. But I didn't. I'm still stuck.*

But how can that be? I was just at home.

Maybe I really have died. Maybe I'm a ghost, and ghosts get to dream about where they would like to be, but when they're no longer ghost-dreaming they come back into their existence, and their existence is wherever they were at the time they died, and that's really what the after-life is, your soul stuck right there doing whatever you were doing when you died.

Lee considered this for a little while, considered his predicament, his conclusions. He thought about Bryn and the kids. He'd left home early Saturday morning. By his best figuring, it was now Monday. Bryn had to be going crazy, wondering where he was. Bryn was practical and nurturing, an award-winning nurse. She'd calmly guided him through the unplanned home delivery of their second and third children. Vinny, the youngest, was born with his amniotic sac unbroken. Lee had to slice it open with a knife before Vinny could draw his first breath. An understanding woman, Bryn continued to allow Lee to throw his surfboard into his van once or twice a year and disappear eight hundred miles into the Baja peninsula for a couple of weeks of surfing and fishing and living off the land. Bryn liked to tell people that she worked hard not to be a bitch. She believed that women were programmed by society to nag, nag, nag. She believed you had to let a man be a man, that he would reward you by being the kind of man you needed him to be. Lee was lucky to have Bryn, and he knew it. A year ago, she'd quit an important job to keep a closer eye on the teenagers, Rhett and Elaine, and after twenty-one years of marriage, Lee and Bryn had lately become closer than ever before. Just about every day they ate lunch together at home, a four-bedroom place with fragrant honeysuckle growing on a trellis outside the front door. He'd cleared the land himself, built the house himself on five acres of a high-desert parcel that was homesteaded in the twenties by his grandfather. Sitting at the picnic table in the grove with Bryn, sipping coffee, eating a sandwich, looking out over the sagebrush and creosote and Joshua trees, toward purple mountains wavering like a mirage sixty miles in the distance, Lee counted himself a lucky man, a $35,000-a-year sandal maker with a priceless portfolio of intangibles, the kind of simple comforts that money could never buy. He felt his lips form a smile. He thought about nooners, the closest a married man could get to heaven on earth. *That's what I'll miss most when I die,* Lee told himself. *That and surfing.* He laughed out loud, his voice echoed. *Why couldn't I have died of a heart attack when I was screwing?*

Lee shook his head. *You've fuckin' gone off the deep end,* he told himself. Blood oozed down his cheeks. He could feel the sickening itchy tickle of ants crawling under his jaw. And then he thought: *Wait a minute—I can't be a ghost. Ghosts don't feel pain.* And then he thought: *How do you know? Have you ever been a ghost before?* And then he thought: *Maybe ghosts do feel pain.* And then he thought: *This sucks. I'm gonna rot here. I'm dead.*

The alarm went off at 3:00 a.m., and Lee padded into the kitchen to turn on the coffeemaker, prepped the night before to save time, as was his custom. It was Saturday morning, March 18, 2000. The first crafts fair of the year was kicking off later that afternoon in Hermosa Beach, a 150-mile drive. Lee was excited, more than ready for the show.

As was also his custom, Lee had spent the whole of the day before, Saint Patrick's Day, in the workshop behind his house, making a few last pairs of sandals. Lee was a creature of routine. Eccentric but predictable, he never wore a watch but always arrived on time. He reveled in the tiny details of life, believed that no task worth doing was too small for intricate consideration and precise execution. Gleefully self-reliant, modestly cocksure, a little bit obsessive, he had, for a time in the early seventies, scratched out a living as a subsistence farmer on his arid piece of land in Lucerne Valley, California, population seventy-five hundred, in the southwest corner of the Mojave Desert.

Like a farmer's, Lee's work was seasonal. And like a farmer, he reaped only what he sowed. He'd spent all winter alone in his shop, cutting and threading and gluing, stockpiling inventory, getting ready for the fairs. With eight styles and fourteen different sizes, black and brown, men's and women's—in multiple widths—Lee liked to lay in a minimum of eight hundred pairs. Come March, he'd load his '91 Econoline van and go to market with his harvest, attending weekend crafts fairs all across the west, from Tucson to San Francisco. When he was really cranking, he could turn out eighty pairs a week. On a good weekend, he could sell about a hundred pairs, $5,000 worth. He wasn't getting rich, but it was honest work, with no one to please but his customers, his family, himself. He rose every morning with an unhurried sense of purpose, wandered naked into his sandy yard with his cup of coffee to greet the sun and check on the chicken. He surfed, fished and skateboarded with his fifteen-year-old, fetched his youngest from school every afternoon, fell dead asleep each night by ten, the powdery scent of night-blooming jasmine filtering through his bedroom window.

Fifty-four years old, Lee had been working with leather for most of his life. During the late sixties, he'd employed fifty workers, wholesaled more than a million dollars a year worth of belts and purses to stores nationwide, even had a sales office on Fifth Avenue in New York. During the eighties, he'd had fifteen people making sandals in his backyard shop, attended thirty-five fairs a year. More recently, he'd reassessed his life and his priorities, decided to downsize, turning his business into a solo operation, focusing on mail orders and a dozen good shows. Like the man, Kiwi Sandals were homey and utilitarian. They looked pretty good and lasted a long time, had a comfortable instep, conformed to your feet with wear. Loyal customers returned every few years to buy a new pair, to spend a little time with the man they called the Sandal Guy—a short, affable surfer dude who tended to go on a bit, whose strong arms and square jaw and squinty left eye put you in mind, rather fondly, of Popeye the Sailor.

Lee picked up the rudiments of his craft as a teen from a friend of his dad's, a salty old-timer who'd made harnesses for Circus Circus elephants and Budweiser Clydesdales. Lee grew up in Torrance, south of Los Angeles, ten miles east of the ocean, then a rural bedroom community of strawberry fields and oil derricks, now a sprawling suburb. His dad was a longshoreman, a union capo who liked his booze and his brawls and his Benzedrine, the kind of guy who came home at night with his trunk full of purloined steaks and lobsters. An uninspired student, Lee frequently missed morning classes to surf. He barely graduated from high school, class of 1964.

After several attempts at traditional careers—tile setter's apprentice, diesel mechanic, dockworker—Lee realized that he'd never make much of an employee. Though he loved working, he hated the notion of having a job. What you did should be part of you, he felt, not just something to make money. Leather was popular with his hippie friends; in time, he hit on the idea of selling watchbands. The materials cost a quarter. The finished product retailed for five bucks. Before long, he'd leased an old bakery in Redondo Beach. Day and night you could find folks crashed in the factory, smoking dope, tripping on acid, making leather goods to sell to the head shops springing up along the coast.

Now, in the early-morning hours of March 18, Lee took a quick shower— he'd shaved the night before to save time—and dressed in his year-round outfit of shorts and a tee, no underwear, adding a long-sleeved flannel shirt against the chill. His feet were brown and calloused, his nails gnarly. A silver ring adorned the long second toe of his left foot. As usual, he slipped on his sandals, the No. I model, simple brown leather thongs, size 10, forty dollars. Lee had gotten married in a suit and sandals. The last time he'd worn shoes was two years ago, at his brother-in-law's funeral. Lee figured he deserved that respect.

Pouring his coffee into a twenty-ounce traveling mug, Lee walked over to the computer, logged on to the Internet to check the coastal surf report. If there had been one constant in his life besides leather, it was surfing. He'd surfed up and down the east and west coasts, in Canada, in Mexico, and all over New Zealand, where he'd lived for two years with his first wife after selling his burgeoning business, fed up with the hassles and complications. Not long ago, he ran into his ex-partner. The company was still going strong, headed for its first $100 million year. Lee felt no regrets. By the time he'd decided to cash out, he was gritting his teeth so fiercely at night that his wife couldn't sleep.

Truth be told, it was the promise of surfing that had clinched the decision to go to the Hermosa Beach show in the first place. Lee was already committed to two shows in Hermosa that year. The Saint Patrick's Day show was a new date on the calendar; he'd signed on as a favor to the promoters. The main attraction for Lee was the setup. At most shows, to save expenses, he'd spend the nights in his booth. At Hermosa there was an oceanfront hotel, quite affordable, right at the site. Lee had reserved a suite for a nice little family vacation to kick off the season. He would drive down first to set up and surf. Bryn and the kids would follow later in the afternoon.

Lee logged off the computer, gathered a few last things into his Dopp kit—a corkscrew, a couple of extra batteries, a Swiss Army knife, a real nice one given to him by a friend, with a hand-carved wooden handle instead of the standard red plastic.

He left at precisely 3:30, juddering along Old Woman Springs Road, turning westward onto Happy Trails Highway. By the time he reached the interstate, thirty miles away at Victorville, the van was warm, his spirits were high. It would be great to see his friends again, the other exhibitors. He liked to think of them as his tribe: the Stained-Glass Woman, the Whirligig Guy, the Batik Couple, the Kettlecorn Folks—he could never get enough of that stuff, sugary and salty at once, perfect for the munchies.

He headed south, through the Cajon Pass of the San Bernardino Mountains, breathtaking in the moonlight.

Speeding through the darkness, yellow lines ticking past in the glowing beam of the headlights, Lee felt a deep sense of peace. Things had never been better for the Rislers. The bills were mostly paid; cash money was just down the highway. Bryn had adjusted famously to being home. Though it had been tough to give up the new GMC Safari—not to mention the health insurance and the income, more than sixty grand a year as a program director at a hospital—it was clearly the right choice. Vinny was flourishing, a sweet and rowdy six-year-old, into his frogs and his snakes. Rhett, a high school sophomore, was getting decent grades, playing noseguard on the football team, surfing and skateboarding like an old hand under Lee's careful tutelage. Elaine, an eighth grader, had always been the troubled child—a budding Kelly Bundy, Lee liked to say—given to wearing T-shirts with slogans like I LIE TO BOYS. The day she came home with an unauthorized piercing in a rather private spot was the day Bryn decided to quit work. Though Elaine still had her moments, she was doing pretty well under Bryn's watchful care. Lee cherished his roles as a husband and father. Four very special people loved him, needed him, counted on him. All of his kids had cornflower-blue eyes, exactly like his good one. He loved the idea that there were three brand-new pieces of himself out there in the world, learning everything all over again, learning everything a little better this time around because he was there to guide them.

Leaving the mountains, turning westward, Lee entered the congested flatlands of Los Angeles County—warehouses, light industry, strip malls, housing developments. By 5:30 a.m., the traffic was still light. He headed south on the 605 Freeway, an eight-lane behemoth that followed the San Gabriel River. Just past the junction with the 5 Freeway—an epic highway, stretching the length of the state—Lee saw the sign for his exit: INTERSTATE 105, 1¾ MILES. From there, he'd take surface streets. Twenty minutes to the beach, max. *I'll probably be surfing before seven,* Lee told himself.

Hurtling along at 70 miles per hour in the number-two lane of the 605, just past Telegraph Road, in the city of Downey, a little more than a mile from his exit, Lee felt a thunderous jolt from the passenger side of the van.

Suddenly, he was careening toward the median, tires squealing. He yanked the steering wheel to the right. The van swerved back across the lanes, fishtailing, heading toward the shoulder, straight for a metal light pole. He took his foot off the gas, cut the wheel back to the left, hit the curb, felt a tremendous thud. . . .

And he was airborne, the nose of the van tilted slightly upward. For a few milliseconds, he felt the way he felt when he was surfing—weightless, adrenalized, oddly calm. He gripped the steering wheel, braced his elbows. *I wonder how this is gonna turn out?*

The van did a somersault and a half twist, landed upside down, nose in the dirt. It came to rest against a pair of towering silk oaks, in a dense thicket on a steep slope near the bottom of a ravine, a man-made basin beneath a vast concrete cloverleaf. As the van slid down the hill, the foliage closed around it.

Lee was stunned, as if he'd just taken a punch on the chin. It was pitch-dark inside the van. He blinked his eyes. Opened or closed, there was hardly any difference in the light. He shook his head to clear the cobwebs. He could hear the engine idling, the pistons knocking. He smelled dirt, gas, oil. *I've been in an accident,* he told himself. *Somebody will be here in just a few minutes.*

Lee inspected himself with his right hand, touching here and there, trying to assess the damage. His scalp was ripped. It felt furry and numb, as if he were wearing a wet woolen cap. His chin was cut, a couple of molars were broken. There was blood in his mouth, all over his face. He worried fleetingly about the possibility of smoke and fire, but he was trapped—that was the first problem to solve. His seat belt was still hooked, but he wasn't in the seat. He couldn't quite tell exactly where he was. He felt along the strap with his right hand until he found the buckle, clicked it loose. He was lying chest down on something hard. His left arm was trapped beneath him. That's what it felt like, anyway, like he was lying on top of something heavy and that his arm was under that. *I don't think I'm badly injured,* he told himself. *Nothing's broken.*

Time passed. The engine sputtered and died. The darkness began to leaven. Looking around as best he could, he figured out that the van was upside down, that he was lying on the roof. He was surrounded by thick branches, two and three inches in diameter. The seats were hanging above him. The steering wheel was behind his head. *Man, that other guy must be really bad off,* Lee thought. *Everybody must be over there helping him.*

He reached up with some effort and sounded the horn, a prolonged blast, then stopped, listened, counted to thirty. He did it again, no response. Then he thought about Morse code. He sent an SOS—three short blasts, followed by three long, followed by three short. *This is weird, you know? Why can't anybody hear me?* He started to become a little worried. He started yelling: "Is anybody out there? Hello? Can anybody hear me?"

His voice echoed, loud and lonely. He listened for a response. There was nothing but the sound of traffic, the rumble and whoosh, cars and trucks buzzing past. And then it hit him: *The other guy kept on going. Nobody stopped. Nobody stopped!*

A wave of outrage and incredulity rushed over him, and he reached up and leaned on the horn. *Can you fuckin' believe this?* he roared inside his mind. *Nobody stopped? A van just rolled off the freeway here! How could nobody have stopped?* The horn blared and blared. Five minutes, ten, the noise like an ice pick in his ear. And then the horn began to grow fainter. Slowly it ran out of juice.

An hour had passed since the accident, maybe two. The sun was up by now. The smells of dirt and mulch began to rise from the forest floor. *Nobody's coming,* Lee thought. *I'm gonna have to do it myself.*

He turned his attention to his left arm. A moment ago he'd been trapped and helpless. Now he had a project, a goal to accomplish. *It can't be later than 7:00. Bryn and the kids will be leaving the house in a couple of hours. There's still time to catch her. She can bring the old van. We can transfer the stuff and still make it to the show.* From what he could gather, he was lying on top of a large cardboard box. His arm was beneath that. The box measured about three by three. He'd fashioned it from a packing crate and some foam padding to hold his Kiwi Sandals sign. The sign itself was elaborately carved out of a two-inch slab of seasoned redwood. He always displayed it in his booth.

He tried sliding the sign out from beneath him, but he couldn't make it move. Because of the way he was lying—at an angle, with his feet elevated about a foot higher than his head—all of his weight was on his chest, which was on the sign.

Feeling around the wreckage, looking for a tool, Lee caught hold of the hunting knife he always kept underneath the driver's seat, an antique with a thick six-inch blade. He went to work on the box.

Ten minutes, a half hour. Blood and perspiration dripped from his forehead and his chin. He sliced up the cardboard, pulled it from beneath him piece by piece. At last, only the sign was left. It was considerably more uncomfortable than the box. His arm was really starting to hurt. It felt as if his hand was caught in a door, only the pain wasn't just in the fingers, it was spread out over the whole arm, up to the elbow, a pain like a bad toothache, a dull type of angry throb. He loved that sign. It was a real piece of art, a beautiful bas-relief rendering of a kiwi bird. He stabbed it with the knife, bending the six-inch blade, breaking off pieces of redwood.

The sign was about half removed when the knife slipped from his hand. *Shit.* It clattered somewhere out of reach. He searched for a while, then gave up. He racked his mind for a plan. By now it was quite a bit brighter inside the van. He could see shadowy forms, dapples of filtered light He craned his neck around and tilted his head back, looking awkwardly over the bridge of his nose, trying to use his good eye to catch a glimpse of the situation over there on his left side.

Twisting and craning, looking upward and around, he spied something odd. His eyes saucered. *My God, I landed on top of a pedestrian!*

A hand was sticking straight out from the branches, fingertips first. It was wedged between two good-sized tree limbs, one across the knuckles, the other beneath the palm. It appeared to belong to an adult white male. A homeless man? A hitchhiker? It looked a bit bloated, more rosy than normal. The way it was posed there, fingers spread and extended, it seemed to be reaching out to him, calling for help. Lee grabbed the index finger. It felt cold. He thought about Vinny, his youngest, the way he sometimes did this very same thing, reached up and wrapped his whole hand around Lee's index finger. And then he thought: *This guy is a goner. He can't be alive.*

Time passed. Every ten minutes or so he'd call out: "Can anybody hear me? Help! I'm trapped!" The longer he lay there, the longer he looked at the hand, the more familiar it started to seem. There was something about the fingernails, the little hairs on the knuckles . . .

And as the sun rose overhead, as the light inside the van continued to improve, as the hand continued to swell—growing fatter, more bloated, the color beginning to change, fading a bit from rose to yellow—he finally noticed: The wrist of the hand was wearing his flannel shirt.

Fishing around in the wreckage for a tool, Lee found his Dopp kit, the Swiss Army knife. The blade was three inches long. He opened it with his teeth. He figured he'd have to cut two or three branches. *I better get a move on if they're going to save this hand,* he told himself. He started out sawing, then switched to a whittling motion. The first few slices went well. The bark was soft; it came away like a potato peel. In order to see what he was doing, Lee had to crane his neck and peer awkwardly over the bridge of his nose. In order to reach the branches, he had to shove his right arm through the crumpled frame of the windshield, through hanging shards of glass and twisted metal. With each stroke of the knife, he gashed his forearm. The inner part of the wood was very hard. All he could take were tiny slivers. The price of each sliver was another painful gash.

After six hours, Lee had whittled the branch down about three eighths of an inch. His forearm was on fire, the knife was getting dull. He needed another plan. *If you can't raise the bridge, you lower the river,* he told himself. *Maybe if I dig under the branches, the weight will shift and I'll be able to pull out my arm.*

He dug and dug, through mulch, through oily dirt, through clay. His fingertips began to bleed. He rested a bit. He dug some more. Every so often, he called out for help. Night fell. He dug.

In total darkness, the thicket came alive. Insects sang and lizards chirped; an owl hooted in the distance. Armies of ants marched across his skin. Small creatures scratched and scampered inside the van. At first, when he heard the noises in the load, he thought it might be a person, some homeless guy maybe, and he shouted out, "Who's there?" The scratching stopped for a moment, but no one responded. *What if they're bad guys?* he worried. *What if they want to douse me with gas and set me on fire?*

The pain was excruciating, worse than anything he'd ever felt, a symphony of throbs and rips and aches. His thirst was unbearable. He was exhausted, but he was afraid to sleep—what if someone walked by? He played the accident over and over in his mind. *I was a mile and a half from my exit.* He never even saw the guy who hit him. He worried about Bryn and the kids. Were they still in Hermosa Beach? He pictured them the way they were in the photo on his nightstand, only instead of smiling, they were grim. It was the longest night of his life.

By mid-morning on Sunday, when the light finally came up again in the van, Lee's hand had shriveled into a claw. Cold and gray, it looked like the hand of a mummy, like something ghoulish, no longer of this world. His left arm had swollen to twice its normal size above the elbow. When he poked the arm with the fingers of his right hand, it felt like he was pushing on a water balloon. It would spring back when he let off the pressure. He lay there for a while in the half light, considering his next move, thinking about those hooks he'd seen people wear, wondering what it would be like to have two little hooks to reach down and pick things up with. He tried to picture the different steps in the process of making sandals, the ways he'd have to alter his shop.

The day wore on. Lee dug and dug. Gradually, as the light again began to fade, he formulated a plan. *I can't spend another night in this van,* he told himself.

He found his wet suit, cut off a piece of the leg, fashioned a tourniquet. Then he took the knife and made a little slice in the webbing between the thumb and first finger of his left hand. He didn't feel a thing. There was hardly any blood, just a thick black paste.

Lee figured he'd go for the wrist. He'd never really thought about the anatomy of the wrist before, but thinking about it now, about the way it worked, he figured there had to be a joint in there, a joint something like a chicken's, where the leg met the thigh. If he could just pop the joint and free himself from the hand, he'd be able to pull out his arm.

He went in from the thumb side, probed around, trying to find the joint. He felt no pain, no pressure. A couple of times he thought he got close to the right spot, but the tree branch was in the way; he couldn't get any leverage.

Frustrated, short of breath, he pulled back to reassess. *How about if I just cut off the fingers?* he thought *If I do that, there will be less to shove through the branches.*

He pushed the tip of the knife into the joint at the base of his thumb, wiggled it a bit to find the right spot. He leaned down hard. . . .

And off it came, a squishy-sounding pop. It hung by a few threads of meat and sinew. *We're getting somewhere!* Lee thought. And then he thought: *There's no going back from here.*

Below him, beside his body on the right, Lee had fashioned a makeshift workbench, a little shelf for things he'd come across in his rummagings. He had his glasses on the shelf, oily and useless, and also a tube of toothpaste, his tourniquet, a couple of strong sticks he'd used for digging. One by one, as he amputated his thumb and three of the fingers of his left hand, all of them except the pinkie, as he popped the joints and cut away the meat, separated each finger from its lifelong position on his hand, he placed them carefully on the shelf for safekeeping. He wasn't going to just cut them off and let them drop in the dirt. They were his fucking fingers, a part of him in the truest sense. *Maybe I'll make a necklace out of them,* he mused. The pinkie was spared. Earlier, trying to free the hand, he'd shoved the pinkie through the branches. It was twisted rather obliquely, probably a compound fracture, but it was already free. Taking the pinkie would have seemed like self-mutilation.

Lee placed the knife on the shelf, alongside the tidy row of fingers. He took up the toothpaste, rubbed it all over his left hand, an improvised lubricant. Reaching up with his right hand, he pushed the left one through the branches. It moved easily. It was free. *All right, baby!* he told himself. *7-Eleven, here we come!*

He shifted his weight to his right as best he could, pulled against the arm . . . But nothing moved.

Fuck! he screamed inside his mind. *Goddammit! I cut my fuckin' fingers off! I deserve to be free!* He jerked frantically at his left arm, trying to pull it free, pulling and jerking and bucking himself, throwing all of his weight against his shoulder and his arm, trying to jar it loose. But the limb wouldn't come.

Exhausted, a little bit horrified, Lee rested for a while, puzzling things out. It was getting darker. His hand was free. His forearm was loose. He could see his biceps and his shoulder. *I've got to be stuck by the elbow,* he told himself.

He took up the knife again, cut away the sleeve of his flannel shirt. Tentatively, he stuck the three-inch blade into the meat above his elbow. That tissue was alive. The pain was nearly unbearable.

He drew a long breath, then shoved the knife to the hilt, to the handle, far enough to hit bone. *Bite the bullet,* he told himself. He sliced and sawed and poked, fishing around, looking for the joint, screaming inside his mind like a man possessed: *Eat this, motherfucker! You think that hurts? Well, take this, you bitch! Take that!*

At last, he stopped. He was breathless. He felt faint, nauseated. He'd always thought of himself as a man who did what it took, who made his own choices. *In for a penny, in for a pound,* he told himself.

He raised his right arm as high as he could. He plunged the knife deep into his shoulder.

The world went white.

When he came to, there were two men in the van with him. They were both surgeons, a father and son. The son was more famous than the father. Lee could tell that the father resented the son. The father was yelling at Lee, "If you'd just let my son do it, we'd all be out of here!"

Lee blinked his eyes. He was on the side of the road. There was a chain gang working with picks and shovels. They were singing a hymn. A fat sheriff in a cowboy hat was sitting astride a horse, a shotgun over his shoulder. He bellowed down at Lee, "If you hadn't lost the knife, you'd be out of here, boy!"

Lee blinked his eyes. It was pitch-dark. Opened or closed, there was hardly any difference in the light. *You're out of it. You're delirious,* he told himself. His arm was killing him. He could feel blood dripping from the fresh wounds.

He was pissed at himself for passing out, disappointed that he hadn't finished what he'd started. He rummaged around, trying to find the knife.

Slowly, he became aware of noises in the load, small creatures scratching and scampering. And slowly, he became aware of a new sound, a wet sort of sucking sound, like crunching, like munching. He got a sickening feeling, and he reached over to the little workbench he'd fashioned for himself.

His fingers were gone.

By noon on the third day—Monday, March 20, fifty-four hours since the accident—the pain had begun to subside. His left hand smelled like rotten meat. Lee felt odd and untethered, as if he were floating. *My body's beginning to shut down,* he told himself. *I'm probably gonna die here.*

Lee continued to dig sporadically. He was weak. He could make only two or three strokes—shoving his hand through the glass and metal of the twisted windshield—before he had to rest. By now, the hole was two feet long, eight inches deep. The skin on his fingertips had been rubbed away. He wasn't really sure anymore exactly why he was digging. *I'm gonna go down fighting,* he thought. *You can't say I didn't try.*

Beneath the bravado, Lee realized now that his only remaining hope was rescue. All morning he'd listened to the rush-hour traffic, cars and trucks whooshing past, barely seventy-five feet from his head. He hoped maybe someone would have a flat tire or even an accident. He was only about fifteen miles southeast of downtown Los Angeles, right in the thick of the commute. On an average day, 247,000 vehicles passed the spot where he lay trapped.

I guess this is about the time when a religious person would begin making promises to God, Lee told himself.

Lee believed in a higher power, but he didn't like to call it God. Over the years, he had settled into his own form of quiet worship. He called it karma; it was about living the truth, about seeing your actions for what they really were, about being responsible. He figured that you got out of life what you gave. Lee had always been the kind of guy who told the cashier when she handed him too much change. He sometimes stopped on the road to help strangers with car trouble. At crafts fairs, when it rained, he passed out his extra tarps. Each pair of his sandals was as near perfect as it could possibly be. Someone would be wearing those sandals. He made them. He owed that much to the universe—to always do the best he could. If it was time for his life force to float away and rejoin the great pool, so be it. He was ready, he supposed.

Lying there in the van, hoping for rescue, Lee racked his brain, trying to think of something he might promise to God if there actually was a God. He reviewed his life, trying to find some chink in his karmic armor, something he wished he hadn't done, something he could bargain with. He thought and thought, but the only thing that came to him was marijuana. A couple of years ago, his daughter had caught him smoking a joint. That was not something she needed to see at that stage of her life. Lee promised Bryn emphatically that he'd never smoke again. Sometimes, however, he still did. Each time he smoked was like telling another lie to the woman he loved most in the world. *If I get out of here, I'll never smoke pot again,* Lee told himself.

So you're making promises to God now?

Not to God. Just to myself.

And that's your big promise?

It's all I can think of.

He started to shove his hand through the windshield, to dig a few more scoops, but then he stopped himself, let his hand rest. He was tired. So tired. *I'm just gonna close my eyes for minute,* he told himself.

A half mile up the freeway, sitting in the cab of a giant Caltrans street sweeper, Ben Sepulveda finished his burrito and checked his watch. It was 11:55 a.m. He still had five more minutes of break. He leaned back in the seat, drummed a few beats on the steering wheel. *Might as well get back to work,* he told himself.

Forty-nine years old, a third-generation Mexican American with a droopy mustache and a singsong Spanglish patois, Ben had always been, in his own words, a "go, go, goer," a busy-type person who was never happy being idle. For many years, he'd been a tree trimmer. This maintenance job was a recent promotion, a little bit of a nod to his age. In ten years, he'd be eligible for his pension.

He threw the sweeper into gear and rumbled south on the 605, hugging the shoulder of the road. Riding along, he noticed that a couple of trees had been uprooted. Then he noticed a large piece of glass lying against the curb.

Ordinarily, Caltrans guidelines call for sweeper drivers not to pick up that kind of large debris but to leave it for a vehicle equipped with a "litter getter." For some reason, however, Ben decided he might as well pick up the glass himself. *It won't kill me, you know?*

He set the brake, climbed down, picked up the glass. He threw it in the back of the truck. Lingering a moment, he let his eyes play along the embankment, down the steep slope, into the dense thicket.

There it was. Lee's van.

When Bryn and Lee were first dating Lee liked to meet her after nursing school. Often, he'd wait in a tree. She'd come walking along with her girlfriends—so cute and proper in their little nursing caps and white stockings—and Lee would swing down out of the tree, barefoot and bare chested, hair and beard flying. He was such a hunk. So much fun. Bryn passed over a couple of professional men to marry him, much to her parents' chagrin.

Now, as she entered the recovery room—followed closely by the kids, her mother and her two sisters, her best friend, her best friend's daughter—Bryn hardly recognized her husband of twenty-one years. He was bloody and dirty, a mass of bandages and tubes and electrodes. His skin was the color of a brown paper bag. His right eye was swollen shut. There were dead ants stuck in the creases of his skin, in his matted chest hair. He was a mess. She'd never been happier to see him.

Lee raised his head weakly. "Hi, hon."

"Hi, yourself," Bryn said, tears welling. She always liked to tell people she believed you had to let a man be a man, that he would reward you by being the kind of man you needed him to be. When she'd first heard that Lee had cut off his fingers, she'd thought, *He would do that, wouldn't he?* Now, in the recovery room, she shook her head and smiled. *My man does what it takes,* she told herself.

Lee looked back at her for a few long moments, ventured a smile of his own. Slowly, his lips curled downward. His face crumpled. "Touch me," he croaked, and then his voice caught, a single shuddering sob. "Please touch me."

Bryn stepped forward, tears streaming down her cheeks. She kissed his forehead tentatively, then touched his face, his arm, his chest, then pulled back the sheet and touched his legs, his gnarled feet. "Your toe ring is gone," she said. "You must have lost it in the accident." The rest of the family stepped forward—Rhett and Elaine and little Vinny, all the rest. They gathered around the bed, kissing him, touching him, and then Bryn got some water and began washing him, scrubbing him, trying to remove all the dirt and the blood and the ants, spilling water and tears across his battered face, his tortured body, washing him, stroking and touching him, doing as he'd asked, welcoming him home.

• • •

After eighteen days in the hospital, Lee came home with a stump where his elbow used to be. With his prosthesis on order, he's trying his best to adjust. He can no longer drink coffee when he drives. He can't cut his food himself. He can't open a door while he's carrying something. Buttons are a real problem. But Lee has never been the type of man who was defined by what he couldn't do. He's learned to rake the sandy yard using his hand and one foot on the handle. He finished the lily pond he'd started in the grove, mixing cement, setting large rocks for coping, doing all of it himself. He is also making sandals again, having retrofit much of his shop to accommodate his loss. Bryn and Rhett have stepped in to help. Last week, the three of them together turned out twenty-eight pairs. Bryn likes to say it's taken four arms to replace Lee's one.

He doesn't give a thought to the hit-and-run driver who ran him off the road. The car left red paint on the passenger side of the van; that's about all he knows, all he cares to know.

"People tell me that I've got to be superhuman to go through this and not have any effects," Lee says, leaning up against the belt sander in his workshop. "If that's the case, then I guess I'm close to superhuman. It sounds flippant, but it's not. See, there's one guy we've been e-mailing with. He's an amputee, and he's trying to mentor us. And this guy tells me, 'Don't worry, it feels funny at first going out in public. It took me eight months to really feel comfortable around people.' But you know what? I never felt like that. If anything, I kind of wear it like a badge. It's like: Here it is, this is me, take it, you know? I did what I had to do."

(2000)

Stairway to Heaven

The members of the Heaven's Gate cult tried to become a genderless, communal mass mind, but they never quite transcended their humanity.

"Here, try one of these," said Rkkody, rummaging through his overnight bag, pulling out a pair of spoons.

"An excellent idea," said Jstody, reaching across the short space between the two beds. He held the familiar artifact before him, studied it a moment—a white plastic soupspoon in a clear sanitary wrapper. He'd been on the planet Earth now for fifty-six years, an eventful sojourn, a mission soon to end. "You know," he said wistfully, "I didn't think of spoons."

"It occurred to me that utensils would be of use," said Rkkody, his voice an efficient monotone.

Jstody pressed his lips into a thin smile. A balding man with close-cropped hair, he wore a black nylon warm-up suit and new black Nikes. "Leave it to you to think of everything."

"I am thankful to the Older Member for giving me his mind," said Rkkody, a gentle correction. Jstody had been living outside the class for several years now, unlike Rkkody, who had continued to follow the discipline, more or less, even after he'd moved away. Rkkody lowered his head, careful not to maintain eye contact for an inappropriate interval. Years ago the class had experimented with hoods in an effort to limit personal interaction. Rkkody never had difficulty keeping to himself. No matter what he tried, where he went—Catholic school, the air force, Fuller Brush, IBM, the streets of Haight Ashbury, the commune of Kriyananda—he'd never felt as if he belonged.

Rkkody's salt-and-pepper pompadour drooped across his deeply lined forehead. His skin was unusually soft and pink for a man of fifty-four years, a side effect of the hormone DES, given to prostate-cancer patients and pre-operative transsexuals to halt the production of sperm. Sensuality had always

387

been a point of slippage for Rkkody, the battlefield in his struggle to over-come his vehicle's human rebelliousness, something that led him to quit and rejoin the class six times over twenty-two years. Recently, Rkkody had seen the Colorado doctor who'd performed castrations on several other class-mates. DES was the first step. Thus far, he'd noticed, the fluids had dried up considerably. But his awareness of his sexuality seemed more dominant than ever. He'd be walking down the street, and his eyes would wander—he couldn't stop them—and the vehicle would just have to indulge itself, acting like a 14-year-old. Sex, he was beginning to conclude after six frustrating months, was as much a mental addiction as a physical one. Unless he cut off his head, he'd always be struggling.

Like Jstody, Rkkody was wearing a new black nylon warm-up suit. His new Nikes were blue. They fit better than the black, so he figured it was OK, though some in the class would have seen his choice as another sign of his vehicle's rebellion, its stubborn attachment to individuality. Most certainly, it would have been recorded in the Eyes Log, where all slippages were duly noted, to be discussed later at class meetings. He pulled a pair of paper nap-kins from his overnight bag, handed one to Jstody.

Jstody began to say something, then stopped himself. Idle conversation was another taboo. His name was pronounced Just-ody, meaning "Little Justin, Child of God." It was a custom of the class that each Younger Member have a similar name: three letters, no vowels, the suffix-ody—derived from Gody, a diminutive form of God. The nicknames signified the classmates' immaturity, their current condition of spiritual and cellular chrysalis. Just as caterpillars cocoon and metamorphose into butterflies, so were the class-mates waiting expectantly for the day they would graduate from their human condition, emerging as members of an incredibly advanced race of galactic caretakers from the Evolutionary Level Above Human, the true Kingdom of Heaven.

In the playful, punning, slightly nerdy spirit of the class, Jstody was also known as Justin Time. He'd been given the handle more than twenty years ear-lier, before the -ody names became the practice, during the Days of Wandering, when the class had been sent into the wilderness by a pair called Bo and Peep to divine their own mission. The classmates were scattered in small cells across the nation, living by their wits, traveling from town to campground to college campus, seeking something—they weren't sure what. One day, guided by his Older Member's mind, Jstody and his partner drove 200 miles in no partic-ular direction and happened upon a group of classmates stranded in the desert. It was high noon when he arrived; the last drops of water had just been drunk. Thereafter he was dubbed Justin Time, an early hero in the evolving mythology of the group that came to call itself Heaven's Gate.

The two men sat facing each other in room 222 of the Holiday Inn Express. They'd paid $59 in cash for one night in the three-story motel five miles north of Rancho Santa Fe, California. It occurred to Rkkody (pronounced Rick-ody) that *Room 222* had been the name of a popular '70s television show. Then it occurred to him that this was hardly the time to be thinking about television, and he chided his rebellious vehicle for this slippage, this weakness, focusing on trivial human matters when he should have been opening his mind to receive the mind of his Older Member, up there somewhere on the Next Level by now, maybe in a spacecraft behind the Hale-Bopp comet.

It was May 6, 1997, about four in the afternoon. Earlier in the day, the two men had flown from their respective cities of residence—Rkkody from North Denver, where he'd been working as a computer consultant; Jstody from Las Vegas, where he'd been working as a maintenance man. They rendezvoused in front of the McDonald's at the San Diego airport, shared a cab to the motel.

Rkkody had chosen this Holiday Inn because he'd stayed here once before. A week earlier, he and Jstody had tried a different sort of venue, a tent in a desert campground an hour outside Las Vegas. It was really hot out there; the vibrations were low. A motorcycle could have driven up at any moment and interfered. Out in the open like that, anything was possible. And since they were so far from civilization, Rkkody worried, there was also a great chance no one would discover their vehicles. Not knowing how things worked once they exited, he was anxious that they wouldn't be able to get to Rancho Santa Fe to meet up with the rest of the class. That was a big concern, being left behind.

When he'd first learned that the thirty-nine classmates had made their exit—when he'd received his Federal Express package with the Farewell Tapes and the directions for him to update and maintain their Web site— he was surprised in one sense, relieved and joyful in another. *They're finally off this planet*, he thought. *That's what they've been wanting for twenty-two years.* He was happy for them, happy they'd been able to do it. Detailed and efficient as always. Their message dispersed in a meteor shower of global publicity. And they had suffered no discomfort whatsoever in going through their transition. As a group, excepting those first years in the wilderness, they were never much into pain, at least not of a physical kind. In this way alone, they pampered their human vehicles, living in large houses in beautiful settings, enjoying the occasional pleasures of frozen pizza, strip steaks and Starbucks Java Chip ice cream.

The class had held many discussions over the years about how their exit might be effected, what options the Next Level might use. In one scenario, there was a confrontation with the Bureau of Alcohol, Tobacco and Firearms, a gun battle like Waco. Another option hinged upon the capture of one of their number by federal authorities. In protest the other classmates would have gone systematically to the steps of the White House, one each day, and effected an exit. The method had not been decided, though self-immolation had been ruled out.

A third, more pleasant scenario involved the arrival of a spacecraft, something like the one in the movie *Close Encounters of the Third Kind*. It would land in their front yard and either take them aboard physically or remove them from their vehicles and leave the bodies behind. There were a number of different ways the beings on the Next Level could do that; they certainly had the technology. In the Evolutionary Level Above Human, 2,000 years of Earth time equaled only forty-eight hours. What it was like there, specifically, was hard to explain. There was no gender, no conversation, no individuality, no sex, no food. It was a physical place, but its exact nature escaped human words and concepts. Just as a dog could not possibly envision his master's factory or law office, the classmates could not comprehend life on the Next Level. One thing, however, was certain: Once they arrived, they would be placed in circumstances 10,000 times more fulfilling than anything on the Human Level. What that meant, exactly, they would have to wait and see.

Now, sitting on their beds in room 222, each man held a plastic soup-spoon and a jar of Gerber baby applesauce, each jar laced with two grams of phenobarbital, purchased over-the-counter at a pharmacy in Tijuana. Rkkody scanned the room, making sure everything was done. They'd sent their FedEx packages with their exit letters, tied rubber bands together to make two bands large enough to fit over their heads. They'd poured their vodka and Minute Maid cocktails, two ounces of alcohol in each, twice as much as called for in the recipe on the Internet, just to make sure. At every step, each man did each task himself. They didn't want any confusion about their intentions. This was no murder. This was no suicide. It was an exit, and they were going willingly, joyously, without any question or doubt. Just as they had known so many years ago, upon hearing the message of Bo and Peep, that they had to leave their jobs and wives and children and join the class, so too did they know that now was the time to exit.

"Good-bye, planet Earth!" said Rkkody, cracking a grin. He dipped the spoon, tidied the lumpy helping against the glass lip of the jar. He raised the spoon. He ate.

"Good riddance!" said Jstody, barely containing a giggle.

"Oh! Jeez!" groaned Rkkody, swallowing hard, his face contorting into a hideous mask. "This is horrible!" He raised the jar, read the label. "Why did you get baby food?"

"I thought these would be nice," said Jstody, holding up his miniature jar, apologetic, the sour taste reflected on his own countenance.

They washed the applesauce down with their cocktails, Rkkody's first taste of alcohol in thirty years. They slid the kitchen-size trash bags over their heads, stretched the rubber bands down past their ears to their necks, as described in the recipe from the book *Final Exit.* They used the thumb and first finger to hold the rubber band away from the neck. When loss of consciousness ensued, the fingers would relax and open, allowing the rubber band to retract and seal the bag. When they were unconscious, all the fresh air gone, their circulation and respiration would slow, and then their hearts would stop, a gentle death.

And then . . . well, they'd find out.

They lay down on their backs, heads propped comfortably on two pillows each, then pulled up their purple shrouds, covering themselves from groin to crown. The shrouds were made of a synthetic material, very shiny and slippery. They kept sliding off the plastic trash bags. Holding the rubber band with one hand, adjusting the shroud with the other, each struggled to get the material to stay in place. "Jeez!" exclaimed Rkkody, the force of his exhalation causing his trash bag to luff.

"This is kind of a hassle, isn't it?" said Jstody.

"I guess the others had classmates to assist."

"I think they put the shrouds on after they exited."

"I guess so," said Rkkody. He lay silent for a few moments, the only sound in the room the scratchy noise of the shroud sliding slowly off his head onto the bed, amplified to a maddening level by the echo effect of the bag. Rkkody reached around with his free hand, grabbed the top corner of the shroud. He tucked it securely between the crown of his head and the pillow, like a napkin between neck and shirt.

They lay silent for a few more moments. "Correct me if I'm wrong," said Rkkody, "but these shrouds are an awfully red-colored purple."

"It's all they had," said Jstody. He yawned.

"I thought what the class used was more of a bluer-color purple."

"Really?"

"Yep. A royal purple, very deep, a sort of wine-colored purple."

"Hmmm," said Jstody, sounding distant. He yawned again.

"OK, well," said Rkkody. He yawned. He felt his eyelids getting heavy. He let them close.

"Collect from Ron. Will you pay for the call?"

"Ronnie? Thank God! Of course I will, operator."

"Go ahead, sir."

"Mom! What's happenin'?"

"Ronnie! Where are you?"

"I'm in St. Louis. On a camping trip."

"Your father's sitting shivah, Ronnie. We thought you were dead!"

"What do you mean?"

"He's asking me what do I mean! You were taken away in a UFO! Walter Cronkite said so, right on television."

"I saw! We—"

"Hold on, Ronnie. Your father wants to speak to you."

Ron Greenberg, now known as Aaron, held the telephone receiver away from his ear and stared at it, shaking his head. Sitting shivah? he thought. *What a bummer!* It was early evening, October 8, 1975. He had just smoked a fat joint of Oregon sense, part of a stash he'd amassed when the Older Members, Bo and Peep, had assigned him to collect all contraband from the newly recruited classmates, including drugs, cash, books, journals, keepsakes and family pictures. Though the bonfire made him think of the Nazis, he was willing to let it slide; he understood that getting into the Trip meant freeing yourself from conventional ties. That's what Bo and Peep had said. Bo and Peep! Dig it! Two gray-haired oldsters with Beatle haircuts and flowing black clothes, talking some heavy shit. But all that pot in the fire? He had to draw the line, man. If it cost him his ride on the flying saucer, so be it.

Aaron's hair dangled in a long ponytail down his back. He wore hiking boots, ripped jeans, a blue oxford-collar dress shirt, a vest from an old pin-striped suit. For the last several weeks, he'd been wandering cross-country with the partner the Older Members had assigned him, this incredibly beautiful hippie chick named Rose. Though Aaron missed his wife—now known as Window—he couldn't believe his good fortune. Sent into the wilderness to divine their own missions, he and Rose camped out, watched the stars, hiked, spent long periods sitting in silence, seeking their Older Members' mind, trying meanwhile not to talk to or look at or touch each other, sleeping chastely side by side every night in a little tent. It was torture, but Aaron let that slide too. In India some time ago, he'd studied Kundalini yoga, an ancient meditation technique. The discipline taught that the electricity generated by the heat of unreleased orgasms caused the serpent inside the body to uncoil and illuminate the pituitary gland, igniting the chakras, setting them spinning, helping to purify the vibrations of the body and the mind. Gurus had practiced it for thousands of years. Why not Bo and Peep?

From where he was standing in the phone booth, on a corner in downtown St. Louis, Aaron could see a store with maybe twenty television sets in the window, all of them tuned to *The CBS Evening News*. Aaron and Rose had been out for a stroll a bit earlier when they passed the store. On the screens was a map of Oregon. The tiny coastal hamlet of Waldport was highlighted. "Hey, look!" he said to Rose. "There must have been a big bust."

Cronkite turned it over to the correspondent, Terry Drinkwater, standing in front of the Bayshore Inn. "Rocket ships from outer space: Buck Rogers fantasy—or is it?" Drinkwater intoned dramatically. "Here along the cloud-covered coast near Newport, Oregon, a mysterious couple appeared three weeks ago, circulating a flyer proclaiming a UFO would soon be ready to take whoever would follow them to another life, another world. They held meetings, one at this motel, to recruit voyagers, who gave away everything—including kids, property, automobiles, boats and money—and just left."

Aaron headed for the nearest phone. His mother never missed Walter Cronkite.

Aaron had grown up on Long Island, the son of Lou Greenberg, one of the few Jewish capos in the Mob, a right hand to Bugsy Siegel known as Louie the Nose. Aaron had lived in a mansion with swans gliding in a pond, two beefy guys standing watch by the columns of the portico entrance. His mother dressed like a movie star. When she wanted a glass of water, she rang a bell. From the age of 6, Aaron wore a suit and tie to dinner. Soon after, his parents shipped him off to prep school. His father hoped that someday he'd attend the U.S. Naval Academy.

Aaron didn't turn out quite as expected; over time his parents came to dread his next collect call. He called collect from boot camp after dropping out of NYU and enlisting in the navy. He called collect from Berkeley, California, AWOL from his ship, which was bound with the rest of its crew for Vietnam. He even called collect from Kathmandu, the last stop along the infamous

Ganja Trail, the hippie highway around the world. He had left Berkeley with a quarter in his pocket. He was gone for three years.

"Ronald? Where the hell are you?" growled Louie the Nose over the telephone. "I'm sitting shivah here, Ronald."

"Dad! You can't believe the media. They have everything all twisted."

"So you tell me. What's all this *mishegaas,* son? They said you and Judy gave away the kids!"

Fresh off the Ganja Trail, Aaron had arrived in Waldport in 1973. Over the last few years, as the scene in California had turned nasty and political, the north-central coast of Oregon had become a haven for refugee flower children eager to get back to the land. In time the town once inhabited exclusively by loggers and fishermen became known as the Hippie Dodge City. There was a natural-food co-op, a head shop, a couple of rock-and-roll bars. People wore flowers and fringe, carried knives on their belts. You could rent a house for $90 a month, buy ten acres with a geodesic dome for three grand.

Aaron bought himself a seventeen-foot boat, became part of a large fleet of hippie dory fishermen, plying the bay with nets. If you fished from April to September, you could make upwards of $20,000. Just about the time the season closed, the fall crop of marijuana was being harvested, and everyone lent a hand. As the cooler weather set in, you'd wake up late, smoke your morning bowl, do a little Tai Chi, head down to Mo's for some chowder around noon. Wherever you went, you'd trip over stoned hippies curled up with books, reading a heavy mix of Tolkien, Steiner, The Tibetan Book of the Dead, Baba Ram Dass, *Siddhartha,* Leary, Huxley, Castaneda, the Cabala. As Aaron liked to say, they were "long-haired, bell-bottomed pioneers of the mind."

Another great pastime in Waldport was Sunday football. Several weeks ago, on September 14, Aaron had been getting ready to host a few of the guys. When Judy came in and told him about wanting to go to some meeting, he didn't know what she was talking about. There had been signs all over the place, but he hadn't bothered to read them. The meeting was being hosted, Judy said, by a pair who called themselves "the Two." They said they were about to leave in a spacecraft. Anyone could come along.

It was a schlepp into town, eight miles over rutted roads, but Judy was his wife, and he loved her dearly. They'd been married recently in a field of wildflowers by a friend of theirs, Robert Rubin, a former yeshiva student from Brooklyn and a card-carrying minister of the Universal Life Church. Judy had two kids by another guy, though the younger one was delivered at home in their A-frame with Aaron attending. They had custody of the kids every other week, a happy little hippie family.

They climbed the steps to the second-floor banquet room at the Bayshore Inn, walked through the door. Aaron was stunned. Two hundred hippies on folding chairs, everybody he knew in town, even some of the guys who were supposed to be at his house watching football. He caught the eye of one of them, his friend Rubin. Rubin raised his palms and shrugged. In the front of the room were a man and a woman in flowing black clothes, both in their late forties, old enough to be Aaron's or Judy's parents. Around them was an aura of preternatural calm. After an interval, the man spoke. "We are called Bo and Peep," he said. "We have come to gather our sheep." He cast his eyes around the room, scanning the crowd. He smiled. It was a silly little grin, a smirk, like maybe he was goofing.

"Far-fuckin'-out!" whispered Aaron.

Bo was the male of the couple. His real name was Marshall Herff Applewhite Jr. His father had been a Presbyterian minister who had devoted his life to spreading the word of God in small Texas towns. A handsome man with bright blue eyes, a big baritone voice and flawless diction, Applewhite Jr. had abandoned his seminary studies to become a professional singer, eventually landing a number of major roles with the Houston Grand Opera. For steady income, Applewhite worked over the years as a music instructor at several universities in the South and as the director of various civic and church choirs. Married, with two young children, Applewhite was popular wherever he went, a tireless volunteer and bon vivant who favored Harris Tweed jackets and Bass Weejuns and the company of well-bred ladies at tea.

Out of the limelight, however, Applewhite was deeply troubled. He'd had numerous affairs with men; he felt guilty about his double life. Applewhite divorced his wife in 1968, after sixteen years of marriage, and thereafter dated both men and women, never feeling comfortable with either. In 1970 he was abruptly dismissed from his post at the University of Saint Thomas in Houston after his relationship with a male student was uncovered. Soon after, Applewhite's father died. Devastated, distraught and deeply in debt, he began hearing voices. Eventually, he committed himself for psychiatric treatment. He told doctors he wanted to be cured of his homosexuality.

In 1972, while he was teaching at a summer theater camp for children in Houston, Applewhite met Bonnie Lu Trusdale Nettles. A plain woman who wore her hair in an old-fashioned bob, she was a registered nurse and a divorced mother of four who was deeply interested in metaphysics and astrology. Guiding her readings of the stars, she said, was the discarnate spirit of a nineteenth-century monk named Brother Francis.

Applewhite and Nettles quickly concluded that they had known each other in previous lives. They became inseparable, sharing a deep platonic love. Together they opened the Christian Arts Center in Houston, specializing in mysticism, healing and comparative religions. When the store went bust, they opened a metaphysical school they called the "Knowplace" in the house they shared. Gradually, they withdrew from friends and family, becoming absorbed in a private world of visions and dreams and cosmic portent.

On New Year's Day 1973, Applewhite and Nettles packed his rusty convertible and left Houston, bound for points unknown. God had a mission in mind for them—of that much they were sure. They were off to discover exactly what it was.

Over the next two years, the pair zigzagged more than 8,000 miles across the country. They slept in a tent, and when their money ran out, they sold blood, dug ditches, tested churches for charity. All the while, they talked and meditated and read and prayed, trying to divine their calling, asking God what they were supposed to do next. Finally, in a field of wild irises and rhododendrons, in a campground near the Rogue River on the Oregon coast, God answered.

Once upon a time, Bo now told his audience at the Bayshore Inn, a group of gods created a physical Kingdom of Heaven somewhere out among the stars. On instructions from the gods, the dwellers in the Kingdom planted humans as a gardening experiment on the planet Earth. From time to time, Representatives of the Kingdom made "soul deposits" into these human plants, preparing them for transplantation to the Evolutionary Level Above Human. When harvest time arrived—roughly every 2,000 years—a Representative would enter a human body, harvest the souls deposited in all the human plants and take them back to the Next Level.

Two millennia ago, the assigned Representative from the Next Level was Jesus. In this era, the assigned Representative was Applewhite, now known as Bo. With the help of Nettles, now known as Peep, he was here to harvest the garden once again. These particular souls had been deposited in 1947. The crew responsible for the seeding had crashed in the desert near Roswell, New Mexico. The U.S. government had stolen their bodies from the site.

Bo spoke for more than an hour. Peep remained silent, speaking only now and then to correct or clarify a point. Bo compared the members of the audience to caterpillars striving to become butterflies. To transform themselves into heavenly beings, to take advantage of their "deposits," they would have to come with him and enter a chrysalis state, separating themselves from the world and turning all their energy inward. The first step, he said, was to walk out the doors of their lives. To give away all their possessions, say all their good-byes. "Man must break from all ties that bind him to this earth: mother, father, brother, sister." They were the same words that Peep had written to her eldest daughter, Terrie, when she'd left Houston.

There was urgency in Bo's voice when he told the gathered that the harvest was drawing to a close. Within a few months, possibly weeks, he and Peep would fulfill the prophecy of the Book of Revelation, 11:3–13. The New Testament passage tells of two witnesses with the power to prophesy, whose message "tormented them that dwelt on the earth." Eventually, the two are killed by their enemies, and their bodies lie in the street for three and a half days, whereupon they rise from the dead, ascending to the Kingdom of Heaven in a cloud of light. That cloud, Bo and Peep believed, was a spaceship. With them would go their harvest of souls. As soon as they left, Armageddon would ensue. The garden on Earth would be spaded under to make way for the next planting.

Aaron stood in the back of the banquet room, blown away by what he was hearing. Like the others attending this meeting at the Bayshore Inn—like the others who would attend similar meetings all across the country—Aaron considered himself a seeker of the truth. Raised as a Jew, he had always had questions about the nature of God and man and the universe that were never sufficiently answered. As an adult, he'd studied every religion and philosophy that crossed his path. There were a lot of ideas out there, a lot of pages in a lot of books. But never any definitive answers. Aaron wanted answers.

Bo and Peep sounded pretty sure about what they were saying. Their rap might have been a little far-fetched, but what religion's wasn't? Reincarnation? Immaculate Conception? Were those concepts any less wild? What Bo was talking about sounded very familiar, as if he'd taken select cuts from all the great cosmologies of the world and mixed them into one outrageous song, a kind of greatest-hits medley of world religions. There were elements of Buddhism, Hinduism, Christianity and astrology. There was a distinct countercultural bent: the whole idea of freeing yourself from bonds and attachments—family, money, marriage, expectations. And as for the UFO part, well, Aaron had done a lot of acid in his day; his doors of perception were wide open. There were a lot of things that had no answers, a lot of things that people just didn't know. Like, who built the pyramids? What happened to the Mayans? What purpose did Stonehenge serve? Is God dead? What is the sound of one hand clapping? If a spaceship touched down in front of him and a great stairway were lowered, sure, what the fuck, Aaron would go for a ride. He could see himself skimming low over the waves off the coast of Waldport, a doobie between his lips, a beer in his hand, waving to the friends who hadn't been audacious enough to sign up.

Bo and Peep said they had answers. Who was to say they weren't right? The truth is, Aaron calculated, no one knows what the Truth is. Maybe Christ wasn't really the son of God; maybe he was just another Jew boy. Maybe Muhammad had no winged steed. Maybe the Pope is a fraud, making himself and his bishops rich while the masses are kept in ignorant darkness. Now here were Bo and Peep, talking a little bit of this, a little bit of that, talking about the Trip, the Process, the Evolutionary Level Above Human. They were promising a great ride on a spaceship; the departure was imminent. It connected the dots in the mysterious universe in a way he could understand. It was Jack Kerouac meets Buck Rogers meets Kriyananda meets Christ meets Tolkien meets the Grateful Dead. As Bilbo Baggins would say, "Adventures . . . make you late for dinner." Aaron knew he would be late for dinner.

As darkness settled over the arroyo, the class gathered on the observation deck for a special briefing. They drifted in two by two, the only sound the muted flap of their bedroom slippers as they took their regular, assigned chairs facing the big-screen TV, beneath which sat a list of approved programs—*60 Minutes, Star Trek, Jeopardy.*

It was sometime in the spring of 1990; the exact day, exact month, is hard to say. If you weren't charged with an out-of-craft task—bookkeeper, computer programmer, sound engineer, office manager—the dates on the Earth calendar were meaningless. Like monks in a monastery, the classmates lived by their own rhythms.

For the classmates who remained in-craft, there was a duty roster with push-pins and name tags. Many years ago, in the campgrounds, jobs were rotated every twelve minutes. You would be kneeling down, getting ready to start a fire to boil water to wash clothes, and a bell would ring, and you would drop everything and go to Central. There you would be directed to bring tea to Bo and Peep. Someone else would be sent to continue the wash. The exercise was meant to keep people attuned to their Older Member's mind; it was also symbolic of the interchangeable nature of the soul deposits, how all were equal in the eyes of the Next Level. By now, however, fifteen years into the Trip, assignments lasted weeks or months; some were even semipermanent. While soul deposits may have been interchangeable, the class came to discover, the vehicles clearly were not. Some couldn't drive a nail straight no matter how fully they opened their minds to the Older Member. Each such realization, each such adjustment in procedure, was greeted by Bo and Peep with bashful candor: *Oops! Guess that doesn't work. Let's try again.* The class was thus in a continual state of evolution, tinkering with its rituals and cosmology, trying to do whatever it was that would kick off graduation. Bo and Peep had admitted from the start that they'd never done this before, never harvested the garden for the Next Level. As they had said from the beginning, when they were calling themselves Guinea and Pig, they were part of a grand experiment. Over the years, the only constant was change.

Leading the in-craft labor force were the dispatchers, who coordinated use of the ragtag fleet of autos and vans. They also had custody of the file box containing all the driver's licenses. If you were leaving the craft for the day, you signed out your license, a wallet, several quarters for emergency phone calls and a $5 bill so that police couldn't accuse you of vagrancy. The ship's medical officers kept track of all medicines. The pursers took care of all claims and paperwork. They helped fill out job applications, computed taxes, set up corporations, kept detailed ledgers of all expenditures and income, even the odd penny found on a sidewalk. Given that most of the out-of-craft workers were skilled laborers, the class's income was often more than $40,000 a month. Added to the coffers were inheritances and trust funds turned over by members of the class.

Though everyone's needs were met, no one owned anything but a toothbrush. The clothes they wore—oversize men's shirts and slacks for both sexes—were kept in a communal wardrobe closet. At one point, the wardrobe contained one purple shirt, size large. After several displays of human emotion regarding its use, it was recommissioned as a dust rag. Dusting wasn't listed on the duty roster. If you had nothing to do at a particular moment, you either dusted or read the Procedure Manual, a phone-book-thick legal-size loose-leaf. As the manual said, "When in Doubt, Dust."

Detailed ledgers were also kept in the "fiber lab," noting every piece of clothing laundered, every sock darned, every button sewn. Recipes were kept in a loose-leaf in the "nutri-lab." As with all assignments, you cooked with a partner. Procedure prescribed dipping the tablespoon into the ingredient, leveling it with a knife, showing it to your partner, emptying it into the mixing bowl. On the Next Level, the fates of galaxies would be in your hands; you had to get things exactly right. Meals were known as "experiments." For a time, the classmates ate only live grasses, grown in trays built along a two-story wall of windows in their craft. For a time, they drank only juices. They'd go three months eating nothing but grapefruit, figs and raw almonds, then all of a sudden have sloppy joes. The idea was not to allow the vehicle to become habituated to anything earthly. An addiction to tofu was just as much against the Process as an addiction to sex or drugs or family ties.

Other classmates were tasked with repairs around the craft—carpentry, plumbing, electrical work—or maintaining the grounds. This last job was usually performed at night to avoid arousing the neighbors' suspicions. In Canyon Lake, Texas, a few years earlier, during a period when they were wearing black hoods to eliminate personal interaction, they all went to the backyard one evening for a game of croquet. The next day, the cops arrived. Though Bo dispatched the cops with ease, explaining that the classmates were grad students studying the effects of light on the diet, he preferred to avoid any dealings with authorities. Back in 1974, Bo had done six months in a county jail in Missouri for auto theft, the aftermath of a run-in with the husband of his and Peep's first recruit.

The craft they were currently occupying was large and luxurious, with dramatic picture windows, seven rest chambers, eight full bath chambers and a three-car garage, set on an isolated ten-acre lot outside Albuquerque, New Mexico. After that night in the summer of 1979—when they'd packed their overnight bags and sat expectantly on rocks until dawn, only to receive the message that their spaceship was indefinitely delayed—they'd given up life in campgrounds. They wintered in the Southwest, summered up north, renting or purchasing as need and funds and whim dictated: a ski chalet near Boulder Canyon, Colorado; a houseboat in Galveston, Texas; a horse ranch in Wyoming; an oceanfront in Newport Beach, California; a survivalist compound in New Mexico; a pair of suburban duplexes in Dallas. They rarely stayed in one craft for more than six months. They paid rent in advance, up to $7,000 a month. They rarely wore shoes inside. Landlords loved them.

The Representative, also known as the Older Member, once called Bo, now called Do, sat to one side of the television on the observation deck, his thin legs crossed, his hands resting primly one atop the other on his knee. Beside him was an empty chair, symbolic of the constant presence of his own beloved Older Member, once called Peep, later called Ti. Five years earlier, her vehicle having succumbed to liver cancer, she had returned to the Evolutionary Level Above Human.

Do sat patiently as the thirty-six classmates took their seats. At one time, before the harvest was closed in 1976 (following the massive publicity over Waldport), there were hundreds of classmates spread across the country, wandering from campground to campground, holding meetings, recruiting more people, trying to divine their missions. Many never met Bo and Peep. Many dropped out when it was announced that the Two would not be killed and rise to Heaven, as had been promised: The character assassination they'd received in the press, they said, was a symbolic death, good enough. Many others, like Aaron and his friend Rubin, dropped out because of exhaustion or boredom or hardship. It was a weeding-out process. Only the most committed would survive the chrysalis.

Do's vehicle was nearing 60 by now. He had an air of weariness about him, like a man on a bench at a lonely station, waiting for a train. He rarely ordered research anymore, as he had in the past, on topics ranging from wheatgrass high colonics to the use of telepathy by the ancient Egyptians. He never played Scrabble or Stratego or helped with the supersize jigsaw puzzles. No one could remember the last time he'd spontaneously broken the class into voice parts for a rousing choral round of "Row, Row, Row Your Boat." It had been years since the last talent show, when Do stood on his head and drank a glass of water, to the great amusement of all.

Since Ti's exit, Do had become increasingly solitary, less able to tolerate the slippages of the Younger Members' vehicles: the inability of Annody (Annie-ody, from Annie Oakley) to keep her face and hair clean; of Lggody (Log-ody, from Logan) to control his imperious temper; of Snnody (Soon-ody, from "sooner or later") to conquer her manic-depressive swings; of Brnody's (Brun-ody, from Brunhilda) to overcome her feelings that age and infirmity made her special; of Tllody (Tall-ody, from his six-foot-plus height) to remember to put salt in the oatmeal; of Dstody (Dest-ody, from Destined for the Next Level) to keep from peeping through bathroom windows at the female classmates; of Pmmody's (Pam-ody, from Pam) to conquer her need to be friendly and outgoing. Such weaknesses were a constant battle for all. Procedure dictated that you keep a log of slippages, share them with the class at the weekly Slippage Meeting. Sometimes, right before the meeting, you'd sit down and write up some stuff, the worse the better. Being hard on yourself was a sign of devotion. It reminded the former Catholics of confession.

Taking their cues from other religions, the class stressed ritual as a means of controlling their darker impulses. There was a proper way to brush your teeth, a twelve-minute time limit on your morning shower and toilet routine, which was outlined in a detailed three-page entry in the Procedure Manual. When you made your bed, the pattern on the top sheet had to face down. You were to sleep on your side or back. Your hands were to remain outside the blanket, above the waist, lest your vehicle take liberties with its genitals while asleep. You were to chew each mouthful twenty-four times.

While in the campgrounds, classmates were required to spend hours every day in quiet meditation, focusing on their Older Member's mind. Later, in one of the houses, they rigged up a room with a curtain, a stool and several grow lamps. You'd sit for hours inside a tube of gossamer fabric, under the eerie lights, trying to visualize your human ties, trying to sever them. You'd visualize your family tree, and you'd see yourself chopping off the roots, chopping off the branches, chopping off anybody from the past who came into your mind. At a certain point, you'd become dizzy and unfocused. You'd begin to see a great beam of purple light coming through the top of your head, your Older Member's mind reaching down for you.

There were procedures for lining up your shoes at the door, for hygiene during menstruation. There were long lists of offenses: taking action without consulting your partner; trusting your own judgment; finding fault with a classmate; comparing yourself with others; having private thoughts; having likes or dislikes; procrastinating; desiring attention or approval; being pushy; being vain; vibrating femininity or masculinity; having inappropriate curiosity; using the *I* or *me* pronoun; allowing your fingernails to get dirty; eating too fast; eating between experiments; using two teaspoons of sugar in your tea.

Now, on the observation deck, all in attendance could tell that something serious was troubling Do; he rarely called meetings anymore, either, allowing the members of an emerging hierarchy to carry out many of his tasks. The class had started out as a collection of equals. This new, multitiered system of Over-Seers, Do's Helpers and Younger Members dredged up ghosts for many: the eternal group dynamic, the in-crowd versus the nerds. The class-mates sat for a while, a while longer. Do cleared his throat. "Dncody has written a note," he said.

Sitting in his regular, assigned seat—third row, fourth from the right—Dncody wedged his thumbnail between his teeth, began grinding his jaw back and forth, a slippage he'd been written up for many times in the Eyes Log. His name was pronounced Dance-ody. For a long time, he was partnered with Sngody, pronounced Song-ody. His vehicle's birth name was Dick Joslyn.

A former air-force lieutenant, Dncody had been discharged from the service after he inadvertently left his journal—with its detailed accounts of his gay activities—at his desk in the nuclear-missile silo in which he worked. Dncody was one of the original thirty members of Bo and Peep's cosmic caravan, recruited at the first big meeting, in North Hollywood, California, in April 1975, five months before Waldport. Back then, living in Los Angeles, he was a waiter and an aspiring actor who'd just returned from a short Broadway run in a comedy called *Tubstrip*, set in a gay bathhouse. The week of the Waldport meeting, he'd gone into a market and found his face on dozens of boxes of Kellogg's Corn Flakes—a beaming all-American boy in a race-car driver's helmet. The Kellogg's job was a day-rate modeling gig he'd landed through Central Talent. Until he saw the boxes, he'd forgotten all about it—a sign to him that something the Two had said was pulling at him, something bigger even than his acting career.

Throughout his fifteen years in the class, Dncody had been close to Do and Ti, but particularly to Do, whose vehicle shared his interest in musical theater. After Ti's exit, Dncody was assigned as Do's partner, though it didn't last long. Dncody's human vehicle was extremely handsome; even the Representative had to battle slippage. Do and five others would eventually undergo surgical castration in an effort to quell their urges.

When he was relieved of his position, Dncody was heartbroken. And he was heartbroken for feeling heartbroken. There was an ornate Spanish-tile bathroom in the craft they were occupying at the time; after Do let him go, Dncody went in and cried his eyes out, his twisted face reflected in all the mirrors. Seething with self-hatred, he pounded his head with his fists, trying to drive out all the emotions. He thought about jumping through the window.

There had been times over the years when Dncody felt successful in taking his internal pain and truly loving it, feeling that there was a value to it, that it could be successfully converted into a closer attunement with his Older Member's mind. But then the dark times would descend. *This is it—I've had it*, he'd think, and he'd cry himself silently to sleep in his bunk bed in a room with three to seven others, feeling hopeless, stupid, loathsome and unworthy.

Always, however, just as things were getting to a point where he was ready to leave, something would happen. Like the night in the desert he'd asked for a sign and was rewarded with a meteor shower. Or the time he was at a truck stop in Nebraska and he looked around at all the people and it came to him that their lives were full of suffering, that there was nothing for him in their world—that the class was his world, come what may. Or the time the class went to see the movie *Field of Dreams.* Movies had always been important to the class. Do and Ti said the Next Level used movies to communicate. When the class saw *Star Wars,* they saw themselves as so many Luke Sky-walkers, trying to harness the force and become Jedi Knights. They were amazed at how much Yoda resembled Ti. When they saw *Close Encounters,* they knew for certain that they were looking at the spacecraft they'd been waiting for. After *Cocoon* they bought a houseboat. With *Field of Dreams,* another kind of message was fortified. Sometimes, the movie taught, people think you're crazy for believing so strongly in something. But, as the voice said, "If you build it, they will come." The class knew exactly how Kevin Costner felt. They just weren't sure what to build.

Now Do read Dncody's note to the class: "I am experiencing a longing to be back in the world. I am experiencing a desire to connect with other people. I have doubts about the Process. And I am sorry, but I even have a doubt about who you are, Do."

The classmates stared at their feet. Do folded the note carefully and put it in his pocket. "Now, class," he said, his voice that of a schoolmarm, "I have checked with Ti on this. She is very insulted. Very insulted. After all these years—"

In the third row of chairs, fourth from the right, Dncody began to sob. No one turned around. "I didn't mean to insult Ti," he croaked.

It felt like sacrilege, like treason, like failure, like plunging a long, sharp, serrated knife into his innards and ripping it back and forth. He didn't mean to insult Ti or Do or anyone in the class. But Dncody had simply had enough. He missed writing songs and singing them for an audience, col-lecting seashells and shellacking them for sale at flea markets. He missed his parents. He thought frequently of old friends and lovers. He missed writing his innermost thoughts in his journal. He missed being allowed to have innermost thoughts. He missed the delightful feeling of being self-absorbed, of being absorbed by someone else, of making lusty, invigorating, sweat-drenched love with a taut young guy.

Dncody was tired of doing the same mind-numbing things in the same complicated way. Every. Single. Day. He was getting older. There was slack-ness in the skin beneath his jaw. His life was draining away. He wanted to hug someone. He wanted to make idle chitchat. While he knew his thirty-five classmates well, had lived with many of them for fifteen years, he knew nothing of their pasts, nothing of their feelings. He didn't even know many of their names. They were the Odys. They were his classmates. They were soul deposits in chrysalis, waiting for a spaceship to take them to the Next Level, where they'd find fulfillment beyond their wildest dreams.

At last the pain had gotten the best of him. The class, the procedures, the whole idea of graduating to the Evolutionary Level Above Human—why did he believe in it anyway? *Maybe there isn't any Next Level! Maybe this whole thing is crazy. Maybe Do is crazy. Oh, I'm such an idiot. I'm a brainwashed member of a UFO cult.*

Or maybe not.

Maybe not.

There was always that chance. Maybe Jesus *was* the son of God. Maybe Muhammad *did* fly to Heaven on a winged steed. Maybe Do knew what he was talking about. If what he said was true, 2,000 years of Earth time equaled only forty-eight hours on the Next Level. They'd hardly waited ten minutes.

Dncody pulled out three squares of toilet tissue, regulation for blowing the nose. He rose from his chair, stretched his arms beseechingly toward Do. "Look," he said, his voice plaintive, "I'm just saying what my vehicle is experiencing. I'm not trying to insult Ti. I'm not!" He broke down again.

Do raised his hands toward Dncody, beckoning him forward. Do patted his thighs. Dncody sat in his lap.

Do put his arms around Dncody, rocked him a bit back and forth. "Some must stay! Some must go. You're doing what you're supposed to do. You must leave us. It is the will of the Next Level."

Rkkody blinked against the bright light, trying to focus. A face swam toward him. It appeared to be female. Bathed in deep shadow, the features were distorted—the eye sockets dark, the head overly large, the crown seeming to jut upward into an odd, triangular peak. Its lips were moving, but he couldn't make out words. Other faces swam into view. They surrounded him.

He tried to move his arms, but it felt as if they were tied. He became aware of a pain in his forearm, wires coming off his chest. He could feel foreign objects stuffed in his nose, his penis, his throat. Everything hurt. He struggled to sit up. An alarm went off, a piercing bleat. Hands forced him back down.

"Mr. Humphrey? Mr. Humphrey? Do you know where you are?"

"Dad? Wake up, Dad."

"Chuck? Come on, Chuck, You can do it. Wake up!"

Slowly, the fog started to lift. The faces, the words, the room, began to take shape. Then it hit him.

Shit! he thought. *Shit, shit, shit!*

Some twenty-four hours after he'd eaten the applesauce, Rkkody had woken up in Scripps Memorial Hospital in Encinitas. It was Wednesday, May 7, 1997. He and Jstody had overlooked one detail: the tracking numbers on the FedEx packages they'd sent from the hotel.

Of the four packages they'd sent, one was addressed to Jstody's daughter, Kelly Cooke. She received it at 10 a.m. in Manhattan and promptly called the New York City police. When they told her to wait forty-eight hours and file a missing-persons report, she called *60 Minutes* correspondent Lesley Stahl. Stahl had interviewed Kelly and Jstody—his real name was Wayne Marshall "Nick" Cooke—after the thirty-nine Heaven's Gate classmates had effected their exit six weeks earlier. Jstody's wife, Suzanne Cooke, Slvody, had been one of the classmates who exited. She and Jstody had joined the cult in 1975, leaving 10-year-old Kelly with her grandparents. Jstody had come and gone from the class several times, the last in 1994. In his interview with Stahl, he'd lamented, "I wish I'd had the strength to have remained . . . to have stuck it out and gotten stronger and continued to be part of the group."

Stahl called the San Diego police; they tracked the package, found the hotel. Police entered the room at 12:17 using a passkey. They found both men on the floor, their shrouds on the beds. Jstody was dead. Rkkody's plastic trash bag had been removed from his head. It lay on the carpet a few feet from him. It had a hole in it.

"How did I feel? I was pissed. I was pissed. Shit! You know! You take all this trouble to kill yourself, and then you wake up."

On an overcast day in May, Rkkody is sitting in an Art Deco hotel lobby in Santa Monica, across from the ocean. He is still a little shaky and slow, an effect of the phenobarbital that is still in his system. He has just been released from the hospital. He is staying around the corner with his daughter, whom he had seldom seen over the past fifteen years. Yesterday he spoke to his parents for the first time in thirty years.

"Something happened; I'm not sure what," he is saying, fiddling with the shoestring of his blue Nike sneaker. "The doctor said there was enough phenobarbital in my system to kill me, with or without the bag.

Yet I'm here. There is no denying that fact. I don't like being here. I tried my best to leave. There must be something they want me to do here.

"Right now a lot of people seem to be interested in the class and the Next Level. The Web site is receiving thousands of hits a day. But the thing is, the opportunity is gone. People can't just say, 'Gee, I want to go to the Next Level.' The exit letters I received made one thing clear: The window is closed. Do is gone. The class is gone. The graduation has happened. They're not looking to harvest anyone else.

"That's generically speaking, of course. Because there are classmates here on Earth who are still part of the crew. We've spoken among ourselves, and that message is also clear in the information we've been given. We came here as a crew. There's X number of people who were on our spacecraft forty years ago when they came and hovered over this planet. They were given an assignment to go down and incarnate into human vehicles. They were to take control of the vehicles, do a little task and then return. And if there are still a few of these crew members down here, they will eventually have to return and pick us up. The Next Level will leave no one behind.

"In a way, I kind of feel like that show *Sliders,* where you're always thinking the guy's not going to make it. That's what I feel like right now. I feel like the vortex is closed and I'm stuck on this planet. I know that's a crazy analogy, but I feel like a slider who didn't slide. I'm marooned here for now. This world is not real to me."

(1997)

The Teachings of Don Carlos

Some say he was a visionary shaman. Others say he was a sham. The mysterious life and impeccable death of Carlos Castaneda.

The Followers doused the headlights of their dusty blue Hyundai and coasted into their regular spot, a no-parking zone diagonally across the quiet intersection from the Sorcerer's low-slung compound. It was a cool Tuesday evening in early August, just past eleven. The sky was unusually clear for Los Angeles; the mystical heavens twinkled invitingly through the tinted windshield of the ten-year-old compact. Crickets sang, a dog barked, the engine ticked off heat. They sat silent for a few moments, enjoying the powdery fragrance of a night-blooming jasmine, girding themselves for another mission.

"You ready?" asked Greg Mamishian, scanning the compound for signs of activity. He was a short man, fifty years old, with close-cropped gray hair and an elfin sparkle in his eyes. A former Army helicopter mechanic with the spare, sinewy body of a vegetarian, he had lived his entire life—excepting his stint in Vietnam—within a ten-mile radius. Self-employed as an electrician, he worked, as a rule, only five hours a day, commute-time included. He lived modestly in a rustic, two-room cabin with a wood stove and no television in the pleasant wilds of Topanga Canyon, favoring quality of life over a big paycheck, self determination over the modern-day treadmill of achievement and acquisition. A talented tinkerer with a fondness for silly jokes, he was a rabid aficionado of slapstick comedies. "Mongo just pawn in chess game of life," he liked to say about himself, quoting his favorite line from *Blazing Saddles*.

"I don't know," said his wife, Gabi, sitting behind the wheel. She checked her watch, knitted her brow, a look of concern. "It's a little early. The Energy Trackers might still be inside."

Gabi was a tiny woman, five feet tall, thin and severe, with jet black, shoulder-length hair parted in the middle. Born in a small town in Bavaria to a school teacher and his wife, she had come early to the conclusion that life held something infinitely more magical than her mother's middle class dreams. Since her teens she'd been on a constant search, exploring philosophy and literature and religion and politics, trying on a world view, shucking it, trying on something else. In her early twenties she was a member of a radical group that contemplated a trip to Hanoi to stop the war. Later, she joined an underground team of Christians who smuggled suitcases full of Bibles into Eastern Bloc countries. After living for a while in Spain and throughout Europe, she immigrated to America to pursue primal scream therapy. Over the next five years, she says, she cried an ocean of tears.

For both, this was a second marriage. Though they'd been together six years, they'd only recently tied the knot. Truth be told, these missions had been the catalyst. Every couple needs a hobby, a binding interest; in an odd, wonderful way, the Sorcerer had become theirs. They were, they'd discovered, one hell of a team. Greg had dubbed them the Followers. The pun, of course, was intended.

Gabi supplied the vision, the ideas, the tenacity. She read the omens, established the energetic connection, tracked the phantom, stood vigil against inorganic predators seeking to appropriate their energy. It was she who'd first brought them into the Sorcerer's world. And, it was she who'd been most hurt when they were cast out so unceremoniously from his inner circle. Greg's role was more focused on the practical. He came up with materials and strategies, added support and enthusiasm and unrelenting good humor, a valuable quality on long, monotonous stakeouts fueled with green tea and McDonald's fries. Where Gabi seemed to be driven by deep personal feelings that she kept masked behind a cool, almost academic exterior, Greg was more emotionally detached, someone who'd come along for the ride and found himself hooked on the adventure, the giddy folly of it all. Maybe he'd never been quite as invested as Gabi; commitment was not really his strong suit—he was a get-along kind of guy who always kept one foot on either side of the line. Or maybe his vivid dreams had shown him something special, something of the Second Attention that she hadn't yet seen, couldn't even imagine. Since he'd begun practicing the ancient ways of the Sorcerer, he'd grown adept at shifting his assemblage point. He'd traveled to other worlds, flown without wings—he'd seen awesome, terrifying, beautiful, incredible things, things that changed his life. So what if the Sorcerer made fun of his sandals?

"What kind of impeccable warrior worries about time?" Greg asked in typical fatuous style, turning now to Gabi, a wicked smile on his face. He raised one finger in the air, Gene Wilder as Dr. Frankenstein, stating the elemental: "Time, my dear, is irrelevant to luminous spheres like ourselves."

"I . . . don't . . . know," Gabi said hesitantly, ignoring his attempt at levity, glancing nervously across the street. She pinched her thin lips with her thumb and first two fingers. Usually, her voice carried the hard residual edge of her German accent. Tonight it sounded soft and anxious. Something was bothering her. Something just didn't feel right. One of the things that irked her most about their estrangement from the Sorcerer was the fact that it had come at a time when she was beginning to make real progress. It had happened towards the end of an evening in the rented dance studio in Santa Monica where the group practiced their Magical Passes—martial art–like movements designed to gather energy. She was listening intently to one of the Sorcerer's three-hour monologues—highly entertaining affairs, Lenny Bruce meets Fidel Castro meets Mescalito, the cricket-like being with a warty green head that embodied the spirit of peyote—when a vortex appeared behind the Sorcerer's head, a kind of liquid swirl in the air, a whirlpool, just behind him to the left. Since then, it seemed, the magic and the revelations had grown stronger and stronger. Over the months of their surveillance, like Greg, she had continued to practice the passes—they had, in fact, just come from their regular practice group, one of the hundreds of independent cells that had formed across the globe. Lately, she'd begun to notice this voice inside of herself, a voice beyond the everyday chatter of the mind, a sort of anchor, a storehouse of knowledge. The Sorcerer called it the Emissary. It answered her questions, guided her choices, told her unwaveringly that this quest of theirs was supported by universal intent. It also told her, on this particular Tuesday night in the summer of 1997, to be careful. Something was different. Something was wrong. She could feel it.

"Let's go," said Greg impatiently, reaching for the door handle.

"Let's just wait a few more minutes, okay?"

The yellowish stucco compound occupied a large corner lot in the tidy neighborhood of Westwood Village, not far from the campus of UCLA. A rambling, L-shaped building with shallow peaks and a shingle roof, it had bars on the windows and a large, internal courtyard, all of it obscured from view by a 12-foot privet hedge that ran along the street sides of the property. From their parking place on the southwest corner of Pandora and Eastborne Avenues, the Followers could watch both gated entrances of the compound, each of which carried a separate address. The right side, on

Eastborne, seemed to be used only by male visitors. According to the Sorcerer's teachings, the right side symbolized experiential knowledge, everything we know—the Tonal. The left side symbolized the mysterious, the unknown—the Nagual. The Sorcerer was also known as the Nagual, the last of a line of shamans that stretched back thousands of years to the Toltecs, the pre-Hispanic Indians who inhabited the central and northern regions of Mexico prior to the Mayans. The left entrance, on Pandora, was used by the Sorcerer and his women: the three Witches, the Chacmols, the Blue Scout, the Electric Warrior, the other female members of the inner circle. The Followers called it Pandora's gate.

To the rest of the world, the Sorcerer was known as Carlos Castaneda. In 1968, at the height of the psychedelic age, he had published *The Teachings of Don Juan: A Yaqui Way of Knowledge*, the first of twelve books describing his apprenticeship in the deserts of Mexico to an Indian shaman, and his journeys to the "separate reality" of the sorcerers' worlds. Like Herman Hesse's *Steppenwolf* and Aldous Huxley's *The Doors of Perception, The Teachings of Don Juan* and its sequels became essential reading for legions of truth seekers over the next three decades. Castaneda himself became a cult figure—seldom seen, nearly mythological, a cross between Timothy Leary and L. Ron Hubbard: a short, dapper, nut-brown Buddha-with-an-attitude who likened his own appearance to a Mexican bellhop.

Though the Sorcerer had ten million books in print in seventeen languages, he had lived in wily anonymity for nearly 30 years, doing his best, in his own words, to become "as inaccessible as possible." Most people surmised that he had a house somewhere in the Sonoran desert, where he'd studied with his own teacher, a leathery old Indian *brujo* named Don Juan Matus, who'd taken his body and his boots and disembarked in a flash of light for the Second Attention many years ago, leaving Castaneda behind to close out his line "with a golden clasp." In truth, Castaneda had lived and written most of that time right here in Westwood Village, a neighborhood of students and professors not far from Beverly Hills. In truth, there were many things that people surmised about the Sorcerer that weren't remotely factual. The Followers, over the course of their investigations, had begun to figure it out. They were particularly proud of their videos. A major tenant of the Sorcerer's way was erasing personal history; he never allowed himself to be photographed or tape recorded. The last major legitimate interview he'd given was to *Time* in 1972; even *they* couldn't persuade him to pose for a full-face picture. The magazine ended up running an abstract drawing on the cover. The story described Castaneda as "an enigma wrapped in a mystery wrapped in a tortilla."

For more than eighteen months now, at least three times a week, Greg and Gabi had made these clandestine pilgrimages. They followed the Sorcerer and his party to restaurants and movies, to inner-circle practice groups. They video-taped him at every opportunity; they'd collected hours of raw footage, the only such cache of its kind.

The Followers weren't sure, exactly, what they were after, but they were certainly hot on the trail. On the one hand, what they were doing felt kind of tacky and intrusive, like they were peeping toms or paparazzi, or maybe more like they were children watching their parents have sex. On the other, it felt like a legitimate—albeit amateur—anthropological exercise. The Sorcerer himself had earned a Ph.D. in anthropology from UCLA; his third book, *Journey to Ixlan*, had served as his thesis. His own journey had begun as a undergraduate inquiry into ethnobotany, a study of the natural hallucinogenic plants of the southwest. In a way, the Followers considered their actions a sort of academic homage. And besides, they knew in their hearts that their motives were pure, that their energetic connection was strong and true. They meant no harm to the Sorcerer. Indeed, they liked him. They respected him. They just wanted to be close. The Sorcerer always talked about seeking non-ordinary reality. It was hard to explain, but this was theirs.

At last, Greg and Gabi exited the Hyundai. They clicked the doors quietly closed, crossed the street, stepping carefully, wearing dark clothes. As was their custom, they started at the Eastborne side of the property, began working their way nonchalantly along the perimeter, arm in arm, like a couple on their evening constitutional. They'd taken a few steps when suddenly, out of the hedge in front of them, there emerged a family of raccoons—two adults, two babies, in a single-file line. Raccoons were certainly not uncommon in the area, but the Followers had been to the neighborhood at all times of day and night and had never noticed any before. They watched raptly as the furry critters perambulated unhurriedly westbound along the sidewalk, a darling little Disney grouping. The last one in line was a bit plump. It struggled to keep up.

The Followers followed the raccoons around the corner, north on Pandora. Twice, the mother broke rank, circled around, coaxed the fat baby with her nose to hurry up, then went back to her place in line. When they reached the gate used by the Sorcerer, the Witches and the rest—Pandora's Gate—the raccoons turned abruptly right and filed through the hedge.

The father, the mother, the first baby disappeared. The last one, the fat one, stopped and turned around. He looked at Greg and Gabi for a long moment, a beckoning type of expression, dark eyes sparkling from within his dark mask, as if to say: "Follow me."

Greg took a step forward. The fat baby vanished through the hedge. Greg took another step forward, bent down to see where he'd gone. A large black moth flew out of the hedge. It hovered in the air for a second or two, right in front of his face, so close that he could feel the disturbance of the air, the flutter of tiny wings tickling the tip of his ample Armenian nose. A palpable sense of alarm overcame him, a strong suggestion to Keep Out. He stood up quickly, his eyes like saucers. "Whoa!" he exclaimed, a stage whisper. "Did you see that?"

Gabi just looked at him. She couldn't even speak.

For several long moments the Followers stood riveted to their places on the sidewalk. They felt a weird tingling up and down their spines. The hair on the back of Greg's neck stood on end. Crickets sang, a dog barked, the leaves on a nearby fig tree rustled in the breeze. And then . . . and then. . . .

Nothing.

Greg looked at Gabi. Gabi looked at Greg. He raised his hands, palms up, shrugged his shoulders. Then he nodded his head toward the Sorcerer's driveway, twenty feet away to the north. Gabi cut her eyes toward the driveway, then back to Greg. She knitted her brow, a look of concern, then took his arm. Slowly, they strolled toward the driveway, toward the large trash can at the curb. Greg reached over, opened the top of the can, peered inside.

Greg looked north, then south. Then, grinning triumphantly, like an archeologist unearthing a pre-Cambrian pot, he began removing bags, translucent white plastic numbers secured at the top with twist-ties. He handed three bags to Gabi, took the remaining four himself.

Neither Gabi nor Greg quite remembered which one of them first came up with the idea of taking the Sorcerer's trash. It just sort of happened spontaneously one night. By chance they'd come on a Tuesday; cans were at curbs all over the neighborhood for trash collection the next day. As the night dragged on, the Followers watched as a cast of marginal characters came one by one on foot into the neighborhood to dig for recyclables. If the homeless could rifle the Sorcerer's trash, they figured, why couldn't they?

And so it was that Tuesday nights became Trash Night. Every week, late in the evening, after practicing their Magical Passes with a group of like-minded (though less literal) followers at a rented dance studio in Santa

Monica, Greg and Gabi would drive the short distance to the Sorcerer's compound and liberate his trash. Once home in their cabin in Topanga Canyon, they'd light a fire in the wood stove, sit on the floor before it, and begin studying the contents of the bags, one item at a time, slowly putting together a puzzle picture of the life of the great and mysterious man. Whatever looked important or significant they kept. Of the leavings, whatever burned went up in smoke.

As you would guess, the Followers learned a great many things from the Sorcerer's trash. They learned that the septuagenarian Sorcerer, who was said to live in celibate solitude, co-habituated with at least five women—two of the three Witches (powerful practitioners and best-selling authors themselves, who claimed that they had also studied with Don Juan), a fiftyish caretaker, a young woman he'd adopted and a disabled old woman who was said to have been "energetically damaged" many years ago during her studies with Don Juan. The Sorcerer and the Witches, who were in their sixties, ate a lot of chicken and eggs—the mounds of bones and shells rankled the Followers' vegetarian sensibilities, stunk up their tiny cabin. They had a fondness for ceramic snakes and Mexican earthenware. Someone in the compound was clumsy: things were frequently broken and discarded; they didn't seem to care for making repairs. The women had a taste for fine clothes—Armani, Barneys, Neiman Marcus. They didn't believe in thrift stores. When they were finished with an item of apparel they would cut it to pieces and throw it away. Sometimes they were not so thorough—Gabi often wore a pair of DKNY leggings they had forgotten to cut up. Later she would find a leather jacket that belonged to one of the Witches. A corduroy jacket with leather elbow patches had belonged to the Sorcerer himself. It fit Greg perfectly; he wore it everywhere, even to practice group. It was his fondest possession.

The Sorcerer and the Witches, the Followers discovered, used wooden stick matches to clear the smells in their bathrooms. They loved word games, anagrams and crossword puzzles. They cut their own hair. There was mail addressed to dozens of different people—over time, the Followers figured out that each of the occupants of the compound had several different aliases. They subscribed to *The Nation* and to *The New Republic*. They loved German chocolates and Diet Pepsi, little airline bottles of vodka, Kotex Light Days pads. There were insulin syringes and acupuncture needles, Chinese paper lanterns, red-handled garden clippers, a prescription for phenobarbital, assorted baby blue boxes from

Tiffany's, literature on health foods and liver cancer, check stubs and bank statements and legal papers, copies of royalty checks, brochures for luxury yachts, ticket stubs from a trip to Hawaii, communications from fans and psychos, tapes full of answering machine messages, a list of home phone numbers for the entire inner circle. Someone in the compound was fond of Eco-tours and Julio Iglesias. The Sorcerer himself seemed overly fond of Las Vegas weddings. Found in the trash were certificates indicating that the Sorcerer had legally married two of the Witches, in ceremonies dated two days apart in September of 1993. A web-generated computer check confirms the marriages, along with several others between the Witches and male members of the inner circle, including the Sorcerer's literary agent, and the author Bruce Wagner, who gave a lengthy and obtuse interview for this story about his association with the Sorcerer but refused to divulge specific details.

Now, on this cool Tuesday night in August, loaded down with their latest gleanings, seven white plastic bags of trash, the Followers walked south on Pandora, heading for their car. As they passed the gate, Gabi noticed, in the far corner of her peripheral vision, a white-clad form leaving the house. She stepped up her pace, but it was too late.

"Hey!"

The Followers froze, turned around. Out of the gate came one of the Chacmols, a thirtyish woman with close cropped hair. The Followers had come to know her during their time with the inner circle. The Chacmols were named for the massive statues of the "fierce dreamer guardians" that stood watch at the Mayan pyramids of Tula and Yucatan in Mexico. On a daily basis, the Sorcerer's Chacmols were bodyguards and helpers. At practice sessions and at paid seminars, they demonstrated the Magical Passes, aerobic movements with names like The Saber Tooth Tiger Breath, The Being From the Ground, and The Crustacean Long Form.

The Chocmol looked at Greg and Gabi with flames in her eyes. "What do you think you're doing?' she thundered.

"It's only *trash*," said Gabi. Oddly, she didn't feel nervous at all. In fact, she felt preternaturally calm, as if someone had disconnected the wires to her fight/flight response. Even her perspective had shifted. It was like she wasn't present at all, like she was watching the whole scene in third person.

The fierce Chacmol ripped the trash bags from Gabi's hands, gestured for Greg to put his down. "You'll never get close to us again," she hissed, gathering up the bags.

That's what you think, thought Greg. He, too, felt inordinately calm. He crooked his arm and Gabi took it, and they turned nonchalantly in the direction of their car.

Walking away, Greg called cheerily over his shoulder, "Tell Carlos we said hello."

There was a knock at the door, and Margaret Runyan smiled quizzically at her gentleman caller, a handsome Jordanian businessman she'd been seeing almost daily for the past two weeks. "Now who could *that* be at this hour?" she sang coquettishly, setting down her cup and saucer, patting his knee, rising from the chintz-covered sofa. Though she'd lived in Los Angeles for nearly fifteen years, her voice still carried the demure, lilting cadence of Charleston, West Virginia. She'd grown up on a dairy farm, the eldest of six children, her daddy's favorite, a sickly little bookworm with jet black hair, Coke-bottle glasses and startling, gold-flecked blue eyes.

It was January 1960, Margaret had just returned from dinner with her wealthy suitor at a fancy Middle Eastern restaurant. They'd sat on the floor on pillows, eating with their fingers, watching the belly dancers, drinking copious amounts of red wine. She was resplendent, as always, on this mid-January evening in 1960, dressed in a clingy black knit cocktail dress with a scoop neckline by the popular designer Clair McCardle. A cousin of the writer Damon Runyon, Margaret was 39 years old, with porcelain skin and Cleopatra bangs, a short strand of pearls around her neck. Though she considered herself unattractive—owing mostly, one would guess, to the thick-framed glasses she wore—Margaret was tall and lithe with an ample bosom. Men were all the time telling her, in the parlance of the day, that she was "really put together." She lived rent-free in an apartment building owned by her aunt, a dress designer. Margaret herself had been bitten at an early age by the fashion bug: she spent much of her paycheck on clothes, many of which were handmade by a South American seamstress. Years earlier, she'd come close to marrying pulp-novelist Louis L'Amour. He penned beautiful love poems to her but lacked an automobile; they went everywhere by bus— she wrote him off prematurely as a failure. As it was, Margaret had been engaged several times to rather eccentric men, and had been married twice, first to a poet and then to a mafia-connected real estate tycoon. Both men insisted she quit her job as chief operator at Pacific Bell and become a full-time housewife. Neither union lasted more than six months.

An odd combination of career gal and man's woman, Margaret was an early prototype of a postmodern Feminist, who believed in paying her own way and making her own decisions, living a life unbeholden to anyone. The great failure of her life, she would later come to figure, was thinking she had to marry a man in order to sleep with him. She was also an early prototype of another postmodern character, the New Age Seeker. Margaret had a keen interest in what were known at the time as the pseudo-sciences—numerology, astrology, parapsychology—and was well-read in philosophy and religion and literature. Herman Hesse and Aldous Huxley were among her favorite writers. Her favorite historical figure was The Buddha. She was also an avid student of a popular mystic from Barbados named Neville Goddard. A spellbinding lecturer with legions of followers, Neville believed that a person could alter the future and achieve personal goals though the manipulation of their dreams, something he called "controlled imagination." Goddard's self-avowed personal goal—promoted through paid seminars, a weekly television show and a popular self-published book called *The Search*—was to shake his disciples out of the dangerous ruts of their ordinary, real world perceptions: to help them, in his words, "To Go Beyond." Goddard believed in erasing personal history, awakening the untapped portions of the imagination, cutting ties with friends and loved ones. He preached something he called the *I AM*, an invocation of the God-like within all of us. Goddard was also said to be imbued with special powers. Sometimes, when he lectured, his face appeared to glow. On several occasions, he was spotted simultaneously in two different places; he claimed to have the ability to generate an "energetic double."

Margaret clicked across the hardwood floor in her sexy black pumps, peered through the peep hole in the door of her fifth floor apartment. Standing in the hallway in the dark olive suit she'd bought him was the short, nut brown, South American anthropology student she'd been dating for the last five years. He called himself Carlos Arana; he was enrolled at UCLA as Carlos Castaneda. They'd had a falling out just before Christmas. She hadn't seen him since. From the appearance of the cozy scene inside her apartment, she hadn't been crushed by his absence. She opened the door about eight inches, stuck out her face. Her blue eyes, framed by her bangs, magnified by her glasses, appeared enormous. "Carlos!" she exclaimed, somewhat abashedly. "You didn't tell me you were coming."

"I'd like to meet your friend," Carlos said calmly in his accented English. He was a slim man, five foot five, with the broad nose, high cheekbones, ample chest and short legs of a high-country Indian. A curly lock of brillianteened black hair hung down roguishly over his forehead. His eyes were large and brown; the left iris floated out a bit, giving the impression that one eye was always looking at something beyond. Though not handsome in a classical sense, Margaret found Carlos to be wildly charming, incredibly magnetic. He called her Margarita or Mayaya; it sounded so exotic when he whispered into her ear. Sometimes, he would listen intently while she spoke, riveting her with his deep eyes, drinking in her soul. At other times, it was if he was alone on a stage, in a spotlight only he could see, riffing brilliantly, passionately, manically for hours at a time, speaking of his life, his art, his dreams and fears and desires. Though he was shy around people he didn't know, he came alive in more intimate settings. He had a gift for story telling and an earthy sense of humor, and he was so present, so absolutely directed, that social intercourse with him was a palpable, exhausting experience—like being drenched by successive sets of huge waves of pure energy, energy directed only at her.

Somehow, over the five years of their association, in his very odd, very intense way, Carlos had made Margaret feel like she was the only woman on earth, the only person in the whole world who mattered, who could possibly understand—except for those frequent periods when he would disappear, often for weeks a time. It was the tradeoff of being with Carlos, she had come to learn. In certain respects, it made her feel terrible. Margaret really and truly loved Carlos, more than anyone before. He didn't have to give her anything or do anything for her, she was just happy to be with him. When he was gone, she felt as if something very important was missing. In other respects, however, his erratic attentions suited her just fine. She'd always had a problem with commitment. If he could be independent, then so could she.

"I don't want you to come in," said Margaret, speaking through the partially opened door. "Please go away. We'll talk later."

"No," Carlos said. "I just want to come in and say hello, speak with him a few minutes."

As usual, Margaret's will was no match for Carlos's. Since the first time she'd laid eyes on him—a brief, chance meeting at her dressmakers' house—she'd been deeply smitten. The second time she saw him—she'd called the dressmaker and insisted on another fitting, hoping the dark stranger would be there again—they'd spoken for a bit. He told her he was a painter, a writer, a sculptor. He said he'd love the opportunity to show her his paintings, to do a bust of her in terra cotta, his speciality. At an opportune moment, when the dressmaker's pretty daughter was out of the room, Margaret slipped him a copy of Goddard's book, *The Search*, inscribed with her name and address, which she'd just happened to bring along to the fitting.

From that night on, Margaret practiced Goddard's techniques of "controlled imagination," hoping to summon Carlos to her side. Every evening, before she fell asleep, she'd lie in bed and concentrate on her personal goal. Goddard taught that the sleeping state sealed instructions given to the unconscious mind, that dreams could become reality if properly nurtured. Six months later, at nine p.m. one Friday evening in June 1956, her goal was finally realized. The doorbell rang and Carlos walked into her life, picking right up where they'd left off, acting as if they'd met only yesterday. Their involvement would span the next decade and a half.

Ten years younger than Margaret, Carlos was a sophomore at Los Angeles Community College, majoring in psychology. He told her he'd been born in Italy on Christmas Day, 1931, the product of an illicit union between a 16-year-old student at a Swiss finishing school and a visiting Brazilian professor. Shortly after his birth, he said, he was taken by his maternal aunt back to Sao Paulo to be raised. At 15, after being expelled from a prestigious private school, he'd begun traveling the world, studying art in Italy, Montreal and New York before coming to Los Angeles to continue his education. He also said he was a veteran of U.S. Army Intelligence. He was vague about his service, mentioning both Korea and Spain; a long ugly scar that stretched from his abdomen to his groin was the result of a bayonet wound, he said.

Carlos and Mayaya seemed a perfect match—two passionate, keen, eccentric minds who'd been lucky enough to cross paths. Though Carlos had very little money—to support his studies, he worked variously as a cab driver, a grocery stock clerk, a liquor delivery man, an artist for Mattel toys, an accountant in a tony dress shop—Margaret was comfortable and generous. They attended concerts and plays, lectures and readings and art openings. They frequented the beatnik coffee houses that had begun to spring up along Hollywood Boulevard, rubbing shoulders with Alan Ginsberg and Jack Kerouac. Gradually, Carlos's interest in painting and sculpture began to fade; he took to carrying a three ring binder with him everywhere, filling it with romantic poetry and prose. One of his poems won a contest and was printed in the LACC student newspaper.

Carlos had a particular fondness for movies: Ingmar Bergman classics, B-grade horror pictures, Russian films. He was fascinated by all things Russian, particularly Soviet Premier Nikita Khrushchev, who had recently taken power in Moscow. In Carlos's eyes, Khrushchev was a determined leader who had come up from the bottom rung of society to grab the reins of one of the most powerful countries in the world. Over time, Carlos developed a fantasy that Margaret would one day meet the great man. To this end, he encouraged her to take her college entrance exams, then helped her enroll in a night-school Russian language course, which she continued for several years.

A dapper man who favored fedoras and pastel Don Loper shirts, nicely pressed slacks and highly polished shoes, Carlos cut his own hair, tailored his own clothes. He'd add months of wear to a shirt by removing a frayed collar, turning it inside out and then sewing it back on, a skill he learned either in the Army or while living with a band of gypsies in Italy—that story, like many, frequently changed. He was partial to Mexican food, Chinese Dim Sum and pizza, long walks on the beach, nightclubs, fine department stores. In a university community populated overwhelmingly with Caucasians, he seemed insecure about his height, his thick accent, his dark skin. On occasion, for reasons Margaret could never fathom, he told people he was a Hasidic Jew. Another thing she could never fathom is why they never had intercourse together. Though Carlos avidly enjoyed giving her pleasure orally, it went no further than that.

Having been exposed by Margaret to her favorite writers—Huxley, Hesse, Goddard and the behaviorist J. R. Rhine—Carlos became an avid participant in bull-sessions with their like-minded friends, holding forth on subjects ranging from astral projection to trance running to ESP. The cozy, spirited gatherings, usually held at the apartment of a friend, would run into the wee hours, fueled by Carlos's favorite wine, Mateus Rose, which he jokingly referred to as "my most valuable teacher." His favorite subject, by far, was Huxley's experiments with mescaline and alternate realities; he chose the topic for a term paper for his second year English class at LACC.

After he received his associate's degree, Carlos enrolled in the anthropology department at UCLA, a change of direction influenced by the publication of a book called *The Sacred Mushroom*, by Andrija Puharich. The book dealt with Puharich's work with a Dutch sculptor who could recall vivid details of his past life in ancient Egypt. Placed under deep hypnosis, the sculptor became Ra Ho Tep, a IVth Dynasty shaman who spoke a lost Egyptian dialect. Puharich's work with Ra Ho Tep revealed that the ancient shamanistic phenomenon of leaving the body was linked to the use of the sacred mushroom, *Aminita Muscaria*. As part of his study, Puharich interviewed anthropologist Gordon Wasson, an expert on drug use among primitive mystics. Wasson told of an ancient mushroom cult that still existed in remote regions of the Mexican desert, in which *curanderos*, or sorcerers, ate psilocybin mushrooms in healing and divination ceremonies. Of particular interest to Carlos was the fact that Puharich had also involved Aldous Huxley in his experiments. With Huxley in attendance, Ra Ho Tep had requested and was given some sacred mushrooms, and then proceeded through the motions of an ancient ritual. Puharich's book also included conversations with anthropologist J. S. Slotkin, who specialized in the study of the Native American Church, which used peyote to reach dream states of non-ordinary reality.

These notions of non-ordinary reality appealed to Carlos. He identified strongly with the Dutch sculptor who brought forth Ra Ho Tep from his subconscious, a man named Harry Stone. Like Stone, Carlos was a foreigner in America, shy and insecure, who'd been trying to no avail for almost a decade to establish himself as an artist. The idea of never reaching his potential frightened Carlos. He often complained to Margaret about the routine sameness of his very ordinary life, how he got up every morning, went to class, went to work, came home, started over again the next day. It was not the kind of future he'd envisioned, a lifetime toting his lunch to work in a brown paper bag. There had to be something more.

And so it was that Carlos found himself in an undergraduate anthropology class called California Ethnography. Needing a topic for a term paper, he decided to continue the work of Puharich and Huxley, Wasson and Slotkin, and conduct a ethno-botanical study of the natural hallucinogenic plants of the American southwest. The professor's assignment carried an interesting caveat: anyone who actually went out into the field and found a live Indian informant would automatically receive an A.

Now, on this January evening in 1960, Carlos walked past Margaret, into the living room of her apartment, and came face to face with her gentleman caller, a wealthy Jordanian businessman she'd been seeing daily for the past two weeks, during which time Carlos had been roaming the California desert, looking for an Indian informant, hoping to secure an A, an early leg up on his new career choice—professor of anthropology.

The two men chatted amiably for a few minutes, and then the subject turned to Margaret, who had resumed her place on the over-stuffed chintz sofa, next to the Jordanian. His name was Farid Aweimrine. He was the brother of another man Margaret had dated in the past; they'd met at a Christmas party. Carlos continued to stand.

"You know," said Aweimrine, "I would have married Margaret the first night I met her if my divorce had been final."

"Over my dead body!" said Carlos.

"Well why haven't you married her?" asked Farid.

Carlos looked puzzled for a moment. He crossed his arms, scratched his chin. "You know," he said wistfully, "I never thought of that." He turned to Margaret, broke a big grin. "Come on, Mayaya! We're getting married tonight!"

On a winter afternoon in 1973, Carlos and Gloria sat cross-legged on the beach near Malibu, a blanket wrapped cozily around their shoulders. The sun was low on the horizon, a blood-orange ball; wispy clouds glowed pink and magenta against the perfect cerulean sky. Seagulls swooped overhead, calling and complaining; sandpipers skittled on stick legs across the sand; surfers in wet suits worked a left-hand break a quarter mile offshore. Carlos took Gloria's hand tenderly in both of his, gazed into her startling, gold-flecked blue eyes.

"You have always been like a bird, like a little bird in a cage," he said, projecting his voice above the rush and pound of the waves. "You are wanting to fly, you're ready, the door is open—but you're just sitting there. I want to take you with me. I'll help you soar. Nothing could stop you if you come with me."

Gloria Garvin was transfixed. Though she was an attractive young woman who'd heard her share of come-on lines during her hippie wanderings of the late sixties, no one had ever spoken to her quite like this. What Carlos was saying was kind of corny, really, the sort of drivel usually reserved for the well-thumbed pages of her mother's romance novels, but somehow it didn't come across to her that way at all—somehow it was new and magical and deeply fetching. She was 26 years old, petite but amply breasted, with porcelain skin and Cleopatra bangs. She had first heard of Carlos Castaneda on a cold day in early 1969, at a long table in the dining room of an old Victorian townhouse in Haight-Ashbury. She and her boyfriend had thumbed up to San Francisco from L.A. to see the Grateful Dead at the Fillmore West. When they returned from the marathon concert, someone made a big pumpkin pie laced with hashish, and they all ate their fill—reveling in the synchronous pleasure of getting high and satisfying their munchies simultaneously. They lay around on pillows on the floor for the rest of the night, dressed in their velvets and buckskins and beads, mesmerized by the glowing light from a paper Japanese lantern that seemed to be receiving them into the universe.

The next afternoon, still pretty wasted, they were sitting around the dining room table, drinking coffee and smoking joints, when someone began reading aloud from a review of *The Teachings of Don Juan*. It was a powerful book, simply written yet deeply affecting, a groovy trip into the heady netherworld of psychedelic drugs and alternative realities—Kerouac does psychotropics. Billed as non-fiction anthropology, issued first by UCLA's University Press, and shortly thereafter by Simon and Schuster, it read more like a novel, an odd combination of Hemingway's bland staccato and Garcia-Marquez's magical realism. Regardless of its genre—about which there would eventually be much debate—the book was perfectly suited to its times, an era of sex and drugs and flower power, of back-to-the-land inno-cence and marvelous cosmic yearnings. Offered in the form of journal entries, the story is set in a hard scrabble desert landscape of organ pipe cacti and glittering lava massifs. It documents the weird, taxing and sometimes antic apprenticeship of a skeptical, slightly annoying young academic to a wily old Yaqui Indian sorcerer named Don Juan Matus, whom Carlos said he met through a friend in the waiting room of a Greyhound bus station, on the Arizona side of the Mexican border, approximately six months after his marriage to Margaret Runyon.

Peopled with indigenous Indians, anthropomorphic incarnations, spirits both playful and malevolent, the book evokes mysterious winds and terri-fying sounds, the shiver of leaves at twilight, the loftiness of a crow in flight, the raw fragrance of tequila and the vile, fibrous taste of peyote. Carlos writes of his meetings with Mescalito, who comes to him disguised succes-sively as a playful black dog, a column of singing light and a cricket-like being with a warty green head. He hears awesome and unexplained rum-blings from dead lava hills; converses with a bilingual coyote; sews shut the eyes of a lizard with a needle and thread harvested from a cactus; meets the guardian of the Second Attention, a hundred-foot gnat with spiky tufted hair and drooling jaws. In dry, detached, scholarly language, he details the preparation and ingestion of *humito*, the little smoke, made from the dust of psilocybin mushrooms, and of *yerba del diablo*, the devil's weed, datura, which causes his head to sprout wings and beak and feet, transform into a crow, and fly off into the heavens. At every development, Carlos remains the skeptical rationalist, a modern Everyman, trying in vain to translate his mystical expe-riences into the kind of concrete understanding which drives the Western mind. As such, his only tools are his questions—his persistent, often fum-bling effort to keep up a Socratic dialogue with Don Juan:

"Did I take off like a bird?" he asks the old sorcerer, upon awakening from an experience with the devil's weed, one of twenty-two drug trips in the first two books.

"You always ask me questions I cannot answer," the old man tells him. "What you want to know makes no sense. Birds fly like birds and a man who has taken the devil's weed flies as such."

Beneath the spectral fireworks and psychedelic drama in *The Teachings* (and in the subsequent eleven volumes that would follow over the course of the next 30 years) is Carlos's quest to become a Warrior, a Man of Knowledge wholly at one with his environment. Agile and strong, unencumbered by sentiment or personal history, the Warrior knows that each act may be his last. He is alone. Death is the root of his life, and in its constant presence the Warrior always performs "impeccably." He is attuned to the desert, to its sounds and shadows, its animals and birds, its power spots and holes of refuge. The Warrior's aim in becoming a Man of Knowledge, the young academic learns through his apprenticeship, is "to stop the world" and "see"— to experience life directly, grasping its essence without interpreting it, coming eventually to the realization that the universe, as perceived by everyday humans, is just a construct based on shared customs and languages and understandings.

In truth, Don Juan tells his bumbling and often frightened student, men and women are not flesh at all. They are made up of fine fibers of light, glowing white cobwebs that stretch from the head to the navel, forming an egg of circulating threads, with arms and legs of luminous bristles bursting in all directions. Through a series of long fibers that shoot out from the center of the abdomen, every man and woman is joined with every other man and woman, and with his surroundings, and with the universe. Don Juan lectures Carlos: "a man is a luminous egg whether he's a beggar or a king and there's no way to change anything." Of particular import in this cosmic anatomy is the Assemblage Point, a place of intense luminosity, located about an arm's length behind the shoulder blades, where perception takes place. By shifting or displacing the assemblage point during dream states, the old Nagual taught, a practitioner could gain entrance into other worlds, something called "The Art of Dreaming."

When Gloria returned to L.A., flush with the new possibilities of Don Juan's worlds, she mentioned the far-out book to her aunt, who was working in the graduate research library at UCLA. The married author, it turned out, haunted the grad library, particularly the rare book room. He was also dating a library worker the aunt knew well. In short order, a meeting was arranged.

Gloria and her boyfriend spent the whole afternoon with the great man in the student union at UCLA. Sitting at a Formica table, amid the hectic bustle of the student body, they spoke about life and death, drugs and sex, meaning and shamanism. At the end of their time together, Carlos took Gloria's hand for the first time. "This was a most auspicious meeting," he said. Then he nodded his head in the direction of her boyfriend. "Too bad you brought that nincompoop along with you."

Over the next few years, Gloria and Carlos stayed in touch by letter and by phone. At his urging, she enrolled in UCLA as an undergraduate anthropology student. Later, also at his urging, she broke off her long-standing engagement to her boyfriend. Carlos, meanwhile, published his second book, *A Separate Reality: Further Conversations with Don Juan,* and then his third, *Journey to Ixlan: The Lessons of Don Juan,* which served simultaneously as his doctoral thesis.

In a departure from the first two volumes, Carlos revealed in *Ixlan* that the drug part of the program was now over. After ten years of study with the old Indian, he wrote in the Introduction to *Ixlan,* "It became evident to me that my original assumption about the role of psychotropic plants was erroneous. They were not the essential feature of the sorcerer's description of the world, but were only an aid to cement, so to speak, parts of the description which I had been incapable of perceiving otherwise. My insistence on holding on to my standard version of reality rendered me almost deaf and blind to Don Juan's aims. Therefore, it was simply my lack of sensitivity which has fostered their use." Now that his eyes had been properly opened, he wrote, it was necessary to focus on what the old sorcerer had called the "techniques for stopping the world." Only then could he become an impeccable Warrior.

"One needs the mood of a warrior for every single act," Don Juan tells him in typical fashion, harsh and judgmental but also loving. "Otherwise one becomes distorted and ugly. There is no power in a life that lacks this mood. Look at yourself. Everything offends and upsets you. You whine and complain and feel that everyone is making you dance to their tune. . . . A warrior, on the other hand, is a hunter. He calculates everything. That's control. But once his calculations are over, he acts. He lets go. That's abandon. A warrior is not a leaf at the mercy of the wind. No one can push him; no one can make him do things against himself or against his better judgement. A warrior is trained to survive, and he survives in the best of all possible fashions."

As it was, by the time his third book was published, Carlos's notion of survival had taken on quite a different hue. By 1973, he had become nothing short of a cult figure; would-be disciples and counter-culture tourists were flocking to Mexico, combing the deserts for mushrooms and Don Juan. *The Teachings* was selling an astounding 16,000 copies a week. *Ixlan* was a hardback best-seller. Sales of the paperback made Carlos a millionaire. He traded in his old VW bus for a new Audi, bought the compound on Pandora in Westwood Village. Before long, *Time* came calling.

In what would be his first and last major interview, Carlos told *Time* that he was born to a well-known family in Sao Paulo, Brazil, on Christmas Day, 1935. At the time of his birth, he said, his father, who would later become a professor of literature, was 17. His mother was 15. He was raised by his maternal grandparents on a chicken farm until he was six, at which point his parents took custody. The happy reunion was cut short, however, when his mother died. The doctor's diagnosis, Carlos told *Time*, was pneumonia, but he believed the cause had been acedia, a condition of numbed inertia. "She was morose, very beautiful and dissatisfied; an ornament," he told *Time*. "My despair was that I wanted to make her something else, but how could she listen to me? I was only six."

Carlos was left to be raised by his father, a shadowy figure whom he mentions in the books with a mixture of fondness, pity and contempt. His father's weakness of will, he told *Time*, was the obverse to the "impeccability" of Don Juan. In the books, Carlos describes his father's efforts to become a writer as a farce of indecision. He told *Time*: "I am my father. Before I met Don Juan I would spend years sharpening my pencils and then getting a headache every time I sat down to write. Don Juan taught me that that's stupid. If you want to do something, do it impeccably, and that's all that matters."

Carlos was educated, he told *Time*, at a "very proper" boarding school in Buenos Aires, where he acquired the Spanish (he already spoke Italian and Portuguese) in which he would later interview Don Juan. At 15, he said, he became so unmanageable that an uncle, the family patriarch—Carlos told people he was Oswaldo Aranha, a legendary gaucho and revolutionary who would later become president of Brazil—had him placed with a foster family in Los Angeles. The year was 1951. He enrolled in Hollywood High School. Graduating two years later, he went overseas to study sculpture at the Academy of Fine Arts in Milan, only to discover that "I did not have the sensitivity or the openness to be a great artist." Dispirited, he returned to Los Angeles and enrolled at UCLA. "I really threw my life out the window. I said to myself: if it's going to work, it must be new," he told *Time* of his resolve to take up anthropology. In 1959, he told the magazine, he changed his name to Castaneda.

"Thus Castaneda's own biography," concluded *Time*, "creates an elegant consistency—the spirited young man moving from his academic background in an exhausted, provincial European culture toward revitalization by the shaman; the gesture of abandoning the past to disentangle himself from crippling memories. Unfortunately, it is largely untrue."

In short order, the reporter for *Time* came up with a radically different account of Carlos's early life, a story later confirmed and appended by Castaneda scholar Richard DeMille, the adopted son of movie mogul Cecil B. DeMille, who has made a life's work of studying Carlos.

According to U.S. immigration records, Carlos César Salvador Arana Castaneda entered the U.S. at San Francisco in 1951, at the age of 26. He became a naturalized U.S. citizen in 1959. He was born in Peru, in the ancient Inca town of Cajamarca, where witches and *curanderos* were not at all uncommon in the town marketplace. Carlos was the son of a watchmaker and goldsmith named César Arana Burungary, who owned a jewelry shop in the downtown section of the city and was himself was the son of an Italian immigrant. Once a promising student, his father was known during his youth as a Bohemian who squandered his academic opportunities after falling in with a fast crowd of artists and bullfighters in the capital city of Lima. Settling down at last to family life as an artisan and shopkeeper, he was a tireless chess player, a constant reader of Kant and Spinoza. His mother was a slender, almond-eyed girl of 16 named Susana Castaneda Novoa. She died when Carlos was 24. He refused to attend the funeral, according to a cousin, and locked himself in his room for three days without eating. When he emerged from his mourning, he declared his intention to go to America.

In his youth, Carlos was an altar boy, attended the local public school. He often went with his father to the jewelry shop; over time he became skilled in working with copper and gold, but he hated selling the things he made. After dropping out of school in Cajamarca, Carlos moved to Lima, where he finished high school and then enrolled in Bellas Artes, Peru's national academy of fine arts. A former roommate remembers Carlos as "a big liar and a real friend," a witty fellow who loved carousing but never drank or smoked, who made a living playing cards, horses and dice while harboring "like an obsession" to go the United States and become rich from gambling.

A former classmate recalled Carlos as "a very capable fellow, likable and rather mysterious. A first class seducer. I remember the girls used to spend the morning waiting around for him at the Bellas Artes. We called him The Smile of Gold because he had, I think, a gold tooth. Sometimes he would go to the market with some used watches which he could only make run for two or three hours. He would sell the watches and then disappear. . . . He was always thinking up unlikely stories—tremendous, beautiful things. At times he sold blankets and ponchos from the mountains."

Confronted by the reporter from *Time*, Carlos was characteristically unfazed: "To ask me to verify my life by giving you my statistics is like using science to validate sorcery," he said. "It robs the world of its magic."

More alarming, perhaps, than the murkiness of Carlos's history, was the debate that raged over the academic veracity of his work. Billed as ethnography, it read like a novel and sold like a best-seller—the envy, no doubt, of many a scholar who had worked in the trenches of anthropology for a lifetime. Though the panel of professors at UCLA who awarded his doctorate continued to stand firmly behind him—in an introduction to *The Teachings*, one of them lauds Carlos for "his patience, his courage, and his perspicacity"—social scientists were skeptical, labeling the work a fictionalized composite in the guise of anthropology, a dramatic rehash that borrowed heavily from the work of others at the expense of accuracy and truth, not to mention credit.

In his two volumes on Carlos, DeMille collected ample evidence of what he considered a fraud. Citing myriad examples large and small, he made a case that Carlos's books were nothing more than cleverly conceived and masterfully executed works of fiction. Among hundreds of well-researched nits, DeMille pointed to the facts that, over his years of apprenticeship to the old Indian, Carlos never learned the Indian names for any of the plants or animals he comes into contact with, and neither did Carlos ever submit a specimen of Don Juan's mushrooms for chemical testing. DeMille quoted experts—Wasson among them—who said that hallucinogenic mushrooms do not, in fact, grow in the Sonoran desert, and that the practice of smoking mushroom powder was unknown prior to Carlos's books. According to Wasson, the godfather of such studies, mushrooms are more usually eaten or brewed into tea, and even when allowed to dry, they normally macerate into shreds, rather than into a powder. In any case, he said the leavings do not burn.

Though much of the story takes place in the desert, an expert on climatology—writing in DeMille's second book, a collection of essays and interviews debunking Carlos's work—said that desert conditions, during the times of year Carlos describes, would have been harsh and impassable. In one of Carlos's entries, for example, dated in August, Carlos writes of hiking to the top of a hill at noon-time "to rest in the open unshaded area until dusk." In another entry, dated in June, he describes the evening wind as being "cold." Summer temperatures in the Sonoran desert are typically as high as 120 degrees by noon. At night, they hover around 100.

Moreover, throughout their extensive desert travels, Carlos and Don Juan went unmolested by the knid of pests and predators—scorpions, rattlesnakes, swarming saguaro fruit flies, razor-toothed desert javelinas—that normally torment hikers. He never mentions some of the more colorful inhabitants of the desert—nine-inch centipedes, tarantulas as big as saucers, gila monsters, chuckawallas and horned toads. During his adventures, Carlos writes of climbing high trees. Yet the trees in the desert—palo verde, ironwood, mesquite—are nearly impossible to climb, and neither are they high. Their branches tangle into thorny thickets. Higher than six feet they are too weak to climb. Carlos catches five quails at once in a hastily assembled trap. He runs down a jackrabbit and snares it with his bare hands. He hurdles breakneck and terrified through the desert, through barrel cacti and prickly pears and thorny scrub bushes, but never once does he mention being stabbed or cut by thorns. And while he wrote in his books that he took notes on everything—his note-taking, in fact, becomes an object of derision by Don Juan and his associates—Carlos never produced any field notes.

A close reading of Carlos's books, said De Mille and his collected experts, revealed Don Juan's teachings to be an amalgamation of American Indian folklore, oriental mysticism, and European philosophy—drawing on, among others, Huxley and Puharich, Slotkin and Wasson, Goddard and Yogi Ramacharaka, a pseudonymous American whose works are still widely available in occult bookstores.

Of equal concern was the existence of Don Juan himself. According to Carlos, the old Nagual was born in 1891, watched his parents murdered by soldiers, suffered through the government-forced diaspora of the Yaquis all over Mexico during that era. DeMille and his experts point out that while many Indian tribes, such as the Huichols, use peyote in rituals, the Yaquis, as a rule, did not. Yaqui sorcerers, they continued, don't take apprentices, either. It didn't help matters that not one known expert on the desert culture of the Southwest had ever heard anything about Don Juan and his party. Or that exhaustive attempts to locate the wily old Indian were unsuccessful. In *Carlos Castaneda, Academic Opportunism and the*

Psychedelic Sixties, anthropologist Jay Courtney Fikes posits that Don Juan was a composite of a number of different shamans who'd been discovered, variously, by Wasson and by several of Carlos's colleagues in the anthropology department at UCLA. Indeed: Why else would a field researcher spend so much time in UCLA's graduate research library?

"Although Castaneda's concocted episodes often have something authentic about them, they trivialize Huichol, Yaqui or any Native American culture . . ." writes Fikes. "Those few kernels of truth Castaneda's books contain are dissolved inside a concoction full of spurious ingredients. Finding ethnographic truth in Castaneda's books is almost as laborious as panning for gold."

Even while debunking him, however, DeMille exhibited a fondness and a overarching respect for Carlos and his work. The continuing saga might have been the product of Carlos's mind—but what a marvelous saga it was, what a valuable mind:

"Castaneda wasn't a common con man, he lied to bring us the truth," DeMille wrote in his first book, *Castaneda's Journey.* "His stories are packed with truth, though they are not true stories, which he said they are. This is not your familiar literary allegorist painlessly instructing his readers in philosophy. Nor is it your fearless trustworthy ethnographer returned full of anecdotes from the forests of Ecuador. This is a sham-man bearing gifts, an ambiguous spellbinder dealing simultaneously in contrary commodities—wisdom and deception."

After the meeting in the student union, it would be four years before Gloria Garvin actually saw Carlos again face to face. Meanwhile, she read all his books, followed all the publicity, participated in the gossip that was rampant in the anthro department at UCLA. Part of the gossip centered around Carlos's very earthly reputation as a Lothario. Some even questioned whether he ever went to the desert at all—his wanderings, they said, were just a ruse to cover his bed hopping. Besides the library worker—who, he would later claim, was energetically damaged during her own studies with Don Juan and would live with him in the Pandora compound for many years—Carlos was also involved with two women in the department, Regine Thal and Ann Marie Carter, who would later change their names to Florinda Donner-Grau and Taisha Abelar. He also began seeing a married mother of two named Judy Guilford, who would later call herself Beverly Ames, and then eventually Carol Tiggs. Tiggs would become especially famous in Castaneda circles as a powerful sorceress who crossed over into the Second Attention for ten years and then returned to help guide Carlos and the others in his inner circle. Together, Tiggs, Donner-Grau and Abelar would form the triumvirate of Witches who surrounded Carlos for the duration of his life. All three would write books about their own, separate apprenticeships with Don Juan.

Gloria talked to Carlos now and then by phone, exchanged the occasional letter, but never saw him in person until one day, walking across campus during the winter quarter of 1973, she spotted him. Their eyes locked, he came over. He acted as if they'd met only yesterday.

And so it was that Carlos and Gloria were sitting cross-legged on the beach at sunset, a blanket wrapped cozily around their shoulders. He had her hand clasped tenderly in both of his; he gazed deeply into her startling, gold-flecked blue eyes. "What this entails is not a normal relationship," he told her. "I want to take you with me but it won't be as a normal man, because I am not a normal man any longer. I want to take care of you. I want you to be my wife. I've always known that. Don Juan has told me that. He's seen you; you've hovered around me in dreams. He has identified you as the woman who is going to be in the center of the hurricane with me. There are other winds in the north, south, east and west, and they are very cold and ruthless women, but you are not that way. I want to take care of you. I will do everything in my power for you, because this is a commitment, one that has existed for a very long time. One that will exist beyond this lifetime."

With that Carlos leaned over and kissed Gloria. It was an intense, directed sort of kiss not passionate, not sloppy, not out of control, just very directed, she can't describe it any other way. At that moment, the sounds of the beach grew silent. Time stood still. She felt herself giving something away to him, something very deep, something of herself she'd never reclaim.

Fast asleep on a futon in his modest apartment, late one night in the spring of 1985, a 32-year-old computer technician named Jeremy Davidson found himself on a mountain top, wearing nothing but his underwear.

He was standing on a rocky ridge, at the edge of a sheer cliff. Eagles soared, riding the updrafts. Clouds floated past; wispy fingers of moisture caressed his face. Beneath him, hundreds of feet below, was a gorgeous clear lake. He turned slowly in all directions, inhaling the crisp air, taking in the view, trying to form a clear and lasting image of the whole place, performing a systematic intake, the way Don Juan recommended. It was a wondrous alpine setting, with craggy escarpments and evergreen trees, snowcaps on the distant peaks. Though it was cold and windy, he was comfortable and warm, filled with a buoyant sense of well-being despite his precarious barefoot perch. A feeling of giddiness overcame him and he took off running—hopping and skipping from boulder to boulder like an astronaut bounding across the surface of the moon. Changing direction, he plunged straight down the cliff face, pausing here and there to flip and spin and twirl, throwing tricks like a free-style ski-jumper, making his way toward the languid blue waters of the lake.

The scene changed and he was standing in a small cove, his toes buried in fine, gritty sand. Thinking it might help to cement the dream, to make it last longer, he decided to look at his hands for a bit. He sat down in the sand, concentrated on his palms, his fingers, his nails. Just then, a big wave rose up and washed over him, enveloping him in bubbles and blue, sending him sprawling.

Rising to his feet, Jeremy moved toward the back of the cove, toward a trail. He walked for a while through the dense woods, then came upon a building in a clearing, a huge Hansel and Gretel type affair, a gingerbread house with fancy trim. He got the feeling it was an abandoned resort hotel. He decided to explore.

The scene changed again and he was inside, in the lobby, a room with a fireplace and overstuffed chairs, a gift shop off to one side, cobwebs and dust everywhere. As he looked around, performing a systematic intake, things seemed to become more and more solid, as if he was watching an image download from the web onto a computer screen. He walked into the gift shop, helped himself to a dry T-shirt that was hanging conveniently on a rack. Off to one side, behind the cash register, he saw an opening, like a door, leading into a blue-green world. He stood a moment, regarding the opening, trying to decide what to do next. Then he spoke aloud: "I intend to go to where the sorcerers are. Take me to the sorcerers. . . ."

Shy and highly intelligent, a bit at odds with the world, Jeremy Davidson had first discovered the writings of Carlos Castaneda in the late seventies, while studying physics as a college junior. He'd always been a seeker, a skeptic, a bit of an outsider, the kind of person for whom the normal order and the normal answers never seemed to ring true. He'd experimented with psychedelic drugs, read extensively on eastern and western philosophy. He'd been a Buddhist and a Scientologist, an atheist and an orthodox Jew. More recently, during a bad period in his life he'd re-discovered Carlos. Starting with *The Teachings*, he'd worked his way through the series, which had grown by now to eight books.

Carlos himself had long since disappeared from the public eye. Smarting, no doubt, from the effects of his exposure in the early seventies, he lived in quiet anonymity in the Pandora compound with the Witches, traveling around the country and to Mexico, churning out books all the while, honing the message and the method, taking it further with each new publication. Though Carlos said that Don Juan left the world in 1973, dying "the immaculate death" of the Warrior, each subsequent book continued to expound upon Don Juan's teachings. Diligent readers noted that the anthropological references seemed to grow fewer as the series progressed, and that the books increasingly bore the traces of other influences, such as phenomenology, Eastern mysticism and existentialism. With Don Juan having left the world, Carlos himself became the heir to the sorcerer's lineage, the Nagual. No longer a disciple, he had become a prophet. As the books evolved, his focus turned more and more toward the Art of Dreaming.

According to Carlos, Don Juan was an intermediary between the natural world of everyday life and an unseen universe called the Second Attention. Though Western minds are conditioned to believe that the world we live in is unique and absolute, it is, in truth, only one in a cluster of consecutive worlds, arranged like the layers of an onion. Don Juan said that even though humans have been energetically conditioned to perceive only their own world, they still have the capability to enter those other realms—worlds as palpable, unique, absolute and engulfing as the ordinary reality that we live in every day.

Don Juan said that in order for people to visit those other realms—the existence of which are constant and independent of our awareness—they had to first recondition their energetic capacity to perceive. To this end, he prescribed a series of techniques designed to displace the Assemblage Point, a place of intense luminosity, located about an arm's length behind the shoulder blades, where perception occurs, where we receive the signals that tell us what we see, feel, hear and understand. Furthermore, said Don Juan, once a person became adept at traveling to the Second Attention, he or she could ultimately remain there as a luminous egg for all of eternity, in a wonderful universe too vast and beautiful and complex and fulfilling to render in conventional language or ideas.

Reading all of this, Jeremy felt invigorated and alive, perhaps more so than he'd ever been in his whole life. Here, at last, was a belief system that felt right to him. It was a system that stressed living every moment to the fullest, as a Warrior and a Man of Knowledge, rising to every trial as a challenge, taking responsibility for everything you have a part in, living impeccably every single day. And, it was a system that explained the place of man in the universe, and the nature of that universe itself. Added to all of this was the promise of other worlds, not just worlds you could visit in an afterlife, but worlds you could visit right now, today. In sum, the Sorcerer's Way was a mode of thinking as well as a mode of acting—a world view that offered its adherents not only ideas and guidelines but also procedures and results. You didn't just sit around believing. You could act.

Jeremy thus embarked on the path of the impeccable Warrior. He sought to live each day as a challenge, as a discipline. He strove to eliminate self-importance, to use death as an advisor, to erase personal history, to disrupt the routines of his life. He tried to have a romance with knowledge, and to write people he cared about a blank check of affection. He practiced gazing and not doing, stalking and the right way of walking. He tried to stop the world and to see. He watched for omens and read infinity, a specific gazing technique where he focused on a fixed point until a violet field appeared, then continued to focus until a little blotch of pomegranate exploded into either written words or visual scenes. He spent hours and hours recapitulating his life—a laborious process in which he reviewed each and every contact he'd ever had with another human being since his first memories after birth, an effort to regain wasted energy. Slowly but surely, he began to become aware in his dreams—he began traveling to the Second Attention.

Now Jeremy found himself in a gift shop somewhere in the mountains, having entered the Second Attention from his futon one night in the spring of 1985. He walked through a doorway into a blue green world, intending to go to the Sorcerers.

As he entered the doorway, a force that he had come to think of as The Spirit picked him up and flew him over a vast area like a huge town square, filled with thousands of people. From his vantage point high in the sky, he could look down and see their faces. Most of them, he could see, were in some state of fear, degradation, agony. Some of them looked up as he soared past. Again he voiced his intent: "I intend to go to where the Sorcerers are."

The scene changed and he found himself on the ground in a dark, smoky gray area. There were small, dark beings surrounding him, and when he focused on them, they turned to face him. They were ghoul-like creatures, with yellowish eyes and a single protuberance extending out from their faces, terminating in creepy little mouths. They began advancing.

Retreating, he entered another area, inhabited by a different sort of beings, tall blocks of dark shadows, like huge sentient rectangles. They too began to surround him, and he found himself standing on something that looked like a gray tombstone lying flat on the ground. Scared of the beings, wishing to leave, he knelt down and clenched his fist, placed it upon the stone. "I want to go where the Chacmols are," he said out loud, but nothing happened. He was about to repeat his demand, using the name of one of the Witches, Taisha Abelar, when a voice told him not to do that, but rather to restate his intention. This time he said firmly: "I INTEND to go to where the Chacmols are."

With that, the scene changed and he was in a cave, with rock floors and walls and boulders strewn everywhere. Though there was no source of light apparent, it was bright as day. He walked around the cave, exploring. Suddenly a man jumped out from behind a rock. He was primitive, vigorous, wild looking, wearing fur clothes. He ran towards Jeremy; Jeremy turned and fled. The cave man chased him through a vast system of tunnels and caverns, gaining with every step, getting closer and closer. Just as the caveman was about to overtake him, Jeremy spotted a hole. It seemed to lead into another chamber. He dove through.

The scene changed and he was flying again, in a prone position with his arms extended like Superman. He felt his mood lighten; up up up he sailed, high into the sky, toward the moon, bright and full. He made a smooth banking turn and headed back toward earth, toward a shopping mall. In his mind, he considered leaving this place, flying out toward the countryside somewhere, but the voice inside his head overruled his thoughts and The Spirit took control of his flight, as it sometimes did, and he began to descend. He flew into the mall, around the atrium, past a fountain and an escalator.

The scene changed. He was inside of a store, a sex shop. There was racy lingerie hanging on the racks, all kinds of toys on the shelves. Drawn to the toys, he was about to pick one up when he noticed a bunch of people in a back room, men and women in various states of undress, an orgy in progress. He stood for a few minutes and watched. A man came over with his attractive girlfriend. He offered her to Jeremy. Though his inner voice clearly told him "No!", Jeremy ignored the voice and took the girl in his arms, began pulling off the remainder of her clothes. She seemed a bit reluctant. Jeremy got the strong impression that she'd never done this sort of thing before, that she was only doing it to please her boyfriend. It bothered him a bit that maybe she wasn't totally into the whole scene, but she was beautiful; it had been a long time since he'd been with a woman. The voice told him No! He reached for her breast. . . .

He awoke in his futon. He sat up, feeling a bit ashamed. He had not acted like a Warrior. He shouldn't have crossed the wishes of the inner voice. He shouldn't have defied The Spirit. It was months before he dreamed again.

At precisely 9 a.m. on Christmas Eve, 1993—the same time as every morning for the past several months—the phone rang in Melissa Ward's Santa Monica apartment. She was in bed with a horrible flu; she just wanted to be alone. The phone rang again, then again. The shrill noise hurt her head. Finally, she picked it up.

"How's my baby girl?" sang Carlos.

"Still pretty sick, I'm afraid."

"You're coming to the dinner tonight, aren't you?"

"I don't know, Carlos," she said, and then she sighed. "I feel like I've been run over by a truck."

"But you have to be there! The whole dinner is for you!"

She rolled her eyes toward the ceiling. They were a startling shade of corn-flower blue, with gold flecks that shimmered in the light. "I guess I'll have to see how I feel."

"Why don't I come over and bring you some chicken soup?"

"No no no!" she said quickly. "Don't bother. Really! I'll be okay."

"Well you have to rest," insisted Carlos. "Don't go to work, don't do any-thing, just rest. You have to be ready. Tonight, you become one of us!"

"Well, er, um," said Melissa, pushing her Cleopatra bangs away from her forehead. He'd been talking about this mysterious dinner for weeks now. Frankly, it gave her the creeps. *Become one of us!* The way he said it made her shudder. It had the distinct ring of something cult-like; she didn't like the sound of it, not at all. "I'm gonna try my best to make it," she said half-heartedly.

"You must make it!" roared Carlos. "Everything is ready. You are the Elec-tric Warrior! We have been searching for you for all of eternity! We have found you just in the nick of time. You must come!"

Thirty-eight years old, petite and attractive, Melissa Ward was born beneath the Northern Lights at a secret military base in the Aleutian chain. Though she was a bit too young to have been a hippie, she grew up with her feet planted firmly in the early seventies counter-culture, into eastern reli-gions and Credence Clearwater Revival, psychedelics, the writings of Gurd-jieff and Huxley. She was 18 when she first read Carlos. She'd just returned from backpacking through Europe; she was severely ill with colitis, in a lot of pain, trying to cure herself naturally with herbs. Staying by herself in a friend's cabin in the woods, lying around naked, trying to fight the sickness, she came upon a copy of *Journey to Ixlan* on a shelf. She opened the book at random, let her eyes drift down the page. "Death is always following you," she read. In her condition, the words rang very true. She turned to the front of the book and started in.

Melissa had been reading for an hour or two when she heard some weird scratching noises outside. She struggled out of bed, looked through the window. There, on the deck, was a giant black bird, the biggest crow she'd ever seen. It was hopping up and down, acting very strangely, like it was trying to get her attention. Stranger still was the fact that crows played a significant part in *Ixlan*. In Don Juan's world, crows were said to be the incarnations of powerful sorcerers and spirits. Under the influence of the devil's weed, Carlos himself had become a crow—his head had sprouted wings, a bill and feet and had flown off into the heavens. Over the next few days, as she continued reading the book, the crow became bolder. It tapped on the window with its beak, hopped from place to place on the deck, knocked over little pots of herbs, generally making itself known. By the third day, her curiosity got the better of her and she ventured out to the deck, sat down with her new companion. The crow hopped up on her chair. She fed it grapes. Though she might have been delirious, she could have sworn the crow had a kind of benevolent presence. In an odd, unexplainable way, it seemed to be there for her, to help her through this rough time. The crow visited every day for a month, until she was fully recovered. Then it disappeared.

Time passed and she went on with her life, forgot all about Carlos. After bouncing around from job to job, she enrolled as an undergraduate at UCLA. By her junior year, in the winter of 1993, her life was full and hectic, more gratifying than ever. She was working part time as a nutrition consultant, writing for the college newspaper, doing an internship at the actress Jessica Lange's film company, taking a full load of classes—looking forward, meanwhile, to graduation and the promise of a job in either journalism or entertainment. And then one day she got a phone call from her mom. She was dying of cancer.

The next nine months were a living hell. Melissa nursed her mom to the end, held her hand as she took her last breath, sat alone with the body for three hours until the man from the funeral home came to take her. Melissa handled all the arrangements, served as executor of the will. Trying to get back to her life, she enrolled in summer school, only to find herself embroiled in a disastrous affair with her older, married creative writing teacher. By the end of the summer she'd dropped out of school and taken to her bed in a deep depression. Lying beneath the covers with the shades drawn, she repeated to herself a manta of despair: "Nobody cares. I've given up hope. Life sucks."

Then one day in September, she ran into a friend at the health food store. He said he was going to another friend's apartment to hear Carlos Castaneda speak to a small group. The session had been arranged primarily though the efforts of a German woman named Gabi Geuther, a New Age enthusiast and veteran of primal scream therapy who'd befriended Florinda Donner-Grau and other members of the inner circle after a reading at a women's bookstore in Santa Monica. For the first time in many years, Melissa thought of the weird and friendly crow who'd helped her through hard times. She decided to come along.

Though Melissa didn't realize it just then, the fact that Carlos had begun to appear in public after a 20-year absence signaled a stunning change in direction for the Nagual and his party. Over the last few years, they'd slowly begun taking on select students for a weekly private class, held in a rented room in a dance studio. Now, apparently, they'd decided to rev things up, to actively promote the ideas and practices of Don Juan on a larger scale, to make them available for public consumption. To this end, Carlos and the Witches had hired a lawyer and formed several corporations, with the stated intent of establishing "a magical relationship between the endeavors of a corporate unit in our modern world and the purpose and will of a bygone era." Toltec Artists was a management agency—run by inner-circle member Tracy Kramer, a well-known Hollywood agent—set up to handle the literary careers of Carlos, the three Witches, and assorted other connected artists. Laugan Productions was a company that sold instructional videos and other saleable products. Most important was Cleargreen, which acted as both a publishing house and as the sponsor of seminars and workshops for something they were now billing as Carlos Castaneda's Tensegrity.

Derived from the words *tension* and *integrity*, Tensegrity was said to be a modernized version of the "magical passes" that were developed by ancient Indian shamans and passed down secretly through 27 generations to Don Juan and then to Carlos and the Witches. By practicing these exercises, Carlos said, Toltec sorcerers had attained an increased level of awareness which allowed them to perform "indescribable feats of perception" and experience "unequaled states of physical prowess and well being." Through the use of the Tensegrity exercises—a sort of combination of martial arts, meditation, yoga and aerobics—modern practitioners could achieve a new level of vigor, health and clarity. And they could gain the kind of energy needed to displace the Assemblage Point and actively engage in the Art of Dreaming, traveling at will to other worlds. While it was earlier believed that the Sorcerer's Way was a solitary pursuit, Carlos now said that the "mass" created by a group of people practicing together caused quicker and more powerful results.

Though Carlos had never before mentioned the "magical passes" in his writings; though other anthropologists insisted that there was no such tradition of body movements among pre-Hispanic Indians; and though Carlos had always eschewed the notion of selling his techniques through expensive seminars, it was Cleargreen's express purpose to disseminate the teachings of Don Juan to a large audience at a high price. What had caused the change of heart was not exactly clear. Perhaps, some suggested, Carlos saw fertile ground in the national obsessions with physical fitness and New Age philosophy—theirs was one heck of a product, a time-saving two-fer, designed to benefit both the mind and the body. Perhaps, some suggested, Carlos was becoming infirm and out of touch and the Witches had begun to call the shots.

Carlos himself acknowledged that Don Juan had always said that the magical passes should be kept secret. This new path, Carlos explained, had been spurred by an extraordinary event. According to Carlos, while following Don Juan's techniques, Carol Tiggs, one of the three Witches, had disappeared from a hotel room in Mexico City into the Second Attention. She had vanished for ten years, Carlos said, in order to act as a beacon from the other side, guiding initiates through the "dark sea of awareness." In 1985, however, Tiggs made a surprising reappearance at a California bookshop where Carlos was giving a talk. Her return had convinced Carlos that the "message of freedom" enshrined in the magical passes should now be passed onto the world at large.

Others had a more cynical view: "Castaneda had built himself up as a prophet through the Don Juan books," said anthropologist Courtney Jay Fikes. "The bible, so to speak, was written; but there was no ritual, so it was necessary to invent one."

Over the next several years, dozens of seminars—some lasting a weekend, some as long as three weeks—would be attended by thousands of Carlos enthusiasts in the U.S., Mexico and Europe. The seminars cost from $200 to $1,000. Tables were set up to sell Tensegrity T-shirts (The Magic is in the Movement) and Tensegrity videos, which had been directed by the well-known novelist and screenwriter Bruce Wagner. Also on sale were Tensegrity tools, for use in concert with the magical passes. "The Device to Enhance Centers of Awareness," was two balls made of Teflon reinforced by a ceramic compound. "The Device for Inner Silence" was a round, weighted leather-covered object for placement on the stomach. "The Wheel of Time" was invented by the Blue Scout; it was a flat disk made of compact foam rubber, extremely pliable, but durable enough to withstand pushing, pulling and twisting. Carlos himself appeared at all the early seminars; both he and the Witches gave long, amusing, passionate speeches. Interspersed with the lectures were Tensegrity demonstrations by the Chacmols, dressed in matching black workout uniforms.

Also over the next several years, serious questions would be raised about the origins of Tensegrity. Some alleged that Carlos's magical passes were nothing more than the appropriated teachings of a kung fu instructor and "energy master" named Howard Lee, with whom Carlos had studied for many years, and to whom *Ixlan* had been dedicated. Though there were allegations that Carlos paid a substantial sum of money and the phallus of a puma to deter the Santa Monica–based Lee from taking legal action against Cleargreen, Lee denied this. Smiling inscrutably, he refuses to speculate upon the actual origins of Tensegrity. He does acknowledge, however, that once Carlos began teaching Tensegrity, the formerly close relations between the two wise men become chilly.

And so, on a balmy night in September 1993, Melissa found herself among a group of 40 people, jammed into an apartment in Santa Monica, listening to the great man speak. Though she'd brought a notebook and had started out taking notes, she quickly gave up. There seemed to be no rhyme or reason to what Carlos was saying, no outline to his talk, just a torrential downpour of ideas and stories and jokes. Though she was frustrated at first, she found herself settling into her seat on the plush pile carpet and letting his words rush over her, concentrating not so much on what he was saying as on his energy. He had about him a really nice emanation, she felt, a nice kind of presence that was warm and fluid, almost like floating around in a Jacuzzi with all the jets on. Whatever this was, it was cool. She felt better than she had for months.

Carlos rambled for two hours, and when he finished he received a standing ovation. Melissa just sat there, kind of stunned. Before she knew what was happening, Carlos was standing over her. He leaned down, whispered in her ear: "You have very good energy," he said. Then he was gone.

The next day, Melissa was contacted by one of the Chacmols, who invited her to a private class, and she went, and Carlos seated her front and center, seemed to be lecturing only to her. The next day, one of the Chacmols called to ask if Carlos might have the privilege of calling her at home. Soon, Carlos was telephoning every morning at nine a.m. sharp, sometimes late in the evening as well. He called her his baby girl. He asked her about her life, her family, her past sex life, her history of venereal disease. He told her that if she smoked pot, she should stop, and that she must completely stop having sex. "You must zip it up! You must not let anyone touch your baby-thing," he'd said. He asked her to tell him her innermost secrets; he asked her to make a list of all her sex partners, to recapitulate each experience. He asked her if she'd ever "been taken away kicking and screaming by men in white coats." Frequently, he'd ask her to lunch or dinner, for sushi or Cuban, his favorites. Usually, she said no. On those occasions when she relented and said yes, one of the Chacmols invariably would call and cancel at the last minute, telling her that Carlos was sick or that had to leave town unexpect- edly. Though they never met alone outside the weekly private classes, Carlos continued to call each morning. He told her that her energy was incredible, that they were soulmates, that he would never leave her. Melissa didn't know what to make of his attentions. Though his tone was distinctly sexual, he never made a move. It was like he had an obsessive need to make women fall in love with him, then to keep them at arm's length. While she had no interest in him sexually, his attentions were oddly addictive—she kept coming back for more, despite her better judgement.

In time, Carlos began telling Melissa that she was the Electric Warrior that they'd been searching for, and on Christmas Eve, 1993, they held a spe- cial banquet in her honor. Though she was creeped out by the notion of what seemed to be happening, she attended the dinner, a classy affair for 18 people with champagne and candlelight at a long table in the banquet room of a four star French restaurant in Westwood. There were toasts and speeches and each of the Witches came in turn to sit next to her and chat. Though the Witches struck her as being very catty and a bit hostile—asking her, for example, what her favorite kind of music was and then berating her for her answer—she got the feeling like she was the bride at a wedding, albeit a bride who was marrying into a family who had mixed emotions about the union. With dread, she sat at the table—Carlos at one head, Florinda at the other— imagining a wedding chamber set to receive her and her sexagenarian groom. To her great relief, when she said she was tired and wanted to leave, no one stopped her. The minute she got into the door of her apartment, Carlos was on the phone. "They all love you! The phone hasn't stopped ringing!" he said excitedly. She could hear the call waiting feature beeping on his line. "Everyone's crazy about you, baby girl!"

From that night on, Melissa was part of the inner circle. She didn't understand what this Electric Warrior thing was all about; nobody bothered to explain. There were others too—the Lecture Warrior, the Blue Scout, the Orange Scout, The Trackers, The Elements, the Chacmols—most of them attractive younger women. It was a little creepy, all this attention from a man old enough to be her father, but nobody was touching her, nobody was really acting inappropriate—though Carlos had this weird obsession with teaching her to make a fist. Truth be told, the inner circle was kind of fun. She hadn't had a group of friends for many years; it took her mind off her problems, and that was a great relief. The members of the inner circle were all smart and well read. They were up on current events, loved nice clothes and making puns, were always joking around and pulling practical jokes, infantile stuff, like a bucket of water atop a door. They had dinner parties at people's houses and at fancy restaurants; they loved going to Tony Roma's for ribs—in short order, Melissa, formerly a vegetarian, gained ten pounds. Once, at Tracy Kramer's beautiful Craftsman house, Carlos prepared a jelly which he said was made of devil's weed. He said it would make them all fly, but nothing happened to Melissa.

Often, there were madcap performances by something the inner circle called, alternately, the Sorcery Theater or the Theater of Infinity. Written by Bruce Wagner, the skits were hilarious. Slickly produced affairs, complete with props and costumes, most of them were didactic, portraying Carlos's philosophy and his rules, but always in a lampoonist fashion. One favorite skit featured a gypsy fortune teller who picked out members of the audience and proceeded to ruthlessly deconstruct their personalities, their idiosyncrasies, their habits, their oddities—fertile ground, to be sure. Another favorite featured the Chacmols doing nude, martial-arts-like movements with sharp knives in their hands. There was a skit featuring a six-foot dildo; another number was aimed at Melissa and the Lecture Warrior—a musical rendition of "I Don't Know How to Love Him" from *Jesus Christ Superstar*. In time, the Witches—all of whom wore their hair extremely short and dressed in designer clothes—seemed to grow to accept Melissa; they began inviting her along to movies and on shopping trips to Century City Mall, which was walking distance from the Pandora compound.

Toward the end of 1994, Melissa began seeing changes in Carlos, in the inner circle. Though Cleargreen was getting stronger, holding more seminars, the group seemed to become directionless, like they were waiting around, trying to figure out what to do next. Carlos even said as much: "We don't know what to do," he told Melissa, "we don't know where to go, we don't know what's happening." Carlos also started complaining about the tyranny of the Witches. He said they were bossy, that they wouldn't listen to what he said. He spent the whole of one Sunday private class railing about the fact that Taisha had made herself a hamburger one night and refused to make one for him. He was obviously having trouble seeing— she heard whispers about diabetes—but no one said anything out loud, though everyone had suddenly taken on a new interest in acupuncture and nutrition—an area in which Melissa was very knowledgeable, a fact that seemed to draw the inner circle more closely around her as she began advising them on meal preparation. One thing was certain: Carlos didn't look very well. His skin had become ashen, his hair had turned entirely gray. He wobbled just a bit when he walked. And sometimes, when he came close to talk to her, or to help her practice making a fist, she noticed this peculiar, sour kind of smell about him; it reminded her of the way her mother had smelled before she died.

Then one day Carlos approached her in private. "I'm leaving soon and I'm taking you and everyone else with me," he said.

Melissa was horrified. The first thing that came into her mind was Jim Jones, Kool-Aid, the mass cult suicide in Guyana. She didn't know what to say.

C.J. Castaneda polished off a tall glass of tap water and turned out the kitchen lights, slowly climbed the stairs to the master bedroom of his rambling, suburban Atlanta house. It was 10:30 p.m. on April 27, 1998, the end of another long and difficult day. The blond, blue-eyed, 36 year old was bone-weary.

A former real estate appraiser and sometime-inventor with a taste for the good life and a near-genius IQ, C.J. had recently started a new business, a chain of drive-up coffee kiosks. The logistics of servicing and running his far-flung mini-enterprise kept him hopping from long before sunup until way past dark, seven days a week. The toll was beginning to show on his handsome countenance; his weight-lifter's build had gone a bit soft around the middle. Sighing, he sat down heavily on his side of the bed, undressed and slipped between the sheets, kissed his wife Lisa goodnight. As was customary, she had settled in with a book, preferring to read for thirty minutes before going to sleep herself. C.J. set his alarm for 4:40, pulled the covers over his head. In moments he was out.

Though few people knew it, Carlton Jeremy Castaneda was Carlos's adopted son, born to Margaret Runyan and a Mormon businessman named Adrian Gerritsen. As with every other chapter in Carlos's life, the story of C.J.'s birth was odd and convoluted.

Six months after Carlos and Margaret were married in Mexico, Carlos had come home to their apartment one afternoon and told her excitedly about meeting an old Indian in a Greyhound bus station near the Arizona border with Mexico. Carlos was enrolled at the time in his first undergraduate anthropology class at UCLA, a course called California Ethnography. His professor had promised an A grade to any student who found an actual Indian informant for a term paper. For months, Carlos had been making trips to the desert, searching for an indigenous wise man to teach him the ancient secrets of hallucinogenic plants. Though he'd once dreamed of becoming a great artist, Carlos now had his sights set on a career as a professor of anthropology. UCLA had a great and competitive department. Surely this desert meeting was an auspicious start on his new path.

Margaret, of course, didn't see things his way at all. She was deeply in love with Carlos; she wanted her husband at home. This was her third marriage, and though it had started out quite romantically—a showdown between two suitors culminating with a midnight road trip to a Mexican justice of the peace—things were already beginning to sour. Besides her suspicion that he was seeing other women, a big stumbling block in their relationship was their respective schedules. While Margaret continued working days as chief operator at the phone company, Carlos was working nights as an accountant in a fancy dress shop in downtown L.A., attending classes during the day. Now, in addition to this hectic schedule, he told Margaret, he was going to start spending his weekends in the desert with this mysterious old man.

Fights and unpleasantness ensued, and soon Carlos moved out of the apartment. Margaret began dating Gerritsen, a tall, handsome Mormon from Utah. Gerritsen was in the clothing business and came frequently to L.A. on buying trips. Finding herself in love with Gerritsen, Margaret asked Carlos for a divorce, and he was surprisingly accommodating. They drove back to Mexico, to the same justice of the peace who had married them. Unbeknownst to Margaret, however, the official didn't actually complete the paperwork for a divorce. Also unbeknownst to Margaret, Gerritsen was an acquaintance of Carlos—it was Carlos who'd actually arranged their first meeting. Furthermore, in a letter filed in connection with a probate case many years later, following Carlos's death, Gerritsen would confirm that Carlos had asked him to father a child with Margaret, a child whom Carlos would then adopt as his own. Margaret and Gerritsen—who was already married to a woman in Salt Lake City—were married in Mexico a short time later. Though the newlyweds never took up housekeeping together, a son was born in August 1961.

Not long after the birth, Carlos came to Margaret and confessed that their Mexican divorce had been a charade, something he'd done to appease her while he did his field work, hoping, he said, that they'd one day reunite as a couple. He explained that they were still married, and that he wanted to adopt her son. As it was, Carlos had been seeing the little tow-headed boy frequently since his birth and had developed a deep attachment. He called the boy Cho-cho; the boy called him Kiki. Carlos took him everywhere—to the beach, to the mountains, to his power spot in Topanga Canyon, to the movies. People got used to seeing the nut brown man carrying the little blond boy everywhere on his shoulders. Often, he brought Cho-cho along to classes at UCLA. When asked, Carlos proudly claimed Cho-cho as his biological son, attributing the obvious difference in coloring to the boy's mother, whom he said was Scandinavian. When Cho-cho was two Carlos appeared at Margaret's apartment with documents from the California Department of Public Health naming Carlos as the natural father of one Carlton Jeremy Castaneda. Her relationship with Gerritsen having long since dissolved, Margaret agreed to sign. A boy needs a father. Carlos was the only one her son had ever known.

Over the next five years, Carlos saw a lot of his Cho-cho; the boy regularly spent nights in his own room at Carlos's rented house. In the mornings, for breakfast, Carlos fed him bananas and raw hamburger to help him grow, then walked the boy, hand in hand, to school. In the evenings, while Carlos worked on his book, the two women who would later become the Witches—Florinda Donner-Grau and Carol Tiggs—read Cho-cho his bedtime stories. Before going to sleep, Cho-cho would stand beside Kiki at his desk. "What are you writing?" he'd ask. "I'm writing a book for you, Cho-cho," Carlos would answer. "You're going to make it the most magical of books, because you're the biggest *brujo* on the planet." Though money was still a problem, Carlos insisted on paying for Cho-cho's tuition at an exclusive Montessori School in Santa Monica—one of his classmates was the daughter of Charlton Heston. Carlos also paid Cho-cho's doctor bills and bought him clothes, sent him for karate and skiing lessons. He would continue paying child support through the mid seventies, when he and Margaret were legally divorced.

When the boy was seven, Margaret and C.J. left L.A., a move that pained Carlos greatly. Carlos continued to correspond with Margaret for many years, writing of his undying love for both her and his Cho-cho, and of his intention to leave any money he might amass to the boy. "I went by your old apt. in the Valley a couple of days ago and got an attack of profound sentimentalism," Carlos wrote to Margaret in August of 1967. "You are my family, dearest Margarita. . . . I owe you a very, very special something. I owe you the most beautiful and magical of all my dreams, *my* Cho-cho. You brought that dream into my life for one instant, and compared to that instant of dreaming all my other dreams are nothing. . . . Take care! And kiss my Cho-cho's big toe for his Kiki. I keep on telling to myself that I will go hiking with him."

The following year, Carlos dedicated his first book, *The Teachings of Don Juan*, to Cho-cho and Margaret, and he mentioned him in several subsequent books as well, discussing "a little boy that I once knew" with Don Juan, telling him "how my feelings for him would not change with the years or the distance." In 1978, Carlos attended C.J.'s high school graduation in Tempe, Arizona; for the next three years, he paid his college tuition. They were reunited briefly once again a few years later in New York.

Starting in around 1993, however, around the time that Cleargreen and the other companies were formed, Carlos ceased all communications with C.J. and Margaret. Despite his repeated phone calls and letters, C.J. was thwarted in his efforts to contact Carlos by members of Cleargreen, who appeared to be handling all of Carlos's personal business with the outside world. Other friends, including an old roommate and one of Carlos's favorite UCLA professors, were similarly thwarted in their efforts to contact the great man. Frustrated, C.J. heard news of a lecture Carlos was giving in October of 1993, and flew to Santa Monica to try to see him.

C.J. waited in the parking lot outside of the bookstore, and when Carlos spotted the strappingly handsome young man, he seemed overjoyed. He embraced C.J. enthusiastically, kissing him on both cheeks, patting him on the back, speaking with warmth and animation. Their reunion was cut short, however, by two of the Chacmols, who took Carlos one by each arm and hustled him away. As they were moving toward the van to leave, one of the Chacmols retrieved from Carlos a piece of paper with C.J.'s phone number on it, balled it up into a piece of trash.

Three years later, frustrated by Carlos's continuing silence, C.J. paid $400 to attend a Tensegrity workshop where Carlos was slated to appear, once again hoping to reunite with his Kiki. At the door of the workshop, however, he was recognized by the Cleargreen organizers. They refunded his money and asked him to leave. When he and his wife went across the street to a mall to get something to eat, members of Cleargreen followed at a discreet distance, keeping them under surveillance.

As the 90s progressed, Carlos's contact with old friends ceased altogether. Though he was by now nearly blind, and had to be helped to the stage for lectures, he became increasingly litigious. Lawyers for Cleargreen filed suits attempting to block the publication of writings of a woman named Merilyn Tunneshende, who called herself "The Nagual Woman" and said that she too had studied with Don Juan. In 1995, a suit was initiated by Cleargreen's lawyers against a Toltec teacher and old friend named Victor Sanchez, claiming that the jacket of Sanchez's book about Carlos infringed on Carlos's copyrights. And in 1997, Cleargreen lawyers launched a suit against Margaret Runyan Castaneda and the publishers of her autobiography, *A Magical Journey With Carlos Castaneda.*

In February of 1997, Carlos made his last appearance at a Tensegrity seminar, in Long Beach, California. A spokesman for Toltec Artists said that Carlos had decided "that the seminars were taking their own course and he did not need to be present." Others had a different view of his absence. "He was taking medication, losing weight," said one Carlos watcher. "People were becoming suspicious. If Tensegrity was supposed to lead to health and well-being, why doesn't he look so good?"

In the winter of 1998, Toltec Artists delivered to his publisher the manuscript for Carlos's eleventh book, *The Active Side of Infinity.* In a departure from his other books, *Infinity* takes a somewhat apocalyptic view of the mystical universe, defining it as predatory and populated by shadowy entities called the Flyers, who prey on a man's glowing coat of awareness. Only by practicing Tensegrity, Carlos suggests, can these dark forces be repelled. He also reappraises once again his encounters with Don Juan, concluding strongly that the "total goal" of shamanic knowledge is preparation for facing the "definitive journey—the journey that every human being has to take at the end of his life" to the region that shamans called "the active side of infinity." "We are beings on our way to dying," Don Juan said. "We are not immortal, but we behave as if we were."

Much attention is given in *Infinity* to the departure of the old Nagual, and the notion that an enlightened sorcerer does not die a normal death but is consumed by "the fire from within," a sort of spontaneous combustion, gathering his mortal energy and carrying the body with him into the next realm. As if preparing his readers for his own leave-taking, Carlos describes in great detail the departure of Don Juan and his party. "I saw then how Don Juan Matus, the Nagual, led the 15 other seers who were his companions . . . one by one to disappear into the haze of that mesa, towards the north. I saw how every one of them turned into a blob of luminosity, and together they ascended and floated above the mesa, like phantom lights in the sky. They circled above the mountain once, as Don Juan had said they would do, their last survey, the one for their eyes only, their last look at this marvelous earth. And then they vanished."

Now, fast asleep in the master bedroom of his suburban Atlanta house on the night of April 27, 1998, C.J. Castaneda, once called Cho-cho by the only father he ever knew, became aware of the insistent buzzing of his alarm clock. He opened his eyes, looked at the time: 4:40. As he reached for the snooze button, he happened to notice, sitting in a chair in the corner of the room, glowing a spectral shade of blue, the great man himself, his Kiki, Carlos Castaneda.

Carlos looked young again, and happy, the kind of face he used to make just before he'd lift the young blond boy up up up over his head, onto his shoulders; the kind of face he used to make in the mornings at his rented house, standing over the sink, cutting the little seeds out of the center of a banana because his Cho-cho didn't like that part. Sitting there in the chair, Carlos smiled at C.J., winked one eye. C.J. blinked, blinked again. Carlos was gone.

Seven minutes later, at 4:47, the alarm buzzed again, and C.J. sat up in bed, swung his legs over the side. Shaking off the cobwebs, he rose, padded to the bathroom to take a shower.

Ten minutes later, at 4:57, dressed with wet hair, C.J. took the dog by the collar and left the bedroom, went downstairs, let the dog out the front door, walked to the kitchen, poured some dog food in a bowl. He looked at the clock on the microwave. It said 11:00. He walked over to the kitchen table, picked up his watch. It also said 11:00.

Puzzled, he let the dog back in the front door and returned to the bedroom. The clock by his bed said 11:01.

"Lisa!" he whispered loudly. "Lisa! Wake up!"

His wife stirred, rolled over, looked at the clock. "What do you want?" she asked. "Why are you dressed?"

"How long have you been asleep?" C.J. asked.

"For a while, why?"

"What time?"

"About eleven."

"Lisa, it's 11:01. What do you mean you went to sleep a while ago?"

"What are you talking about!" exclaimed Lisa, growing annoyed.

C.J.'s mind raced. If Lisa had gone to bed at 11:00, how was it that he'd awoken and snoozed and showered and gone downstairs? It was now 11:02. All of that would have had to have taken place in one minute. It was at least twenty minutes worth of activities—she would have still been still reading when he first awoke! The whole thing didn't compute, not at all.

"Why don't you get back in bed?" Lisa suggested, rolling back over, putting her head down on the pillow.

"Holy shit!" said C.J.

"What?"

"I just remembered!"

"What?"

C.J. felt a weird tingling up and down his spine. The hair on the back of his neck stood on end. "I think Carlos is dead."

The Follower parked his dusty blue Hyundai at the curb in front of Spalding Mortuary, a nondescript brick building in a run-down industrial district just east of Culver City. It was Monday, June 22, 1998, around ten a.m. Though the morning sun was bright, the air was cool; Greg Mamishian was wearing his favorite jacket, a tan corduroy sportscoat with suede elbow patches that once belonged to Carlos. Greg sat silent for a few moments, listening to the engine tick off heat, a short man, fifty years old, with close cropped gray hair and an elfin sparkle in his eyes, girding himself for another mission.

For the past two and a half years, Greg and his wife Gabi had made a hobby of following Carlos. They'd sat outside his compound for hundreds of hours, watching the comings and goings, trying to read between the lines. They'd trailed the Nagual and his party to restaurants and movies, to inner-circle practice groups. They'd videotaped him at every opportunity, collected and processed his trash, made what they considered an anthropological study of his life. Along the way, they'd learned much about the great man and the doings of his inner circle, and much about themselves. Every couple needs a binding interest; in an odd, wonderful way, Carlos had become theirs.

It had been more than nine months now since that magical summer night when the fierce Chocmol had caught them red-handed stealing the trash. Though they'd promised the woman from Cleargreen that they were done with their innocent surveillance—thereby avoiding a formal complaint to the police—they'd only lasted about a week before their curiosity and determination had gotten the better of them, and they'd renewed their activities in earnest. Besides changing the time of their trash runs to 3 a.m., things proceeded pretty much as before. The Followers, as Greg had dubbed them, were back in business.

Then, one Sunday afternoon in late February 1998, sitting at their regular post, in a no-parking zone diagonally across the quiet intersection from Carlos's low-slung compound, the Followers saw a car pull up to the Pandora Avenue gate, a blue Ford Crown Victoria that belonged to one of the Chacmols. As it slowed to a stop, several members of the inner circle came quickly out of the house, moved toward the back door of the car. Riveted, Greg and Gabi watched in disbelief as they ministered to the great man, helping him gingerly out of the back seat, hauling him to his feet. For some time it had been obvious that Carlos's vision had been failing; they'd found insulin syringes and prescription medicine bottles in the trash. Now it was clear that his health had taken a dramatic turn for the worse. Carlos was thin and fragile, floppy like a rag doll. His skin was grayish green, his hair was very short, there were dark circles around his eyes; he had the skeletal appearance of an internee in a concentration camp. He didn't so much walk as shuffle, supported on either side by Chacmols, steadied from behind by the Blue Scout.

Gabi looked at Greg, Greg looked at Gabi. A wave of extreme sadness washed over them. There was no mistaking the fact that Carlos was dying, that their marvelous folly would soon be coming to an end. At the edge of the sadness was something else, a sort of bitter aftertaste of disappointment: If Carlos was planning, as he'd promised, to leave the Earth in full awareness with his boots on, in a flash of light for the Second Attention like Don Juan, he had better hurry. From the looks of him, he didn't have much time.

Over the next weeks and months, the Followers saw no more of Carlos. His public appearances at seminars and workshops ended; the private classes at the dance studio came to a halt; he never again went out for a movie or a meal. Meanwhile, the level of activity at the compound increased dramatically. People came and went in shifts several times a day, bringing with them medical supplies and covered dishes of food. The members of the inner circle all got new cars, mostly mid-sized Fords. A new roof was put on the house, many other small repairs were made as well; the Followers got the feeling that the place was being readied for sale. When landscapers arrived and began tearing up the internal courtyard of the compound, the Followers wondered if they were digging a grave. Then one evening they observed Taisha Abelar packing her van with stacks of files and documents and a big cooler full of supplies. She was in an obvious hurry. The Followers wondered: Were they taking Carlos to Mexico to die? In mid-April, Gabi and Greg observed what seemed to be a flurry of packing and cleaning and organizing. Their trash take that week was unbelievably fruitful: clothes, statues and knicknacks, flatware, curtains, supplies—there were 16 bags, more than twice the normal amount. Once upon a time they'd have been overjoyed by such fabulous gleanings. Now they felt only curiosity and sorrow.

During the week of April 22, Greg and Gabi left off their surveillance in favor of a rare, seven-day vacation to Kauai, the honeymoon they hadn't yet gotten around to taking. When they returned, tanned and rested, the first thing they did was drive to Carlos's compound.

The place was empty. There was no one there. No cars, no people, no furniture inside. The only thing in the trash can was some construction debris and a few fast food wrappers. Several trips over the next few days confirmed their suspicions: The Sorcerer and his party had disappeared.

For the next six weeks, things at the compound remained unchanged. Meanwhile, phone lines and Internet chat rooms were buzzing with speculation. There were rumors that Carlos and his party had bought a big luxury yacht and had embarked on a world cruise. Others said that the inner circle had taken Carlos to Mexico to "leave." Still others posited that Carlos had died and the Witches had committed suicide in solidarity. Everyone associated, it seemed, had an opinion. Cleargreen remained suspiciously mum, continuing to schedule new seminars, carrying on business as usual.

Then, in mid June, C.J. Castaneda received a notice from the probate court in Los Angeles. On April 27, 1998, the letter informed him, Carlos Castaneda had died. Though C.J. and Margaret were mentioned in the will, they were left nothing of the estate, which some estimated to be worth as much as $20 million. In the six-page document, which was signed and dated April 23, Carlos explicitly distanced himself from his Cho-cho, stating in Article I that "although I once treated him as if he were my son, C.J. Castaneda is not my son, natural or adopted." All monies and property and future rights to his work were bequeathed to something called The Eagle's

Trust, the officers of which were members of Carlos's inner circle, men and women who also served as the officers of Cleargreen, Toltec Artists and the other corporations. Outraged that Cleargreen had failed to exercise common decency and notify him of his Kiki's death, hurt that he'd been disavowed and disinherited by the only father he had ever known, C.J. called the *Los Angeles Times* and tipped them off to the death. Later, he would initiate a suit against Cleargreen and Carlos's executors, claiming that the will was a fraud. After nine months of legal wrangling, C.J. would drop the suit.

The story ran on the front page of the *Times* on Friday, June 19. "Carlos Castaneda . . . apparently died two months ago in the same way that he lived: quietly, secretly, mysteriously."

According to his death certificate, the *Times* story said, Carlos had died of liver cancer on April 27, at the age of 72. In typical Carlos fashion, the death certificate listed his occupation as "teacher," and his employer as the Beverly Hills School District, for which he'd never worked. It also said that he had never been married. Immediately following the death, it was reported, his body had been cremated, his ashes spirited away to Mexico. Explaining why no one was notified about his passing, Carlos's long-time lawyer, Debra Drooze, was quoted as saying: "He didn't like attention. He always made sure people did not take his picture or record his voice. He didn't like the spotlight. Knowing that, I didn't take it upon myself to issue a press release."

The next day, on their website, Cleargreen issued a statement to the faithful. Their position was a bit different than the lawyer's. "Carlos Castaneda left the world the same way that his teacher, Don Juan Matus did: with full awareness," the statement read in part. "The cognition of our world of everyday life does not provide for a description of a phenomenon such as this. So in keeping with the terms of legalities and record keeping that the world of everyday life requires, Carlos Castaneda was declared to have died."

Having read both the article in the *Times* and the posting on the Web, Greg and Gabi, like many others, didn't know what to think. So many odd and wonderful things had happened in connection with Carlos, so many mystical events and occurences that seemed to have no explanation in the world of ordinary reality. Now they wanted to know how the story ended. They needed to know the truth. Had he died like a man? Had he left like a sorcerer? Which was it? For so many years now, Gabi and Greg and countless others around the world had set their reality compass by the teachings of Carlos and Don Juan. There was a need for some kind of closure. It didn't help any that all the Witches had disappeared. When asked, Cleargreen would only say that the Witches were "traveling."

Using the detective skills he'd honed to a sharp edge over the last several years, Greg tracked down Carlos's death certificate. A little leg work revealed that Carlos's body had not been taken to the mortuary that was specified, but to a different place, one with an unlisted telephone number called the Spalding Mortuary.

And so it was, on the Monday morning following the announcement of Carlos's death in the *L.A. Times*, that Greg got out of his car and walked through the unlocked door of a nondescript brick building in a run-down industrial district just east of Culver City. He was going to get to the bottom of this mystery, once and for all.

He was met in the hallway by a tall, elderly black gentleman, who kindly asked his business. Standing there in the dark hallway, wearing the corduroy sportscoat that had once belonged to Carlos himself, Greg explained that Spalding Mortuary had recently cremated the remains of a man named Carlos Castaneda. This man, Greg continued, had claimed to be a great and powerful sorcerer and had followers all over the world. Though his teachings were many, Greg explained, first among them was the notion that an enlightened sorcerer does not die a normal death, but rather is consumed by something called "the fire from within," a sort of spontaneous combustion, wherein he gathers his mortal energy and leaves for the next realm, taking his body with him.

"I am here to find out the truth," Greg told the elderly gentleman in his typically earnest but ironic style. "What I want to know is this: Did he burn with the fire from within? Or did *you* burn him?"

The gentleman regarded Greg for several long moments—trying, no doubt, to decide what to do. Greg seemed harmless enough. He was polite and appeared sane. He was obviously deeply aggrieved. But what Greg was saying, well—he'd seen and heard many things in his years in the mortuary business, but this took it all: he'd never heard anything so ridiculous in his life. "Please sit down," he said at last.

After ten minutes or so, a well-dressed, older woman appeared before Greg and asked him to repeat his business. She listened intently, nodding her head, wearing a sympathetic face. Until, that is, he got to the part about "the fire from within." She reared back her head and laughed out loud.

Greg looked at the woman and smiled. He raised his hands, palms up, shrugged his shoulders. She was a tall, heavyset, regal woman, the model of a family matriarch. She leaned down and put her arms around Greg, gave him a tender, motherly hug. "He has gone to a better place," she said, patting his back.

Greg stepped back from her embrace. "I know that," he said, regarding her quizzically. "But what I want to know is: *which* better place. Are you sure you cremated him?"

"I watched it myself," she said confidently.

"You're positive?"

"His spirit is gone, baby."

Greg thanked the woman, turned and went outside, to his car. He opened the door, started to get in, then stopped himself. He felt numb, an odd mixture of disappointment and relief. For what must have been the one millionth time over the six years, the words of scholar Richard DeMille floated through his mind. *Castaneda wasn't a common con man, he lied to bring us the truth. His stories are packed with truth, though they are not true stories, which he said they are. . . . This is a sham-man bearing gifts, an ambiguous spelbinder dealing simultaneously in contrary commodities—wisdom and deception."*

Greg removed his favorite jacket, the tan corduroy sportscoat with suede elbow patches that once belonged to Carlos, and threw it unceremoniously into the back seat of the car. It was time to move on.

(1999)

Acknowledgments

For many years I have anticipated with great relish the chance to thank the people who have generously helped, fostered, sponsored, inspired, befriended, fed and mentored me:

David Granger, Peter Griffin, Jann Wenner, Bob Love, Morgan Entrekin, Art Cooper, Don Graham, Bob Woodward, Bill Regardie, Jack Limpert, Walt Harrington.

Ann and Harry Sager, Jacob Levin, Sarah and Lee Rosenberg, Dora Simons, Al Baverman, John Bugge, Jonathan Prude, Steven Cohen, Steven Sulcov, John May, Henry Schuster, Albert Murray, David Kelley, Steve Jones, Diana Ries, William H. Sager, Tom Sherwood, Charles Jackson, Rudy Maxa, Stan Hinden, Tom Morgan, Gene Bachinski, Loretta Toffani, Bill Gold, Andrew Mayer, Herb Denton, Ken Ringle, Jay Lovinger, Peter Mehlman, Diane Landis, Geoff Diner, Terry Dale, Terrell Lamb, Kathy Robbins, William Greider, Jeff Stein, Marshall Keys, David Rosenthal, Carolyn White, Bob Wallace, Robert Vare, Eric Etheridge, Kurt Andersen, Lynn Nesbit, Elliot Kaplan, Lisa Henriksson, David Hirshey, Terry McDonnell, Pete Earley, Clay Felker, Bonita Hauge, Sam Freedman, Lisa Hintelmann, Philip Raskind, Jeffrey Frankel, James L. Brooks, Douglas Wick, Jerry Bruckheimer, Chad Oman, Ken Norwick.

Thanks to Avalon Publishing Group and Thunder's Mouth Press: Will Balliett, Clint Willis, Maria Fernandez, Blanca Oliviery.

Thanks to Jay McInerney, whose work inspired the first paragraph of "The Rise and Fall of a Super Freak."

Thanks to everyone who has taken their time to grant me an interview or to aid in my research. And thanks, especially, to the legion of people—alive and dead—upon whose bones I have made mine. Above all, I hope I have done justice to your stories.

Finally, most deeply, I wish to thank my wife, Rebekah, and my son, Miles, around whom I revolve.

The following stories were first published in the same or slighty different form in *Rolling Stone*: "Inhuman Bondage" 3/24/88; "The Death of a High School Narc" 6/2/88; "The Devil and John Holmes" 6/15/89; "Rob Lowe's Girl Trouble" 8/24/89; "The High Life and Strange Times of the Pope of Pot" 6/13/91; "The Rise and Fall of a Super Freak" 6/27/96.

The following stories were first published in the same or slightly different form in *GQ*: "The Corruption of Ed O'Brien" 5/90; "Murder, My Sweet" 5/91; "Damn! They Gonna Lynch Us!" 10/91; "The Temple of Doom" 6/94; "Little Girl Lost" 11/94; "Requiem for a Gangsta" 11/95; "Janet's World" 6/96; "The Martyrdom of Veronica Guerin" 3/97; "Raised in Captivity" 6/97; "Stairway to Heaven" 9/97.

The following stories were first published in *Esquire*: "An Imperfect Weekend" 9/00; "The Final Days of Gary Condit" 9/02.

MIKE SAGER quit law school after three weeks to work the graveyard shift as a copy boy at *The Washington Post*. Eleven months later, he was promoted to staff writer by Metro Editor Bob Woodward. He left the *Post* after six years to pursue a career in magazines. Currently he is a Writer-at-Large for *Esquire*.

A former Contributing Editor of *Rolling Stone* and Writer-at-Large for *GQ*, Sager has also written for *Vibe*, *Spy*, *Interview* and *Playboy*. For his stories, he has lived with a crack gang in Los Angeles; ex-pat Vietnam veterans in Thailand; a 625-pound-man in El Monte, CA; teenage pitbull enthusiasts in the Philadelphia barrio; Palestinians in the West Bank and Gaza Strip; heroin addicts on the Lower East Side; Aryan Nations troopers in Idaho; U.S. Marines at Camp Pendleton; Tupperware saleswomen in suburban Maryland; high school boys in Orange County. Many of his articles have been optioned for film. A graduate of Emory University, he lives with his wife and son in La Jolla, California.